Nameless Indignities

TRUE CRIME HISTORY SERIES
Harold Schechter, Editor

NAMELESS
INDIGNITIES

Unraveling the Mystery of One of Illinois's
Most Infamous Crimes

SUSAN ELMORE

The Kent State University Press
Kent, Ohio

© 2013 by The Kent State University Press, Kent, Ohio 44242
ISBN 978-1-60635-159-8
Manufactured in the United States of America

Cataloging information for this title is available at the Library of Congress.

17 16 15 14 13   5 4 3 2 1

A GENERATION BACK

We are apt to think of the present times as sadly out of joint,
To sigh, and then towards ages past, the revered finger point.
Of model husbands, model wives, say we there was no lack—
Of manners, moral pride and worth, a generation back!

The girls were modest, neat and fair, the boys were brave and true!
They labored on from sun till sun, with joys and pleasures few!
The children went to bed at dark and seemed to have the knack,
Of being seen and never heard, a generation back!

And thus it is from age to age, and thus 'twill ever be,
The scenes enacted long ago, with partial eyes we see.
Our offspring in the years to come will tread the beaten track,
And praise the conduct of their sires, a generation back.

—*Anonymous,* Decatur (Illinois) Review, *August 17, 1882*

CONTENTS

ILLUSTRATIONS

See photo insert

1 Emma Bond

2 Abner Dobbins Bond II

3 Delia Delile Sabine Bond

4 Justice James B. Ricks

5 Judge Jesse J. Phillips

6 Christian County Courthouse (1856–1901), Taylorville

7 Montgomery County Courthouse, Hillsboro

8 John G. Drennan, State's attorney, Christian County

9 Judge Amos Miller, State's attorney, Montgomery County

10 Judge Horatio M. Vandeveer, prosecuting attorney

11 Judge Anthony J. Thornton, defense attorney

12 J. C. McBride, defense attorney

13 Shelby M. Cullom, governor of Illinois, 1877–83

14 Palmyra Sanitarium in Palmyra, Wisconsin

15 John C. Montgomery and family, 1911

16 Delia Sabine Greene

MAPS

PREFACE

Much family history is handed down by word of mouth. It was through this very tradition that I first learned of a tragic episode in my own family's past. In 1977 my mother interviewed her aunt, Delia Sabine Greene (then in her mid-eighties), to record her reminiscences for posterity. During that interview, Delia spoke of her aunt Emma Bond who, as a young schoolteacher, was gang-raped at her deserted country schoolhouse on the last day of school in June 1882. Delia's details were sketchy, and her recollections filled only a third of a typewritten page. As it turned out, Delia had the basic story correct, but many of her details would later prove wrong. While I always found the story fascinating, it was merely a footnote in the larger context of my family's history. So I tucked it away in the back of my mind. Every now and then, I would come across the transcript of that interview and wonder about the whole incident. Then back it would go to its lonely place in an old file box.

When I inherited my family's archives in the mid-1980s, my long-simmering interest in family history began to heat up. In the next decade, there was a great explosion of genealogy websites on the Internet, and, like most family researchers, I was drawn to their pages. While perusing one such site a few years ago, I came across an unexpected entry in *The Portrait and Biographical Record of Christian County, Illinois* (1893). There, in a biographical sketch on J. G. Drennan, one of the county's notable lawyers, was a reference to "the famous Emma Bond case." I knew instantly that this had to be my great-great aunt. Apparently, her story had attracted far more attention than even Delia realized. My original curiosity quickly turned into an obsession as I searched old newspapers for specifics on the case. The more I found, the more hooked I became. Days turned into weeks and weeks into months as I hunted down anything and everything connected to the case. Not surprisingly, I ran into a few brick walls, but the mounting intrigue kept me moving forward.

What eventually revealed itself was a spellbinding whodunit. The story was stranger than fiction, verging on the downright unbelievable. It seems that the Bond case captured the nation's unwavering attention for the better part of two years as readers faithfully followed it in the daily press. It was Victorian suspense at its best—a story fraught with human interest, intense controversy, deep family loyalties, conniving characters, unexpected twists, dark innuendoes, and, ultimately, heart-wrenching consequences. But, above all, it was a mystery that went unsolved, and that gave it a certain staying power. Rumors and speculation persisted for decades beyond the trial's end.

This story, however, is far more than just a true crime mystery. It is also a chronicle of life in rural mid-America during the late 1800s. Woven into its fabric are the sacrifices and toils, joys and sorrows, dreams and disappointments that marked our ancestors' lives at every turn in a changing era—the expansion of the railways, arrival of telephones and electricity, rapid evolution in science and medicine, and great manufacturing boom would alter their lives and the American landscape forever.

But perhaps more than anything else, this is a tale of ordinary Americans thrust into extraordinary circumstances. At least three hundred local residents took part in the investigation and trial. To conduct a trial of that magnitude in 1883 was a major feat. Unfortunately, the investigative standards of that day were woefully lacking; suffice it to say, had the crime occurred more recently, the mystery would have been easily solved and the guilty parties readily convicted. But this crime took place long before law enforcement officers knew the value of securing a crime scene; long before there were trained criminologists to properly collect evidence; long before fingerprinting, handwriting analysis, and criminal profiling came into widespread use; long before computers gave easy access to a suspect's background; and long before the development of DNA testing, with its irrefutable pinpointing of the guilty. Even geography presented a barrier of sorts, as long-distance travel and communication were sometimes difficult.

Because of all these limitations, the original investigators cannot be blamed for their failure to crack this complicated case. They were profoundly restricted by the available knowledge, techniques, and tools. Fortunately, most of our country's historical records and documents are readily accessible today, and they revealed some surprising and relevant details about some of the men involved in this case.

Ultimately, the Bond case was—and might still be—the most notorious one in Christian County, Illinois, history. The details of this senseless crime continue to astound. And, as I eventually learned, the facts proved much more complex and absorbing than those recalled by my great-aunt Delia in 1977. I can only wonder what she would have thought of this more accurate and in-depth account of the crime and its far-reaching consequences.

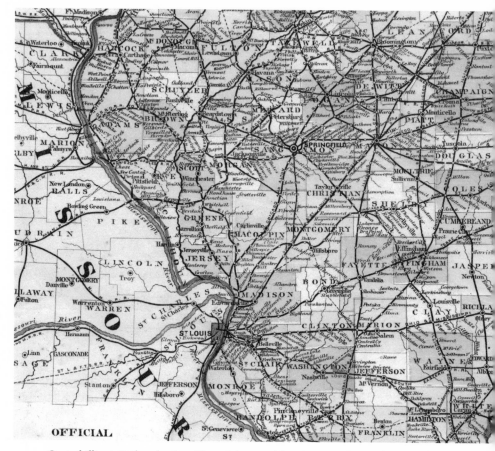

Central Illinois Railroads, 1875. (Copyright www.historicmapworks.com)

PROLOGUE

If the men are guilty, no punishment known to the law is too severe to visit upon them, but let them first be shown guilty beyond a reasonable doubt.
—Decatur Review, *Friday, August 11, 1882.*

In a small and quite ordinary town in central Illinois, the August day began like any other. Yet by nightfall, what was about to unfold there would put the name "Taylorville, Illinois," on the lips of men and women everywhere. Although local residents would argue that taking justice into their own hands had been the right, even the only, thing to do, others would disagree. Luckily, by the time the news reached the nation's larger journals, the locals had come to their senses, or so it seemed. Certainly, lynchings occurred in other parts of the country, but rarely in a peaceful place like Taylorville.

Before the summer of 1882, the people of the town and surrounding Christian County had been quite content with the lives they'd honed for themselves on the Illinois prairie. Just a few decades earlier they had been perched on the edge of the untamed American wilderness. Now, however, they were no longer living on the geographical fringes of society but were firmly entrenched in America's heartland. And then came the tragic events that would leave the small town with a notoriety that few places east of the Mississippi and north of the Mason-Dixon Line could claim.

On Friday, August 11, the town's merchants arose early, kissed their wives and children goodbye, and hurried off to their storefronts on the square to tidy up in anticipation of a good day's business. In outlying regions, farmers arose earlier than usual, heading for their barns and fields even before the rooster's first crow. There was a general determination to finish up their work quickly so that they could scramble into town, grab a hitching spot near the square, and be among the first to hear the news.

On the three days leading up to Friday, Taylorville—the county seat—had been abuzz with activity, due to the preliminary hearing at the courthouse. That hearing marked the first public airing of evidence since the disturbing events of June 29 had sent shockwaves rippling through the county. Local residents were appalled and angry, their sympathies with the victim and her family. Almost everyone agreed that once all the evidence was revealed in court, there would be nothing to do but put the scoundrels on trial for their monstrous act.

Tuesday's crowd was large, as expected. Throughout the day, trains brought hundreds of interested spectators from surrounding communities. Many more came in wagons and on horseback, and the town's residents turned out in droves. Hence, the usually adequate courtroom quickly jammed to capacity. The numbers would ebb and flow throughout the week, as would the public's sentiment. Tuesday's testimony turned slightly in favor of the defendants, which resulted in a smaller turnout on Wednesday. As a consequence, the potential for unrest seemed to subside—at least until Thursday night, when it became apparent that Justice James Ricks would issue his ruling the following day.

For that reason, Friday's attendance was the highest yet. In summer, the courtroom could be stifling, and on August 11, it was exactly that—packed to the hilt with overheated men and overdressed women. Latecomers were forced to mill about on the lawn. At noon, word filtered out that the hearing was over and that Ricks was sending the case to the grand jury, having released only one of the five accused men for lack of evidence. Those who had squeezed into the sweltering gallery soon began to spill from the north entrance of the courthouse, grateful to feel the fresh air. As they mingled with those waiting outside, they eagerly shared their takes on the proceedings with anyone who would listen.

Inside, Sheriff William Haines and his deputies stood armed and ready for any altercation. Within an hour, this contingency exited the courthouse with nervous prisoners in tow. Amid angry jeers and shouts, the suspects were hustled off to the jail, two blocks southwest of the square. There, they were taken at once to the upstairs cellblock. Only then did deputies dare to relax. But as the afternoon wore on, the crowd failed to disperse; people lingered, as if waiting for something more to happen. With the majority expressing strong approval of the court's decision, only a brave, outnumbered few voiced disagreement, which fell on deaf ears. Most of the women, needed at home, departed by late afternoon. Yet, not until the sun dropped behind the west-side stores did the crowd truly begin to thin. The most vociferous, however, stayed behind, and when night brought out the curious, some visibly intoxicated, the gathering grew louder. Soon, a clamor for action took root, punctuated by demands for a more exacting kind of justice.

On the ground floor of the jailhouse, Haines and his deputies kept an uneasy watch over their charges. Try as they might, though, it was impossible to tune out the growing din of discontent that wafted on the night air like the cadence of locusts—at times growing louder, then fading, only to rise up again. The sheriff had done all he could, had even warned the governor he might need reinforcements. Haines, a conscientious lawman, was well aware of the potential for violence and had solemnly vowed to protect the suspects to the best of his ability. At this point, however, all he and his men could do was pray that the idle ruminations would not turn into a dangerous reality.

The suspects had every reason to be concerned, and it showed on their faces. Few words passed among them as they strained to hear the disturbance coming from the square. Their worries intensified when they realized that the noise was moving in their direction. Minutes later, there was a great commotion downstairs, where the deputies stood guard. Any earlier confidence these men had placed in the officers' ability to protect them was suddenly nonexistent. It was now a little after nine o'clock, and the late summer dusk had given way to a velvet, moonless night, engulfing the terrified prisoners in a shroud of darkness.

1

THE CRIME
AND THE
INVESTIGATION

June 29, 1882–August 7, 1882

1

The heavy storm of Wednesday night caused considerable damage in the vicinity. The vivid flashes of lightning and the terrific crashes of thunder made many people tremble with fear. The old sinners must have thought that the end had come.
—Decatur Review, *Friday, June 30, 1882*

On the night of Wednesday, June 28, 1882, a violent electrical storm swept across the prairies of central Illinois—damaging buildings, tearing off rooftops, turning fields into mud. Despite the tempest's savagery, the clouds moved out quickly and the sun—just days past its zenith—made its appearance right on schedule the next morning, around four-thirty. Local farmers were in the middle of a wheat harvest, but the storm had dumped enough rain to keep them from their fields for a day or two.

When young schoolteacher Emma Bond awoke that Thursday, blue skies and the smell of moist, black earth greeted her. The overnight storm had washed away the previous day's heavy heat and humidity, and that was a blessing; the long skirts, heavy petticoats, and high necklines of Emma's day were much more bearable in mild weather. Thursday promised to be easy, since it was the last full day of the school year and she was expecting just one pupil—little Charlie Masters. The eight-year-old had to finish up a few reading and spelling lessons if he wanted to take part in the school's year-end festivities on Friday. Emma planned to set him straight to work and then give him a short mid-morning break while she crossed the road to rehearse some music for Friday's ceremony with the Pettus girls. Minnie and her younger sister, Ona (short for Iona), were in their mid-teens and only slightly younger than their teacher.[1] But that was not unusual in a time when a girl in her late teens needed only to pass a written exam to become a rural school teacher.

Emma had accepted the position at the Montgomery School just three months earlier. As it happened, Minnie's and Ona's older sister, Cora, had also applied for the same job, but it had been awarded to Emma. Perhaps Emma was given the position because she, along with her five sisters, had been educated at home by a governess. Their father certainly had the means to provide his girls with more privileges than most farm children enjoyed. Their dress, while not extravagant, seemed slightly out of place in rural Christian County. The girls even got piano lessons; Emma had mastered the ivories quite nicely, which was why she was going to accompany the Pettus girls on Friday.

When Charlie arrived at school to finish his lessons, Emma was there to greet him. Upon entering, he glanced up and noticed that the scuttle hole leading to the attic was ajar. He pointed it out to his teacher, but she seemed unconcerned and dismissed the matter. Charlie shrugged, took his seat, and set to work in his reader. At ten-thirty, his teacher sent him out for recess, saying she was going over to the Pettus house and would return in thirty minutes.

The Pettus home belonged to Mrs. Margret Pettus, widow of George, and stood kitty-corner across the road, about two hundred yards from the school. Margret had raised her children alone after George's passing in the mid-1860s; however, by no means was she in dire straits. Her husband had left her with a substantial piece of first-rate farmland, and her widowed brother, Robert Johnson, had stepped in to help her keep the place going. Of her eight children, Margret had already married off five. The four oldest girls had chosen husbands from the local stock of farm boys. None lived more than a short ride from their mother's home. Cora, the schoolteacher, had wed most recently—in April. Margret's older son, George, was also married. Her younger boy Lee, at twenty-one, still lived at home and worked with his uncle on the family farm. But the property was large, forcing Margret to hire one of Lee's sidekicks—a young Spaniard named Emanuel Clementi.

On Thursday, June 29, Pettus and Clementi were also enjoying an easier than usual day, just like the schoolteacher, but they had Wednesday night's bad weather to thank. They spent the morning repairing a fence that some of the farm's mules had knocked down during the storm. At noon, the two young men walked back to the house for dinner, always the biggest meal of the day. Two of Pettus's sisters, Cora and Mattie, and their husbands, Owen Hart and John Montgomery, had stopped by, so it was a larger-than-normal gathering.

After dinner, Pettus saddled a horse and drove some errant cattle back across the branch while Clementi climbed atop a nearby fence rail to watch. Pettus soon joined him, and the two perched there and talked for a while. By mid-afternoon, both decided it was time for a rest, so they headed back to the house, fetched a pipe and a newspaper, and settled into the spring wagon in the front yard. When Clementi dozed off, Pettus climbed out and went back to doing nothing much around the house. He had some weeds to cut in the fence corners before dark, but there was plenty of time for that. His friend dozed away the afternoon in the wagon bed, waking just before supper. The day proved to be a welcome respite from their usual, more demanding routine.

When Emma arrived to rehearse with Minnie and Ona, the sisters were too busy to practice and asked their teacher if she could return in the afternoon. She agreed, strolled back across the road, fetched her idle student from the schoolyard, and returned with him to the classroom. It was high noon before the two took another break. Charlie carried his lunch pail outside and, as boys will do, quickly devoured his food—paying little mind to what his teacher was doing. At one o'clock, Emma called him back inside and checked over his morning work. She was pleased to see that he'd made good progress. Three more hours and they'd both be done for the day.

At two thirty, sharp, she sent Charlie outside for recess and headed off to practice with Minnie and Ona. Charlie dashed off toward the school's coalhouse and scrambled up onto its roof—the perfect vantage point for a boy who had nothing better to do than watch the clouds go by. Emma waved to him, saying that she'd be back in thirty minutes. This time, the Pettus girls were ready. They sang, and Emma played—their melodies wafting through the open windows and across the road to Charlie's ears. Lying there, soaking up the sun and the music, the boy did not notice the two men coming down the road from the north. As they drew even with the coalhouse, Charlie looked up and saw John Montgomery, the elder, on horseback, and his grown son, also named John, on foot. The younger man hollered out, asking the lad why he wasn't playing with the other schoolchildren. When Charlie answered that there weren't any, he shouted back, "Well, wait and I'll come back and wrestle with you."[2]

The two men waved to the boy and continued on down the road. Charlie, his reverie thus broken, hopped down and crossed the road to get a drink from the Pettus well. He then hurried back to the coalhouse roof, eager for John's return. But to his dismay, his teacher reappeared first—at three o'clock, just as promised. As the two reentered the classroom, Charlie mentioned he had heard noises coming from the attic during his recess. Emma reassured him that it was nothing more than rats.

At three thirty, the youngster announced he had finished his work. Before sending him on his way, Emma made sure of it. As he bolted out the door, she picked up her broom to sweep the floor; she wanted her classroom to look perfect for Friday's ceremony. Then, after stacking up the completed report cards and tidying up her desk, she picked up her belongings, made one final glance around the room, and headed toward the door. Though she would miss the place over the summer, she looked forward to teaching there again in the fall. She dearly loved teaching—almost as much as playing the piano.

Where Emma intended to go after school that day was uncertain—at least to everyone but herself. At the Bond homestead, four miles south, her father and stepmother and five sisters must have thought she was going to spend her last night of the school year at the home of Ed and Amanda Montgomery, where she boarded during the semester. The young married couple lived a short distance north of the school. Ed, busy with his chores, and Amanda, busy with their toddler, must have assumed Emma was going home that evening. So when the teacher failed to show up at either place by nightfall, nobody was the least bit concerned.

Light from a nearly full moon slipped through the school's south-facing windows, casting a soft glow across the worn, wooden floor. Slowly but steadily, its beams inched toward the crumpled body of the young schoolteacher, lying beneath the scuttle hole. As they edged across her motionless form, she began to stir. Several more minutes went by before she lifted her head, dazed and disoriented. A heavy silence filled the classroom, and the pale light that surrounded her gave no clue to the hour.

When she struggled to rise, waves of nausea washed over her. She collapsed forward, her face and nose taking the brunt of the impact. A sudden, searing pain pierced her midsection, and her hands dropped to find a shawl cinched tightly around her waist. She tugged at it in vain, trying to ease its unbearable constriction. In time, she would be tormented by haunting flashbacks of that night: her own handkerchief being doused in chloroform and forced over her mouth; the shawl growing ever tighter as she was hoisted roughly up through the small opening in the ceiling; the feel of unforgiving wooden planks beneath her body; the cruel pressure of coarse hands pinning her down; the repeated acts of rape and the terrifying verbal threats. The ugliest of those threats had been backed up with a knife, its blade used to inflict numerous lacerations on her face, neck, and wrists. Any attempts to pull free, to fight, had been met with more doses of the noxious chemical. And throughout it all, her desperate pleas for mercy had been callously brushed aside.

Fortunately, she had drifted away—for much of the time, at least—into blessed nothingness. Unfortunately, the chloroform's effect had not been constant, and she had suffered through more than a few lucid moments. In one of those, she had threatened that "she would die before she would submit to them."[3] Emma had no idea that in the days to come, she would experience serious regret over her inability to carry out that vow. But as fate would have it, she was alone now and, incredibly, still alive. The memory gaps caused by the chloroform had left her in a state of total confusion. The angle of the moonlight suggested that the hour was quite late. She felt for her watch. Gone. Her favorite scarf pin, also gone. So, too, was her engagement ring—the cherished token of her recent betrothal to a young man named Adams. Her clothing was in utter disarray—not only torn but stained from the knife wounds on her upper body.

She needed to get home, but home was miles away. Help was within reach, however, if she could traverse the two-hundred long yards to the Pettus home. So, with little choice, she staggered to her feet and made it out the door and down the steps. The moon, now sinking toward the horizon, was still high enough to light her way. Step by excruciating step, she crossed the schoolyard and the road, aiming for the dark Pettus house. By the time she stumbled onto the front porch and managed to rouse someone in the sleeping household, it was well past midnight. The very first newspaper account of the crime gave the details: "Mrs. Pettus heard her knock at the door and upon asking who it was, the faint answer came 'Emma Bond.' The door was then thrown open and the poor girl was found fainting and exhausted upon the door step. The pitiful story was told in a few words, and she was taken into the house and laid upon a lounge. Upon examination, Miss Bond was found to be in a pitiable state. She was bleeding profusely, her garments were torn and covered with blood, and she could barely talk."[4]

The knotted scarf at Emma's waist did not want to relinquish its hold but Margret finally succeeded in undoing it. She then guided the young teacher to a settee in the family parlor. Awakened by the sound of the late night visitor, Minnie joined her mother at Emma's side. Within minutes, Lee—who slept downstairs—was also awake and wanting to know what was happening. It was obvious to Margret that the girl needed immediate help but, given the ungodly hour, she thought the most sensible course would be to nurse Emma and her wounds until first light and then fetch the doctor and send word to the Bonds. Margret tried in vain to calm her distraught guest, but Emma wanted no part of it and pleaded to be taken home at once.

Unable to soothe the suffering girl, Margret told her son to wake their hired man and prepare the wagon. Clementi was upstairs, sleeping soundly, despite the commotion going on downstairs. When he finally appeared and saw the wounds on Emma's face, neck, and arms, he insisted that the young woman was in no condition to go anywhere. Margret, with a mother's compassion, told the boys to get moving anyway. Both hesitated, with Clementi concerned "that Mr. Bond was a very excitable man and might suspect them of the crime."[5] But Margret wasn't going to accept that one; she ordered them to get the horses hitched up at once.

When the wagon was ready, the injured girl was laid out on blankets in the back. Margret climbed in beside her while her son took the reins, with Clementi at his side. The group set off in the deepest hours of the night. They were barely underway when one of the boys decided to make a slight detour. They turned the wagon north, toward old man Montgomery's house, so they could send someone to keep an eye on Minnie and Ona. Before the wagon came to a complete halt, Lee hopped down and disappeared inside. To Emma, it felt like he was gone for an eternity. Whether her injuries muddled her sense of time or whether, in fact, Lee did take an inordinate amount of time is uncertain, but the wagon did not reach the Bond farm until just before dawn.

When the group finally pulled up in front of the Bond house, the weakened victim called out for her father. There was no answer from the sleeping household, so Clementi hollered out for Mr. Bond. At last, the old man appeared in his nightshirt, took Emma in his arms, and carried her inside. Before the good Samaritans departed, Mr. Bond took a description of the assailants from his daughter, wrote it down on a piece of paper, and handed it to Lee: "Two large men, dressed in dark clothes, wore white shirts, one had whiskers."[6] This would be repeated—virtually word for word—by at least three different people during the eventual trial, indicating that perhaps this particular piece of paper was its basis.

Varying descriptions of the assailants appeared in the local papers in the coming days. The first claimed that "one of the villains [was] thirty-five years of age with dark hair, dark chin whiskers and mustache, and one with sandy hair. Both were large men, and wore dark clothes, both being in their shirtsleeves. One of the men wore a new pair of rubber boots."[7] The second account gave a slightly different version: "The one who first assaulted her [had] dark hair, a dark mustache and chin whiskers and [wore] a suit of dark clothes. . . . The other she did not see closely but that his hair is red there can be no doubt as a handful was found in the loft yesterday morning, which the poor girl had pulled from the wretch's head."[8]

Other specifics about the crime were disclosed early on. The assumption is that these, too, came from the victim within hours of the crime. The attackers had used chloroform to repeatedly subdue her. And, apparently, Emma had gotten a good look at their feet. For in addition to the new rubber boots worn by one man, she had noted that the other wore low shoes with red stockings.

With the speed of Wednesday night's treacherous storm, news of the schoolhouse outrage swept across the county. At home in her own bed, Emma weakened rapidly, and a bedside vigil began. Over the next twenty-four hours, she drifted in and out of consciousness. Dr. D. K. Cornell, the family's physician, was summoned to examine the victim. He observed many wounds on her body and suspected serious internal injuries as well. In spite of that, his prognosis was cautiously optimistic. He expected Emma to recover without suffering any lasting effects from her injuries. But he also alluded to something else—some injury that sounded far more disturbing than those of the typical rape. His veiled insinuations were mentioned in the papers, yet no specifics were given. After all, this was the Victorian press, and certain boundaries were simply not going to be crossed—especially when it came to a discussion of the human body, more specifically, the female body.

Although "rape" was a term seldom used in the nineteenth century, the act itself was not uncommon, and the press did not shy away from reporting such crimes. In fact, there were a number of other despicable outrages committed against young girls and women in the vicinity, not long before and after the schoolhouse attack.[9] But the press did steer clear of overly explicit details. To avoid being too blunt, the *Chicago Tribune* stated that the perpetrators were "not satisfied with outraging her person and torturing her in the cruel manner already stated, they gratified their malice by submitting their victim to OTHER INDIGNITIES, which shall be nameless, but which combine to render their crime, as has already been stated, one of the most diabolical ever committed in a civilized community."[10]

Although the journals refused to elaborate, those things too grisly to put into print seemed to be common knowledge among Emma's friends and neighbors. Details of the horrors she had suffered were being spread from woman to woman in whispered snippets and from man to man in hushed conversations. The public's outcry over this crime—and its absence in the other rape cases in the area—suggested that the locals knew something.

2

To call it ordinary is not to imply Taylorville was an unappealing place—quite the opposite, really, for it had its fair share of neat streets, modest clapboard homes, well-tended yards and gardens, four schools, and several churches. In all aspects, it was the typical American town of its day—a place of friendly, upstanding citizens going diligently about their business, raising their families, working hard to make ends meet. Day in and day out, with few complaints. For that was the American way. And in 1882, Taylorville, Illinois, was as good a place as any to call home.

Of the area's many thoroughfares, two crisscrossed diagonally through the county and intersected in Taylorville. Thus, on a map the town appeared to be a hub. Residents could hitch up their wagons, head northwest, and be in Springfield, the state's capital, in half a day or less, a trip of only thirty miles. Decatur, another decent-sized town, sat to the northeast and could be reached in a similar amount of time. So could Hillsboro, to the southwest. The smaller town of Pana sat a little closer—sixteen miles southeast.

Taylorville was luckier than most small communities, because it was served by two rail lines. The Baltimore, Ohio & Mississippi ran straight through the heart of town and offered the easiest means of travel to Springfield or Pana. Its modest depot sat a block and a half north of the square. The other line, the Decatur-St. Louis Railroad (also called the Wabash), was the busier of the two. Any man with a couple of bills in his pocket could catch a train bound for Decatur and from there make his way to the great metropolis of Chicago, two hundred miles to the north. Or he could ride in the opposite direction to the southwest, and within four hours, give or take, he could be in St. Louis—gateway to the West. For all its traffic, the Wabash depot was unremarkable, and it was situated an inconvenient half-mile south of the square, on the outskirts of town.

The town square, of course, was the heart and soul of the community, just as it was in many other American settlements. Merchants sought to establish their shops and trades on its perimeter, with their doorways and windows facing the town's centerpiece. In some towns, that centerpiece might be a circular bandstand in the middle of a bucolic park. But in the case of a county seat, it was invariably the courthouse. As with most county seats in the heartland, Taylorville's future was further secured by the fertile earth that surrounded it. That earth supported the local farmers who came to the town square to buy, sell, and barter goods. More often than not, the town's merchants would sell them on credit the necessities for feeding and clothing their large families and for running their farms. And, as the county's name implied, the families in this area were all good Christians, sprung from honest, hard-working, God-fearing stock. For this reason alone, Taylorville's merchants had no qualms about granting their customers a little leeway; they knew that just as soon as the autumn harvest was in, farmers would stop by to settle their debts.

The arc of land north of Taylorville was an especially fine expanse of prairie. An occasional stand of trees—oak for the most part—peppered the landscape. Here and there, farm houses broke the monotony. In early summer, the fields became a two-toned patchwork for as far as the eye could see. Dense winter wheat begging to be mowed stood in stark contrast to the rising stalks of green corn, reaching toward the sky. In a good year, the late June corn might easily surpass the "knee-high by the Fourth of July" benchmark.

The dirt lane running due north out of Taylorville was called the Mt. Auburn Road, simply because that's where it took you if you stuck with it. Between the two towns, the road ran straight as an arrow except for two sets of right-left jogs. Each consisted of a ninety-degree turn to the right, followed very shortly by a ninety-degree turn to the left, which put the road right back on the same northerly course—all the way to Mt. Auburn.

Eight miles out of Taylorville, past the first set of turns and down a small dusty track to the east, sat the Bond family home, where Emma and her five sisters had come into the world. Four miles past the Bond lane came the second set of turns. There, one could leave the main road, head west, and be in Grove City in a matter of minutes.[1] Home to one hundred friendly souls, the Grove was the next best thing to going clear into Taylorville. The little village offered local farmers all the basic necessities: a blacksmith, a harness and saddle maker, a grocer and druggist, a boot shop, a dry goods store, two doctors, one dentist, a church, and a post office. Plus, there was Sam Snyder, who served his neighbors in their saddest and happiest moments. When the local undertaker wasn't preparing someone for the final resting place, he was making homemade ice cream to be sold out of his parlor at the front of the same building.

Emma had close ties to Grove City. Her mother's family, the Housleys, had settled at the southwest corner of the village in the early 1850s, when it was called Buckhart Grove. A good many of her relatives lived there still. One uncle, Rufus Housley, owned the local house- and sign-painting business. Another, Dan, had served as the town's postmaster and was part owner of its popular dry goods

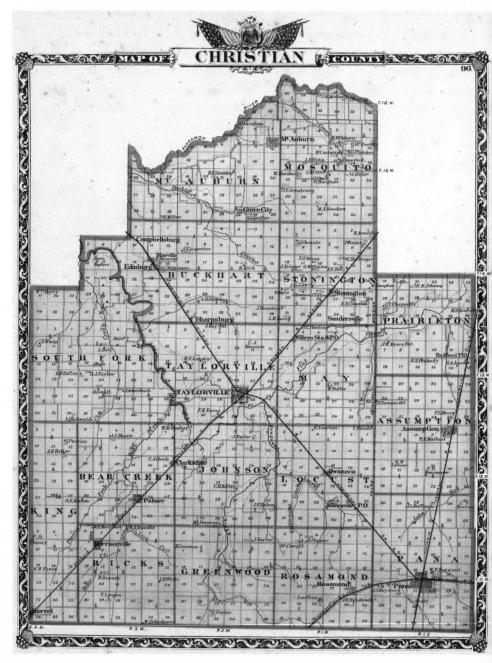

Northern Christian County, state Atlas, 1876. (Copyright www.historicmapworks.com)

business. The storefronts that lined the Grove's Main Street provided a popular gathering spot for local farmers. If weather kept them from their fields, they would often pass the time of day there, chatting with neighbors. The Grove was a busy village, with people constantly coming and going. It was the kind of place where everybody knew everybody. Back out on Mt. Auburn Road, just beyond the second set of jogs, one would pass the Pettus farm on the east side, and then the elder John Montgomery's just beyond that. Montgomery also owned the land on the west side of the road, where the Montgomery Schoolhouse stood. He leased that land to his cousin Joe Younker, whose house was located south of the school. A little farther north sat a cluster of Montgomery homes, including Ed and Amanda Montgomery's, where Emma boarded during the school year.

Like their Taylorville brethren, the farmers of Christian County held an abiding love for this place they called home. They knew its promise of a good life for those willing to work hard. To the farmer, that meant six days of backbreaking toil, the tedium interrupted only for the Sabbath. Following Sunday worship, families would come together for well-deserved feasts. Such gatherings were large and joyous, shared with siblings, aunts, uncles, cousins, and grandparents. Invariably, those same loved ones lived just up the road, around the bend, or across the creek. Never far away. Always handy when you needed them. In fact, many who had started out back east as good and trustworthy neighbors over time became in-laws. They followed the trails west together, bought new land in the same townships, then helped erect one another's homes. When their children grew up, they usually married into the families down the road; thus, after another half century or so, nearly everyone who lived within a couple miles of each other was somehow related.

The eagerly awaited Sunday gatherings meant good times, of course. The women set out hearty spreads while the men sat around chewing on talk of crops, livestock, and politics. Children of all ages romped together in clover fields and barnyards, the older ones taking charge of the younger ones. And then, after all had broken bread together and had had their fill of pie, young and old alike would indulge in some lively singing and dancing. But Sunday gave way to Monday, and the drudgery of the workweek resumed. For the farmer, this pattern seldom varied from week to week or month to month. It was a simple way to live, and when all was said and done, a farmer knew he had every reason to be thankful, even if all he had to his name was a good piece of land and a couple of strapping sons to help him work it. If he took into account the solid roof over his head, the decent food on his table, the devoted family and friends nearby, he could truly count his blessings and go contentedly to his grave.

One farmer in Christian County who considered himself more blessed than most was Emma's father. For Abner Dobbins Bond Jr., however, life had not always been easy. He was born in Indiana in 1827, and his mother had died at or shortly after his birth. Having no other children, Abner Dobbins Bond Sr. placed his son in the care of grandparents and a married uncle in Belmont County, Ohio. There, young Abner spent his formative years as part of a large Quaker family but without the benefit of his surviving parent. It is not known when, or even if, the lad ever rejoined his father in Indiana. Nevertheless, the father made sure that his only son received a good education at Miami University in Ohio.[2] When the younger Abner emerged from that school, he possessed a great independence and a driving ambition.

Having majored in German, he immediately took to the roads selling Seth Thomas clocks to German immigrants. As he wandered the Midwest peddling his timepieces, his ability to speak to his customers in their native tongue proved a boon, and his business flourished. The venture was a partnership between Abner the son and Abner the father; in time, the two were joined by a third relative who, coincidentally, shared their name. Abner Faye Bond was a first cousin of Abner Dobbins Bond Jr., and five years younger. The eldest Abner was strictly a financial backer for his son and nephew, while the two younger men traveled the back roads from Ohio to Kansas. The cousins were persevering fellows, willing to endure the lonely life of the traveling salesman. Abner Jr. ordered the clocks from Cincinnati and kept meticulous records of every transaction, and both young men took to the byways separately, delivering the goods to their delighted but isolated customers.

After five years of wandering, however, Abner Jr. began to yearn for a family. He was approaching his twenty-eighth year, well beyond the age most young men put down roots. Having seen much of the Midwest firsthand, he knew the earth in central Illinois was some of the best to be had. It was a landscape of infinite possibilities for a young man who'd already lined his pockets with $20,000 in gold coin. So when he rolled into Christian County in 1855, atop his handsome clock wagon pulled by a team of six magnificent road horses, he decided to stay. He turned the clock business over to his cousin, keeping only his own wagon and horses, which he planned to sell and put the profit toward establishing a farm.

But here he fell victim to his emotions. He simply could not conceive of a life without his favorite steeds, especially after all that man and beasts had endured together; his horses had been his constant and devoted companions as he'd crisscrossed the open range. They had shared lonely campfires with him, stood alert as he slept under the stars, and whinnied their soft approval of the melodies he coaxed from his favorite violin. And so it was that the two best of the bunch, a clay-colored stallion named Beauregard Billy and another he called Roan Jim, were granted a reprieve. With the cash from the sale of his other four horses and his clock wagon, Bond invested in three spans of medium-sized mules. Aided by these sturdy work animals and his two favorite horses, he set to work building a place he could call home for many decades to come, one that would reflect his worthiness as a good provider.

The acreage he chose sat on the Blackhawk Prairie, north of Taylorville, and boasted rich, black, loamy soil. Adding to its appeal was that it was fairly level terrain, except where it sloped gently down to Buckhart Creek. Gazing out over it, Bond could envision his newly acquired land bursting at the seams with bountiful crops. But, being pragmatic, he also realized that breaking the virgin prairie sod was going to be more work than one man could handle. So, to see the job accomplished more quickly, he reluctantly parted with another chunk of his hard-earned cash. He then erected a spacious two-story frame house with several outbuildings and fenced in the entire property.

By 1856, Abner Jr. had established his homestead—the envy of more than a few of his new neighbors, who included the large Housley family. George and his wife, Eliza, and their nine children had come to Illinois around 1850 from the German settlement of Canal Dover in eastern Ohio. George knew that the youth and brawn of his six sons was the key to a successful farm. And for their contribution, his sons would one day inherit the family land. Eliza and George also had three daughters: Maggie, Minnie, and Becky. They, of course, contributed by helping their mother with the household chores and lesser farm duties. But they would not inherit any of the land. George's greatest hope for his girls was that each would find a good and decent husband—one who would provide for her adequately and love her unconditionally. In return, she would treat her husband with deference and respect, maintain a well-run home, and grace him with a large family of his own—including a son or two, at the very least.

Yet in this period of ongoing western migration, there always loomed the possibility that a daughter would marry a man with an adventuresome spirit—one who would leave for uncharted territory. If that happened, a father might never lay eyes on his beloved daughter again. So when young Abner came calling at the Housleys, asking for Maggie's hand in marriage, George was pleased: his first-born would be delivered into the hands of a man who not only lived just across the fields but had also so recently established himself that he wasn't likely to leave any time soon. Nor did it hurt that Maggie's suitor had proven himself to be hard-working and prosperous. Thus, with her parents' blessings, Abner Dobbins Bond Jr. and Margaret Housley were joined in holy matrimony in September 1856.

Cousin Abner continued to cover the partnership's established sales routes for another decade, peddling clocks and amassing a decent fortune of his own. The two Abners maintained their brotherly bond, with the younger often stopping at his cousin's place in Illinois as a respite from the road. Inevitably, Abner Faye Bond also began to tire of the wandering lifestyle and, not surprisingly, he too chose to settle in Christian County. Like his cousin, he had a knack for picking prime land, and by 1870 he'd purchased some of the best in the county.

Now all he needed was a bride of his own. He set his cap for the oldest daughter of Dickson Hall, one of the area's earliest and most respected settlers. And so in September 1870, Abner F. Bond wed Miss Lizzie Hall.

Over the years, the two cousins became highly respected citizens of their county. But outside of the family circle, there existed a persistent confusion over the two men's exact relationship. More often than not, they were thought to be brothers—suggesting that not everyone knew that they shared the same first name. Perhaps that was because the elder cousin went by either "Ab" or "A.D.," while the younger one was widely known as "Sonny."[3] Sonny, however, assumed the greater role in the public arena, going on to serve several years on the county board of supervisors. He eventually became the better known of the two—at least until the schoolhouse attack.

Ab and Maggie settled quickly into married life, producing six daughters over eleven years. As was common then, their firstborn, Arabella (Belle), arrived within nine months of their marriage. In 1860, little Maggie was born and was named after her mother. The couple's next three children, Emma, Henrietta (Etta), and Frances (Francie) entered the world during the dark years of the Civil War. Josephine (Josie), their last, was born in 1867.[4] Bond's farm had prospered from the start; thus, he had the means to give his daughters the very best. Sadly, the one thing that he could not assure them for long was the presence of their mother. Maggie Bond died in December 1868, leaving behind her girls, ranging in age from one to eleven.

Their father saw at once that he was going to need some extra help. Although he doted on his daughters, their care was way beyond one man's capabilities, and so he hired a young lady from nearby Sangamon County. Delia Delile Sabine arrived at the farm in early 1869 and fell quickly and naturally into the task of caring for the six motherless girls. Their father's initial plan called for her to tutor them in academics as well as teach them the essential household duties their mother would have taught them, had she lived. Delia was so kind that the girls soon began to think of her as more than a teacher. Her winning ways must have appealed to their widowed father as well, for in less than eighteen months, the two became husband and wife.

The capable governess quickly became the adored stepmother, allowing life at the Bond home to return to normal. At the time of the marriage, Ab was pushing forty-three; however, his new bride was just shy of twenty-seven when she found herself in charge of a large, ready-made family and an oversized farmhouse. Luckily, she came to the job with plenty of firsthand experience; her own mother had died when she was just thirteen. As the only remaining female in her family, Delia had taken over the day-to-day task of mothering her infant brother, Lester—then only eight months of age.

That the Bond girls dearly loved their new stepmother, there was no doubt. And their love was reciprocated. Only fourteen years older than Belle, Delia seemed more like a big sister than a replacement for their mother. And, of course, she shared that mutual and significant connection with them—of having lost her own mother at an early age. Delia even endeared herself to the Housleys, the family of the woman whose shoes she now filled. With his new bride now busy running the household, Ab decided to bring in a new tutor for his girls. Whether it was his overprotectiveness or his desire to give them the very best schooling, he never entertained the thought of sending them to a conscription school, even though the nearest one sat less than a mile away. His decision "to hire a teacher at home rather than to ask his girls to paddle through mud, water, rain, snow or windy weather" made perfect sense to him, especially since his house was big enough to accommodate a classroom on the second floor.[5] The new tutor—a versatile Ohioan named Agnes Wells—guided the girls through their studies and coached them in the finer arts. Piano lessons were of the highest priority, since Ab wanted to instill in his girls his own delight in and appreciation of music.

While Ab was a good man, he was also a complex and, perhaps, conflicted one. He could be gentle and understanding one moment, temperamental and volatile the next. It seems he had fallen away from his Quaker religion by this time. Perhaps his first marriage to Maggie, a non-Quaker, was the cause, or maybe it was his insatiable love of music and fiddle. In any case, it was obvious that he still held certain tenets of his faith. Quakers, or members of the Society of Friends, supported equality for the races, the sexes, and the downtrodden. However, they could be condemned for such inappropriate and frivolous behaviors as dancing, playing an instrument, singing, gambling, or fighting with others in their community.

Many of the rules at Ab's farm reflected his Quaker upbringing. He allowed no drinking, gambling, card-playing, or swearing, not even in the bunkhouse—though he admittedly broke the rule about swearing on more than a few occasions. But his greatest temptation—at least in the eyes of the Friends—was music, especially the violin. His granddaughter Delia Sabine Greene later described his passion:

When we went to Grandpa's, he would call out requests. Sing "The Cat Came Back," he'd say, or "Grandfather's Clock." "Lead, Kindly Light" was his favorite hymn. A difficult one to play, its music and tempo were sweet and its words were comforting. Afterwards, he would reach into his pocket and give them each a silver quarter. No mean sum in those days.... On top of the piano lay a magic box—his violin. Once it had been broken into fifty pieces, crushed under a wagon wheel during his early days as a traveling clock salesman. Repaired so there was no visible evidence of its adventure, the violin came forth to liven our hearts with tunes to stir the pulse. . . . My mother or one of her sisters played the simple accompanying chords on the piano, with Grandpa tapping his slippered feet in time to the music. Woe to the child who dared touch a single low note below his flying hands. A single sound, "Ar-rah!!" from Grandpa was enough to stop any such nonsense and discourage all other attempts.[6]

Obviously, Bond followed his heart when it came to his musical transgressions. As for the Quaker belief in equality of the sexes, the man was surely put to the test—first with six daughters and then with nine of his first ten grandchildren being girls. Fortunately, he was ahead of his time regarding traditional gender roles. That was evident from Delia's description: "After dinner, Grandpa tied an apron around his waist and washed all the table dishes, stacked and scalded them. Then he untied the apron, handed it to my mother or one of my aunts, saying, 'I'm no pot-scullion,' and he then proceeded to the living room."[7] Such intrepid conduct by a man of his day was, indeed, rare.

Quaker beliefs included more fundamental principles as well. Members could be disowned without recourse for such things as marrying outside of the faith, enlisting in the military, and owning slaves. When the clash between the North and South erupted, Quakers faced a personal dilemma that many found hard to resolve. In remaining true to their faith, most chose not to fight in the Great War but instead found alternative ways to contribute. Thus, Bond could not conceive of taking up arms against his fellow man—not even the slaveholders of the South. So when his wife's brothers—Samuel, Levi, and George Housley— departed for the battlefront, he stayed behind. A family member later explained how Bond dealt with his inner conflict: "When the Civil War broke out, Mr. Harmon, with Hiram Hoagland, Mac Adrian, and 'Big Dutch' Hen[shie] were working for Bond and he persuaded them to enlist; then when they came back, he helped them to buy farms, lending them the money to start with."[8]

Bond's Quaker values were every bit as evident in matters of racial equality. After the war, he hired a number of former slaves, knowing the risks involved in doing so:

The best one of all was Plinny Richardson [whose] master used to keep him for breeding purposes just as he did his racing horses. . . . [While working for Bond] his greatest pleasure, or you might say "hobby," was to gather a few white boys of fourteen to sixteen years, sing to them, tell them stories and, after a year or two, he would drop them and get a younger set again. As these boys grew to be men, they remembered the stories of [Plinny's] slave days and the way he used to play games with them and they always had the utmost respect and love for Plinny.[9]

As early as 1868, the *Decatur Republican* alluded to Ku Klux Klan activity in the area, but this never deterred Bond from upholding the principles that he'd learned as a child.[10] That he allowed Plinny to bend the ears of his farm's younger employees was strong proof that he sanctioned Plinny's hobby.

Ab, while lenient on some issues, could be quite strict when it came to his family. Living in a home overrun by six rambunctious girls, a much younger wife, and a governess had to be a challenge of crazy proportions. So rules were a must, and he was quick to lay down the law. As a result, the Bond girls knew exactly what was expected of them. Delia, gentle to a fault, provided the perfect counterbalance. Yet seldom, if ever, did Emma and her sisters dare cross their father's boundaries. It was simply out of the question.

Not long after Delia wed her employer, her brother Les—by then in his early teens—came to live with the Bonds. For Ab that was akin to being blessed with a son of his own, at long last. By the time Les arrived, he had set up a small sleeping space for the boy under the main stairwell. Les took classes with the girls, upstairs. In his spare time, he worked around the farm, earning $5 a month. As he and the older girls grew toward adulthood, good times prevailed. There were wagon and sleigh rides and parties with friends, as well as Sunday school classes and singing lessons and social events at the Methodist church in the Grove. Ab tolerated most of the high jinks and teasing that are the norm in large families, but he never spared the seven youngsters a good tongue-lashing when they deserved it. He held the highest expectations, not only for his own six daughters but for anyone who lived under his roof. Nobody was exempt, except perhaps Delia.

Furthermore, Ab was not one to bend, even in the face of a good excuse—like when Les, the four oldest girls, and some friends had gone to a birthday party for Sam Sadler in the Grove. As they were returning home that evening, one of the back wheels of Bond's spring wagon fell off. "The boys found a rail nearby and, with the aid of the hitch strap, raised the bed so they could drag the wagon home. Only one could sit in the seat and drive, so Emma drove and the rest walked the four miles." Consequently, Les and the girls arrived home much later than expected. And for this, "plenty was told them at the breakfast table next morning."[11] Although the head of the house kept a tight rein on his brood as they approached maturity, he also displayed an easygoing and humorous side— with both his children and his grandchildren; as any wise parent knows, children behave much better when they are never quite sure which parental persona is going to show up in a given moment.

Of course, the youngsters weren't without responsibilities. Because of the farm's size, Ab would add as many as three dozen men to his harvest workforce. It took a substantial and collective effort to feed that temporary crew. His kitchen staff consisted of Delia, the six girls, an older black woman named Hattie (who normally worked at the Long House Hotel in Taylorville), and another young black woman, whom he affectionately dubbed "the Striker" because of her feistiness. They all worked elbow to elbow from dawn until dark to feed the ravenous farmhands their three meals a day. The final cleanup often lasted well beyond the end of the harvest, but the girls all pitched in, willingly and cheerfully.

Despite Ab's unpredictable nature and the devastating losses of their respective mothers, all seven youngsters were well-grounded and resilient individuals. Belle, the oldest, wed Hank Goodrich in 1877. Their first child, Roxanne, arrived within the year, making Ab a grandfather at the age of fifty. The couple gave him another granddaughter in February 1882. Meanwhile, Les and the second Bond girl, Maggie, fostered a romantic attachment. In April 1882, they married; hence, Ab became not only Lester's brother-in-law but also his father-in-law. He offered the newlyweds the use of a small house located on the railroad quarter of his farm so they could begin married life close to family. During this same April, Emma— the third oldest girl and an accomplished young lady in her own right—received a proposal of marriage from a local farm boy named Adams.[12] And so it was that 1882 began as a year of great promise and joy for the entire Bond family.

3

Dr. McFarland, of the Illinois Insane Asylum, who came here at the twelfth hour to testify for the defense that Guiteau is insane, had, it was stated in court, no other grounds for his testimony than the fact that he had read the case in the newspapers, and had some knowledge of the peculiarities of Guiteau's father.
—Chicago Tribune, *January 5, 1882*

The last day of June 1882 was forever linked to the fate of presidential assassin, Charles Guiteau. On that Friday, June 30, his countrymen were awaiting news of his hanging in the nation's capital. Six months earlier, Guiteau had been tried and convicted of the shooting death of President Garfield. During the previous summer, the man had entered the train depot in Washington, D.C., walked up to within three feet of the president and unloaded two bullets into his side. Amazingly, even at that close range, his aim was flawed. Consequently, Garfield had lingered for almost three months before infection finally claimed him. Now the Friday evening papers were expected to confirm what nearly everyone believed was a just and fitting end to the man responsible—nearly everyone, that is, except for one Dr. Andrew McFarland, superintendent of the Illinois State Hospital for the Insane in Jacksonville.

McFarland had aspired to testify at Guiteau's trial in January, stating that he knew the man to be insane—a conclusion he'd reached based on the fact that the assassin's father, Luther, had been insane. The doctor firmly maintained this conviction, even though Luther had never been his patient. Now, it was possible that the younger Guiteau was, indeed, mentally unstable. At the very least, he was egotistical and bizarre. But ten eminent doctors had already examined the accused and presented their assessments of him at the trial. Their opinions were varied and inconclusive, but they had each grabbed a few minutes of fame by participating in the legendary case. However, McFarland had been denied his chance to impress from the stand, thanks to Judge Walter Cox's decision that the court had heard quite enough of the insanity debate. As a result, the sulking McFarland decided to grant the *Washington Post* an interview. When asked about the mental condition of Luther Guiteau, the father of the accused,

McFarland's response had reeked of arrogance: "Allow me to preface the answer with the remark at the opinion given by one or more of the gentleman who have testified as experts in the trial of Guiteau, that insanity is not hereditary is a most astounding one, coming from such a source, as it has long been recognized as an established fact, by the medical faculty . . . insanity is one of the most hereditary of all diseases."[1]

The trial had dragged on for weeks, marked throughout by Guiteau's brazen remarks and tedious grandstanding. He'd set the tone during jury selection, by instructing his lawyers to see that "no nigger be allowed on the jury."[2] Over the course of the trial, everybody—especially the jury—had grown weary of the defendant. As to whether he was sane or not, his defense team had failed to sway the jurors with the combined testimonies of some top doctors. Ultimately, the jury of eleven white men and one "colored man" had gotten the last word.[3] On January 25, 1882, Charles Julius Guiteau was sentenced to swing from the end of a rope at high noon on Friday, June 30.

After granting the interview to the *Post*, McFarland, with his limelight rapidly fading, had decided there was no reason to stick around for the verdict. By the time the trial was over, he was already back at his regular post in Jacksonville, Illinois, knowing he would get other chances to show off his expertise. One came a few weeks later, when he testified at C. W. Stickney's murder trial in Denver, Colorado.[4] There, McFarland labeled Stickney's "fits" as epilepsy. But when he tried to say that those fits were what drove Stickney to commit the murder, his testimony was blocked.

The narcissistic doctor, it seems, had a penchant for getting his name into print, and not usually with a positive slant. In the 1860s, charges of "cruelty and oppression" and "financial mismanagement" had tarnished his reputation as the head of the Illinois Hospital for the Insane.[5] His name had also come up in connection to a nasty scandal involving a patient named Mrs. Elizabeth Packard. Committed against her will by her preacher husband—allegedly with McFarland's aid—she had made some serious allegations against the doctor who, in turn, had leveled some seamy accusations against her. Eventually, a court of law declared her legally sane and granted her release. As payback, however, she went on to write a number of tell-all books, in which she described the deplorable conditions and treatments forced on helpless patients behind the institution's closed doors.[6]

Shortly after the scandal and resulting state investigation, the doctor resigned from his Jacksonville post and took over as head of a private asylum in the same city. Like the State had before, the owners of the Oak Lawn Retreat soon grew unhappy with McFarland's management skills. When they decided to sell the place out from under him, what followed was pure chaos. "Dr. McFarland . . . refused to surrender. The buildings are barred and bolted and entrance denied to all outsiders. The gates have been closed and locked. Officers of the law will probably seek to enforce an entrance . . . and eject the occupants."[7]

Not long before the attempted lockout at the retreat, McFarland did something even more outrageous—something his colleagues found hard to explain. In St. Louis in May 1877, he chose to have his marriage to Miss Abby Knox performed in front of the entire group on the last night of the aptly named annual meeting of the Insane Superintendents of the Country.[8] This decision left those in attendance shaking their heads in disbelief. As McFarland must have seen it, there was no better way to trumpet the fact that his bride was the daughter of the well-to-do Isaac H. Knox, president of the National Stock Yards in St. Louis.

Four months after Guiteau's conviction and two months before his appointment with the gallows, McFarland made one last stab at drumming up some publicity for himself. He suggested that a committee of physicians should visit President Arthur and urge him to put a halt to Guiteau's execution. This was necessary, he claimed, because his own expert testimony had been denied at the trial. To this, one newspaper responded: "It is well known that Dr. McFarland is a good deal of a crank and it is not probable that there'll be any postponement of the execution on his request."[9] It seemed Guiteau and his champion had been cut from the same cloth. In the end, the doctor's outspoken efforts on the assassin's behalf were for naught.

Just past high noon on Friday, June 30, 1882, the man who had murdered President Garfield paid the ultimate price. As hundreds of spectators looked on, Guiteau emerged from behind the heavy gates of the Washington, D.C., jail, surrounded by nine guards. With wrists secured tightly behind his back, he moved slowly across the jail yard, showing no emotion. At the waiting scaffold, he was marched up a flight of twelve steps to a platform where his legs were bound together at the ankles. A noose was slipped over his head and tightened at his neck. And then the traditional black hood was pulled down over his face to obscure it from the gawking masses, so eager to view history in the making.

The warden watched for Guiteau's predetermined signal—the release of a piece of paper that the convicted man held in his hand. It supposedly contained a prayer. At exactly 12:40 P.M., the paper fluttered to the platform as a defiant yell of "Glory! Ready! Go!" escaped from underneath the faceless mask. In that instant, the floor dropped away and the man's body snapped to the end of the rope. The *Washington Post* described Guiteau's final exit in vivid detail:

> For at least forty seconds after the drop fell, the body hung motionless. Then there was a slight shiver or shudder due to muscular contraction, commencing in the legs and spreading up into the shoulders. Three minutes after the trap fell, the body was lowered to be examined by the physicians. There was

a decided action of the heart for fully fourteen minutes, and the pulse fluttered two minutes longer. When the body had hung with the feet just touching the ground for over half an hour, it was lowered into the coffin which was waiting for it under the scaffold.[10]

When it was over, the warden announced that anyone who so desired could file past the coffin to view the deceased. There was a general rush as a line quickly took shape. Two hours later, a team of physicians gathered around Guiteau's body in the jail chapel to perform an autopsy. They removed the criminal's brain to look for some hint of abnormality that would have explained his deviant behavior. One Dr. McWilliams said he observed nothing unusual about the gray matter of Guiteau. A Dr. Hartigan thought perhaps the brain showed signs of something that might have suggested insanity; however, he admitted that he'd seen those same signs in the brains of men who were known to have been of perfectly sound mind while alive.

As tenacious stories have a way of doing, the Guiteau tale had grown tiresome, thanks to more than a year of obsessive coverage. But in the Gilded Age, replete with its yearnings for the niceties of life, there still lurked a primitive fascination with the darker side of man's existence. And the country would now be needing something to fill the void left in the wake of Guiteau's departure; to that end, the Bond tragedy sat poised and ready. Actually, the timing couldn't have been better. For on the very day that marked the end of the assassin's long and unworthy saga, word of the schoolhouse outrage burst into the nation's headlines.

In central Illinois, any interest in Guiteau's execution was overshadowed by the news of the schoolhouse attack. The local story spread quickly, via word of mouth. Charley Montgomery, the youngest of John Montgomery's boys and the one sent to keep an eye on the Pettus girls, wasted no time in doing his part. Likewise, while making her way home after delivering Emma, Margret Pettus felt compelled to stop off at Laurence Heinlein's and share what had happened. By the time she and Lee and Clementi stopped there, the eastern horizon was already glowing.

Laurence was Margret's brother-in-law, married to her sister Elizabeth. A knock at the door at such an early hour made him cautious. He called out, asking who was there, and Margret answered back that it was she. Heinlein ushered her in. While the two young men waited outside, Margret spewed out what she knew of the attack. As she babbled on, Laurence asked Lee and Clementi to come in. He wanted more specifics. When the two hesitated, Heinlein slipped on his boots and stepped outdoors to quiz his nephew. However, his suggestion that they go at once to "alarm the neighbors" was met with a decided lack of enthusiasm.[11] After all, they'd been driving up and down Mt. Auburn Road much of the night. But when the visitors departed, Margret promised to stop at a couple more places on their way home to alert the neighbors. Before that, however, Clementi decided to head off alone, on foot. He was going to borrow a fast horse, he said, and go in search of the guilty parties himself.

Meanwhile, Heinlein set out immediately for the schoolhouse, stopping on the way to rouse his neighbor Martin Swick. Upon hearing the news, Swick tossed on some clothes, and the two left in haste. As they neared the school, they saw a lean figure of a man, pacing back and forth out front; they recognized him as William J. Montgomery—another of the Montgomery boys. The sun was just peeking over the horizon when the three met up.

During the early hours of June 30, someone from the neighborhood had had the good sense to fetch Sheriff Haines. Just who that was and how quickly that task was accomplished is unknown. Unfortunately, the sheriff lived in Taylorville proper.[12] So by the time a man could saddle up a horse, ride the fifteen or so miles into town, awaken him, tell him of the affair, and then return with him to the schoolhouse, a lot of valuable time was going to be lost. Heinlein and Swick, then, must have figured the sheriff could use some help. So together with William Montgomery, they entered the deserted schoolhouse at daybreak.

The pitch-black opening over their heads told them that they would need a lantern if they wanted to look around the windowless loft. The older men sent William to fetch one while they waited. Upon his return, Heinlein and Swick went up, lamp in hand. In spite of the limited light, their initial search yielded several pieces of good evidence. First, they noticed some of Emma's belongings lying in the rafters near the opening. Her scarf pin and parasol were both there, as was her hat. There was no floor in the loft, but they could see that a crude platform constructed of weatherboarding had been laid across the open rafters. Stuck to the north end of that platform was a handful of hair. At the very west end of the attic, on the rear wall of the building, they noticed what appeared to be a freshly cut, narrow rectangular opening. It looked as if a dull knife with a nicked blade had been used to carve the opening.

Once they were back down in the classroom, Heinlein noticed blood on the floor directly below the scuttle hole. Scrawled across the blackboard at the front of the room were some words that had nothing to do with schoolwork. Though the exact wording was never revealed, its message was something like "Beware, young woman," "Look out," or "Beware of your fate."[13] The note was apparently unfinished, but the handwriting would surely implicate someone. The only item found in the classroom was Emma's pocketbook. Somehow, Swick and Heinlein had missed it earlier. Now, William handed it to them, saying he spotted it while the two older men were searching the loft. A quick inspection showed that it was empty.

As the day brightened, curious neighbors began to arrive. Many, if not all, of these would-be detectives proceeded to swarm through the unsecured crime scene. Such a breach would trigger severe criticism today, even from the least experienced of investigators. But the concept of a compromised crime scene meant little to lawmen back then, and to the nosy men and women traipsing through the schoolhouse, it meant even less. Despite the neighbors' transgressions, they recovered more evidence, apparently overlooked by Heinlein and Swick, including a section of a Chicago newspaper and a piece of an envelope. And there was something else that might have been easily missed. A keen-eyed local man named Charley Dickerson spotted a small toenail paring as he scoured the attic in mid-morning.[14]

As the hours ticked by, the crowd at the school grew steadily larger. Meanwhile, lawmen were noticeably absent. Nevertheless, an official investigation was already underway. Sheriff Haines had decided to stop at the Bond farm en route to the school. There, he had learned all the pertinent details, although it was unclear whether those came directly from the victim or from her father. While this visit delayed his arrival at the crime scene, the decision to stop may have been a wise one. For as Friday wore on, Emma's condition grew worse. By nightfall, she was drifting in and out of consciousness. Days would pass before she could provide any more information. What the sheriff gleaned during that first interview was that as Emma reached for the school door, she was accosted from behind by a man who dropped down from the attic hatch. He slammed her hard, face-first, into the door while applying a ferocious grip on her throat, which in turn caused her to faint. Worst of all, she had gotten nary a glimpse of the man since something had been thrown over her head immediately; one report claimed that it was her shawl, and another said it was a coat.

In any case, her shawl was definitely used to hoist her aloft. Her assailant cinched it tightly around her waist, securing the knot on her right side. Then, while standing on a chair or desk, he pushed her upward from below while another man waited above to grab the end of the shawl. Together, they hauled the victim up and out of sight. This knowledge prompted Deputy Chris Hamel and two other men—Charley Dickerson and Thomas Hart—to attempt an experiment. The three tried to lift Dickerson up through the scuttle hole. Although they picked a man of about the same weight as Emma, they apparently failed to take into account several other variables that might have influenced the outcome of their practical test. These included the height of the victim versus that of her stand-in, the fabric and length of the scarf used, and the manner in which that scarf was tied around the victim's waist. Less significant, though perhaps still critical, was the slight difference in weight, plus its distribution in a female versus a male. At 127 pounds, Emma weighed slightly less than her stand-in.[15]

And, obviously, the strength of the perpetrators was unknown, which made a fair comparison impossible.

Throughout Friday, the investigation picked up steam by the hour. Lawmen in surrounding towns and counties were alerted. All up and down the rail lines, trains were detained while officers boarded them in search of potential suspects. They walked the aisles slowly—scrutinizing the faces, demeanor, and clothing of passengers. Meanwhile, word of the outrage continued to spread like a prairie wildfire whipped by an unrelenting wind. In no time, it jumped the boundaries of Christian County and made its way into adjacent counties. Decatur, in the direct path of that inferno, was the first large town to learn of the crime when Laurence Heinlein's son Sammy, postmaster and merchant in Grove City, apparently telephoned the *Republican* with the particulars of the crime perpetrated "on Miss Emma Bond, the nineteen-year-old daughter of A. D. Bond, a well-to-do farmer residing near Taylorville."[16] From there, the telegraph lines jumped to life, scattering the news far and wide—first around the state and then across the nation. With the Guiteau story having ended, the story coming out of central Illinois would be the start of a new fascination for readers, and one that would not subside any time soon.

4

They are not tramps as has been reported, but notorious characters residing in the vicinity of Grove City, a small village in the northern part of Christian County.
  —Chicago Tribune, *July 4, 1882*

Sheriff Haines knew what the people of his jurisdiction wanted, and he wasted no time in giving it to them. Within twenty-four hours, he had three local men in custody for the horrendous crime against Emma Bond. The accused had themselves, more than anyone, to thank for their speedy arrests; their strange behavior and remarks the day after the crime suggested a possible involvement. The first man arrested had acted most suspiciously of all. When picked up on Friday, Emanuel Clementi was hanging around the Blue Mound depot, supposedly waiting for the 4:19 P.M. train to St. Louis.

After leaving Lee and Mrs. Pettus just after dawn, he turned up at George Housley's door at about five o'clock. He seemed to know the Housleys owned some very fast mounts; George's brother Hank had long been involved in the business of race horses. However, he seemed unaware George was Emma's uncle when he asked to borrow George's "best horse" so he could ride toward Blue Mound in search of "some tramps who had outraged Miss Bond at the schoolhouse."[1] Upon hearing the shocking news, George willingly saddled one of his horses and handed it over to Clementi.

The village of Blue Mound sat about eight miles east of the Grove, just over the Macon County line. The place had its own tiny train depot, which offered more convenience to the people of northern Christian County than did the larger station in Taylorville. Shortly after borrowing the horse and while making his way toward Blue Mound, Clementi ran into a local man named James Armstrong. James was the brother of Bill Armstrong, another of Emma's many uncles; Bill was married to Becky Housley, Emma's aunt. Clementi stopped just long enough to tell Armstrong of the crime. Then, without explanation, he reined his horse around and headed back west, toward the Grove.

Later that morning, three local men passing near the schoolhouse also ran into Clementi. To Pleasant Venters, John Hawkins, and C. F. Knight, he repeated the story of the attack and his plan to track the two culprits toward Blue Mound. After talking, the group—Clementi included—decided to form a scouting party to track down the brutes. The four headed off in the direction of Blue Mound, based solely on the word of the farmhand. After going only a short distance, however, Clementi suddenly stopped—saying he was going to cut across the fields to search for signs of the assailants. He promised to rejoin the others on the road near Armstrong's place.

Clementi then veered off into the Pettus pasture, still soft from Wednesday night's heavy rain, while the others continued eastward on the road. Yet when the others arrived at the designated rendezvous, they were left waiting for Clementi far longer than expected. He should have easily beaten them to their meeting place. And something else was gnawing at them: each had noticed the inappropriate manner in which he had spoken of the rape. Later, they would say that they were taken aback by how he "frequently laughed in speaking of the affair."[2]

Growing weary of waiting, the three decided to return to the spot in the road where Clementi had split off. There, they set out across the Pettus pasture. One of them knew that his mount belonged to George Housley and that it was shoed; this made horse and rider easier to track. Traversing the Pettus property, they came upon a spot where other tracks appeared to join up with Clementi's. It appeared as if the farmhand had met up near a small bridge with someone on a mule and someone else on horseback. It also looked like the three riders had milled about, without dismounting, while their animals grazed on the weeds underfoot.

Just how long it took the men to catch up with Clementi is unclear, but all four finally rode into Blue Mound around nine o'clock in the morning. There, they ran into C. H. Crosley, the local train agent, and a lively discussion ensued about possible suspects. Crosley said he had noticed two strangers hanging around the village the night before. Hotelkeeper John Stumpf approached the group. Yes, he had seen the two unfamiliar men as well. They'd entered his hotel around ten o'clock on Thursday night. But they had seemed like ordinary fellows—both "neatly-dressed, nice-looking men." He described their clothes and shoes as clean and dry and confessed that he "did not notice anything peculiar about them."[3]

Stumpf assumed that when the two strangers left his hotel, they had gone to the depot to catch the next train. Hearing this, Clementi announced that he wanted to wire Mr. Bond about the men. He asked for a piece of paper, jotted something down about two strangers having gone west on an early morning freight train, and then handed it to Agent Crosley. Again, no one questioned Clementi's assumption that the suspicious parties had fled to the West on a freight train.

However, based on the rail lines of the time, to go west, one had to board a northeast-bound train to Decatur and there transfer to a westbound train. Decatur also offered other options for escape: one could go east to Indianapolis or north to Chicago, the perfect place in which to get lost. But traveling west from Blue Mound required that rather circuitous route. In fact, two passenger trains did pass through Blue Mound each night, bound for Decatur. The first steamed through the small village around quarter after ten and the second, around eleven thirty. Maybe by "west," Clementi actually meant southwest—toward St. Louis, for example. Of the St. Louis-bound passenger trains, one left Decatur at 4:15 A.M. and reached Blue Mound at 4:45 A.M. From there, it made its way through Taylorville, then Litchfield, and points farther south and west before it crossed the Mississippi and pulled into the St. Louis station. At 5:45 A.M., another passenger train came through Blue Mound on the same route.

Of course, as Clementi theorized, the two strangers might have hopped a freight train. Freights passed through Blue Mound at all hours of the day and night, and catching a free ride on one, as a train slowed to pass through town or stopped to refuel or unload goods, wasn't so implausible.[4] The village of Edinburg—just west of the Grove—had a small depot too. From there, one could ride northwest to Springfield or southeast to all sorts of places beyond Pana, a coal-mining town where several major rail lines intersected. And trains weren't the only means of escape. Dirt roads led out of the county in all directions—a few well-traveled, others less so. But Clementi was bent on the notion that the men had fled to the West. From Blue Mound. On a freight train.

Unfortunately for Clementi, none of these routes provided him a swift getaway. Late on Friday afternoon, Officer H. P. Crowe picked him up at the Blue Mound depot. As he was being taken into custody, he couldn't resist shooting off his mouth: He was innocent. He had an alibi. And he would get even with the people responsible for his arrest. The last comment only served to stoke his already fiery reputation, which followed him wherever he went. The *Tribune* depicted the farmhand as "a Spaniard who has seen a good deal of the world. He has worked on farms in this and neighboring counties for several years past, but while nothing de———[unreadable] against him was known, he has been LOOKED UPON WITH SUSPICION by the community as one who probably had some dark pages in his history."[5]

By late Friday evening, Clementi would have the company of two more suspects. Though the evidence was largely circumstantial, the sheriff thought it was enough to warrant the arrest of Clementi's two closest friends—John C. Montgomery and Lee Pettus. Both men were among those who showed up at the schoolhouse on the morning after the outrage. Montgomery arrived some-

time between eight and ten. According to him, he stayed just forty-five minutes. During that time, he went into the loft to have a look around. Later, as he
stood outside in the schoolyard, a neighbor rode by and called out, "You have
got yourself into a devil of a fix at the schoolhouse." Montgomery, taken aback,
asked the man "how he had found it out." The man replied that "he had heard
it."[6] Montgomery then explained to the man that he and his father, the elder
John, had run into each other near the school's coalhouse on Thursday afternoon and had stood there talking, unaware of the crime taking place inside.

Although Lee also stopped by the schoolhouse on Friday morning, he seemed
indifferent to the excitement there. About ten o'clock, he saw Ed Housley—one
of Emma's many cousins—standing in the schoolyard, and he asked him if he
wanted to go for a swim. Ed said he did. But when they reached the swimming
hole, Lee refused to go in the water. At the time, Ed paid no mind to his friend's
sudden change of heart.

As the crowd slowly dispersed on Friday, many gravitated toward Grove
City. By early afternoon, a substantial number were gathered along the town's
Main Street. None were inclined to leave, for fear they'd miss the latest on the
hunt for the assailants. Naturally, the attack had generated an uneasiness in the
once-trusting neighborhood. The women, especially, worried about their own
vulnerability. Not a one felt immune to the horrors that had befallen Emma.

Early that afternoon, John Montgomery and his cousin Hiram Montgomery
made their way to the Grove. Lee Pettus turned up there at about the same time.
As John and Lee mingled with their neighbors, they said and did some things
that seemed odd. The first of the incriminating encounters took place about three
o'clock, when Martin Swick and his friend Laurence Heinlein ran into Lee. The
young man was acting tense, and John—standing nearby—appeared to be the
reason. Swick tried to elicit more details about the previous night from Lee. As
Lee began to describe the condition of Emma's clothing, John came up and ordered him to be quiet, saying "he didn't know what he was talking about."[7] The
latter sheepishly obeyed, his uneasiness now more obvious than ever.

About this time, word circulated through the Grove that Clementi was under
suspicion and would soon be arrested. Upon hearing this, John started pumping
Martin Swick for information. Was Clementi still in Blue Mound? Did he say
anything about who had done the writing on the blackboard? Did he make any
sort of statement at all—or a confession, perhaps? Had he brought up his (John's)
name? When Swick said that he didn't know, John urged him to find out more.

John appeared more nervous with each passing minute and continued to
press Swick for more information. What was known about the crime, how did
the people feel about it, and was there a possibility of mob action? Lee and John
then stepped away, out of Swick's earshot. As they stood off to the side talking,

Lee repeatedly turned a worried look in the direction of Mr. Bond. Emma's father was there to learn what evidence had been recovered. Understandably, his need to know was so overpowering that within days, his impatience would prompt him to hire a private investigator.

It was late afternoon when the concerned crowd finally began to disperse. John left around four o'clock, and shortly after that, his life began to unravel. When confirmation of Clementi's arrest worked its way back to the neighborhood, John set out to find Henry Crowe, the arresting officer. According to the officer, John wanted to know "if Clementi had given him away." That he dared pose that particular question was evocative. Crowe refused to elaborate but did tell him about Clementi's threats, directed at unnamed persons. When the nervous young man asked what exactly the threat was, Crowe answered: "To make those who caused his arrest suffer."[8]

Meanwhile, the neighborhood's self-appointed detectives, Martin Swick and Laurence Heinlein, were busy hatching a scheme. They would seek out Lee Pettus and John Montgomery and tell them Clementi had confessed and had named the two of them in his statement. Although this was an utter concoction, maybe it would encourage the brothers-in-law to talk. Early Friday evening, Lee received the first calculated visit from his uncle Laurence and Mr. Swick. They informed him that Clementi had implicated him, and then pressed the lad to tell everything he knew. He looked them squarely in the eye and insisted he knew nothing. When he failed to give the men what they were after, they left to find John. They used the same approach on him, insisting Clementi had pointed the finger at both him and Lee. John said that he already knew about it but "didn't see how that could be."[9]

Actually, John seemed more concerned about the escalating anger among his neighbors. A discussion developed, centering on the possibility of an irate mob forming and what John might do to protect himself in such an event. Heinlein reassured him he had nothing to worry about if he was innocent. But those words brought little solace to John's racing mind. Here, the older men fibbed again, telling the now panicked John that "the people didn't think he was in the thing, but that he caught the other boys, Lee Pettus and Emanuel Clementi, in the schoolhouse."[10] When this tactic didn't get them very far either, they again switched gears, telling John that Lee had also implicated him. The young man cried out, "My God, what shall I do?"[11] Failing to secure any real admission from their agitated subject, Heinlein and Swick finally gave up and left.

Later that evening, as the sun dipped toward the western horizon, they again met up with John on the road to Grove City. This time he was with Lee's brother George. Another interrogation ensued. Who said what? Who knew what? As darkness settled over the prairie, more neighbors arrived on the scene and gathered around to listen to John and his denials. But the more he talked, the more he incriminated himself. He asked what would happen to him if he told what he knew. Somebody suggested that he and Lee should figure out a way to "fix up their story and throw it all on Clementi."[12] John seemed to warm to that idea and asked that the plan be relayed to his brother-in-law, with instructions to Lee "not to admit anything or give anything away."[13]

Unbeknownst to John, however, it was already too late. As the scheme was taking shape, a neighbor rode up, confirming that Lee had just been arrested. In that instant, all of John's resolve evaporated. Picturing a noose around his neck, he begged for reassurances that he would not be harmed if he told what he knew. A voice in the group promised him a safe escort to the Taylorville jail. As the men stood there discussing his dwindling options, an officer of the law rode up on horseback and, within seconds, John C. Montgomery became the third man arrested for the rape of Emma Bond.

It was common knowledge that the three friends "were almost constantly together."[14] Montgomery was married to Lee Pettus's sister Mattie, and the friendship between the two went well beyond that of brothers-in-law. Both had deep roots in the community—unlike the outsider Clementi. Their families had been part of the great influx of pioneers who'd come to Illinois in the 1850s and were among the area's most respected names. For decades, the Pettuses and the Montgomerys had lived on adjacent plots of land at the south end of Mt. Auburn Township. Over time, the two clans had become intertwined through marriages, grandchildren, and the inevitable merging of property through inheritances. So John and Lee shared that common bond.

There were, of course, notable differences among the three. Lee was barely twenty, a youngster compared to John, who was nearing thirty-three. Clementi, whose twenty-sixth birthday was approaching, fell midway between the two. John had the responsibilities of a wife and children, whereas Lee and Clementi were still young, single, and carefree—each with an eye for the young ladies.[15] Clementi was a hired farm laborer. However, John ran his own successful farm, and Lee had a personal stake in his mother's farm, for he stood to inherit half of it. Their futures held the promise of success and prosperity, whereas Clementi's future bore no such promise; like most hired hands, he was reputed to be a drifter.

Young men born into less-than-fortunate circumstances often took to the roads in search of temporary farm work. Some stuck close to home, but the drifters kept going and never looked back. The work did have its perks—namely free room and board. But, it was grueling labor, suitable for only the young and the fit. Wages were a pittance, and there was no such thing as job permanence. These laborers usually squandered away what little they earned on gambling or drinking or prostitution, if not all three. Then the work would dry up, the money would run out, and the drifters would move on—out of boredom and discontent and, only rarely, in search of something better. Clementi, though, had lingered in the county longer than most men of his ilk. He must have found something there to his liking. Maybe it was the comfortable upstairs bedroom inside the Pettus house that anchored him. Or maybe he stayed because of his bond with Pettus and Montgomery, but that alliance was bound to weaken in time, mainly because of his background. Nevertheless, in the summer of 1882, the three men were as thick as blood brothers. Could their friendship withstand the coming test, or would it crack under pressure?

Constable William Eltzroth transported John Montgomery to Taylorville, without incident. Deputy Sheriff Hamel escorted Lee Pettus to the jail. Clementi was already there to greet them. It would later be noted that the three suspects had reacted quite differently when arrested. Clementi had immediately thrown out the word "alibi," letting it be known that he had one. Lee and John, on the other hand, made no attempt to explain their whereabouts on Thursday—which would later come back to haunt them. In the end, second-guessing their reactions was pointless. For very early on Saturday morning, July 1, the three friends were officially booked into the Christian County jail, charged with a crime that would soon pit relative against relative and neighbor against neighbor.[16]

5

The evidence against the prisoners is well-nigh conclusive and should Miss Bond die from injuries received at their hands, a mob will doubtless hurry their souls off to the final tribunal by the hemp route.
—Decatur Review, *July 22, 1882*

In 1880, Christian County was home to 28,227 mostly law-abiding citizens. In just thirty years, the pioneering souls who had come to settle there had increased its population tenfold. The jailhouse in use that year was the county's second. Completed in 1870, it was a more than adequate facility, considering the disposition of the people it served.

It had become obvious that the county needed a larger jail. The new structure—a solid, two-story brick structure—was erected at a cost of $5,360.[1] Its only shortcoming was its location, two blocks southwest of the courthouse. Prisoners were housed on the second floor of the jail, where ten cells lined a central hallway—five on each side. At two men per cell, the place could accommodate twenty inmates. If the citizenry really got out of hand, the surplus could be housed in the seven-foot-wide center corridor. The county claimed it could squeeze in as many as forty or fifty errant citizens, if need be. But that was never going to happen—not in a place like Christian County.

When the three rape suspects were booked into the jail on Saturday, July 1, they joined a handful of other detainees. Charles Meyers had been there since the previous fall—awaiting his day in court for murder. His accomplice in the crime, George Traughber, was there, too. John Dunn, himself accused of a rape, had been incarcerated since April. Edwin Burritt had been locked up in May on charges of burglary and larceny. The latest addition to the cell block was Benjamin F. Scott, booked in early June for assault to commit murder.[2] By any county's standards, this was a tough bunch. For the jail's existing residents, the arrival of three new prisoners provided a break from the usual monotony.

Conditions at the jail weren't that uncomfortable. Mrs. Clark, the jail's widowed housekeeper, prepared some good home-cooking for her boys behind bars.[3] With the jail nowhere close to full, each man had a cell all to himself. And Sheriff Haines wasn't exactly a stickler for rules. During the daytime, cell doors were unlocked and prisoners were allowed to mingle in the center hallway. The sheriff apparently bent the rules even further on occasion. Apparently, on that Saturday, July 1, he allowed John to go over to the square, alone, to secure his own bond.[4] The Pettus family members intended to bail out Lee just as soon as they could manage it, but it was going to take them a bit longer to round up the necessary cash. The chance of Clementi's coming up with bail was almost nonexistent; he lacked any financial means of his own and had no family nearby to help him out. He did have a mother, Maria, who lived in Milwaukee; but whether she could get to Taylorville, let alone help her son out, was doubtful. John's jail stay, at least, would be a short one. First thing Monday morning, his bond was paid, and he was released.

Sheriff Haines had moved swiftly to put the three suspects behind bars, but that accomplishment had not tempered the public's wrath in the least. A. D. Bond was one of the few who was willing to let the justice system do its job; however, those who did not know him personally marveled at his self-restraint. While the world expected a much different reaction from the father of a victim such as Emma, his closest friends weren't surprised that he was standing strong in his convictions:

> His bearing throughout this trying ordeal has been deserving of the highest praise. Under ordinary circumstances, he is an impetuous and easily excited man, and he was expected to lose no time in seeking revenge. . . . But to him is due the credit of preventing all attempts at mob law. When a body of determined men . . . announced their readiness to follow him in an attack upon the jail, Mr. Bond dissuaded them from their purpose and prevailed upon them to wait until the guilt of the prisoners was established more conclusively. A large number of his neighbors have been ready to lynch the suspected men had Mr. Bond said the word, but his advice and that of Judge Vandeveer . . . have made it improbable that any acts of violence will be attempted.[5]

The accused probably had Mr. Bond's Quaker upbringing to thank for his exceptional self-control. Not everyone in the county reacted with that kind of restraint, however. By Monday, a mentality of revenge had secured a foothold in the county, and its instigators seemed hell-bent on taking matters into their own hands, with or without Mr. Bond's permission. That afternoon, a belligerent crowd showed up at the jailhouse, ready to storm the building. When the angry participants heard John was no longer on the premises, they began chanting for Lee.

Somehow, the sheriff managed to keep control during the confrontation. But it was a real eye-opener; once the crowd dispersed, he decided it was time to implement countermeasures. He fired off an urgent telegram to Governor Shelby Cullom, asking for backup. In response to the volatile situation, Cullom "instructed [Sheriff Haines] to call out a posse and telegraphed to the Capt. of the local militia to hold his command in readiness to assist."[6] Captain James Culver's Guard soon took up watch near the jailhouse, armed to the tooth. As added insurance, the captain let it be known that his men would take whatever action necessary to protect the prisoners.

Luckily for Montgomery, he'd gotten himself out of jail *and* out of town before the fracas erupted. A timely move—or perhaps not, given one dire prediction in the *Decatur Review*: "The feeling against Montgomery seems to be especially bitter and he is set down as the ringleader and chief instigator of the crime. So strong is this opinion that should he venture to return to his home, he would be very roughly handled."[7] There seemed good reason for the mounting suspicions. Although the evidence against John was deemed circumstantial, there was that nagging matter of the toenail bit found at the scene and the hole hacked out of the rear wall of the loft; these particularly troublesome pieces of evidence were both being linked to him.

No time was wasted in trying to match the toenail paring to someone's large toe. Two days after the crime, this minute piece of evidence—after having passed through an untold number of hands—found its way to the jailhouse. There, it was decided that a comparison should be made, particularly because John's toenails looked to have been recently trimmed. He agreed to submit his big toes to scrutiny and was removed to Judge McCaskill's office, where Sheriff Haines and State's Attorney John G. Drennan conducted the test in the presence of several witnesses. The initial assessment was that the loose paring "exactly fitted the nail of one of Montgomery's toes."[8] Most damning was a rough ridge or seam on the clipping, which seemed to line up with the one running down the middle of the suspect's toenail.

Though this consensus would later come under question, the case against Montgomery was further bolstered by the fact that when taken into custody he was found to be carrying a knife on his person—specifically a dull one with two nicks in the blade, the very kind thought to have carved the hole in the rear attic wall. With these two strikes against him, it didn't help that he also closely fit the description of one of Emma's attackers. This opinion was based on his age, size, and "chin whiskers."

Before his release from jail, Montgomery's lawyers tipped him off about the brewing hostilities, and, wisely, he paid heed. After posting bond, he sought refuge at a relative's home rather than risk returning to his own place. And while the evidence did not bode well for him, other clues—just as damaging—suggested that his brother-in-law Lee also had some explaining to do. The section of newspaper and the piece of envelope were both thought to belong to Pettus: "The paper, which they claim to have been reading that afternoon under the tree has been found in the schoolhouse loft, also a piece of an envelope, the counterpart of which was found on the person of one of the prisoners."[9] Although the paper didn't say who "they" were or on whose person the piece of envelope was found, another article offered this: "The evidence against Pettus is based on a piece of paper found in the loft. This piece is part of a *Chicago Times*, the remaining portion of which was found at Pettus's home."[10]

While Montgomery and Pettus faced a tough road ahead because of the evidence, Clementi was plagued by his reputation. Meanwhile, the press was in disagreement on who was the real mastermind behind the attack. While the *Decatur Review* was taking aim at Montgomery, its larger and more prestigious counterpart to the north, the *Chicago Tribune,* had the itinerant farm worker squarely in its crosshairs: "He has more brains than Montgomery and Pettus together, is cool, calculating and cunning, and is now believed to have been the one who planned the plot so successfully carried out."[11] Of course, opinions were one thing. Irrefutable proof was another.

The investigation, meanwhile, harbored some glaring shortcomings of its own: the leads not pursued, the details overlooked, and the questions asked too late or not at all. Not until Saturday, a full day and a half after the crime, did anyone scrutinize the suspects' clothing for blood. In view of this oversight, it seems even more doubtful that the men's bodies were checked for telltale scratches or cuts.

Emma had given a fairly generic description of her assailants' clothing. They'd been wearing dark pants and white shirts, she said. Her observations on their footwear had been much more explicit, however: one wore a new pair of rubber boots and the other, low shoes and red stockings. Still, with that kind of information floating around, it wasn't likely that the perpetrators would be caught dead in that footwear. And yet nobody followed up to determine whether any of the accused owned such things. And other pertinent clues fell by the wayside: the tuft of red hair, the handwriting scrawled on the blackboard, the two men seen near the Blue Mound depot—all possibly relevant, but all given little attention during the early investigation.

As was to be expected, not everybody believed the right men were in jail. Family and close friends of the accused held to a much different version of what had taken place, and all of them were ready to come forward and back up the men's alibis. The elder John Montgomery attempted to dispel the most detrimental evidence against his oldest son, as reported in the *Decatur Review* the following Wednesday:

> His father says that John was at his house from two till three o'clock in the afternoon of the day the outrage was committed; that he went with him nearly a quarter of a mile past the schoolhouse to Younker's where he, John, remained until about six o'clock, when his father returned from the Grove, when he and his father went up to Mrs. Pettus's, which is still nearer the schoolhouse than Younker's. He claims he can prove the whereabouts of John from 10 a.m. till 8 p.m. of the day; that the paper evidence is a myth; that the toenail alleged to have been found will fit any ordinary toe, and that the knife marks are genuine, for John did cut a sliver from the hole in the gable the morning after, when a search was being made. He says that his son did conceal himself from the mob, not from a sense of guilt, but from necessity; that he will be present at the preliminary hearing on Wednesday next, the 12th inst., and that he will show himself innocent.[12]

Likewise, the other two suspects had a whole slew of Pettuses lined up, ready to vouch for how they'd spent their Thursday. Nevertheless, questions continued to surface in the press, reasonable ones, like: "Why have not the men, if innocent, and their friends sought out the guilty parties?" The writer offered his own answer, which was every bit as logical as his question: "If all reports be true, they have had about enough to attend to take care of themselves for the past few days." He added this postscript:"Yesterday, Mr. Montgomery and one of the Pettus brothers were at Blue Mound looking up the fellows who came there the night of the occurrence. These fellows were seen at Litchfield next day, and were seen to hide what has been found to be a bottle partially filled with chloroform. Yesterday, Mr. Freshwater of Blue Mound, who saw the fellows in that village, went to Litchfield. And securing that bottle and a further description of the men, went to Waverly in pursuit."[13] Never mind that a full week had elapsed before the hunt commenced or that the pursuit was initiated by someone other than a law officer. This development sounded promising. Sure, it could have been a smokescreen, fanned by those loyal to the suspects, but to ignore this kind of information indicated a lack of thoroughness on the part of those charged with solving the crime.

The Litchfield connection raised some additional questions. Who first noticed the two men in Litchfield and assumed they were the same tramps seen in

Blue Mound? From whom did Mr. Freshwater secure the bottle of chloroform and that further description? Were there identifying marks on the bottle to prove it was connected to the schoolhouse crime? What prompted Mr. Freshwater to proceed on to Waverly? And, more to the point, why did his search end there? Curiously, this particular bottle, its contents, journey, and final whereabouts would go unaddressed during the court proceedings. Finally, if this was such a solid set of leads, why didn't the sheriff take that "further description" and go in search of answers? Perhaps he had already determined that the leads were dead ends—or possibly contrived.

The writer of the *Review* article did raise one point in favor of the accused, however: "For the arrest and conviction of the guilty parties, Mr. Wilkenson of Taylorville has offered $500; Mr. Bond $100; Mr. Pettus $500; Mr. Montgomery $—[illegible]. There is enough to tempt detectives and no doubt more can be secured if any effort is made."[14] Of course, the article did not specify which Mr. Pettus or which Mr. Montgomery had contributed to the cause. It could have been the elder Mr. Montgomery rather than his son or George Pettus rather than his younger brother, Lee. It wasn't even clear which Mr. Bond had chipped in—the victim's father or his cousin Sonny? The general belief that the suspects had no shortage of resources was also being promoted by the press, which declared: "Their people have plenty of cash."[15] That may have been an erroneous assumption, at least in regard to the Pettuses, since several days had elapsed and they had yet to raise the cash for Lee's bail. Luckily for him, by the end of the week, the unrest had mellowed to the point that the sheriff felt safe in sending home the militia.

Surprisingly little was said about motive. The first mention of one did not appear until a full week after the crime when the *Review* submitted this explanation: "Lee Pettus was in love with the girl, but she repulsed his advances. Montgomery and Clementi interceded for him but without changing Miss Bond's feelings. Pettus then grew desperate and to ruin the girl and prevent her marriage with young Adams, he planned the outrage and secured the aid of Montgomery and Clementi in its execution."[16]

If the public needed a reason, a theory—something, anything—that would account for the crime's viciousness, well then, there it was in black and white. The *Tribune* presented its own take on a motive but without naming any names:

Miss Emma Bond . . . is a young lady of attractive appearance, whose accomplishments are superior to those usually possessed by young women with her opportunities. She was not only equal to the best in all the domestic duties so essential in the education of a farmer's daughter, but had also received a good education, and was able, on a moment's notice, to leave the kitchen and appear to advantage in the parlor. In fact she was fitted to adorn any station in life which she might be called upon to fill, and it was probably her superiority over most of the young women of the neighborhood which led to her recent misfortune. Being a girl of irreproachable character and of high spirit, she disdained to associate with those whom she did not consider worthy companions, and never allowed any such low characters as those now suspected of this crime to have any more communication with her than was absolutely necessary. It has been learned that HER INDEPENDENCE in this respect had been unfavorably commented upon by some of the men of the neighborhood who had manifested a desire to become better acquainted with her and the horrible manner in which she was treated renders it probabl[e] that the perpetrators were actuated as much by a spirit of malicious revenge as by anything else.[17]

Although this made the victim sound a bit snobbish, the *Tribune* did praise her admirable qualities, singling out "HER INDEPENDENCE." Regrettably, in Emma's day, a good portion of the male population still considered a woman's "independence" an undesirable trait. The bold lettering probably reinforced their belief that the Bond girl had gotten just what she deserved. In fact, her independence may have been the very thing that had provoked her attacker. According to modern-day profilers of sexual predators, rapists who know their victims seek to dominate, humiliate, retaliate. To accomplish that, they resort to violence, sexual aggression, and gross torture—with verbal threats and personal ridicule as added insurance. In such an abuser's mind, the victim is always at fault. She has ignored him or rejected him or defied him in ways only an independent woman would dare.

Assuming the paper's reference to Emma's independence was meant as a positive one, it sharply contrasted everything being written about the suspects. Yet, as the *Decatur Review* so succinctly pointed out: "Where there is so much excitement as in this case . . . reports become exaggerated and mere hints or suggestions soon grow into reports and facts."[18] Opinions often came across as truth, and facts were seldom verified. But to call the evidence against the suspects "well-nigh conclusive" may have been pushing it—especially since the suspects had yet to set foot in a court of law.[19]

Certainly, prejudicial and inflammatory remarks about the suspects appeared in many papers; the press has always enjoyed the widest of latitudes in exercising its First Amendment rights. But as this case unfolded, journalists repeatedly pushed the limits of free speech. Words bordering on libel were frequently aimed at the suspects. In fact, some of the pretrial commentary came perilously close to affecting their rights to a fair trial. Language that could incite civil unrest and violence was perhaps the most risky, and yet the press seemed to be goading the public in that very direction. However, the U.S. Supreme Court has always held that the burden of proof is virtually insurmountable in matters of free speech, and in this case, the press corps clearly trusted its immunity without reservation.

While the public's indignation seemed to be abating, the condition of the victim was growing steadily worse. Dr. Cornell issued frequent updates on Emma's health. On July 14, he downgraded his initial prognosis, saying: "She is in a critical condition . . . unable to turn herself in the bed and every movement is attended by agonizing pain. Her spine is badly injured, caused by the shawl that the fiends bound so tightly around her body, the shawl knot pressing against her spine during all the time the devils were ravishing her person."[20] With this discouraging turn, the original date for the preliminary hearing was postponed, in hopes that the victim might yet be able to testify.

At her home, Emma's sisters, stepmother, and close friends were coping with the realization that her days might be numbered. Only her father refused to surrender to that fear. Instead, he reaffirmed his belief that Emma would, indeed, recover; he simply could not accept the idea of losing his daughter. As everyone prayed for some positive news of her condition, the days dragged by and the investigation ground to a halt. Then in mid-July came the news of Mary Todd Lincoln's death. The story momentarily captured the country's interest, though hardly its sympathies; the multitudes who had so revered her husband never warmly embraced the poor widow. Mrs. Lincoln's death temporarily distracted the public from the Bond story, but within a week, the more intriguing Christian County affair was again at the center of public interest.

After the speedy arrests and the initial glut of disturbing details on the crime, there'd been the disappointing news that the hearing would have to be postponed, forcing the journalists to drum up something more to sustain their readers. Consequently, the rumor mill began to churn. There were hints that other unnamed parties were involved. As many as three private detectives were said to be working the case. Locals believed that Emma's father was the driving force behind the expanded manhunt, although Bond himself was mum on the subject.

Where Bond was not inclined to talk with the press, others were more than willing to do so. Speaking candidly, the sheriff announced that "only a small portion of the gang interested in the outrage has been apprehended" and that "startling developments will follow the discovery of the person who purchased the chloroform used on the girl."[21] State's Attorney Drennan had some things to say publicly, too. In referring to the local suspects, he let slip that "he does not think that they can be the guilty parties, their people are so respectable."[22]

Understandably, that was not what the victim's family needed to hear from the lawyer who would be leading the offense. Drennan must have had second thoughts about his lapse in judgment, or perhaps someone enlightened him. On July 20, the *Tribune* alluded to Drennan's reversal: "He would give nothing of the new testimony, but admitted that he believed it was sufficient to convict the parties under arrest." The article concluded: "This is an important statement, in view of the fact that Mr. Drennan has heretofore held a different opinion."[23]

Punishment—or vindication, perchance—was not going to come swiftly. As July wore on, it became increasingly clear that a timely trial was a pipe dream, thanks in large part to Emma's slow recovery. Dr. Cornell now believed she would not be up and about for at least three more months, if at all. The preliminary hearing had been postponed twice—first pushed back to July 22 and then to August 1. Meanwhile, rumors hinted of more arrests and a resurgence of mob activity.

In late July came the grim news that Emma had lost so much strength that she would probably not survive. With the advent of antibiotics still decades away, infection from her external wounds was unavoidable. The severity of her internal injuries, however, was more difficult to assess. She was said to be in constant pain, which forced her doctors to ease her suffering with "restoratives," which were most likely opiates. Being bedridden and unable to move, she had quite possibly developed pneumonia. There was no way to know if she would ever make it to court.

Naturally, nobody was more anxious for the proceedings to get under way than the two men still behind bars. Neither had been able to come up with bail. On July 20, a *Tribune* reporter stated, "Pettus and Clementi were visited at the jail this morning but refused to talk. Both are ordinary-looking country youths. Clementi is quite sick with throat trouble and looks thoroughly terror-stricken."[24] Another five days went by before Pettus's family scrounged up the cash to gain his release. However, Clementi wasn't so lucky; it was beginning to look like he might be stuck in jail indefinitely.

As Sheriff Haines promised, another suspect was about to be charged in the crime. On July 30, William J. Montgomery—younger brother of John C.—was taken into custody.[25] Like the other three, he was officially charged with both rape and robbery, even though his arrest seemed to stem from the pocketbook incident at the schoolhouse. Evidently, Heinlein and Swick thought it odd that they had missed the item initially and that it had miraculously appeared in William's hands, right after they'd come down from the loft. William, of course, had been there at dawn—before anybody else. Of his own admission, he had rummaged through the pocketbook. And it didn't help that he was also related to one of the suspects. Still, the case against him seemed thin, at best. William—like his brother John—had no trouble posting bail, and he was back home before nightfall that same day.

In spite of this fourth arrest, the unofficial hunt for coconspirators continued, with the press dropping the vaguest of hints. Those already charged "are not the only ones concerned in the case," declared the *Republican,* adding, "People will be surprised when the whole truth comes out, and the attorneys for the defense will be more surprised than anyone else."[26] Bond's probe was said to be progressing, even though he still wasn't talking. And if anybody else knew what was going on, they weren't talking either. Then on August 1, a *Tribune* headline confirmed that Emma's father was "on the Track of Another Suspected Party."[27]

It was true. A. D. Bond had hired a private detective, C. W. Page of St. Louis. Page's investigation led him and Bond to Springfield, if not other places, in pursuit of a drifter named Hobbs. There, at the army's recruiting office, Sergeant Ricketts confirmed that he had recently escorted a Private Hobbs and eleven other enlistees to the barracks in Columbus, Ohio. Bond and Page explained to him that they had "pretty conclusive evidence" linking Hobbs to the schoolhouse outrage.[28] Very little was written of this latest suspect or why Bond and Page suspected him. But, like Clementi, he was a drifter with a questionable background. An Indiana native who was about the same age as the victim, Hobbs had been in Omaha City, Nebraska, in 1880, working as a teamster. By 1882, however, he was in Christian County, doing farm labor. Then, shortly before the Bond outrage, he had picked up and moved on again. According to the *Tribune,* he had joined the army in Springfield on July 21.[29]

One day after the *Tribune* leaked the story about Hobbs, two thousand people converged on the Taylorville courthouse, expecting the preliminary hearing to commence. To their surprise, they were turned away; it had been postponed again. Even A. D. Bond showed up, unaware of the change. The new date was set for exactly one week later, Tuesday, August 8. By the time it finally got underway, the number of suspects had risen to five, although only four would be present in court. That fifth man—enlistee Elliott Hobbs—still sat a world away in his Ohio barracks.

2

THE HEARING AND THE INDICTMENT

August 8, 1882–December 6, 1882

6

Sheriff Haines, who has decided to rely on his civil power to preserve order, feels confident that his forces will be equal to the emergency.
—Chicago Tribune, *August 8, 1882*

Tuesday, August 8, 1882. Christian County's residents had had enough of all the hearsay and conjecture about the Bond crime. They were more than ready to learn the real truth in a court of law, and a good many of them were about to descend on the county courthouse to do so.

Taylorville, because of its central location, was predestined to become the county seat. That title had been bestowed upon it in 1839, and the county's first courthouse had been commissioned that same year. Built of hand-hewn oak and walnut, the small, humble structure had two floors, with a simple office upstairs and a stark courtroom downstairs. The courtroom was barely large enough for a circuit-riding judge, a couple of lawyers, the sometimes necessary jury, and a few curious onlookers, to say nothing of the requisite chairs, tables, and benches. Despite its modest size, its walls had once echoed with the eloquence and humor of Illinois's most famous lawyer, Abraham Lincoln.

By 1854, however, that historic two-story log structure had outlived its usefulness. In its place, the county decided to erect a more substantial center of law and justice. Local citizens wanted something akin to eastern courthouses, like those they remembered from their childhoods. These were typically majestic, constructed of natural stone, and topped with stately domes or clock towers. But Christian County's was a practical and frugal citizenry, to whom bricks and a modest cupola seemed the most sensible choices. This second courthouse was completed in 1856 for just over $13,000. A continuous fence separated its inner courtyard from the sometimes muddy, sometimes dusty, streets that surrounded the square. Unfortunately, the people had forgotten to address one very annoying and constant problem—its solution: "Steps were to be made over the fence around the courthouse and the south steps were to be fixed to keep the hogs out of the courthouse."[1]

Inside, county offices occupied the first floor. The second floor was where the Bond hearing would take place. It housed a room for the circuit clerk and two small jury rooms, one of them doing double duty as the circuit judge's office. The rest of the second floor was taken up by the courtroom itself, which was indeed impressive: "Two stairways from the lower hall furnish access to a large hall or vestibule above, which is separated from the courtroom by a large double door."[2] The courtroom's gallery could accommodate five hundred people and was separated from the bench by the usual low wooden railing, strategically placed to keep spectators at bay. Carpeting helped soften the loud and contentious exchanges that took place within its four walls.

The courtroom's splendor, however, did not make up for its one major flaw: nobody was ever truly comfortable within its confines. A scathing 1890 report summed up its pitfalls: "For inconvenience and for being uncomfortable, if there is a room in the state that can excel it, we have not yet seen it. With gas and smoke filling it without ventilation, it is a wonder men can live, much less do business in such a place. One third more business could be done each day, if the room were properly ventilated."[3] In summer, with the poor ventilation, the place could quickly turn into a Dante's inferno; too many people on a warm day, and everybody would start to simmer like a slow-cooking stew. That was bound to be the case in mid-August 1882.

The good citizens of Christian County could overlook their own discomfort but not the fact that Emma was still bedridden, unable to lift her head from her pillow, which only fueled their impatience for the hearing. A "Special Dispatch," dated August 7, revealed new details on the victim's state:

> The most serious injury from the rough handling she received [has] re-
> sulted in congestion of the spine, and this increased until it has occasioned
> neuralgia of the heart. Miss Bond has been suffering from very severe par-
> oxysms each alternate day, which have usually lasted several minutes at
> a time. . . . Last Saturday, one of unusual violence came on, and even the
> doctors . . . believed for a time that she was dead, her pulse and breath-
> ing having ceased for as much as three minutes. The physicians, however,
> revived her by the use of restoratives. . . . Today the acute paroxysms ex-
> pected did not trouble her. . . . She is still liable, however, to be carried off
> by any of these severe attacks. . . . She bears her terrible sufferings with re-
> markable courage and, while conscious of her nearness to death, is cheer-
> ful and hopeful of recovery. She made a full statement of the affair Friday
> [August 4], being at that time in full possession of her mental faculties.

This has not been made public, but it is believed that she has identified some of her assailants and given a clear account of the outrage.[4]

The mention of a statement given by the victim and detailing her assault confirmed that Emma Bond would not be present at the preliminary hearing.

Long before eleven o'clock, when the hearing was set to commence, people began streaming into Taylorville from all directions. Hitching posts on the square proved hard to come by, forcing many who came by wagon to park their rigs down the side streets. Fakirs, or vendors "of the class that attend country fairs and follow in the wake of a circus," set up shop on every walkway near the square, hawking whatever the locals could be cajoled into buying.[5] Trains had taken on more and more passengers along their routes so that by the time they pulled into one of the town's two depots, they were jammed to capacity. Those arriving on the Wabash faced a healthy half-mile hike in the August sun.

As the starting hour drew near, the atmosphere in and around the courthouse was one of pandemonium, the likes of which had seldom been seen in the region. The crush at the courtroom entrance was described thus: "For an hour at least, these people endured the suffocating atmosphere of the closely packed stairway leading to the courtroom and when the doors were finally opened, the rush for seats was a spectacle worth seeing. In a few moments every inch of standing room was occupied. . . . Attempts were vain to compel the crowd to take seats. This was found to be impossible, but the spectators maintained very good order despite the fact that they were packed together like sardines."[6]

With the courtroom filled to overflowing, many were turned away. The latecomers were "obliged to content themselves with wandering about the streets and picking up such scraps of information as were carried outside by those unable to stand the pressure of the crowd in the courtroom."[7] Nevertheless, the possibility of getting into the afternoon session kept the majority from leaving.

Justice James Brooks, who was set to hear the case, had foreseen the onslaught and had pressed every deputy into service.[8] Additional hands, whom the sheriff had sworn in in advance, also stood at the ready. Haines expressed confidence that his men were up to the task. In addition to the influx of spectators, dozens more were present in a much different capacity. In fact, between them, the State and the defense had issued more than 160 witness subpoenas.[9] As the first matter of business, lead defense attorney Anthony Thornton asked that Justice Brooks step down on grounds of prejudice. The papers failed to note a specific reason for this request; however, Brooks agreed, and Justice James B. Ricks was summoned to take over. As the court awaited his arrival, a stenographer busied himself near the front of the room.

A small entry in Monday's *Republican*—noting that Thornton would travel from Decatur to Taylorville in the company of that stenographer—brought to light one of the case's stranger coincidences. For his name was none other than John Montgomery, John T. Montgomery. Unlike the two Abner Bonds, however, stenographer John T. and lead suspect John C. were evidently not related—at least not closely enough that anybody could determine.[10] Still, the name was bound to cause confusion; hence, in subsequent press accounts, the stenographer's middle initial was usually included in his name. At the time, trained court reporters were few and far between, so John T. Montgomery's talents were in great demand. The courts in the region depended on him to work their most important cases— usually those involving murder, rape, and other felonies. And the Bond case was one of the most important to hit central Illinois in a long, long time.

While waiting for Justice Ricks to arrive, State's Attorney John G. Drennan took a few moments to contemplate the challenges he would face in the days ahead. He knew that all eyes and ears would be focused on him, and he certainly had no intention of letting down his electorate. In 1880, on the heels of a meteoric rise up the legal ladder, he'd been elected state's attorney. His admission to the bar had come just two years before that—on his twenty-fourth birthday; he had passed his bar exam on his first attempt, outscoring all of the seventeen other young hopefuls who had taken the exam with him. In time, he would be touted as one of the most successful lawyers and businessmen in his county, "a man of pleasing address, frank and open in manner . . . quick, logical and resolute."[11]

But on this day, still months shy of his twenty-eighth birthday, he found himself at the helm of a stellar prosecuting team, preparing to tackle an extremely sensitive case. It promised to be a daunting task. Young, definitely, inexperienced, probably—but foolhardy, Drennan was not. He had assembled some of the best legal minds in the area to sit at his side. Chief among them was veteran attorney Horatio M. Vandeveer. Another of Taylorville's eminent attorneys, James Muirson Taylor, would also assist.

Vandeveer was an icon; born in Indiana in 1816, he was one of the best known and most respected lawyers in Illinois. After becoming the first member of the bar from Christian County, he had dedicated his life to public service. There wasn't much he hadn't done during his long and illustrious career. He'd held numerous local and state offices, and for most of the 1870s, he had presided over the circuit court, demonstrating his "ability, integrity, and impartiality."[12] His credentials were impeccable. But more important, at sixty-six, he could boast of more years of legal experience than Drennan and Taylor combined.

His family's name and reputation were equally renowned throughout the region, indeed across the state. The Vandeveers had tapped the land's riches, and their success was visible throughout Christian County. In 1868, Horatio had organized a bank bearing the family name; at one point, it ranked as "the strongest private bank" in the entire country, "its financial stability fortified by thirteen thousand acres of land located in Christian County."[13] His family was also responsible for the new Vandeveer Opera House. Under construction and due for completion in 1883, it promised to greatly enrich the fabric of a community that might otherwise have been shortchanged in the arts.

The third man at the prosecution table, James M. Taylor, had more experience than Drennan, but not nearly as much as Vandeveer. He'd been born in Scotland in 1839—the same year Vandeveer had been admitted to the bar. He'd come to the States before reaching adulthood, his heart and mind set on making the most of what his new country had to offer. When he'd lost his right arm due to a gunshot wound in the Civil War, gangrene had slowed his recovery. Never one to be deterred, he had redirected his energies into the study of law, gaining admission to the bar in 1868, at the age of twenty-nine. Soon, he had established a lucrative private practice in Taylorville, his adopted hometown. Together, the members of the prosecution team represented a formidable force. Emma Bond, her family and friends, and nearly everyone else were counting on this triumvirate to bring about due justice.

Justice Ricks entered, took his place at the bench, and bade the prosecutor to begin. Drennan stood and with barely a pause launched into his opening remarks. He kept them brief. Without giving too much detail, he laid out the sequential events of the outrage, beginning with Emma's dismissal of her pupil, Charlie Masters, on June 29. The crime, said Drennan, took place between four o'clock on Thursday afternoon and one o'clock Friday morning. He emphasized the abhorrent nature of the act and warned the court that most of the evidence presented would be circumstantial, "because men who designed such a crime did not take witnesses with them."[14] He expected his team to further show that the rape was a conspiracy, planned in advance. Finally, he alluded to the defendants' suspicious behavior in the aftermath of the crime—behavior they had yet to explain to anyone's satisfaction.

The floor was then turned over to the defense team, with its equally impressive alliance of legal minds. Alexander McCaskill would make the opening statement. A native of Illinois, he was closing in on fifty. Like many of his colleagues, he'd been admitted to the bar at a young age, in his case in 1856, at only twenty-three. The next year had brought him to Christian County where, besides running a private law practice, he'd served five years as county superintendent of schools, four as state's attorney, and five as a county judge. He'd also put his verbal skills to good use in politics, dedicating much of his free time to campaigning and speech-making. Known as "a clear reasoner, a logical thinker, [who] carefully weigh[ed] evidence," McCaskill was a natural in both legal and political arenas.[15] Joining him at the defense table were former judge Anthony Thornton and private attorney J. C. McBride. The defense team had much the same balance as the prosecution's: Thornton had been practicing law since 1836, so, like Vandeveer, he was a veteran of the judicial system, and McBride, like Drennan, was viewed as an up-and-coming star on the legal horizon.

Thornton had amassed forty-six years at the bar, during which time he'd earned the highest respect of his peers. Like Vandeveer, he was still addressed as "Judge" or "Your Honor." He had graduated in 1834 from the same school as Emma's father—Miami University in Oxford, Ohio. In preparation for his law career, he then studied under an uncle. In 1836, he stopped in Shelbyville and found it so much to his liking that he decided to stay and establish his law practice right there.

If anybody had accumulated more credentials than Horatio Vandeveer, quite possibly it was Anthony Thornton. In his younger days, he had traveled the same Illinois circuits as Abraham Lincoln, and the two had sparred, frequently and respectfully, in various courtrooms. They had even faced off in a public debate, a year before the Lincoln-Douglas debates. As a member of the state's constitutional conventions, Thornton had helped shape Illinois's judicial system. In the 1860s, he had served in both the state legislature and the U.S. Congress, only to realize that he preferred practicing law over creating it. In the 1870s, he spent several years on the state's supreme court, as "one of its ablest members."[16] But again, the unique appeal of the lower courts had beckoned, and so he had given up his seat on the State bench to return to private practice. In 1879, he moved to Decatur to form a partnership with esteemed colleagues, Eldridge and Hostetler. Arguably, his legal genius was second to none. Not only was he focused, fervent, and articulate, but he'd also been blessed with certain physical traits that greatly enhanced his courtroom performances. At six feet, four inches and more than two hundred pounds, with "cold, gray eyes" and "a rich powerful voice," he had a commanding presence.[17] And he knew how to use his talents and stature to utmost effect in front of a jury.

McBride, at thirty-seven, the youngster of the defense team, had been admitted to the bar in 1870—a year after his graduation from Lincoln College in Illinois, so he had more than eight years on his counterpart, State's Attorney Drennan. McBride's passion for literature and debate had served him well in his career, and his private practice was one of Taylorville's most successful.

McCaskill's opening statement, like Drennan's, was short and to the point. Wisely, he began by offering sympathy for Miss Bond. And then he declared that his clients were innocent, insisting they had absolutely no motive for attacking the young teacher. Furthermore, he said, they all had alibis. When McCaskill was done, Justice Ricks called for a brief recess. As the gallery emptied, a detective approached one of the spectators and informed him that he, too, was being charged in the Bond case. The man did not resist and was quietly removed to the jailhouse. The new suspect's name had first cropped up on July 29, when Mr. Bond had told the press that he and investigator Page had enough evidence to implicate Dr. William H. Vermillion.

Initial reports stated that the Grove City physician had been taken into custody as early as August 3. But again, the rumors proved wrong. The jail register confirmed that he wasn't arrested and booked until Tuesday, August 8—officially charged with "aiding in committing the crime of rape of the person of Emma Bond"—in other words, complicity.[18] His arrest was blamed on something he had supposedly said prior to the schoolhouse attack. The *Tribune* alleged that not only had he furnished the chloroform used on the victim but that he'd also been present during the commission of the crime. What's more, the State had a witness ready to swear he had seen the doctor dispensing chloroform to one of the suspects. Bail for Vermillion was set at $5,000—the same amount required of the main suspects. Even though he was a practicing physician, that amount was beyond his grasp; consequently, he would not be returning to the Grove any time soon.

When the courtroom finally cleared, the doors were securely locked. Many retired to nearby stores and cafes, while others walked the busy square. And wherever two or more gathered, talk immediately turned to the hearing. All expressed disappointment in what had transpired so far. The midday break was just long enough to make everyone forget how uncomfortable they'd been during the morning session; thus, when the doors were flung open shortly before one-thirty, there was another chaotic push to gain entrance:

At one o'clock the courthouse yard was crowded and the halls and stairways were a living mass of humanity, men being literally crowded together like sardines in a box. One of the attorneys for the defense and the official stenographer were twenty minutes in making their way from the bottom of the stairway to the courtroom door, so dense was the crowd. When the door was opened by the sheriff the living mass of humanity surged in, and the room was filled in an instant. Eligible seats were in demand and so great was the desire to get near the attorneys that the bar railing was broken down and the room completely filled.[19]

The lawyers, the witnesses, and the defendants and their families all had to push and shove and jostle their way up the staircase along with everyone else. Among those caught up in the madness was Emanuel Clementi's mother, Maria. Her son's whereabouts had been unknown to her for some time; but now that she knew where he was, she'd come down from Milwaukee to lend him support. John Montgomery's wife, the former Mattie Pettus, was also swept along in the surge, clutching her fourteen-month-old son tightly to her chest. Close on Mattie's heels came the baby's grandmother, Margret Pettus, whose own two children—Lee and Mattie—needed her now more than ever. But by and large, those who managed to squeeze into the seating area that day were there in support of the Bonds.

When the massive doors at the rear of the courtroom were finally slammed shut, a loud chorus of dismay arose from those still trapped in the outer hallway. Inside, spectators immediately fell silent as Ricks instructed the prosecutor to call his first witness. With photojournalism still in its infancy, the challenge of bringing a news story to life fell to the journalists, and the good ones could paint a verbal image more vivid than any drawing or photograph. One Decatur reporter did just that in describing the State's first witness: "The father of Miss Emma Bond is a very large, broad-shouldered, deep-chested man, who will weigh probably 260 or 300 pounds. He has a large, partly balding head, wears burnside whiskers, and though a kindly light beams from his full blue eyes, he has withal a look as fierce as a tiger's, showing most plainly in every lineament of his countenance, 'I am no man with which to trifle, and most certainly not a man to rest content under the most heinous wrong.'"[20] A sympathetic hush fell over the room as Bond came forward. There was no need for him to place his hand on the Bible and swear to tell the truth, the whole truth, and nothing but the truth, as that had been accomplished beforehand, with all of the day's witnesses taking the necessary oath en masse.

Drennan immediately began his questions. The first two concerned Emma's state when delivered to her home early Friday, June 30. Drennan asked Mr. Bond "to state what she then said as to the cause of her condition." The defense raised an immediate objection, arguing that "no testimony of that character was admissible except the fact that she complained of having been ravished."[21] This triggered an hour-long debate on legal technicalities. Apparently, the State also wanted Mr. Bond to read aloud from the statement, given by Emma in early August.[22] Justice Ricks decided to allow the reading but, to the disappointment of the spectators, it added nothing new to the case. During cross-examination, Bond admitted that his daughter "could not and did not identify any of the four men arrested."[23] The witness was excused.

The next to be called, Martin Swick, was one of the State's key witnesses. He told of talking with John and Lee on Friday and said both men behaved as if they had knowledge of the crime but were unwilling to discuss it. He continued: After repeated attempts to get them to talk, Lee finally agreed. He said Miss Bond's dress was torn. He also described her underclothing. About then, John walked up and ordered Lee to keep his mouth shut because "he didn't know what he was talking about." John was on edge, wanting to know what people thought of the case and if he was in danger from a mob. He also said that maybe he and Lee should "get the thing off on to Clementi." One journalist couldn't help but point out the obvious: "How could Pettus describe Miss Bond's underclothing unless he had seen it, and there is no probability of his having seen it unless he was one of the outragers."[24]

During cross-examination, Swick admitted that, yes, he did make some suggestions to Montgomery about what to do and say, but the latter went along with them willingly. Drennan seemed satisfied with Swick's performance. Little did he realize that his next key witness would fall far short of expectations.

Of all those subpoenaed, Laurence Heinlein was "believed to have a full knowledge of the case." And yet his demeanor on the stand was that of a man holding something back. Throughout his testimony, he spoke so softly that those in the gallery could barely hear his answers. First, he described his early morning search of the loft and how it had turned up several of Emma's belongings as well as "a handful of hair cut from her person."[25] This was an interesting supposition on the witness's part and one the State might well have probed further. An early reference in the *Review* had mentioned a "handful" of red hair, suggesting that it had come from the assailant's head. Now here was a witness saying that the hair had been cut from the victim. It seemed a crucial point, yet the State pursued it no further.

Drennan fully expected Heinlein to corroborate Swick's testimony about what John C. Montgomery had said to the two of them on June 30. Yet here again, the prosecutor came up short. Heinlein, supposedly a friendly witness, sounded more like he was there to help the defense's cause. In fact, he confirmed that the guilt-ridden remarks attributed to the suspect were nothing of the sort but "rather suggested by Swick and assented to by Montgomery."[26] Rebounding quickly, Drennan asked Heinlein if he was related to any of the defendants. The latter had no choice but to say he was, since he was married to Margret Pettus's sister. Pettus was his nephew, and Montgomery's wife, Mattie, was his niece.

The prosecutor next asked Heinlein about the odd circumstances surrounding William Montgomery's discovery of Emma's pocketbook. He answered in a straightforward manner, but when the questioning returned to his conversations with John Montgomery, Heinlein became withdrawn again. Drennan had to fight to elicit what he was after: John's expressed concern over a mob uprising and his remark that he and the other suspects "had all talked it over, that Clementi was solid, and had given nothing away."[27] The hour was now approaching eight o'clock, so although Drennan had more questions for Heinlein, Ricks decided that those could wait until the next day. The prosecutor had to be discouraged that his hour-long inquisition of Heinlein had done so little to help the State's case. He could only hope his witness would be more forthcoming when testimony resumed on Wednesday.

7

It was estimated by good judges that there were at least two thousand people in town yesterday.
  —Decatur Daily Republican, *August 9, 1882*

Wednesday, August 9, 1882. The throngs and excitement that had marked Tuesday's session were much more subdued the following day. The atmosphere on the streets was one of tentative composure as stores went back to business as usual and many residents resumed their normal routines. Farmers could ill afford to ignore their work for two consecutive days. With predictions that the hearing could last all week, many stayed home to catch up. Justice Ricks didn't expect a replay of Tuesday's disruptions, which the *Decatur Daily Republican* described: "A number of times during the hearing yesterday, [Justice Ricks] stopped the exam and compelled the officers of the court to force the crowd back, and at other times made those in front kneel down so the railing around the bar would not be entirely crushed in. At other times by his order, the doors were closed, shutting out the seething mass of humanity from those starving to gain a footing. . . . Strong braces have been placed inside the bar during the night in order that the railing may not be crushed in again."[1] If things did get out of control again, Ricks was prepared to exercise his full authority, using whatever means necessary.

Both sides arrived feeling cautiously optimistic. Emma's supporters felt confident that once the prosecution really got going, it would have enough "to involve the accused in a network of circumstantial evidence which, when all the little incidents and events are considered in their relation to each other, will convince the public of their guilt."[2] They firmly believed that in due course the State would produce the necessary preponderance of evidence.

Friends and family of the suspects were encouraged for much the same reason. Plainly, all the prosecution had up its sleeve was a hodgepodge of circumstantial evidence. Ricks would be hard-pressed to explain sending the case to the grand jury if the State failed to come up with any cold, hard facts linking the suspects to the crime. The veteran defense team didn't dare take anything for granted, however. It planned to employ a full gamut of legal maneuvers. With dozens of witnesses still scheduled to appear, both sides were ready to continue.

Laurence Heinlein was called back to the stand. Drennan continued to struggle to get decent answers; he dug into Heinlein and Swick's plan to coax a confession out of John Montgomery and Lee Pettus. Yes, Heinlein reluctantly confessed, he did hear Montgomery voice some concerns about Pettus. Were they specific concerns? Yes. He was worried about what his brother-in-law might say. A frustrated Drennan hammered away at Heinlein, finally getting him to admit that John wanted someone to tell Lee "not to give anything away or make any confession."[3]

With Heinlein's loyalties now in question, Drennan turned the floor over to his adversary Thornton. Thornton asked the witness if he was aware that rewards had been offered for the arrest of the guilty parties. He was, but he had never hoped to earn part of that money for himself by playing detective. According to Heinlein, he never planned to "touch a cent of the reward." Nor was it entirely his plan to lie to John and tell him that Clementi had already confessed. That was something he and Swick came up with together. However, Montgomery never really admitted any guilt, said Heinlein. And when Pettus learned of Montgomery's message to him, he insisted that "he had nothing to give away."[4]

Heinlein did make one very candid admission that morning, however. Again, the prosecution had to pull it from him. He revealed that he believed he was in danger. Quietly, he told how Montgomery "had asked him what he was going to swear to and threatened that if his testimony did not suit him or he told too much, one or the other of them would be no more when this thing was settled."[5] That disclosure shed at least partial light on Heinlein's guarded demeanor.

Next up was Henry Crowe, the officer who had arrested Clementi. Crowe repeated the suspect's threat against the unnamed parties responsible for his arrest. On cross-examination, he recounted what the suspect had told him about his activities on June 29, including that he, Pettus, and Montgomery "had eaten supper together in Mrs. Pettus's about six o'clock that evening."[6] The State called the dispatcher from the Blue Mound depot, C. H. Crosley, to describe what had transpired when Clementi and the posse rode into town the morning after the outrage. On cross, the witness confirmed that the group had talked at length about the two tramps and that he might have suggested that Clementi send a telegram to Bond, telling him about the two strangers.

When Emma's doctor, D. K. Cornell, testified, the audience sat riveted on his every word. He described his first examination of the victim at her home: "Her breathing was difficult and accompanied by a groan at every breath. There were scratches on her neck and wrists, bruises on her side, and an apparent fracture of the tenth rib." Here, the paper alluded to the unspoken aspects of Emma's injuries: "Witness made an examination which showed that a terrible outrage had been committed, but it is not necessary to publish the horrible details of his investigation." There it was again—something so appalling that the press refused to name it. The doctor wrapped up his testimony by saying that he believed Emma Bond "would not recover from her spinal injury."[7] Worse yet, any hope that she would survive had lately grown dim.

Next came Pleasant Venters, C. F. Knight, and John Hawkins—the three men who had joined with Clementi to search for the two tramps. All told virtually the same story about Clementi's prolonged detour across the Pettus property, and all remarked on the farmhand's peculiar behavior that Friday morning. Venters was also quizzed about the telegram to Bond. According to the witness, Clementi led him to believe that Bond did get the telegram, that he was at the Taylorville dispatch office when it arrived. When asked whether he believed Clementi, Venters replied that from what he knew, Bond wasn't even in Taylorville at that time. This line of questioning was obviously meant to expose the suspect's propensity for lying.

Hawkins also told of how the group doubled back to follow Clementi through the Pettus pasture. What he said next, however, could only be classified as pure conjecture, and, as such, it must have provoked a rousing objection from the defense. The witness described how the trio came across a trampled bed of weeds and grass by the creek, where Clementi had apparently met up with two other individuals. According to Hawkins, the two were thought to be Pettus and Montgomery, and Clementi's rendezvous was for the "supposed purpose of consulting with them."[8]

Taylorville constable W. R. Eltzroth, who was present when the toenail paring was compared to John's toe, testified that the piece in question was an eighth of an inch wide and had a distinctive ridge down the middle. In his opinion, it matched John's nail "close all the way round, though on one side another paring seemed to have been cut off, so that [it] did not fit close on that side."[9] Furthermore, the ridge appeared to correspond with the one on John's toenail.

The prosecution called Thomas McNeil—the mail carrier whose route took him past the school around three o'clock every day. When asked whether he noticed anything out of the ordinary as he went by on Thursday, June 29, he replied that he had seen Pettus, Clementi, and another man standing near the schoolhouse, talking. He evidently failed to get a good look at the third man, or else he didn't recognize him. McNeil was also part-owner of a Grove City store—one that sold chloroform. He continued, explaining that right after he heard about the attack, he went to his store to check the supply of the drug and was surprised to find that four to six ounces were missing. McNeil's business partner later backed up this fact, testifying that they had dispensed only two drams of the drug between June 20 and July 3—and from a different bottle. Neither man could explain why chloroform was missing from the other bottle.

Waiting, fidgeting, outside in the hallway throughout the morning was the youngest of the witnesses. Everyone was keen to hear what little Charlie Masters would have to say. After all, he'd been Emma's only pupil on June 29 and presumably the last person to have seen her before the attack. Like nearly all of the students at the Montgomery School, this one—while not directly related to the school's namesakes—had relatives who belonged to the Montgomery clan. His uncle and aunt were William and Amy Masters, and Amy was a sister of the two Montgomery suspects.[10]

By mid-afternoon, when his name was finally called, the frightened lad wanted no part of the goings-on. As the imposing wooden doors creaked open at the rear of the courtroom and all eyes turned in his direction, Charlie balked. No amount of cajoling was going to persuade him to walk down the aisle and take a seat in the daunting chair next to the judge. The prosecution team approached the bench and conferred with Ricks, whereupon it was agreed that the boy could give his testimony in the small, adjoining jury room. There, away from the inquisitive stares in the larger room, the youngster shared what he remembered of his last day of school, seven weeks earlier. He recalled that the scuttle hole was open that morning when he went inside. And he remembered hearing noises in the loft, but he thought that was during afternoon recess, when Miss Bond was over at the Pettus house. When asked whether he'd seen anyone go by during that recess, he answered that he had. Charlie said he saw young John and old John go by, together. John was walking and his father was riding. John called out, saying he'd come back and wrestle with the youngster. The witness also confirmed that these were the only people he saw.

The defense asked the lad if he'd left the schoolyard at any time during his afternoon recess. Yes, he went to get a drink of water from the Pettus well. The boy was excused and sent back to his parents' side. At this point, the prosecution caught everyone off guard by announcing that it was resting its case. In two days, the State had paraded 130 witnesses in front of the court, although the majority had answered only a brief question or two.

The first witness called by the defense was the elder John Montgomery. The sixty-five-year-old father of John C. and William proceeded to give an accounting of his sons' whereabouts on the day in question. At one o'clock, John stopped by his house, and the two headed off together around two-thirty. They went south toward the Grove, and as they passed the schoolhouse, they saw the Masters boy sitting atop the coalhouse. Father and son parted company just past the school, and the younger man veered off to Joe Younker's house. When the elder was returning home around six, he ran into his son again near Younker's place, with several other people. The witness stopped to talk with them. After a few minutes, father and son left and started back up the road together. They passed the schoolhouse again, and when they reached the Pettus lane, the father bid his son goodbye, and the younger man veered off toward the Pettus house, where his wife, Mattie, was waiting for him. When the witness arrived at his own place, he saw his other son, William, leaving for home with his family. John Sr. appeared calm and straightforward in his responses.

On cross, however, Vandeveer asked the witness "if he had not told Mr. Bond that about five o'clock on the evening of the outrage, he and his son John had met at the coalhouse in the school house yard and had remained there in conversation for fully one hour. Mr. Montgomery answered that he had not told Mr. Bond anything of the kind nor had he made such a statement to any man."[11] The lawyer pursued the matter relentlessly, but John Sr. held firm in his denial. Before leaving the stand, he wanted it to be known that he "had expressed his regret to Mr. Bond that he and John did not know about the outrage when they stood near the schoolhouse talking for several minutes that afternoon, during the time when the devils had her there."[12] It sounded like a fitting and genuine expression of sympathy from one father to another, though perhaps not an entirely accurate one.

A whole string of witnesses then came forward as alibi witnesses. John Clancy recalled seeing John around two in the afternoon and again between five and six o'clock. Sherman Yockey said something similar.[13] A man named Duff recalled passing William Montgomery going home in his wagon about six that evening. Next came Joe Younker, the tenant farmer on the land owned by John Sr., just south of the school. He confirmed that John Jr. had come by his farm after parting company with John Sr. on the day in question.[14] The defense was determined to build a solid alibi for each of its clients. But glaring discrepancies began to crop up almost at once. On the one hand, John Sr. put the time that his son had turned off to the Younker farm at shortly after two thirty. On the other hand, Sherman Yockey thought John Jr. showed up at Joe Younker's place around two o'clock. Now here was Younker, adding to the confusion. If the Tribune's version of his testimony was correct, his memory fell woefully short, because, according to the paper, he stated that "John Montgomery was at his house during the afternoon of the outrage from the time he went there with his father until he went away again."[15] Although that was decidedly vague, it was probably better to be vague than to perjure oneself.

The relevant question might be: did any of these eyewitnesses actually own a watch or clock, or, as farmers often did, were they simply estimating the time based on the sun's position in the sky or the length of its shadows on the ground? With defense witnesses contradicting each other right and left, it looked as if Drennan's team might be regaining the upper hand. Still, the *Decatur Review* voiced some valid criticisms of the State's case, suggesting that it had dropped the ball on certain matters:

> The prosecution proved yesterday that a hole had been cut in the weatherboarding of the schoolhouse loft by one of the ravishers, and that the knife used was a dull one. It was then shown that John Montgomery had a dull knife in his possession when captured, but this does not prove that Montgomery had cut the hole. If it had been shown that the knife blade which was used in the cutting contained nicks which left small ridges . . . and that Montgomery's knife contained corresponding nicks, then the evidence might be accepted as having weight; but as this was not shown. . . . the fact that Pettus . . . refused [to go swimming] is no evidence that his clothes were soiled by the blood from the person of Miss Bond. . . . If the prosecution had [shown] it was Pettus's invariable custom to go in swimming with his companions, then . . . his refusal to do this . . . on the 30th of June . . . would be a strong circumstance pointing to his guilt.

For weeks, the press had stoked the embers smoldering beneath the surface of an already inflamed public. Now, for the first time, one journalist dared criticize the State's case. This signaled an apparent shift in sentiment, albeit a slight one. On the other hand, before he could wrap up his commentary, the writer seemed to have second thoughts: "All in all, the case is hard to understand. It is surrounded by many mysterious circumstances, which must be explained if the parties accused expect the public to believe in their innocence. While the people generally hold that the prosecution has not made out a case, they are yet not willing, under the circumstances, to say that the accused should be discharged."[16] In truth, this summary was probably an accurate reflection of what everyone was thinking.

8

Many are in the position of a well-known Christian County farmer who declared, in commenting upon the case last night, that he was upon the fence and that today's developments would determine on which side he would get down.
—Decatur Review, *August 10, 1882*

Thursday, August 10, 1882. Many believed Wednesday's evidence had turned slightly in favor of the defendants. However, any advantage thus gained was about to go the way of a spring snow on freshly turned earth. Prevailing opinion held that Thursday would be the last day of testimony; as a result, the turnout was up again.

Attendees were anticipating some high drama, should the justice system falter. And, accordingly, one suspect wasn't taking any chances. Right before court resumed, Lee Pettus was found to be carrying a loaded revolver. The other prisoners were then searched for weapons, but they came up clean. Paying a fine of just $10, Lee got off relatively easily, considering that a new state law had specified a $25 to $200 fine for carrying a concealed weapon.[1] Pettus probably figured that if he won his release, all hell was going to break loose—in which case, he wanted to be ready for it. Of course, it was just as possible that all hell would break loose regardless of the final ruling.

Even if the State came up short in the eyes of the law, everyone firmly believed that the case would go to the grand jury. Some even surmised that the prosecution had purposely held back, not wanting to tip its hand by revealing all its evidence before trial. That was a risky approach, to say the least, because if the evidence wasn't compelling enough now, there would be no trial later. The State was probably counting on public pressure to influence the justice's decision. Then again, if the prosecution failed to show just cause, the justice was duty-bound to set the accused free.

But the hearing was not over yet. The defense still had a few more witnesses waiting in the wings, ready to shore up its clients' alibis. John Morgret, who was also at Joe Younker's on June 29, testified that he saw John there "between four and six o'clock."[2] Whether that meant that John had been present the full two hours or had stopped by sometime in that window is unclear. To this point, the alibi testimony had focused largely on John's whereabouts. Now it was time to give the other defendants their due.

Newlywed Mrs. Owen Hart, the former Cora Pettus, confirmed that she spent Thursday, June 29, at her mother's house, where she saw her brother and Clementi "every little while."[3] She also observed Clementi in the wagon that afternoon, reading a paper. When asked about her brother-in-law, she said he had brought his wife, her sister Mattie, by and stayed through the noon hour. After the family ate dinner together, said Cora, he left. She had seen Emma Bond that day, too, when she came to practice with her sisters, sometime between two and three o'clock. The teacher stayed half an hour.

After Cora was excused, the other three Pettus girls—Minnie, Ona, and Mattie—were brought forth in succession. Except for Mattie, they corroborated everything Cora had said on the stand. It was ruled that because Mattie was John's wife, she would only be allowed to testify on behalf of her brother and Clementi. She, too, acknowledged seeing the two around the house throughout the day. In the course of the interrogation, she did add one new detail. She stated that she had taken supper with both Lee and Clementi at her mother's home at seven o'clock that evening; this was a direct contradiction to the six o'clock mealtime Clementi had professed to his arresting officer. The defense called George, the oldest of the Pettus siblings, and asked him about the conversation he'd witnessed between his Uncle Laurence and his brother Lee. According to George, his brother's exact words were that he "didn't know anything."[4]

Among the Montgomerys who testified that day were John and William's two youngest siblings. Their newlywed sister, Amanda, and her husband, James Allen, still lived at the Montgomery homestead with her parents. Amanda stated that William had been at the family home between three and four and again between six and seven o'clock on Thursday. The youngest of the family, nineteen-year-old Charles, testified on behalf of both of his brothers and agreed that William had stopped by their father's house between three and four o'clock on June 29. He recalled seeing William with mail carrier Thomas McNeil by the road around four o'clock and also noticed three men talking together near the Pettus home that afternoon. These he assumed to be his brother John, Emanuel Clementi, and Lee Pettus. And, yes, his brother John came by the farm that day, too, around one o'clock.

Overall, the alibi witnesses were standing pat on their stories—so pat, in fact, that the *Tribune* offered this observation: "Like the other relatives, this witness seemed to have a very distinct recollection of everything the defendants did that afternoon and every place they went but found it difficult to remember anything else that happened about that time."⁵

Amanda's husband, James, was another who'd seen Pettus and Clementi "about the Pettus place" that afternoon. Asked about his two brothers-in-law, John and William, the witness recalled seeing both at their father's house: John at one o'clock, when he came by to help hive the bees, and William around four o'clock. William and his wife, Rebecca, left for home at six. While Allen seemed confident of his facts during his direct exam, the State apparently had no trouble dismantling that confidence in short order. According to the *Tribune*, "On cross exam, the witness did not appear to have a very clear idea of the hours he mentioned except from what he had been told by others."⁶

John Stumpf, the proprietor of the hotel in Blue Mound, took the stand to describe the two strangers seen in his village on Thursday night. One, said Stumpf, was tall and lean and clean-shaven. The other was a little more stout and had chin whiskers. Both wore white shirts and dark or black coats. The defense hoped to show that the two unfamiliar faces closely fit the description Emma had given and that "Clementi had some foundation for the telegram he sent to Mr. Bond from there the following morning."⁷ However, on cross-exam, Stumpf admitted the visitors' clothes were clean and their boots dry. The prosecutor's point was well made. Neither looked as if he'd just fled a violent crime scene and then hiked several miles in the dark.

Two non-family members came forth in William's defense. Mailman McNeil appeared for the second time in two days, confirming that around six o'clock in the evening, he had seen William leaving John Montgomery Sr.'s house. And William and Rebecca's hired girl, eighteen-year-old Eliza Desper, stated that William had taken his family to his father's farm about ten o'clock on Thursday morning. According to Eliza, he then came home, ate his midday meal, and whitewashed the kitchen. At three o'clock, he went back to pick up his family and was home in time for the evening meal. When the couple, their two small children, and Eliza retired for the night, it was still early. Of course, the term "early" was open to interpretation. Almost certainly, Eliza did not own a watch. Local sunset on the day of the outrage occurred about seven thirty. So by the time it was dark enough for sleeping, "early" was no doubt closer to eight o'clock or later.

A doctor named James Cussins disagreed with the State's witnesses on the toenail paring. It seemed thicker to him than John's toenail. On cross-examination, however, he admitted that John's nail looked as though it had been scraped down. With the hour nearing six o'clock, the defense announced that it was resting its case. Some of the spectators who'd watched the proceedings all day got up and left, unaware that the prosecution still had witnesses to call in rebuttal. One after another, the State brought five different men to the stand. Their testimonies, taken in total, delivered a severe uppercut to the defense.

Sam Sadler dealt the first blow when asked if John Montgomery Sr.'s Wednesday testimony coincided with what he'd heard the man say shortly after the outrage. Before Sam could answer, Thornton jumped to his feet with an objection. Justice Ricks listened patiently to the heated debate that followed. The crime was "the result of a conspiracy between these four defendants and was of such a character that it could not have been witnessed by others and must be proved by circumstantial evidence," Vandeveer argued for the prosecution. He further charged that "the alibi testimony presented [by] the defense had been arranged and rehearsed for this hearing, which made it necessary for the prosecution . . . to show contradictory statements made by these witnesses."[8] After considerable discussion back and forth, Ricks sided with Vandeveer. The witness was allowed to continue. No, Mr. Montgomery's statements did not coincide with what he'd told others, said Sadler. He told Mr. Bond something entirely different about his late-afternoon encounter with his son on the twenty-ninth. Sadler also said he was surprised that Mr. Montgomery denied his earlier statements under oath.

Following Sadler's revelation, A. D. Bond, Edward Housley, Laurence Heinlein, and Frank Heinlein (another of Laurence's sons) all came forward and swore to having been present at that same conversation. Each insisted that the elder Montgomery had lied about his remarks while under oath the previous day; in fact, what they'd all heard him say was that "he met his son John right by the schoolhouse about five o'clock and stood there talking for an hour or more while the girl was being outraged."[9]

One other point remained to be made. For that, the State recalled Martin Swick, who confirmed that he'd passed the Pettus house that Thursday afternoon at about three thirty. He was looking for Clementi, to see if he wanted to help with some work, but he never found him; the only person Swick saw was Mrs. Pettus's brother, Robert Johnson. On cross-examination, however, the defense proceeded to poke a hole in Swick's testimony. When asked whether he had ridden past the Pettus house rather quickly, with "only a passing glance at the premises," Swick admitted it was true, that he didn't actually stop.[10] And with that, the testimony concluded.

Ricks announced that closing statements would take place on Friday morning and then he would consider the evidence and issue his ruling. Given the air of unrest, the defendants were happy to return to their jail cells when Thursday's session came to an end. Spending the night behind bars was a small but necessary sacrifice. Friday morning would dawn soon enough, and then, God willing, they would be absolved and allowed to return safely to their homes.

Although closing arguments were yet to come, the public consensus was that both sides had scored some points; likewise, both sides had come up short in certain aspects. In his opening statement, McCaskill had promised to show that his clients had "no motive," but that subject had gone unaddressed. And although the defense had established alibis for each of its clients, the *Tribune* couldn't help but note the obvious: "The defense . . . made out a very complete alibi as to all of the defendants, but this was done by the testimony of interested relatives, and the people are still ready to believe, notwithstanding the completeness of the alibi, that the family have been thoroughly drilled in their parts, and but repeated a story arranged since the outrage to clear the prisoners . . . and that none of these witnesses were positive as to the time of any occurrences except at certain hours, which they all fixed positively."[11]

In the State's favor, its remedial efforts had smoothed over some of the damage inflicted by the defense on Wednesday. Decatur's *Review* praised the prosecution for its thoroughness regarding John Sr.'s apparent deception:

The evidence given by John Montgomery Sr. as to the whereabouts of his sons in the aftermath was riddled by the prosecution. The feature of the day, in fact, was the successful attempt of the prosecution to prove that his statement in a very essential point was false. . . . Thus a link in the chain of evidence proving an alibi for Montgomery was lost, and the entire defense weakened. The prosecution was sagacious enough to have each witness for the defense excluded from the courtroom until he was called to the stand, so that the evidence of one would not influence that of another. The wisdom of this course was clearly seen in the result, as the testimony was of the most conflicting character.[12]

The prosecution pointed out that, despite the alibi testimony, "there were times during the day when it might still have been possible for Pettus, Clementi and John Montgomery to have taken part in the outrage."[13] There were vague time frames given all around, and nobody had really confirmed seeing the suspects continuously between four and seven o'clock that Thursday afternoon. And why had old man Montgomery chosen to distort the truth about his five o'clock, hour-long encounter with John near the schoolhouse? With so many conflicting statements by so many different people, perhaps it was impossible for the prosecutor to make heads or tails of the defendants' whereabouts throughout the afternoon in question.

In spite of what was going on upstairs that Thursday, on the first floor of the courthouse business went on as usual. In typical government fashion, the county board of supervisors was wrapping up its July meeting—on August 10.

The Bond case may have been partly responsible for the delay, or perhaps there were simply no pressing issues on the board's summer agenda. Naturally, its members were just as interested in the courtroom drama as everybody else. But the crime had hit very close to home for one particular member. Sonny Bond, now in his sixth term as a supervisor, had taken the news of Emma's misfortune almost as hard as her father, his favorite cousin, had.

Sonny's holdings sat southeast of A. D. Bond's, on the very northeast edge of Taylorville. He was Taylorville Township's representative on the county board. In 1882, the splendid home he shared with his wife, Lizzie, overflowed with the happy chatter of five youngsters. The oldest, Elbie, was eleven that year; Nellie, nine; Mary, eight; and Dickson, three. The baby, eight-month-old Abner Faye, had arrived shortly before Lizzie's fortieth birthday.

In 1854, when Lizzie was just twelve, her father, Dickson Hall, had died. But he had left his widow and her brood a hefty estate. Nearly all of the land adjoining Sonny's property belonged to Lizzie's relatives—her mother, her grown sisters and their husbands, and her only brother.[14] And everyone for miles around knew that, like his in-laws, Sonny Bond was "in good circumstances."[15] He'd transferred his entrepreneurial flair, honed in the clock business, to land investments. That, combined with his success in "farming, trading and shipping stock" had paid off quite handsomely.[16] One figure bandied about rather freely was that Sonny was worth upward of $100,000—a substantial sum at the time. With such a large fortune and fine family, his was clearly a life to be envied.

Nevertheless, Sonny was well liked. With the exception of 1880, he'd been elected to the county board of supervisors every year since 1876. Familiar around town, he was considered an outstanding public servant—one who "looked carefully after the interests of his county and locality." In fact, "none [were] more respected for their worth as a man and citizen than Abner Bond."[17] As a private citizen, he was "charitable to the poor," and in both his civic and personal relationships, he strove to be "courteous to all."[18]

At the meeting that Thursday afternoon, four members of the board were absent. But Sonny Bond and the thirteen other supervisors hurried through their agenda in hopes of catching at least part of the action taking place upstairs. As business wound down, Supervisor Carey stood to introduce a resolution:

> Whereas on or about the 29th day of June 1882 at a school house in the Township of Mt. Auburn in the County of Christian State of Ills some person or persons did assault and outrage Miss Emma Bond who was at that time engaged in teaching a school at that place and so injured her as to endanger her life. And whereas certain parties have been arrested [and] charged with committing the crime and are now undergoing a pre-

liminary examination, therefore be it resolved that in case the said accused parties shall prove themselves innocent of the crime alleged against them, then the Sheriff be and is hereby authorized to offer in the name of Christian County a reward of Five Hundred Dollars for the arrest and conviction of the guilty parties. J. J. Carey

Bond moved to adopt the motion, and it was quickly seconded. A vote was taken, and the resolution passed handily. The $500 incentive was rescinded the next morning, however, in favor of a reward in the amount of "two-thousand dollars."[19]

Sheriff Haines was sitting in on Thursday's board meeting. He, like the others present that day, expected the proceedings in the courtroom to be settled at any moment. And if the accused were released, he knew he'd have to reopen his investigation. At least now, thanks to the board's resolution, there would be a decent reward to use as leverage to that end. Nevertheless, he didn't relish the idea of having to start over from scratch, should the current suspects be discharged.

Whether or not the right men were in custody, Haines had a more pressing concern on his mind that day: if the accused *were* allowed to walk, he'd have to deal with some loud protests, at the very least, or with a mob uprising, at the very most. That was the last thing he wanted, but that slim possibility nagged at him. He'd heard the idle talk, the "rumors of a lynching matinee being possible before morning."[20] So a battle waged inside the sheriff's head. Maybe he shouldn't assume anything. Maybe he should even go ahead and ask Governor Cullom to send reinforcements. In the end, he decided his forces could handle the situation alone.

As soon as the defense announced it was resting its case on Thursday afternoon, a few self-appointed town criers went forth and spread the news. So by seven thirty, when the courtroom actually emptied out, the town was already filling with the curious and the concerned, who "seemed to have come from different places and directions by some preconcerted agreement."[21] As the sun slipped below the western horizon, what began as a trickle swiftly grew into a torrent. A half mile east of town, two fired-up contingents—one from Assumption and one from East Prairie—ran into each other and merged into one large, single-minded force. It descended on Taylorville, marching in phalanx formation toward the square. By nightfall, more angry men joined the fray, pouring in from every direction.

Rumors surged though the gathering crowd. The hearing was over, and the suspects "had been conclusively proven guilty."[22] A group was marshaled outside of town, waiting for Mr. Bond to say, "Let's finish it tonight."[23] No, Mr.

Bond would never say anything of the sort. The Montgomery boys and the other two were hunkered down in their cells, fearing for their lives—no, they'd already flown from town. Clementi was on the verge of a confession—no, also impossible, for there wasn't a truthful bone in his entire body.

Nine o'clock came and went, and the numbers continued to grow. Then, like a rolling fog, a modicum of truth began to seep through the crowd, dousing the fiery emotions of even the hottest-tempered souls. So the hearing wasn't over yet? Closing arguments had yet to be heard? "When these people discovered . . . how unfounded these reports were, and that the case made out against the accused was by no means conclusive, they returned to their homes quietly."[24] To the sheriff's huge relief, another volatile situation was narrowly avoided, even though the racket lasted until well past midnight. With Friday morning now just hours away, the sheriff could only hope that the people would use every ounce of common sense that the good Lord had given them and that sanity would thus prevail.

The *Review,* however, was putting the responsibility squarely in the State's lap: "The prosecution holds the key to the situation. In the present state of popular feeling, a few intemperate words would doubtless precipitate trouble, and it is to be hoped that the [closing] speeches will be characterized by a spirit of fairness . . . it can be said with reason that if the speeches of the prosecuting lawyers are of a sensational or inflammatory character, the prisoners stand but little chance of escape from summary punishment."[25] Of course, the man ultimately charged with maintaining civil order had no way of knowing what daylight would bring. The conclusion of the hearing on Friday might draw hundreds, if not thousands, from near and far. In view of the evening's unsettling activities, Sheriff Haines was beginning to have second thoughts about his decision not to call in help. But for now the hour was late, the crowd was gone, and he was bone-tired.

9

That there is a strong presumption of their guilt no reasonable man will deny, yet it cannot be said that the prosecution presented enough evidence at the preliminary examination to convict them in a court of record. The case is still a mystery and the end no man can see.
—Decatur Review, *August 11, 1882*

Friday, August 11, 1882. Court was to resume at eight o'clock but started a half an hour late; it took that long for all the bodies to squeeze into the courtroom and settle down. As soon as Justice Ricks appeared, the noise in the chamber dropped to hushed whispers and then absolute silence. The State's attorney was directed to begin his closing arguments.

Had the State shown "reasonable probability of the guilt of the accused?"[1] According to Drennan, it had. Of course, anyone who could have attested to the suspects' guilt would have been brought forth to testify. But, as Drennan pointed out, the "fiends took care to have no witnesses to their foul deed."[2] He summed up the physical evidence found in the loft, including the toenail paring and its similarities to John Montgomery's toenail. And what, asked the state's attorney, could possibly account for the suspects' suspicious remarks and odd behavior the day after the crime? He reminded the court that the alibis presented by the defense "bore the appearance of having been made up by conspiracy and perjury on the part of the relatives of the accused." He wrapped up his remarks in short order and returned to his chair. Judge Thornton then caught everyone off guard by announcing that the defense would "submit the case without argument." Was this a strategic move? Or had the defense accepted the inevitable? Certainly, the situation called for delicate handling, given "the intense bitterness of the feeling against the accused on the part of at least three-fourths of the people of the county."[3]

Justice Ricks wasted no time in rendering his decision. He summed up his findings by saying, first of all, that there was no doubt that an outrage had been committed. Reading from the statutes, he next explained what was required to bind the accused over for trial—that being probable cause as to guilt. He noted how that differed from the evidence needed for an actual conviction at trial. In his opinion, the men were definitely in the immediate vicinity of the crime scene on the day in question. Furthermore, he was not convinced that their alibis were full and complete. More incriminating, in his mind, was their behavior on the day after the outrage and the statements that they'd made to Heinlein and Swick.

Ricks next addressed Emanuel Clementi's alleged involvement. One paper offered this interpretation of the justice's remarks: "It was singular that none of these defendants except Clementi said anything immediately after the outrage as to their whereabouts that afternoon, which would have been the most natural thing for an innocent man to have done." But since Clementi's and Pettus's comings and goings were "intimately associated together all that day," Ricks had some concerns about the unaccounted-for gaps in their day—times not covered by their alibi witnesses.[4]

As for John Montgomery, there'd been plenty of conflicting testimony on his exact whereabouts on June 29, particularly in regard to the late afternoon. His own father had not helped matters, as five State witnesses had sworn that the old man had given two different versions of his son's activities on the day in question—one to the five men in the Grove and another to the court. However, Ricks believed that there was insufficient evidence to suggest that John's brother William was involved. So on August 11, the justice's first order of business was to discharge the younger of the two brothers: William Montgomery was free to leave at once, and he did.

Emanuel Clementi, Lee Pettus, and John C. Montgomery, however, were not going to be so lucky. According to Ricks, "there had not been a particle of evidence to show that it might have been someone else."[5] He stressed that he was not the jury nor was his ruling a finding of guilt against the three. Nonetheless, he felt that there was enough evidence to justify turning their case over to the grand jury when it convened in November. As he finished speaking, there was not one sound in agreement, nor one utterance in disagreement—absolutely nothing to indicate the gallery's reaction. But then, suddenly, "there was a movement among the spectators towards the prisoners." It was promptly "checked by the sheriff and his posse."[6] The suspects themselves showed no emotion, except for Clementi: "Lee Pettus received the decision with the same appearance of stolid indifference that characterized his bearing throughout the examination, giving no expression of any feeling except a slight weakening of the eyes. John Montgomery also bore himself with utmost composure, but Clementi became very nervous as the result became evident, while his mother burst into tears."[7] As his last order of business, Ricks announced a bond reduction for the three prisoners: Montgomery's and Pettus's were lowered to $4,000 each, Clementi's to $3,000. Court was then adjourned. The time was eleven o'clock.

Family and friends of the suspects were visibly upset with the justice's decision. Emma's supporters, while believing it was the right one, were just as upset
over the lowered bond amounts. The men would surely get themselves out of jail
now, and then they'd never be seen or heard from again. Ricks explained that he
"made [the] concession to Clementi because he had no property nor relatives to
assist him," a statement that would not sit well with the public.[8]

With rumblings of displeasure coming from both camps, the law officers
grew nervous when the courtroom was slow to empty. If one of the suspects
had managed to smuggle a handgun into the courtroom, some of the onlookers
could have done the same. For this was still, by and large, a gun-toting society. To make matters worse, people were lingering in the vestibules outside the
courtroom or dallying in the stairwell and on the first floor. Nobody was in a
hurry to leave. William Montgomery may have been the one exception, having taken off as fast as his legs would carry him. The officers in charge of the
remaining prisoners realized the atmosphere was nothing if not a powder keg
of discontent, so they waited patiently until the moment seemed right. Finally,
with weapons drawn and visible to all, they formed a circle around their charges
and headed for the jailhouse, two blocks away.

There was some talk that John's father might be able to cover the bonds for
not only his son but Pettus and Clementi as well. But since that would take
some doing, the three friends quickly resigned themselves to spending yet another night in jail. At least there, they'd have the protection of the law. Before heading back to Milwaukee, Maria Clementi scraped together some of the
money necessary for her son's release, but her cash in hand fell far short of the
amount required. So she approached John Sr. with a deal: she'd give him what
little she had as an advance, on the promise that if he would cover the difference
and get her son out of jail she would pay him back. This was an undeniable risk
for John Sr., since it was generally assumed that if anyone was going to skip out,
it would be the farmhand who had nothing to tether him to the area.

Noon came and went, and the thermometer held in the mid-seventies. On
the boardwalks and streets, in front of churches and homes and stores, people
congregated to discuss the hearing's outcome. With pencil and paper in hand,
news correspondents circulated among the masses. Mr. Bond was asked how
he felt about the ruling; he expressed his satisfaction. Initially, he wasn't sure
the right men had been arrested. But now he was fully convinced. And when
the case finally made it to trial, he expected the prosecution to present more
incriminating evidence, things deliberately held back during the hearing. He
had no doubt that justice would in time be served and that the accused would
have to pay for what they'd done to his daughter.

Fortunately, wisdom prevailed throughout the daylight hours, but as afternoon eased into evening, the crowd grew, rather than diminished. Most of the women departed before nightfall, but in their place came a more vocal sector of the male populace. Although there was not a single saloon in town, it was clear that some of the loudest had fortified themselves for the task ahead. As one reporter observed: "It only needed whiskey to place such a mob in a frenzied condition. There was some whiskey in the town on Friday evening, but not enough to go around."[9] As dusk took on the more ominous shades of night, the mood of the crowd also began to darken. The absence of moonlight afforded a sense of anonymity to those who now called for action. Their words went from accusatory to coaxing and finally to incendiary as they worked the crowd, trying to convince the undecided that something had to be done at once. Because, insisted the rabble-rousers, once the prisoners made bail, they'd be long gone.

With the hour now approaching nine o'clock, a dam stood ready to burst in tranquil Taylorville, and nothing would be able to stop it. The full scope of the events would be chronicled in publications across the land—from some of the oldest and most prestigious presses back east to the greenhorn journals of the far West. Sure, readers were familiar with the Emma Bond case, but over the long summer, many had lost interest in the slow-moving drama taking place in that little farming community in central Illinois.[10] Now, however, the story was about to reemerge with a sensational new twist—one that would lodge it in the national psyche and keep it there for weeks, months, and, yes, even years.

10

At the time of this writing, it is known that a mob at Taylorville took pos-session last night at the jail of that place in which were confined the persons accused of the outrage upon Miss Emma Bond last June.
—Waukesha Daily Freeman, *August 12, 1882*

The malcontents working Taylorville's square on Friday night expected support to arrive from the outlying areas. But when no organized parties appeared, the mob grew restless and began edging toward the jail. There, just minutes past nine o'clock, a group of angry men approached the jailhouse door, demand-ing that the sheriff hand the prisoners over to the people. When the door was slammed in their faces, a sudden cry went up to "break the door in and bring them out."[1]

The push to gain entrance could not be denied as the hostile mob shoved and jostled its way through the tight doorway and up the narrow staircase to the second-floor cellblock. The sheriff and his men—unable to stop the surge—quickly abandoned their posts, dousing their lamps as they went. Only a few of the intruders carried lanterns, and those cast an eerie light over the bedlam. When Americans picked up their local dailies that weekend, they were treated to absorbing accounts of the raid:

After half an hour's work, Pettus and John Montgomery were pulled out through an opening in the top of the cell and handed over to the mob. A brand new rope was suddenly produced and thrown around the necks of the men. Then ensued the most horrible language on the part of the mob. They endeavored by blows, threats, and every means known to them, to induce the wretches to confess. "I am innocent, and, gentlemen," cried Pettus in an agonizing voice, "hang me if you will, but I'm innocent." "You lie, damn you, you know you did it." "I know I am going to die, but as God is my judge, I am innocent." . . . Montgomery was, in the meantime, whining, "I am innocent. I don't know anything."[2]

Clementi, it seems, had vanished. Determined men, faces covered with hand-kerchiefs, went from cell to cell, prying them open with crowbars and shouting out his name. When it became clear that he was nowhere to be found, the mob headed back outside, with just the two prisoners in tow. With so many tempers flaring in such tight quarters, it was a miracle that no one was hurt during the exodus: "The rush down-stairs was awful. The passage-way was narrow, and in their haste to follow the prisoners the crowd pushed those ahead of them until suffocation was imminent. But such a crowd could stand pushing, and in a short time, they were in the jail-yard yelling for the prisoners' lives."[3]

Wherever Clementi was hidden, his safety was short-lived; in the time it took to drag Montgomery and Pettus over to the square, he was found and thrown back to the wolves with his buddies. Along the route to the courthouse, every tree drew scrutiny. Fortunately for the suspects, they were all relatively young specimens. The courthouse yard had some much sturdier ones, so the march continued in that direction. At one point, when it looked like Montgomery might talk, the crowd slowed. But when he again declared his innocence, the procession forged ahead toward the square, with Pettus repeating over and over, "I'm innocent. I am innocent."[4]

The first tall tree in the courthouse yard brought the mob to an abrupt halt. It looked more than adequate for the task at hand:

> Some nimble fellow climbed the tree, and threw the end of a rope into a forked branch. A dozen hands caught the loose end, and John Montgom-ery was jerked off his feet, just for trial. The poor wretch still pleaded his innocence. They were called upon by a hundred voices to speak out and tell their story. "I have no story to tell. I am innocent. I know no more about this matter, gentlemen, than you." The voice was as weak as a wom-an's, and as pathetic as a child's, pleading for mercy. The infuriated crowd hooted and cried at him, saying that he was dead anyway and he might as well confess. "I am innocent," repeated Montgomery. "Up he goes, then," cried those at the end of the rope and up he did go. The body was pulled up about four feet from the ground and kept there for a full minute. The hanging man never strangled, but being exhausted and weak with fear, the men who held the rope let him down and he was called upon to tell his guilt. The man could not speak at first, but laid limp on the grass. After he recovered his breath, he finally said, "Gentlemen, I know I am dying and tell you I am as innocent as you are."

At this point, the crowd sought out the father of the victim. Mr. Bond stepped forward and also tried to elicit a confession from Montgomery. Again, he refused to cave. For a full hour, the angry mob "bullied, stormed, and threatened" him, but to no avail. The "abject wretch repeatedly reiterated his innocence."[5] Prosecutor Drennan soon appeared and attempted to tame the insanity, but he was quickly "hooted down."[6]

Clementi, being held on the fringe of the crowd, had witnessed the madness: "Cowering down with his head on his breast, his neck drawn in like a turtle's, he shook and shivered and when goaded, chattered out his innocence." Of all the men in jeopardy, Pettus clearly displayed the most courage: "He loudly and boldly proclaimed his innocence, and told the mob to go on and hang him." But it seemed it was Montgomery's soul the mob craved most, as "men on the outskirts of the crowd yelled themselves hoarse with cries of 'Hang him!' These loud-mouthed persons never dared to squeeze into the crowd, but barked and bayed where they were, free from possible danger, like so many bloodhounds."[7]

The chant grew more deafening and the noose was again tightened around John's neck. As he was about to be hoisted aloft for the second time, A. D. Bond's Quaker conscience took over. He stepped forward, pulled out a knife, and cut the rope, dropping John to the ground. Whether because of Bond's reluctance to proceed or Montgomery's resolute denials, the group finally backed off: "The men who held the rope had too much heart to hang the man after his repeated declarations, and gradually their manner softened. A cry to 'turn them loose,' was yelled down, but after a few minutes the cry was repeated, and generally taken up."[8]

And then, as if on command, "a light in the western part of the town drew attention away from the prisoners." Word rippled through the crowd that the Goodrich barn was on fire, and many of the bystanders took off to have a look. "This had the effect of dampening the spirits of the rest, and their passion for a midnight adventure and thirst for blood being satisfied, the prisoners were, after consultation among the leaders, taken back to jail and placed in their cells."[9] The press would later praise A. D. Bond and State's Attorney John G. Drennan for saving the suspects from certain death.

Oddly, the papers did not mention what happened to the other prisoners housed in the jail that night. Besides them and the elusive Clementi, where was Dr. Vermillion, who had been arrested just days earlier? It seems he was not dragged to the square during the early melee—or even later, as Clementi was. Perhaps the sheriff and his deputies were in the process of trying to remove all of their inmates from harm's way and simply ran out of time.

Another detail may represent something more than coincidence. The name of the man whose barn caught fire that night was "G. D. Goodrich." Emma's oldest sister, Belle, was married to Henry Augustus Goodrich, and the young couple lived on a farm on the western edge of Taylorville. Henry's father, who owned substantial acreage in Taylorville Township, was named William Augustus. The "G" could have come from "Gus," the shortened form of the middle name, or perhaps "G. D." was a nickname for one of them. If the barn belonged to either Goodrich, perhaps the conflagration had been a diversionary tactic. Regardless, it proved to be a godsend for Montgomery, Pettus, and Clementi; if not for the blaze, they might well have exited center stage prematurely.

In the earliest hours of Saturday morning, three very grateful prisoners were returned to the dubious safety of their cells. In the jail register, entries by each man's name noted that they were brought back "by John Drennan for protection from mob violence."[10] However, they now faced a difficult choice: post bond and face the hostilities on the outside, or remain in the jail. At the height of the fracas, the state's attorney had promised the mob that the prisoners would be kept behind bars. Legally, of course, that was not his call. Rather, it was up to Justice Ricks, and he had already set their bail. So in an attempt to keep his word, Drennan turned to the defense lawyers, hoping they might convince their clients to acquiesce. The accused did not have to think twice. All opted to stay put, for however long it might take for things to cool down; if that was until the trial, then so be it.

Clearly, the prisoners had suffered horribly. But if nothing else, their close call brought them one unexpected benefit: some of their former detractors were now having second thoughts about the men's guilt. At least one, a journalist from the *St. Louis Republican,* was genuinely swayed by the suspects' defiant refusal to admit guilt under extreme duress. The reporter sought an interview with the men the next morning. He was either lucky or persistent, for the sheriff granted him that singular privilege. At seven in the morning, he was taken to the cellblock to talk with the three suspects. They greeted him with a handshake and quickly warmed to his questions. As a result, the interviewer came away with one of the best scoops since June 30:

> "That was a close call you had, John." . . . "Yes, I know," said Montgomery weakly. "I thought I was a goner. I am aching all over. My joints are all sore." Montgomery said that he experienced death when he was hung up, that he lost all consciousness, and that before losing it, thought that he was passing from the world. He revived though, immediately after he was let down. Pettus was as happy as the proverbial clam. He smiled all over and danced around in glee over his escape. "Why, they didn't hurt me at all. They just kept me there with a rope around my neck. I knew just the minute that I got out of this jail that those fellows did not have the

nerve to hang me, and I was as sure that I'd get out of it as I am that John is here by me." . . . Clementi, who had been lying on the floor of the cell . . . crawled forward then and greeted the reporter. His face was as white as death, and he looked haggard and wan. His voice was as weak as an invalid's as he inquired where all the people were, and when he was told they had all gone home . . . , a little flush of relief passed over his face.[11]

The repercussions from Friday night's calamity were at once obvious. Genuine regret and embarrassment became the new order of the day. How far the locals were ready to go in believing the suspects, however, was still undetermined. Supposedly, three or four thousand people had witnessed the spectacle.[12] If only a small fraction of those had experienced a change of heart, that would surely work to the suspects' advantage.

A few now expressed the opinion that the men's staunch refusals to confess under the circumstances was proof of their innocence. Others still weren't prepared to go that far but acknowledged that the suspects deserved a fair trial, at the very least. In any case, the *Review* noted that "the prejudice against them has lost much of its bitterness."[13] One outspoken Taylorville resident tendered his opinion: "The statements which are being industriously circulated by some papers to the effect that people in Taylorville believe Pettus, Clementi and Montgomery innocent, are false. The belief is that they are the guilty parties and had it not been for the weakening of Bond, their souls would have been tossed over into the future by the mob Friday night."[14] Another local observer offered a slightly different perspective: "Of course, they'd say they were innocent; they'd be blanked fools if they didn't; for if they had said they were guilty they would be hung anyhow, and so long as they protested their innocence, they'd have a chance for their lives."[15] That made sense, given Mr. Bond's instructions not to hang the men unless they confessed.

Bond's detective, C. W. Page expressed his own frustration over the failed lynching, calling it "badly managed." Furthermore, he said, "they swung up the wrong man." Just who would have been the right man, Page failed to note. But, he continued, "if they had taken these men out, each in a separate wagon to the grove south of town, and tied one end of the rope around a limb and the other around their necks and told them they would give them thirty minutes to prepare to die before they hitched them off, they would have confessed."[16]

With all that had taken place on Friday night, Emma's struggles were momentarily forgotten. But on Monday, August 14, her doctors announced some encouraging news—she was actually faring better of late. Her terrible fits, called paroxysms, had slowed, giving her doctors more cause for optimism than they'd had in weeks. For her father, who'd been clinging to a mere wisp of hope, there was no better news.

For the sheriff, however, the chaos of Friday night had created all sorts of problems. There was no denying that the incident had occurred in his jurisdiction and under his watch. So naturally, questions were being raised and fingers were being pointed. Somebody was going to have to shoulder the blame. Politicians at all levels are well known for passing the buck. In this instance, Haines was apparently praying that the buck would stop in Springfield—on Governor Cullom's doorstep, to be precise. The *Tribune* concurred, chastising the governor "for having failed to prevent the mob from taking the prisoners from the jail Friday night."[17] But Cullom disagreed. In a terse response to the *Tribune*'s charge, he spelled out the steps he'd taken prior to the disastrous events in Taylorville.

First of all, he reminded his constituents that he was the one who had called up Christian County's local militia in early July, when trouble first began brewing. Captain Culver's Guard had kept the peace for several nights in a row; yet, according to Cullom, this had been "strongly objected to by leading citizens of Taylorville as reflecting upon their ability to maintain order." So, at their insistence, he had called off the guard. Nevertheless, he had urged those same citizens to be prepared for any and all adversities during the hearing. In fact, he'd even sent Adjutant General Isaac Elliott to Taylorville right before the hearing, to see if any additional help would be needed. Furthermore, said the governor, he had written and telegraphed Sheriff Haines—not once but several times—reminding him of his duty to maintain civil order. And throughout the hearing, Cullom had kept himself abreast of the volatile situation. He had been prepared to order the militia back to duty, and even to send the Governor's Guard from Springfield—if only the sheriff had asked. But as late as Thursday, August 10, Cullom was being assured that the situation was under control and that no outside reinforcements would be needed. On Friday, he had fired off one last telegram to the sheriff. The exact wording of that telegram was shared with *Tribune* readers:

Spfld., Ill., Aug 11—To Wm. C. Haines, Sheriff, Taylorville, Ill.: Do you anticipate any trouble? Rumors have come to me indicating trouble at the end of the trial. You ought to be prepared for any emergency. It is your duty to prevent mob violence at all hazards. S. M. Cullom, Governor[18]

Clearly, the State's top official wasn't admitting to any failure. If his claims were true, then it sounded as if the blame *did* rest in Christian County. But who was going to shoulder that blame—the sheriff or Taylorville's mayor or those unnamed "leading citizens" who had raised such a loud resistance to outside help? Each, no doubt, bore some of the blame. Of course, elected officials are famous for saying, in hindsight, that "something" should have been done. But as usual, they can never seem to agree on who should have done what and when it should have been done.

With Emma now apparently on the mend, her father took off for Springfield on Monday, August 14, with his investigator. No one was inclined to elaborate on what the two were up to. But during their visit, they spoke with a Springfield correspondent and reaffirmed their conviction that the right men were in custody. Page also implied, as Bond himself had done, that other pertinent facts would soon be revealed.

This particular trip obviously had something to do with Elliott Hobbs, the army enlistee. For one day later, Detective Page was on his way to Columbus, Ohio, with an arrest warrant in hand. It seems that after their first visit to the recruiting office, in which they had voiced their suspicions about the man, Sergeant Ricketts took it upon himself to go to Ohio and question his new recruit. When confronted by his officer, the soldier acted every bit as guilty as the other three suspects had. According to Ricketts, Hobbs "manifested an anxiety to learn whether a soldier could be taken from the post to answer to a crime committed elsewhere."[19] The sergeant, now equally convinced that Hobbs was involved, hurried back to Illinois to relay the information to Bond and Page. The three then agreed that the detective should leave at once, arrest the soldier, and return him to the proper jurisdiction.

On Wednesday, August 16, Page walked into the Columbus barracks and—with the army's blessing—arrested Private Hobbs for "complicity in the outrage on Emma Bond."[20] He then transported the almost twenty-two-year-old to Illinois by train and turned him over to Sheriff Haines on Friday, August 18. Per the jail register, however, the official charge against the soldier was not complicity, as first reported, but rather "Rape of the person of Emma Bond."[21] So, of the six suspects thus far arrested, five were now accused of having taken a direct part in the sexual assault.

11

The prisoner was led into the room where the still weak and dangerously ailing girl was lying.
—Decatur Daily Republican, *August 24, 1882*

As if the Bond case didn't present enough bewildering circumstances, another showed up via the postal service—in the form of an intriguing letter. It arrived at the Bond farm on Wednesday, August 16. Upon returning home that evening, Mr. Bond sat down, weary from his day, and glanced at the envelope. He noted its Chicago postmark, its two two-cent stamps, and his own name and address in unfamiliar handwriting on the front. Why was someone sending him mail from Chicago? He opened it carefully and pulled out a single sheet of paper, which contained a message written with blue ink in a neat and even hand:

Chicago, Aug 12. To Abner C. [*sic*] Bond. . . . You should have let the mob take their course. It would be only a just punishment for the three brutes, and Dr. Vermillion, who is not so bad, because he had no part in the outrage, but he knew what was going on just the same. My wife wished me to write a week ago to you but I thought the law would deal justly. Now that I see that those money-grabbers have been bought over, it's time to speak. Remember I want no reward but I am a lover of justice. I happened to be going through Taylorville that same day. Shall not mention why, but those who outraged your daughter are the very three who have been arrested. Pettus and Clementi were the two concealed upstairs. John Montgomery was the second in outraging your daughter and Clementi last. Montgomery's brother came and was afraid. He told the other three to fly for their lives as some G—— D——d spy was around. John Montgomery and Clementi came out together from the schoolhouse. One of the two made the remark, "She will not be stuck up after this."

That was all I heard. I am the tramp that they mentioned. Montgomery knows me well and I respect the old man but the —— [illegible] should predominate. Respectfully,

A Spectator[1]

Bond was taken aback. He read the message and then reread it. Whoever had composed the letter knew at least four of the suspects well enough to call them by name. Referring to the fifth as "Montgomery's brother" indicated that the writer was less familiar with William; yet he did claim to know the elder John Montgomery. This alone should have prompted law officers to immediately press John Sr. about the "tramps" he knew. If nothing else, that the author was familiar with the neighborhood and some of its residents suggested he had spent some time in the northern part of the county.

While most of the writer's accusations were straightforward, his statement that "those money-grabbers have been bought over" was confusing. If the author had firsthand knowledge that money had changed hands, thus preempting due justice, then clearly somebody was in serious trouble. Perhaps his inference of impropriety was aimed at the prosecutor who had made the careless remark about doubting the suspects' guilt because they came from such respectable families. Moreover, the words "going through Taylorville" sounded like a smoke screen, meant to explain the man's presence in the county without giving away much else. But if he wasn't from the area, he should have attracted some notice while traveling past the schoolhouse on Mt. Auburn Road, the thoroughfare so heavily used by locals going to and from the Grove. Yet not a single resident had mentioned seeing an outsider near the schoolhouse or in the Grove on the day in question. The only unfamiliar faces were of the two tramps seen in Blue Mound on Thursday night.

The letter was dated Saturday, August 12—the day after the failed lynching— and it was postmarked Monday, August 14, at 7:00 A.M. Perhaps the most telling clue was the wording, the neat handwriting, the overall character of the message— none of it looked to be the work of an uneducated person, much less a tramp. The author had crammed an incredible number of accusations, albeit ambiguously, into his short note. But as fascinating as it was, the letter was virtually worthless without the author's name. The *Republican* published its own take on the matter: "It is the opinion of the Decatur people who have watched the development in this case since June 29 that the writer of the letter, whosoever he is, was not near the schoolhouse when the outrage was committed and if he was and his identification can be established, he should be arrested and jailed along with the quartette Pettus, Clementi, Montgomery and Vermillion."[2]

Rather than ruminate for the press, Bond preferred to play it close. The Decatur paper summarized his reaction in one sentence: "Mr. Bond thinks he knows who the writer is and that it is someone who resides in the Grove City neighborhood and who was in Chicago when this letter was written but does not wish the name disclosed until he is better informed."[3] Bond wanted the sender to reveal himself, so he put out word that $100 would be handed over to the man if he would come forward. In the end, nobody took the bait, so perhaps the letter was nothing more than a grand hoax. Besides, Bond was satisfied that, with the arrest of Private Hobbs, all of the guilty parties were now in custody.

Like Clementi, Hobbs was claiming to have an alibi. As soon as he was officially booked into the county jail, Detective Page escorted the newest inmate, in handcuffs, to the Bond farm to answer to an anguished father. He was first taken into Emma's room, where the bedridden victim failed to identify him as one of her attackers. The suspect was then hauled back to the parlor, where the two older men questioned him mercilessly. Where had he been, and what had he been doing since he'd left the county? Where was he on June twenty-ninth, last? Could he prove his whereabouts on that day? What about the days right before and right after that? And why had he enlisted when he did?

According to the suspect, at the time of the crime he had been working in the tiny village of Mitchell, in western Illinois. Upon being fired from his job there on Friday morning, the thirtieth—for oversleeping—he'd packed up and headed to Springfield, with the idea of joining the army. The pay wasn't great, but it was steady. And, yes, he could give them the name of someone in Mitchell who would vouch for his story.

Not long after the interrogation, Hobbs and Vermillion were both taken into court for arraignment. The latter waived his hearing, hoping to get a swifter trial and, thus, a swifter acquittal. His bond was lowered to $3,000. It was becoming increasingly clear, however, that he wouldn't be able to raise one nickel of it. Hobbs's bail was set at $5,000, pending further investigation. Both were returned to their cells—Vermillion to pray for a windfall and Hobbs to wait for someone to check out his alibi.

Obviously, Emma's father wasn't about to immediately accept the soldier's word at face value. It was imperative that someone travel to Mitchell to confirm his alibi. The village of Mitchell sits across the big river from and slightly northeast of St. Louis, only a few hours from Taylorville. But, oddly, nothing appeared in the press to indicate whether Bond, Page, or even Sheriff Haines ever made that journey. Presumably, somebody went, because toward the end of August, word circulated that Hobbs had been cleared of any involvement in the outrage. But for some reason, he was detained at the county jail until mid-September, when State's Attorney Drennan finally ordered his release.[4] Along with his freedom, he was handed just enough pocket money to return to his army post.

About two weeks after the preliminary hearing, the victim changed her mind. She was now firmly convinced that three men, not two, had raped her. And she now believed she could identify the man who had pulled her up into the loft. This was in contrast to her statement two weeks earlier, in which she said she did not think that she would recognize the guilty parties and could only give general descriptions. Around this same time, word slipped out that "the suspects would be turned loose under the cover of darkness and allowed to make their escape"—in truth, not an escape so much as a mad dash to their homes to avoid any potential harassment.[5]

The accused, with the exception of Dr. Vermillion and Private Hobbs, had been free to go ever since posting bond. Evidently the elder John Montgomery had come through with Clementi's bail, too. So the suspects had only to muster up the courage to leave, but they obviously valued their necks more than their freedom. Plus, there was Drennan's pledge to the public to keep them behind bars and their subsequent promise to comply. Of course, that agreement was in no way binding. With the harvest season fast approaching, Montgomery was feeling the tug of his land. Pettus, too, worried about how his mother and uncle would manage without his and Clementi's help. Sure, there was always a chance that the latter would take off, once he got out of jail. But if he was that stupid, he'd better watch his back constantly, because John Sr. would be out a good amount of cash and would surely hunt him down.

While the sheriff was busy skirting the rumors that the men would be sneaking out late at night, he was secretly planning for their safe departure in broad daylight, barring any worsening of Emma's condition or, God forbid, her death. The sheriff was only willing to concede that the men's release would probably come before the end of the month. On August 31, after almost three weeks of voluntary incarceration, the three slipped away in the late morning without attracting any notice. They headed straight for the Wabash Depot, on the southern edge of town. There, they caught the 10:59 A.M. train to Blue Mound. Family members had no idea they were coming, so nobody was at the depot to meet them; hence, they had to hike the last nine miles to their homes.

As summer waned and the suspects got back to farming, Emma had a setback. She was now enduring recurrent fevers and constant pain, slipping in and out of consciousness. Her doctors—now two of them—were at her side more often than not, and she was said to be "gradually dying of exhaustion."[6] Her family hovered over her day and night—looking, praying for any glimmer of hope.

Even the defendants expressed their concern over her health; of course, if she died of her injuries, they'd have to face murder charges, not to mention a situation more volatile than the one that had already shaken them to their core.

That her physical injuries were so slow to heal was, understandably, the biggest concern of her doctors. Their reports on Emma changed so frequently that nobody knew what to believe. One day, the press would write that "her death is hourly expected."[7] The next, it would say she was "resting easier today."[8] One reporter, unsure of what to make of the victim's status, decided to pay a visit to the Bond house and assess the situation. The family kindly allowed him into the sanctum of Emma's bedroom, where he encountered a heartrending scene: "The bed on which Miss Emma lay [was] surrounded by anxious, weeping friends, who knew that death must come, and yet would ward off the dreadful monster. As I entered the room I found Miss Emma in an insensible condition, which lasted for four hours, and her appearance was more like that of the dead than the living."[9] Her breathing became so shallow at one point that her loved ones thought the end had come. But to their amazement, she revived. Some days, she would babble incoherently one minute, then rant about her memories of the crime the next. According to her father, "in her delirium, she went over the scene of the outrage, telling precisely the same story she told the prosecuting attorney."[10]

It was unclear what caused Emma's latest downturn. The world was offered countless descriptions of her agonies but few theories on their origins. The spinal injury was always considered the most serious, even though its exact nature was never explained. And she was also said to be suffering from "neuralgia of the heart." This, surmised her doctors, was a side effect of the spinal injury and the cause of her violent paroxysms. In turn, those fits were now lasting anywhere from a few minutes to several hours. Besides administering the usual restoratives, there was little else her doctors could do for their patient.

Luckily for the suspects, she continued to live, though barely. Her doctors declared that if she did pull through, she would forever be a cripple, due to the severity of her back injury. On one September night, it took four men to restrain her as she writhed in spasms of pain. Then came this grimmest of updates: "Her stomach now refuses to retain nourishment of any kind, and her physical power can last but little longer. The paroxysms which have so long baffled the skill of the attending physicians have disappeared, and vomiting has set in and is of so violent a nature as to be beyond the reach of medical skill."[11]

The mental state of Mr. Bond—the last bastion of strength at the family home—sounded almost equally pitiful: "A gentleman who visited Tuesday afternoon says that the poor old gentleman was almost heartbroken with grief, and the lines which furrowed his face told too plainly of the days and nights of anxious watching and care that he had experienced. He said that he had given up all hope and that the end was near at hand."[12]

Emma's suffering was not purely physical. In her day, nobody—not even doctors—addressed the latent psychological effects of a sexual assault, not in the immediate aftermath or ever. And that was bound to have serious repercussions for her, sooner or later. In 1882, there was another and more troublesome force to be reckoned with. This one had the potential to severely affect Emma's extended prognosis, probably more so than any discussion or lack of discussion on the rape. Hysteria, the Victorian enigma, had reached epic proportions by the late 1800s; nevertheless, the public *and* the medical community had almost no understanding of it. The list of symptoms pinned to this condition was virtually endless; so, too, were its presumed causes and treatment protocols. The condition was always thought to be a predominantly female one, which originated in the womb.

By the latter half of the nineteenth century, the list of symptoms grouped under the blanket diagnosis of hysteria had grown exponentially and ranged from mild to severe. At the mild end were such nuisances as dyspepsia, crying fits, insomnia, loss of appetite, taking to bed for long periods of time—all things that today would likely point to mild depression. In the extreme, however, Victorian patients could suffer anything from paralysis to amnesia. Some patients went for weeks without food. Others lost their ability to speak, swallow, walk, talk, or awaken. And any combination of these symptoms could draw a diagnosis of hysteria.

Plaguing the most severely afflicted were the classic paroxysms, or "fits." These were not seizures as we know them today; the patient's body (or portions of her body) would go completely rigid, with the arms and legs assuming grotesque positions and the face contorting into all sorts of inhuman expressions. For the patient's family—who could do nothing but stand by and watch helplessly—this was the most distressing and least understood aspect of hysteria.

Emma's recurring paroxysms did appear to be the typical spasms associated with hysteria. But it was also possible that her spinal injury was responsible for at least some of her other symptoms. Unfortunately, more than a century after the fact, there is no way to decipher the many complexities of her mental and physical state. But one thing was certain: nobody close to her truly understood how Emma's many ailments would come to affect her life—a life that had held so much promise just a few weeks earlier.

12

*He said that he had given up all hope and that the end was near at hand. In
speaking of the parties now in custody, he expressed himself freely and bitterly.*
—Decatur Review, *September 21, 1882*

With the grand jury not scheduled to take up the Bond case until late November, everyone half-expected the story to die down for awhile. Fueled by the public's insatiable curiosity, however, it did not. On the day after his return home, John C. Montgomery set out for the *Republican*'s office in Decatur with his brothers-in-law J. C. Paxton and George Pettus.[1] The suspect had more than a few things to get off of his chest, and he wanted the paper's editor to print them all. First, he wanted people to know that he was innocent. He could vouch for Pettus and Clementi, too, because he'd seen them both at the Pettus place "between sundown and dark."[2] And, yes, he had gone straight home from the jail the day before, just like the other two. That was ample proof that none of them intended to run.

John wanted to believe that his troubles were easing up. After all, didn't people have better things to do with their lives? Ideally, the answer would have been yes. But when word got out that he was in town, the *Republican* office was besieged by a throng of gawkers, their faces pressed up against the building's windowpanes to get a better look at the now-infamous suspect who had barely escaped with his life in August.

Action from Mr. Bond was still in great demand, but no amount of prodding was going to drive the man to revenge. The diehards persisted anyway, with letters from all over the nation arriving daily at the Bond home, advising him "to take the law in his own hands."[3] And should he follow through, those same letters promised him absolution. But as someone who preferred to let the courts handle it, Bond wasn't listening. However, someone else was, and he was worried enough to purchase a "sixteen shooter rifle." John Montgomery, it was said, intended to "give variety to the next entertainment gotten up for his benefit."[4] And who could blame him after all he'd been through in August? But another man was about to become the center of attention, which would give John a much-needed and long-overdue break.

Vermillion's court appearance, scheduled for Monday, September 18, promised to be as big a draw as the August hearing had been. It came close and did not disappoint. Once again, Taylorville was overrun with noise and dust and wagons and horses as country and city dwellers converged on the town from all directions. Fifty of the previous witnesses were again subpoenaed to testify. At one o'clock, the defendant was ushered into the courtroom. The spectators' curiosity was matched only by Vermillion's anxiety: "He wore a scared, nervous look, which led a great many to believe him guilty. He was smoking at the time. As he would take the cigar from his mouth, his hand would tremble so visibly as to be perceptible, all over the room, and a sickly pallor overspread his face."[5]

The suspense in the room evaporated instantly when attorney McCaskill announced that some of the witnesses were absent, as was L. F. Hamilton—the lawyer who was to assist him. Consequently, his client wanted to waive his examination until the next term of the circuit court. Ricks then granted the doctor a second bond reduction. The original $5,000 had already been dropped to $4,000. The new amount was set at $2,500—a decent gesture on Ricks's part. The justice, however, had no way of knowing that even this was way beyond the doctor's reach. It seems Vermillion had no family in the area to turn to for help. Being stuck in jail was likely a good thing for him, however, since his house in Grove City sat within a stone's throw of four belonging to Emma's relatives, the Housleys.[6]

Other than the confusion with the two Abner Bonds, the newspapers were doing a fairly decent job of sorting out the intricate family connections of those involved. However, one family link had escaped their notice. In November 1879, Dr. William Vermillion had married Mary C. "Kate" Hart, who had died of tuberculosis just one year later. And Kate had been the sister of Owen Hart, who was married to Cora Pettus, Lee's sister.

Although Vermillion repeatedly proclaimed his innocence, almost nobody was convinced, and choosing to waive his hearing did very little to improve his lot. Rather, it pointed all the more to his guilt. Then, in an unexpected twist, Bond named him "the chief instigator" of the crime. Previously, that dubious distinction had been arbitrarily assigned at various times to Montgomery or to Clementi. The day after Vermillion's court appearance, a family friend stopped by the Bond farm, where Emma's father shared his feelings. As someone who had previously called for public restraint and cautioned against mob law, he now expressed an unusual show of contempt:

"Would you interfere in the case of another mob?" asked the visitor. "No," was the reply, "I would not, but I would be the first to pull on the ropes that would send their guilty souls to hell." Being asked about another mob, he answered, "Mind, I don't say there will be a mob, but if there is, there will not be another fiasco." . . . [T]he feeling against Vermillion and his accomplices is so bitter that a mob could easily be raised to lynch them. When Miss Bond's death is announced, a recurrence of the scenes of August 11th is almost a foregone conclusion.

Both Montgomery and Clementi dared to show up for Vermillion's court date, and afterward Clementi was seen "walking around, showing friends the places that will long be remembered by him where he was interviewed by the mob."[7] Pettus, the only one who did not put in an appearance, had more pressing matters to deal with.

The latest turmoil in his life had begun a couple of weeks earlier, when young Allie Hill announced to her father, John, that she planned to marry the young suspect on Saturday, September 16. The Hill family lived just up Mt. Auburn Road to the north and were longtime neighbors of the Pettuses and the Montgomerys. Mr. Hill, "one of the wealthiest and most influential citizens of the county," had not so much as blinked three years earlier when Lee's brother George had asked to marry Allie's older sister Effie.[8] In fact, both families had embraced that union wholeheartedly. But now that Lee was in hot water up to his eyebrows, Mr. Hill would not hear of the wedding and voiced his strong disapproval. As can happen with parents and nearly grown children, however, the father's objections fell on deaf ears. In a fit of youthful defiance, young Allie told her father in no uncertain terms that she intended to marry Lee anyway.

Then early on the morning of September 12, just days before the planned wedding, Coroner John Kittle was summoned to the Hill farm, where something horrible had taken place overnight. When Kittle arrived, he was led to the family's barn. There, high overhead and swinging from the rafters, was the family patriarch. After making an initial assessment of the scene, the coroner lowered the not yet cold body of John Hill, age sixty, to the ground. Kittle needed to assemble a coroner's jury, and, in rural areas, nearby friends and neighbors were usually called upon to assist in that capacity. Pressed into service that day were Laurence Heinlein, W. Y. Croswait, Deal Davis, O. Z. Housley, Daniel Masters, and John A. Armstrong.

By the time the six jurymen gathered at the Hill farm, morning had broken. The inquest into Hill's death proceeded on the spot, in the barn's stark surroundings. The verdict was straightforward: "We, the jury, find that the deceased, John M. Hill came to his death by hanging by the neck with a black rope at his barn in said County about five o'clock on the morning of the twelfth day of September 1882." From the body, Kittle removed "one pocket book containing 172.00 dollars, 2 deposit checks for 322.67 on H. M. Vandeveer and Co., also a lot of checks."[9] These items were handed over to Hill's widow, who watched the entire inquest, along with four of the dead man's eight children: Henry, the eldest; Allie, the defiant one; John Jr., in his teens; and Maggie, the youngest, at twelve. Also present were several Montgomerys and Pettuses, plus Mr. and Mrs. Owen Mathews, George Smith, and a Dr. Lawrence.

Apparently, Mr. Hill had shared his thoughts on Allie's future with somebody who, in turn, shared them at the inquest: "The evidence before the coroner's jury was to the effect that he would rather die than see his daughter marry Lee Pettus, one of the suspects in the Bond outrage case."[10] After all, who in his right mind would hand over a beloved daughter to a man he thought capable of the shameful act committed against Miss Bond? Many a father could sympathize with Hill. Allie's father had obviously made up his mind about Lee's guilt and was overcome with humiliation because of his daughter's plans. Wisely, Lee and Allie postponed their nuptials.

The press latched onto the Hill story right away. Granted, it didn't offer the same high drama as the hearing, but it was connected by a thread to the bigger story. In its follow-up, the *Republican* wrote:

> The friends of Mr. Hill for miles around were at the inquest, and the name of Lee Pettus and John Montgomery were repeated in every little group of men that congregated around Hill's house. John Montgomery and the Pettus family, with the exception of Lee, were at the inquest and Montgomery seemed anxious to know what the girl [Allie] would testify to, and said that was what he came to the inquest for. He and a citizen of Christian County were in the room alone with the body, and the citizen remarked that a small rope could make an ugly mark around a man's neck. Montgomery, after a critical examination of the old man's neck, replied: "Yes, it makes a worse mark and hurts more than a large one."[11]

Although the newspapers often used unnamed sources for information, they didn't always check those sources' accuracy. About two weeks later, the *Republican* was obliged to present an alternate version of what had taken place at the Hill inquest. This time, the information came directly from John C. Montgomery; and if anybody had the right to challenge the papers on their affinity for half-truths, then it was him—the man who had been walking around for three months with a bull's-eye painted on his back, courtesy of the press.

Grove City, Ill, Sept. 28. EDITORS, DECATUR REPUBLICAN: I do not believe that you would intentionally do me a wrong in publishing sensational articles . . . charging me with nearly all the crimes in the criminal code, all of which was reported at the time by a Decatur merchant who was traveling down in Christian County, or "an interview with Col. Bond," or a "special correspondent," "a reliable citizen," etc. . . . I desire to make what will be a very surprising assertion. . . . It is this: that I have never been guilty of a dishonorable act in my life, and I challenge any one to specify such an act over their own signature—especially the aforesaid authors. Furthermore, that each and every one of them has been guilty of acts which the statutes classify as criminal, and will include in this declaration the self-styled detectives who have been so conspicuous in the matter . . . in regard to my presence and reported remarks at the inquest of Mr. Hill. . . . I expressed no anxiety to any one as to the testimony of Miss Alice Hill. She stated that she knew of no cause why her father committed the rash act. . . . She afterwards . . . denied there being any such conversation as stated in the communication to your paper. Mr. Hill was not happy in his family relations, which fact was generally known. A gentleman stated to a lady in the neighborhood the week before that he . . . would not be surprised if Mr. Hill killed himself. As to my being alone in the room with a citizen and making my remarks about the rope or its effects is false. There are well defined reasons why he killed himself, but the cesspool in which we are involved furnished a convenient receptacle in which others hastened to hide their dirty linen. John C. Montgomery.[12]

Most likely, John was not privy to the precise cause of Hill's suicide, for who can say what goes on behind a neighbor's closed door? One thing the papers failed to mention was John's widow was the stepmother of his children. So there may have been other undisclosed family dynamics at play—things that only the Hills knew.

The Bond case wasn't the only one attracting attention in the region that year. The county had a rash of other contemptible felonies awaiting the court's action. Among the most prominent was a senseless murder of a good and decent farmer, Joseph McKinney. There were also two other rape cases pending.

The 1881 McKinney murder remained a high priority on the court docket. George Traughber and Charles C. Meyers, who had shared the cellblock with the Bond suspects in August, had been charged in the slaying. They hoped to get off easy by showing that they had been rendered half-crazy from too much liquor; the pair, whose heroes were the notorious James brothers, had gone on a long drinking binge before setting out in search of their own victim. They soon came upon poor old McKinney, riding along on his horse and minding his own business. When he ignored their drunken tauntings, they asked him if he would trade horses with them. He flatly refused, so they rode on ahead and lay in wait behind some roadside bushes. As he came even with them, they took aim and felled him with four bullets. Well, Traughber had actually pulled the trigger—after Meyers called him a coward for hesitating. McKinney never knew what hit him. Meyers had a lifelong reputation as a troublemaker, while it was said Traughber had simply fallen in with the wrong man. In the end, however, Traughber would face the scaffold and Meyers would go to the state penitentiary.

Of the other two rape cases, one involved a fourteen-year-old servant girl named Anabel Nave, who had been deflowered by her drunken employer. The second case closely mirrored the first, except Nina Ortman was only twelve and the guilty man had not been under the influence of alcohol when he'd forced himself upon the young girl, whom his wife had hired.

Nobody could say which straw had broken Governor Cullom's back, but clearly, the man was still smarting from the scolding he'd taken over the Taylorville riot. With that and many other problems across his state, he had had his fill of criminal actions and mob reactions. So rather than sit back and wait for the proverbial other shoe to drop, he drafted a warning letter—really, more of a retroactive reprimand—to those in charge of the state's local jurisdictions. The *Tribune* called it a "timely and forcible reminder" to the state's "conservators of the peace." It read:

> I call your attention to the following provisions of the statutes of this State. . . .
> "SHERIFF. Chapter 125, Sec. 17. Each Sheriff shall be conservator of the peace in his county, and shall keep the same, suppress riots, routs, affrays, fighting, breaches of the peace, and prevent crime. . . .
> "MAYOR. Chap. 24, Sec 21. He may exercise, within the city limits, the powers conferred upon Sheriffs to suppress disorder and keep the peace . . . Sec 26. He shall have power, when necessary, to call on every male inhabitant of the city over the age of 18 years to aid in enforcing the laws and ordinances, and to call out the militia to aid in suppressing riots and other disorderly conduct . . ."

In his caveat, the governor urged local officials to be more diligent in their pursuit of "the vicious persons infesting our cities and towns . . . to the end that crime may be reduced to the lowest possible limit in Illinois."[13] So there it was, right off the pages of the Illinois statutes. Specifically, while sheriffs were charged with suppressing riots in their counties, within city limits, the mayors also had the power "to call out the militia." It sounded as if the governor was also faulting Taylorville's mayor for ignoring his offer of help during the August riot.

As the days of autumn grew shorter, Emma experienced some new and disturbing symptoms. In early October, news came that her latest affliction resembled lockjaw. The effect was so extreme that the young woman could not open her mouth; and had anyone wanted to pry it open, they could not have done so. She had also reportedly lost her sight. Not only that, but ever since the attack, her weight had been dropping steadily. She was now down to a skeletal seventy-five pounds. So desperate was her condition that the press was ready to pound the last nail into her coffin. Phrases such as "when Miss Bond's death is announced" left no doubt about her assumed fate.[14]

As concerned citizens and friends awaited the inevitable, new plans to avenge Emma's impending death were taking shape. That the defense was talking about a change of venue further antagonized the mood of the people. A replay of August's catastrophe seemed unavoidable. On October 4, the *Tribune* wrote, "The people there are organized, and . . . they do not intend to let justice be thwarted by any trick."[15] The renewal of vigilantism combined with Emma's almost certain death prompted Montgomery to start stockpiling weapons at his farm. He had every intention of protecting himself and his family and of going down fighting, if necessary. That should have been an indication that he intended to stay put until the trial. Nevertheless, detectives continued to track his every move, just in case his plans suddenly changed.

Yet, the weeks went by, and nobody fled. Nobody stoked the embers of unrest. And nobody died. The pessimistic news of Emma's battle to survive tapered off. Little was written of her progress throughout October, until the *Review* published the first real ray of hope: "After months of painful suffering, Miss Emma Bond is reported improving and the prospects are favorable for her recovery. Her old time health and robustness of constitution, however, can never be fully regained, even under the most careful treatment."[16]

Thus, a standoff of sorts—however fragile and temporary—marked the passage of autumn. The grand jury was scheduled to convene on the third Monday in November. Based on the opinions expressed right after the hearing, the State's case was going to need a substantial boost. Ideally, Emma would be healed enough to appear in court. However, nobody really expected that to happen. What they did expect, almost without exception, was that the accused would be indicted for their contemptible criminal acts.

13

Notwithstanding the numerous crimes already reported from this section of the State, Christian County again comes to the front with a rape case, the details of which are indeed horrifying in the extreme.
　　—Chicago Tribune, *November 18, 1882*

Decatur's *Herald* perfectly expressed the question on everyone's mind that November: "The situation presents an opportunity for the vindication of our jury system. Will Christian County accept it?"[1] Meanwhile, friends and loved ones of the accused were trying their best to convey optimism, maintaining that there would be no indictment. And even on the outside chance that there was one, they truly believed that no jury would ever convict.

Other than the Bonds, nobody was more thankful to learn of Emma's progress than the accused. On a visit to Decatur in November, John C. Montgomery expressed his own relief that Emma was growing stronger with each passing day. Montgomery was in Decatur to get a copy of the testimony of a particular witness from the stenographer John T. Montgomery. That the defendant was allowed to pick up said document seemed highly irregular, since the lead defense attorney, Anthony Thornton, lived right in Decatur and could have easily obtained the document himself.

John C.'s trip to John T.'s office occurred just two weeks before the circuit court was set to convene. Then, one week before that anticipated date, another young woman was gang-raped in nearby Pana. The attack, while not nearly as brutal as the one against Emma, was just as reprehensible. The culprits singled out a completely helpless victim, a "simple-minded girl about twenty-years-old, a stranger in the place and without money."[2] Young Lena Zinn's parents had put their girl on a train in Mattoon, bound for Beardstown. When she missed her connecting train in Pana, she found herself alone in a strange town after dark. Not having any experience in such matters, she asked the Pana stationmaster if she could spend the night in the depot. He agreed but then left for his home around ten, leaving her alone and at the mercy of three hooligans who sensed she was easy prey. Two of them approached her in the depot, posing as a policeman and a hotel employee. They offered to secure her an overnight room at the local hotel, and she gladly accepted. They picked up her bags, and she followed them, unknowingly, into an ambush. At a nearby schoolyard, a third miscreant joined them, and they forced their naïve young victim into the school's outhouse, where each took a turn raping her.

Fortunately, the guilty parties were rounded up quickly and thrown into the Christian County jail. The timing of the Pana rape wasn't going to help the Bond suspects one bit; with this latest outrage coming so close on the heels of the Montgomery schoolhouse attack, it would take a miracle to calm the stormy waters. The *Decatur Herald*'s response sounded like a revival of the earlier calls to action: "The opinion is quite evident that in order to save this county from further crimes, an example should be made of some of the fiends now in jail." A citizens' group, known as the "Tower Hill Horse Company and Vigilance Committee," was supposedly en route to Taylorville with ropes in hand. Yet when hours passed and nothing developed, Decatur couldn't help but take a poke at its neighbors in the next county over: "It is rumored that a mob had been organized in Taylorville to lynch the fiends; but this was evidently a mistake, for the mob failed to materialize. Besides, people have come to understand that a Christian County mob is a harmless kind of thing. It lacks the distinguishing feature of a successful mob—determination. It is heavily charged with bluster but is devoid of courage. It is, so to speak, a blank cartridge, as harmless at the business end as it is at the breech. Even the criminals laugh in their sleeves when the thing begins to fizz."[3] As painful as that was to read, at least in Christian County, perhaps it held some measure of truth—excluding the part about the criminals laughing in their sleeves. In all likelihood, the Bond suspects weren't laughing at anything; instead, they were probably praying that the offenses of the Pana gang would not come to bear on their own imminent case.

Circuit Judge Jesse Phillips of Hillsboro was sitting on the bench when court convened in late November. A tall man with an imposing presence, he had run his own law practice after the Civil War and until his election to the Fifth Circuit bench in 1879. When H. M. Vandeveer had stepped down that year, the voters had gladly transferred their trust to the much younger Phillips. He held one of three judgeships in the circuit, sharing duties with two highly regarded men: W. R. Welch of Carlinville and Charles S. Zane of Springfield. The Fifth Circuit encompassed a fair swath of the middle part of Illinois and included not only Christian and Montgomery Counties but also Shelby, Macoupin, and Sangamon. Both Zane and Welch had been on the circuit for years; but because of the division of the workload, Christian County's cases fell to the newcomer Phillips.

After reviewing the cases on his winter docket, Phillips cut straight to the Taylorville uprising, declaring that any violence against prisoners was a "menace to the rights, liberties and protection of the people" and, as such, would not be tolerated in his jurisdiction.[4] He charged the grand jury with thoroughly investigating the attempted lynching of the Bond suspects, promising not only the court's complete support but also its protection throughout the probe. But before the jury could tackle that issue, there were other cases to be considered. With multiple rape cases on the docket, the grand jury's task was not going to be an easy one. By Tuesday, it was clear that the Bond case would come up on Wednesday; and, naturally, that news was leaked. Sheriff Haines expected large and unwanted numbers to show up at the courthouse, even though grand jury proceedings were closed to the public.

On the upside, however, Emma had made so much progress during the fall that Mr. Bond was bringing her to town so that she could testify before the grand jury. Although not fully healed, "she never lost courage and became despondent, but, on the contrary, maintained and expressed the belief that she would recover and be able to come before the Grand Jury to testify against the accused."[5] Whether those were Emma's own sentiments or somebody else's, it is impossible to know. If they were truly hers, she was displaying a fundamental inner fortitude that would prove invaluable in the days ahead.

The trip would be her first real physical test. She had not seen the outside world since that excruciating day back in June. As the date for the proceedings drew closer, she must have experienced a certain degree of dread. Was it asking too much of the fragile victim? The journey was more than eight miles, over bumpy dirt roads, in the open bed of a spring wagon, in the chill air of late autumn. It was bound to take a toll on her body. Then again, this was the same young woman who had survived the unthinkable, albeit as "a shadow of her former self."[6] She had endured unrelenting pain and frequent bouts of dissociative states and had been unable to eat for weeks. And still, her "cheerful nature had begun to show itself" of late.[7] However, this same young lady would soon be forced to relive the most intimate of horrors—a challenge made more daunting by having to describe them out loud, not only to strangers but to strangers of the opposite sex.

On Tuesday, November 21, A. D. Bond bundled up his girl, placed her in the back of his wagon, and set off for Sonny's house on the outskirts of Taylorville. Of course, Sonny offered whatever help he could, without hesitation. If his cousin needed moral support, he would be there with a compassionate shoulder. If he needed money, now or in the future, Sonny would dig deeply into his own pocket. He had already nudged the county board into posting a nice monetary reward, and then he'd upped the ante by throwing in a generous chunk of his own cash. The total incentive now stood at an impressive $31,000—no small sum in a day when a loaf of bread cost less than a nickel, a quart of milk averaged seven cents, and a pound of beef could be had for a dime.[8] It was typical Sonny. Every ounce of the burden that the older cousin had carried around for months, the younger one had taken on as his own. This wasn't surprising, of course, since the same Quaker anvil that had forged A. D. Bond had also shaped Sonny.

The ride to town was exhausting for Emma, but she endured it with no obvious setbacks. With the trip out of the way on Tuesday, the next day would be easier, at least physically. Midmorning on Wednesday, she was loaded into Sonny's comfortable carriage for the short ride to the courthouse. With her father and one of her sisters at her side, she peered anxiously out the window. The crowds lining the streets grew thicker as the carriage drew closer to the square. Emma spotted an occasional familiar face, but most belonged to people she did not recognize. And although the chaos that had marked the August hearing was nowhere to be seen, the arrival of the long-secluded victim was not to be missed:

The wagon stopped at the north gate of the courtyard and Miss Emma was tenderly lifted to the ground, and from there to the steps leading to the Grand Jury. She walked slowly, supported on one side by her father, on the other by a sister, while her back was supported by Mr. John Price and Dr. D. K. Cornell. As she wearily walked along, the sympathizing throng was as quiet as if in the presence of death. At the foot of the stairs they halted and Miss Bond was placed in an easy chair and carried to the jury room above. During all this time not one in the large crowd spoke above a whisper, and as they remembered the terrible ordeal through which she had passed, and coupled that with her present weak and almost helpless condition, the hearts of that vast crowd were moved to pity and strong men almost gave way to tears.[9]

The members of the jury, concerned about overtaxing Emma, hoped to keep their questioning as brief as possible. Dr. Cornell was standing by, just in case his patient should need him. When Emma was felled by one of her paroxysms, just a few minutes into it, Cornell rushed to her side and administered the usual restoratives. After a short break, the inquiry resumed. But right away, Emma was hit by another attack—this one coming with a vengeance. Her doctor reappeared, and the medicine again worked its magic. The jury pushed forward, but when a third spasm overcame the young woman, the doctor had to be summoned again.

With so many interruptions, Emma's interrogation lasted three hours. Then, as she was preparing to leave, she was struck down by the most violent attack of the entire day. She was carried off and laid down, and still the spasm did not abate. At one point, her torment became so extreme that it took several men to hold her down. While her father, the doctor, and the some of the jurymen tended to her inside the courthouse, outside "her heartrending screams could be heard all over the courthouse square." One account even claimed that her cries were heard several blocks away. The victim's ongoing struggles were familiar to all, but the men who witnessed her agony that Wednesday were completely unprepared for it. As they listened in disbelief, they "cursed the fiends that perpetrated the damnable outrage upon her."[10]

A full hour went by before Emma was up to leaving, but she obviously couldn't make the trip home. So she was taken back to Sonny's house. There, under the attentive care of her physician and the gentle nursing of Lizzie Bond, the troubled girl was soon restored to relative comfort. By Thursday, it was reported that her recovery would not be greatly affected by the previous day's physical and emotional demands.

The grand jury continued with its investigation throughout that week, amid rumors that Emma's testimony had produced some new "revelations"—namely, that certain elements of her suffering had yet to be told. But with the grand jury sworn to secrecy, nobody was ready to predict what it might do—except A. D. Bond, who expressed confidence that the main suspects would all be standing trial. He also expected Vermillion to be indicted for aiding and abetting the other four. He had waived yet another hearing and was still confined to jail. Perhaps he hoped that if enough time went by, the court would simply dismiss the charge against him. Meanwhile, the other defendants were considering pressing charges of their own—"against the leaders of the mob which took [them] so near to the borders of the dark valley."[11]

On the sixth day of December, the grand jury handed down its decision. John Montgomery, Lee Pettus, and Emanuel Clementi were named on the indictment. So too was William Vermillion, which came as no surprise to anyone other than the doctor himself. But a fifth and unexpected man would also be facing trial—William J. Montgomery, the only one discharged at the preliminary hearing for lack of evidence. In addition to his discovery of Emma's pocketbook and the persistent rumors that he had acted as a lookout for the assailants, one other thing had worked against him. It seems he had "disposed of most of his property and tried to run off" in mid-July, only to be caught in Chatham, just southwest of Springfield.[12]

Upon learning that William's name was also listed on the indictment, Judge Phillips had no choice but to issue a new warrant for his arrest. He wanted William back in his courtroom the following Friday, at which time he would set a new bond amount for him. The grand jury had conducted a thorough, painstaking investigation into the Bond case, leaving no room for future criticism.

3

THE INTERIM

December 7, 1882–December 9, 1883

14

Under the circumstances, Judge Phillips cannot well do otherwise than grant [the change of venue].
—Decatur Review, *December 8, 1882*

With the indictment in, the waiting began. It was going to be long but hardly uneventful. Nine days after the Bond indictments, the second-floor courtroom again filled to capacity. This time, the matter was a simple one: the defense team was seeking a change of venue for the accused—Vermillion being the only exception. The reason for the defense's request was, foremost, that none of the defendants could get a fair trial in the place where "a mob had gathered and forcibly taken them from the jail and swung them up."[1] Thornton addressed the court for more than two hours, quoting often from the area's newspapers. Their damning commentary illustrated how unjust it would be to try the men locally. H. M. Vandeveer spoke for the State, arguing vehemently that because of Emma Bond's health, there was no guarantee she would be able to attend a Taylorville trial, much less one in the next county over.

Judge Phillips retired to his anteroom, where he took a respectable amount of time to consider the petition. But, as expected, he granted the change of venue. The trial would take place in neighboring Montgomery County—in Hillsboro. Much was made of the absurd argument that the defense was trying to dodge justice. The *Reno Gazette* even theorized that "the defendants are only trying to defer the trial until their victim dies."[2]

Only the doctor expressed a desire to stand trial right away and in his own county. He got half of his request: his trial would take place in Taylorville, but he'd have to wait until the court's March session. The Hillsboro trial for the remaining defendants was set for April 2. Judge Thornton and his defense team insisted they would be ready and would not ask for a continuance. Of course, Emma's recovery was of the utmost importance for the State, since there was no chance of getting a conviction without the help of its primary witness, truly, its *only* eyewitness.

At Sonny and Lizzie's house, that witness was still confined to bed, her grand jury appearance having put a much greater strain on her than was first thought. Worse yet, the paroxysms had come back with a vengeance. Three days after giving her testimony, she was persecuted by one lasting several hours. Some physicians would later speculate that her paroxysms had no organic basis whatsoever, that they were simply the manifestations of a hysterical woman. Still, the press kept hinting at a possible physical cause, referring to one injury in particular: "The protrusion in the small of her back, which up to this time was not very large, now [has begun] to grow and become exceedingly painful."[3]

Clearly, Emma wasn't going anywhere soon, so Sonny and Lizzie graciously converted their downstairs bedroom into a sanctuary for her. Regrettably, the succor of Sonny's family was no match for Emma's complicated condition. Her doctors were running out of ideas. As a last resort, they tried "a plaster-paris support for her back," but that quickly became "a source of great annoyance and irritation" and, ultimately, "one of extreme anguish."[4] Soon, they were cutting it off of her torso.

Meanwhile, winter spread its own dose of hardship across central Illinois. First, the region was socked by an intense blizzard. Then temperatures plummeted to fourteen below, and "chickens, exposed to the wind, froze and fell from their roost."[5] Illinoisans were used to such extremes—just not so early in the season. The mercury failed to climb above zero even at midday. If this was a sign of things to come, it looked like Emma might be trapped at her cousins' home until the spring thaw.

During that bitter cold December, Charles Meyers—the former jail mate of the Bond suspects—went on trial for his part in Joseph McKinney's murder. It was an easy case, and Meyers was quickly dealt a guilty verdict and sentenced to ninety-nine years at the Chester State Penitentiary for his part in the senseless killing. His partner, George Traughber, pleaded guilty a week later. His appointment with the gallows would be the first-ever court-ordered execution in Christian County.

Although Governor Cullom granted him a brief stay of execution, Traughber's final day on earth would be January 26, 1883. The scaffolding was erected adjacent to the jailhouse, with direct access from the jail door, and a high wall was raised around the entire site to keep out the general public. Only sixty-two observers were allowed into the enclosure. Among them were the jurors, some reporters, several sheriffs from the area, a handful of physicians, and, perhaps, the Baptist preacher who had been trying to save Traughber's soul. At high noon, after refusing his final breakfast and dinner, the doomed man—dressed in a dark suit—was led into the jail yard. Sheriff Haines guided him up the stairs to the gallows. Around the outside of the temporary barricade, Culver's Guard held off the public with fixed bayonets, visible to all. As reported in the *Decatur Herald*, Traughber's last utterance was: "I have nothing against anyone. I bid you all goodbye. That is all I have got to say"—no hint of remorse, just the simple words of a man who had come to terms with his fate. The *Herald* rendered its opinion on the execution: "The hanging will have a healthy effect on Christian County. . . . What the County needs is a hanging for every outrager and every murderer until the awful power of the law should strike terror in the hearts of criminals."[6]

In small-town newspapers, the "Personal Mentions" and "Local News" sections were always popular. Subject matter was varied and usually included comments on the weather, the comings and goings of local residents, social and church events, court cases, and other similar tidbits. The Bond case made perfect filler for these catch-all columns. So, too, did the work of the court reporter, John T. Montgomery. Several mentions in these columns indicated he was employed by various courts throughout east-central Illinois on a case-by-case basis. One mentioned his work on "the Freeman poisoning case" in nearby Sullivan.

In January 1883, the board of supervisors—in control of the county's purse strings—asked John T. to compile a "transcript of evidence" in the Bond case, with the stipulation that he complete his work in time for the trial. Given the unusual wording, it is unclear whether that document was based on witness statements taken during the investigation or on a verbatim transcription of the hearing testimonies. Either way, it was bound to be a monumental task, given the number of witnesses. In fact, it would take the stenographer many months to complete, even with his newfangled machine, the Caligraph. Similar to Remington's earlier typewriter, it first hit the market in 1880, providing stenographers with a level of speed and efficiency far beyond what they could achieve using shorthand.

Meanwhile, Emma settled in at Sonny's place, where, in a pleasant room on the first floor, she would spend the rest of the winter. Her room sat on the south side and an outside corner of the sizeable house. During the daytime, the low angle of the winter sun infused her bedroom with a golden glow and welcome warmth. The room was connected to the downstairs living area of the home by a long, narrow hallway, which gave Emma a degree of quiet and privacy away from Sonny and Lizzie and their young, active family. It also had its own door to the outside, not that Emma would be venturing out any time soon. But at least her visitors could come and go without disturbing the family. The only distraction, really, was the intermittent, loud rumbling of trains as they passed on the tracks adjacent to Sonny's property.

Although Emma's accommodations were comfortable, that winter she lost much of the ground she had gained during the autumn. Her doctors marveled at her "continued clinging to life," and even Emma seemed to accept the idea that she might not survive.[7] Her friends, still worried about her possible death, convinced her to give a deposition; it was the prudent thing to do. Prudence on the part of the defendants was not in short supply either. The *Republican* reported that the homes of Montgomery and Pettus had been turned into "arsenals" and that "one member of each family is constantly on guard armed with Winchester rifles." The same article said that John was "defiant" and prepared to shoot down anybody attempting to enter his home.[8] Three weeks later, however, John asked the paper to issue a retraction: He wished to put the whole arsenal story to rest; his house was not full of repeating rifles; and there were no armed guards on his property. Furthermore, all disbelievers were welcome to stop by his house and see for themselves.

Details on Emma's relapse were conspicuously vague, until late February when another confusing update appeared: "She is suffering from curvature of the spine, doubtless the result of her fall from the loft of the school house . . . to the floor below."[9] Apparently, "curvature of the spine" meant something different than it does today. Exactly what kind of back problem did Emma have? And was it connected to the large protrusion at the base of her spine—the one her doctors had tried to treat with a plaster cast in December? And what about her "neuralgia of the heart," mentioned on more than one occasion?

Perhaps her physicians were finally on to something when they concluded that their patient was suffering from an enlarged spleen. In fact, they felt certain that her spleen had been damaged during the attack. While a ruptured spleen might have killed her in short order, a small splenic tear will often heal itself.[10] In addition to her ongoing infirmities, however, she had developed some new symptoms, described as "fifteen or twenty nervous chills a day" and "frequent sinking spells," the latter a Victorian euphemism for fainting.[11] All of these symptoms—combined with her weight loss, fatigue, and anorexia—suggested two very serious, and possibly related, underlying conditions.

The first was endocarditis—an infection in the heart's lining and valves, which can develop when large numbers of bacteria enter the bloodstream from other parts of the body and migrate to the heart. Its primary symptoms are fever, chills, and lightheadedness (which can result in dizziness and fainting). It can also cause weight loss and fatigue. With no antibiotics to treat a primary infection, bacterial endocarditis was not implausible. Furthermore, with endocarditis the spleen can become enlarged when it is called upon to fight off the heart infection. Because an enlarged spleen exerts excessive pressure on the stomach, there is often it pain in the upper left quadrant of the torso and loss of appetite. Thus, several of Emma's symptoms might have been the result of endocarditis or an enlarged spleen—if not both.

Whatever the case, two things seemed undeniable. The patient faced a long road to complete recovery, and the passage of time had not lessened the public's interest in the case one iota. Contradictions, propaganda, and half-truths persisted at every turn. Discussions were still marked by disagreement about who had said what and when and who had done what and why. Informants were always plentiful but not necessarily well informed. Assertions from all sides were "as varying as the wind"—much like the reports of Emma's health.[12]

And the victim was not the only one struggling. Her father was dealing with his own personal hell. The *Tribune* noted, "His constant care and anxiety for his daughter is telling upon him fast, and he looks but a wreck of his former self."[13] In spite of that, Bond continued his search for new evidence. There were recurring leaks that he had uncovered more information "bearing on the guilt of the accused."[14] Again, he was not inclined to share the details, but his discoveries may have been related to an unidentified witness who surfaced in February: "A traveling seller of pumps . . . will swear that he saw one of the three accused standing in the door of the schoolhouse at the time the outrage was being committed. The seller knew not at the time, of course, about the outrage, but his memory now tells him that at the time of day when these inhuman acts were being perpetrated, he saw one of the accused as above stated."[15]

This story had an eerily familiar ring to it—reminiscent of the mysterious Chicago letter of the previous summer. But instead of a tramp, this was a traveling salesman. And instead of hearing things, this man had supposedly seen things. The author of the Chicago letter had attributed his six-week delay to a fickle memory. This traveling salesman had waited several months to come forward, so his memory might prove even more fickle. If this witness was to testify at the trial, as the article implied, then his identity must have been known to the prosecutor. In contrast, the earlier letter writer had chosen anonymity. Whether the two witnesses were the same, the bigger questions were these: How could either have traveled down Mt. Auburn Road so heavily used by locals, and escaped notice in broad daylight? And if someone had observed an unfamiliar man on that road, why hadn't he been tracked down by investigators? Finally, why such long delays in coming forward?

In early March, Emma's physicians announced she was not well enough to appear at Vermillion's trial, set for the thirteenth of the month. The doctor was doing rather poorly himself. At the time of his arrest in August, he'd been hale and hearty. Six months later, his friends and acquaintances barely recognized him. Definitely the odd man out, he seemed to have very few supporters, certainly nobody who was willing to lend him a financial hand. Even the itinerant and ill-reputed farmhand Clementi had managed to finagle some help from the Montgomerys. So while the four accused of the actual rape had gone on with their lives, to the degree it was possible, the man charged only as an accomplice bore the telltale signs of countless days and nights spent in a cold and dingy cell, devoid of fresh air and sunshine.

As the doctor's court date approached, his attorneys promised the citizens no further delays. As part of their advance strategy, they also let it be known that they would be making some concessions, chief among them that Emma Bond had indeed been the victim of a foul outrage. Yet they maintained that their client was not involved and they intended to show that by using the ever-popular "he can prove an alibi" defense.

Early on Tuesday, March 13, Vermillion was escorted into the courtroom, looking "much reduced in flesh and pale as a sheet."[16] As her doctors had warned, Emma did not appear, although nearly everyone else with a stake in the matter was present. Emma's father, the Montgomery brothers, and Pettus and Clementi were all there. Time dragged as the court worked through a thick docket of menial cases. Vermillion could only sit patiently and wait. His fellow defendants, of course, had no such constraints, so when the proceedings grew monotonous, they disappeared into the fading light of late afternoon, feeling like they'd wasted an entire day.

Naturally, as soon as they left, the *People v. Dr. William Vermillion* case was called. The State asked for another continuance, explaining that since the doctor's appearance closely matched Emma's description of one of the assailants, it was imperative that she see him in person. However, she couldn't possibly attend court until the next session, if then. The defense team asked that the trial go forward anyway and that the doctor be allowed to address the court directly. Judge Phillips consented. Vermillion stood and, sounding like a child smarting from the pangs of a cruel teasing, stated that "the charges were harshly unjust, and that a time was coming when he would stand before the world a free man, and those who had misjudged him would plainly see their mistake." Phillips listened quietly but then sided with the State by postponing the case until the next term of court. While Emma was not yet ambulatory, said Drennan, he was confident she would be up and about by summertime. Well, maybe up and about wasn't the best way to put it, since her doctors had declared that she would "ever remain an invalid," due to her severe back injury.[17]

The judge took pity on Vermillion by again lowering his bond—from $2,500 to $1,000. It was a mediocre consolation, but when court adjourned, several people rushed forward and promised him financial help. Seemingly oblivious to the doctor's plight, his fellow suspects had attended that day, not so much to lend Vermillion their support but to assess the public's current sentiment. With their own court date drawing near, they had to be concerned about the mindset of the potential jury pool, as expressed in a January editorial: "We can advise the good people of Christian County that those five criminals—John C. and William Montgomery, Lee Pettus, Emanuel Clementi and Dr. Vermillion—will get their legal, if not their just deserts at the hands of a Montgomery County jury. Criminals stand precious little show in this county of getting out of trouble on technicalities."[18] It had been a long and dreary winter, which gave the defendants plenty of time to mull that one over.

15

Her family . . . attempted to keep the facts from the public, but it leaked out to a few and gained headway until it has become public property.
—Decatur Daily Republican, *March 18, 1883*

As winter slowly faded, the sun began to trace a higher arc through the sky, and the frozen earth softened underfoot. With the promise of spring embracing every living thing, it was hard *not* to feel better—even for Emma. Wisely, she had put her marriage on indefinite hold, at the recommendation of her family and friends, who had urged her to take all the time she needed. And her fiancé, Mr. Adams, had promised to wait patiently for his hometown girl. So in the spring of 1883, it was her sister Etta, not Emma, whose wedding plans were in the works.

Now in her late teens, Etta had finished her schooling, and Ab knew he might soon be handing her over to another man. His two oldest girls had used remarkably good judgment in selecting their mates, and he approved of Etta's chosen partner as well. The Taylorville man, a successful miller and son of a Baptist preacher, was named Charles Logan.

What kind of man Emma's fiancé was remained to be seen. Young Adams had been far removed on June 29, working somewhere out on the western plains.[1] Only time would tell if he would return for his intended, as he had promised. Everybody wanted to believe he was a man of his word; Emma needed that kind of support. But in a day when many men viewed rape victims as damaged goods, that was a tall order. There was another class of males, however—those who considered themselves defenders of the fairer sex. These were the same men who now marveled at Adams's incredible restraint, and the same ones who wanted to "get it over with" by making the fiends pay for what they'd done. Perhaps it was a blessing that hundreds of miles separated young Adams from the turmoil back home, for if he was harboring a burning desire for revenge, distance was enough to thwart any such action.

In any case, Etta's nuptials were to take place in early May. On Friday, March 16, she went to Sonny's house to visit her sister. With her wedding only weeks away, it isn't hard to imagine what the two young women discussed that day. Emma was especially upbeat, her health and spirits apparently back on track—perhaps that is why, with Emma's blessing, Etta decided to take supper in the dining room that night, with Sonny and Lizzie and their children.

She propped her sister up in bed, turned up the bedside lamp, and handed Emma a book. But then she hesitated, saying that maybe she should stay and take her meal in the room after all. No, insisted Emma, she should go and enjoy her supper with the others. So Etta crossed the room, checked the lock on the outside door, circled back to kiss her sister lightly on the forehead, and then disappeared down the hallway. When she entered the dining room, Lizzie inquired after Emma and suggested that maybe Nellie or Mary should go and sit with her.[2] Etta didn't think it was necessary. Her sister was having a good day, and she would be fine. Midway through supper, however, Lizzie sent one of her girls to look in on Emma anyway. What unfolded next was pure chaos.

"The little girl came running back at once, crying 'Oh, Mamma, the room is dark and Emma is gone.'"[3] Hearing the alarm in the child's voice, everyone sprang to their feet. Mrs. Bond screamed and, lifting her skirt hem, took off down the narrow hallway toward Emma's room. The others followed, but before they could reach the bedroom, more screams from Lizzie confirmed their worst fears. Emma's bed was empty, and her reading lamp was out, cloaking the room in darkness. Someone fumbled around and relit the bedside fixture. It only took a cursory glance to see that the door leading to the outside stood wide open. As the frigid night air poured in, the room's appearance sent a collective shiver down the backs of those gathered there—Etta's, most of all. When she'd left for supper, her sister had been tucked safely into her large and heavy bed in the southwest corner of the room. Now that bed commanded a spot in the center of the room—several feet from all four walls. More pandemonium ensued as the family realized the missing girl might be in grave danger. The adults spread out in every direction, calling out Emma's name: "They searched the house and yard and found the afflicted girl outside, around an angle of the house, lying on the ground, partially unconscious. They carried the girl back to her room, and while doing so, heard with horror her mutterings, and looked with blanched faces at her apparently dreadful fear, as she would rave of men with black masks on their faces."[4]

In the aftermath, the press reported that Emma was confused and drifting in and out of consciousness. Yet, as frightening as the episode had been, by Monday she was able to speak of it. She recounted the horrifying details of a kidnapping attempt that began right after Etta had left for supper:

Immediately, two men with black masks stepped into the room from the hall. One unlocked the outside door and the other extinguished the lamp. The one at the door said, "Where is the other girl?" The two men then seized Miss Emma, who from fright was unable to speak, and carried her out on the porch, thence to the ground along the front of the house, about twenty feet around the corner. At this time, the folks in the house had discovered that the light was out and the girl's bedroom door was open and they began screaming. Miss Emma says that she heard the screams and one of the men said, "D—— it, drop her." Then they went down the backyard through a gap in the fence, released her and ran. She, while partially conscious, could neither move nor speak. This is the story told by the girl in her rational moments. During her sinking spells, she mutters in her delirium and seems to think the men came back and got her a second time and that she is still in their power.[5]

More specifics were revealed in the coming days. The bed had ended up in the middle of the room, said Emma, because she had held on for dear life while the men sought to remove her from it. The harder they pulled, the tighter she gripped the bedposts until, finally, she *and* the bed were dragged several feet from the wall, at which point Emma gave up her battle.

The Bonds, fearful of further attempts to harm Emma, tried to remain tight-lipped about the mysterious turn of events: "The serious reticent air assumed when speaking of it is proof of the awful possibilities that the matter has called up in their minds, and of the frightful consequences that may follow this event in the horrible career of this unfortunate girl."[6] It was one more chapter in the family's ongoing nightmare—and one best forgotten. The damage to Emma's already delicate psyche was their greatest concern. In her tortured mind, the line between reality and imagination was so blurred that she sometimes imagined she was still in the hands of her abductors.

Within hours, theories were being advanced on street corners and around supper tables. The most popular one coincided with Mr. Bond's belief that his daughter had been snatched to prevent her testimony at the trial. Needless to say, there were doubters who wondered about a simpler explanation, one originating deep within Emma's soul. Monday's *Republican* described that premise: "Others think—and at this writing it is the most accepted theory—that she is in a temporary aberration of mind, wandering from her room to the yard, where her strength failed her, and she sank to the ground, still laboring under the hallucination probably of former hideous scenes that had driven her from the house."[7]

That was not such a far-fetched notion. Even Emma's doctor had considered it. On the night of the debacle, he first examined the bottoms of her feet, looking for any clues that she had walked barefoot out of doors. He gave his opinion: "There was no sign that she had stood on them, and I do not think that she could have walked in the yard without leaving perceptible marks of the trip on her feet." Feet that hadn't touched the floor in almost four months had to be especially tender and pristine—a virtual telltale canvas incapable of hiding the slightest use.[8] But on the chance that others would not be convinced, the doctor decided to put his theory to a further test: "He bared his own feet and went over the same course. When he returned to the house he could find numerous indications of his journey."[9] He concluded that there was absolutely no way Emma could have walked that far, outdoors, barefoot, and kept her feet so clean. It was even more unfeasible that his patient, who had not left her bed since early December, could have walked anywhere without assistance.

Adding further credence to the kidnapping theory were some new rumors, which surfaced almost immediately. One alluded to some suspicious goings-on during the previous week, when "some men of doubtful character [were] seen quite often secreted in some nook or corner late at night, talking earnestly to one of the men under bonds."[10] The *Daily Republican* presented its own frightening theory: "The Wabash Railway passes just in the rear of Mr. Bond's house and it is thought by some that the intent was to lay Miss Bond on the track and whatever the result might be, it would be believed that she wandered there herself."[11] This same article asserted that two thugs had been paid to grab the helpless victim.

If desperate individuals were hoping to prevent Emma's testimony, they could put their worried minds to rest for awhile. For a trial postponement was in the works. Days after the State's primary witness was found mumbling incoherently behind Sonny's house, Amos Miller—the state's attorney of Montgomery County—asked the court for a continuance, and it was duly granted.[12] The big trial would most likely take place during the court's winter session.

A week after the incident at Sonny's house, an obscure note—so tiny it was easy to miss—appeared in the *Republican:* "Emma Bond has recovered to some extent from her fright on Friday night and was able to have her picture taken on Tuesday."[13] On Monday, she was said to be in a "semi-unconscious condition" while on Tuesday, just four days after the scare, she was posing for a photographer.[14] That had to be an encouraging sign for her family.

By April, Emma began to talk of going home. What she truly needed most was to sink into the embrace of her own bed, surrounded by the comforts of home and her closest family members. At the farm, she could immerse herself in the gentle delights of springtime in the country. If all those things didn't speed her recovery, then nothing could.

Sonny and Lizzie and family had been exceedingly generous, having cared for Emma over the entire winter. This, plus Sonny's contribution to the reward fund, must have had Ab Bond wondering how he would ever repay his cousin for his support, even though Sonny probably didn't expect repayment—ever. Besides, Ab had nothing to offer at the moment, due to Emma's extensive medical bills, the cost of hiring Detective Page, and the fact that he'd been neglecting his own farm ever since the tragedy.

Emma's father was a proud man who had never asked for, wanted, or dreamed of taking financial help—especially from complete strangers. However, something had to be done soon to get his family's finances back on track. So a "quick fix" made perfect sense, at least to him. Regrettably, his solution was ill-conceived and likely caused the first crack in the armor that had thus far shielded his Emma.

Way out on the California coast, trouble was brewing, spawned by a caustic editorial that appeared in the *Los Angeles Times* on April 10. The headline set the tone for the damning innuendoes that followed:

Emma Eye to Business—(From the *Stockton Herald*)—"About a half year ago the press contained accounts of a shameful outrage committed upon Miss Emma Bond, a young school teacher of Taylorville, Ill. . . . Tons of editorials have been written in a sympathetic strain of this innocent, intelligent, and refined girl, lying prostrated in body and all but crazed by reason of the physical shock and unbearable shame of the outrage. How deserved all this sympathy has been may be judged from the following advertisement, which appeared in the *Chicago Times* a few days ago: 'PERSONAL—EMMA BOND'S PICTURES—By repeated urging of friends, Emma Bond has permitted her pictures, cabinet size, to be sold. Any orders, inclosing [*sic*] $1, will receive prompt attention. Address EMMA BOND, Taylorville, Ill.'"

It is evident that Emma Bond is shameless. If she ever was outraged . . . it is certain that her sufferings in consequence—if she has suffered—have been purely physical. Her effort to turn into money the peculiar notoriety that has been given her is one of the most extraordinary strokes of business enterprise ever heard of.[15]

Much like his counterparts a half a continent away, this story's author was undoubtedly guilty of distorting the truth. First, he assumed that the plan to sell the pictures had been Emma's. But the idea that she came up with the idea seems absurd. She was a young and naïve country girl, barely into her twenties—and one whose worldly travels had been limited to Christian County or Springfield at the farthest. Furthermore, she was bedridden, in physical pain, and emotionally traumatized. Her awareness of America's fascination with her story would have been minimal, if it existed at all. And a young woman of her standing would have had little to no experience in raising revenue.

Yet some readers eagerly embraced the notion that Emma was sophisticated enough to concoct such a moneymaking scheme on her own. She was in no condition to give the slightest thought to finances. In fact, it was unlikely that her father ever discussed his money situation with Emma or her sisters. Chances are, none of the girls had any idea how much he or Sonny had spent on anything—doctor bills, the private detective, boosting the reward fund, or supporting the prosecution. To add insult to injury, the *Times* writer concluded: "There is a dreadful possibility that the attention of theatrical advertisers will be attracted to it, and then instead of stories of actresses being robbed of diamonds, we may ere long have flaming and harrowing accounts of their loss of a still more precious jewel than the sparkling stone. If this fear be realized, there will be a deep and general regret that Emma Bond's ruffians, if they ever existed, did not kill her when they were at it."[16]

In appalling contrast to the more genteel considerations afforded the victim back east, this cynical columnist intimated that Emma was a money-hungry ne'er-do-well whose story was now in serious doubt—who, perhaps, didn't even deserve to be alive. And yet there was no denying that a picture had been commissioned and that the subject of said picture was now a household name across the land. Maybe that was the crux of the problem—Emma Bond was a name and a name only. A face attached to that name was bound to be worth a lot more. Assuming people were curious enough (and most were), and assuming they would be willing to pay the price (and many would), then it's understandable that Mr. Bond would have seen it as a solution to his money problems.

That photographic solution portrayed a fashionable and refined-looking young lady, her hair done up elaborately, with tiny, precise ringlets framing her face. The rest of her hair was pulled close to her head, neatly sectioned and twisted, making it impossible to tell whether it was long or closely cropped. Her clothing looked like her Sunday best—certainly not what a farm girl would wear most of the time. The dress was light colored, with a delicate overlay of black lace. A lovely cameo necklace or brooch graced her neck. Her eyes appeared very light—perhaps pale blue, the color so prevalent among her family members and their descendants. And yet, behind the expressionless facade, one could sense a veiled sadness in faint betrayal of the secrets trapped within her soul.

The most revealing part of this cabinet card, however, was not the picture itself but rather the printing on the card's lower border. As was always the case for the front of Victorian cabinet cards, this one bore the name of the photographer;

"G. N. Burleigh of Taylorville" was stamped in neat, small letters across the very bottom. Directly below the actual photograph, in a much larger and more elaborate font, was the name "Emma Bond," even though cabinet cards very rarely included the subject's name. And between Emma's and Burleigh's names was the inscription "Copyrighted 1883 by A. D. Bond." This suggested that Emma's father had indeed initiated the sales scheme.

Bond, no stranger to business dealings, would have known that a copyright notation on the front of the finished product might discourage the hucksters. A search of the U.S. Copyright Office in Washington, D.C., however, failed to turn up an application for this particular photograph—under Bond's name or Burleigh's. Normally, the photographer owned the rights to his works.[17] In this case, however, Burleigh may have transferred those rights to Bond, who had then asked the photographer to add the copyright notation as a deterrent to those who would do anything for their own gain

On April 19, Emma finally went home. She suffered only minor setbacks the following day. Her family was delighted to have her back, and Etta would be able to enjoy her wedding day with all five of her sisters gathered around her. On a fragrant spring evening in mid-May, she and Charles exchanged their wedding vows at the Bond home and, for the first time in nearly a year, the family was able to enjoy some happy moments together.

As the distractions of May gave way to the toils of June, interest in the Bond case and anything connected to it began to wane. In late June, an unnamed Chicago man, acting alone, sent the Bonds a check for $350. Two weeks later, another good Samaritan, identified as a "traveling man named Avery" sent them $300, which he had personally collected from around the state.[18]

June 29, 1883—the first anniversary of the schoolhouse outrage—came and went with nary a hiccup. Perhaps of greater significance was the passing of one year and one day—for reasons more important to the suspects than to anyone else. As the *Republican* pointed out: "If their victim had died within a year and a day from the date of the assault, they would have been liable to trial for murder, but now they can be tried only for RAPE."[19] Actually, the point was irrelevant: if Emma had died at any time, there wouldn't have been enough rifles in the county to hold off the mobs that would have come calling for the suspects with rope in hand.

16

She declares that she will be there, and expresses confidence in her ability to stand the ordeal she will have to undergo. . . . The young lady has endured almost untold sufferings, and all must rejoice to see her present degree of health.
—New York Times, *October 28, 1883*

As the days and weeks of summer passed, Emma's health continued to improve. Naturally, that kind of news didn't make for the best of headlines. So with the trial still several months away, press coverage of her story grew even more sporadic—until July, when the two biggest intrigues of the spring suddenly resurfaced. In March, a loyal family friend had tried to put the fuss over the cabinet card to rest, but for reasons unknown, his rebuttal, titled "Why Miss Bond's Photographs Are Sold," was ignored by the *Los Angeles Times* until July 12:

> To the Editor of the *Chicago News*. Chicago, March 31. Lately there have appeared in various newspapers articles criticising in adverse terms the sale of Miss Emma Bond's photographs . . . [and assigning] a desire on Miss Bond's part to make capital out of her misfortune. . . . Her long and severe illness has been a great expense to a family far removed from wealth—so much so that they have been reduced almost to poverty. This being the case, . . . she naturally accepted the kindly suggestion to sell her pictures. . . . Miss Bond's family have been influenced in this matter only by the pressure of necessity. It is hard to imagine this poor woman . . . at times delirious and hovering between life and death, entertaining thoughts of working upon the sympathies of the people for the sole object of making money. Four or five devils have wrought a great and terrible injury to an unoffending household, and instead of uncharitably denouncing an honest endeavor on their part to raise means for relieving their distress, the press could well afford to lend its encouragement to this and suggest to our citizens other means of contributing financial aid to this stricken family. E.L.T.[1]

Whether or not this advocate possessed an intimate knowledge of the Bonds' money situation is hard to say; however, he had used the term "kindly suggestion," which implied that the scheme to sell the picture may have originated with him or some other family friend—someone who saw it as a way for the Bonds to generate a little extra cash. Alternatively, newshounds have always hankered for the likenesses of well-known figures, so it is just as possible that one of them offered to pay Bond for a picture of his daughter and thus unwittingly planted the seed of an idea.

As for the alleged kidnapping, Emma's father still worried constantly about her safety. Unable to accept that the kidnappers had gotten off scot-free, he tried to smoke them out in July:

> $500 Reward . . . A. D. Bond has issued the following circular: "On the evening of March 16, 1883, Emma Bond was abducted and carried out of the house of Abner Bond, just northeast of Taylorville, and dropped on the ground. I will pay $500 for the arrest and conviction of the persons who were engaged in the abduction. And $100 will be paid to anyone who will give information that will lead to the conviction of any of the guilty parties. If either of the parties engaged in the abduction will give the information, he will be paid the reward and will not be prosecuted."[2]

With the offered reward exceeding the June contributions from Chicago and with the family so strapped for cash, someone else—possibly Sonny—may have put up part or all of the money. In any case, if just one of the perpetrators could be enticed into coming forward and snitching on the others, then the reward was all his, no strings attached. But alas, nobody broke rank, and the reward went unclaimed. Perhaps the incident really had been nothing more than a figment of Emma's imagination.

The press and the public barely noted several other events related to the case. The first occurred on July 14, when Dr. Vermillion was finally released from jail, after spending almost a year behind bars. At his March court date, his bond had been reduced to $1000, which led to immediate promises from his friends to procure the cash. It evidently took them another four months to raise that amount.

Also, late in July, it was announced that the "transcript of evidence"—which the board of supervisors commissioned in January—was finally complete and on its way to Taylorville. There was no mention of where the transcript was sent; but its size was said to be "voluminous," consisting of "1,037 pages of foolscap, embracing 103,700 words." For his labors, John T. Montgomery billed the Board of Supervisors for "$207.50."[3] At its July meeting, however, the board's committee on claims rejected the stenographer's bill and sent the matter back to the full board, which also deemed the amount excessive.[4] Instead, Montgomery was offered $125. He countered that he would accept $167.50; and with that, the two sides came to an impasse. According to the board's September minutes, it had "made a liberal offer to the said John T. Montgomery under the circumstances, which is well known to the Board, [and] your committee would beg to report the whole matter back to the Board without any further recommendations."[5] The full board voted to stick with its original offer, so it looked as if John T. wouldn't get one penny unless he relented. Since there was no indication that he ever did, he may have gone unpaid for his extensive effort.

Although the transcript was ready when the circuit court convened in early August, the Bond case was put on the court's winter calendar, with the trial set to begin on or about November 30. As soon as the court adjourned, subpoenas started going out to the scores of witnesses. While nobody was surprised to get one, everybody dreaded having to travel to Hillsboro in winter. But now, in the dead of summer, the people had heard just about all they needed or wanted to hear regarding the victim's perpetual ups and downs. They had also developed an equally ho-hum attitude toward the suspects. The most exciting thing that could be said of the accused, in fact, was that they were "working on their farms near Taylorville."[6] Of course, no one doubted that the enthusiasm for the story would revive once the trial finally got under way.

The controversy over the photograph faded of its own accord. People either belonged to that small group of skeptics who thought Emma was a clever manipulator who had concocted the perfect scam for lining her pockets with scads of the green stuff or were part of the majority who believed that she had been victimized a second time and thus deserved every ounce of compassion that she could get.

September arrived, bringing welcome relief from the summer heat. That same month, one of the suspects found relief of his own—the everlasting kind. On the twelfth of the month, State's Attorney Drennan announced that William J. Montgomery had died from a progressive case of consumption.[7] Tuberculosis had claimed another adult in his prime; the young husband and father would never see his thirtieth birthday. Whatever William knew of the crime, if anything, he took to his grave: "So far as the world knows, he made no mention of the crime on his deathbed, and this is accepted in some quarters as proof of his innocence. On the other hand, it is said that none but members of his own family were allowed to visit him during his dying hours."[8] If William had spoken of the outrage on his deathbed, it was doubtful his family members would have shared that information.

The cooler days brought Emma relief of a different sort. Several times that autumn, she and her father visited her new physician in Springfield. That she was able to make the trip at all was heartening. Better yet, she was now walking without help, her back supported "by some kind of surgical appliance."[9] As further cause for optimism, more than three months had elapsed since her last paroxysm.

With the trial fast approaching, both the State and the defense were promising to be ready. As reported in the *Atlanta Constitution,* State's Attorney Drennan held a press interview, hoping to get a head start in the war of words.

"I think there is no doubt of our ability to convict them," State's Attorney Drennan said.

"Besides the proof we had at the preliminary hearing, we have additional testimony that tends to further fasten the guilt upon them."

"What is this new testimony?"

"I can't tell you that. We don't want to show our hands now."

"Have you anything to positively show that they are the guilty ones?"

"Yes; we can identify them as closely as men can be identified without their being actually pointed out. We do not depend solely upon Miss Bond's testimony to show they were then in that schoolhouse, but her statement, together with other evidence we have, will positively show that they are the guilty ones. We had a better case at the time of the preliminary trial than we made out or attempted to make out."

"Why didn't you bring it all out then?"

"We set a trap for the defense and they fell right into it. For instance, we had two ways of showing that John Montgomery was concerned in the affair. We used the weakest method for the purpose of committing the defense to a denial of that evidence, and now we have them where they cannot shake the other testimony."

"You think you can convict them, then?"

"I certainly do. I think the proof will be so strong as not to admit of a doubt as to their guilt."[10]

To everyone's dismay, the trial date was pushed back to December 10. The defense, it was said, planned to introduce a new theory that would "implicate parties whose names have never been connected with the case."[11] Of all the defendants, only John expressed a defiant optimism, declaring "he had been 'dead three times, but wasn't dead yet.'"[12] All he asked was a fair trial, insisting that he was not the least bit concerned about the outcome. The trial was expected to run through most of December, with predictions that it might last more than three weeks. With 280-plus witnesses holding subpoenas, that didn't seem unreasonable.

As the anticipation mounted, so did the concerns over Emma's safety. Her family and friends worried about her state of mind, but their biggest fear was that there might be another attempt to silence her. To ward off that possibility, she was secluded in a place known only to her family. Physically, she appeared to have turned the corner. Her weight, which had dropped to a piteous seventy-five pounds the previous year, had rebounded throughout 1883 and was now back above the one-hundred-pound mark. That was still far below a healthy weight for her tall frame, but at least she was beginning to look more like her former self. The *Atlanta Constitution* confirmed another encouraging milestone in her recovery: "Miss Bond's improvement is noted mainly in the increased facility of her expression of ideas in writing. In the past two months her writing has changed from incoherent and nervous epistles to sensible and well constructed letters."[13] Given her love of teaching, that was especially good news.

In late November, Vermillion received some good news of his own. Initially, his stated desire "to be tried at home and among his own as well as the friends of Miss Bond," had come across as pure insanity.[14] But in retrospect, his refusal to seek a change of venue may have been a smart move. His trial, slated for late November in Christian County, was suddenly in doubt when the prosecution announced that it would probably enter a *nolle*, short for *nolle prosequi*, whose literal translation is "we shall no longer prosecute." In other words, the charges against him would likely be dropped. This action usually indicated that either the State's case was short on evidence or the accused was thought to be innocent. In this instance, however, the decision appeared to be a carefully calculated legal move. As the State's attorney put it: "If the *nolle* is entered, it will be upon the theory that to try him first would be to give the other defendants the benefit of knowing all the proof against them in advance."[15] So, thanks to a last-minute legal strategy, it looked like Vermillion might walk free—for good. And he did.

On the weekend preceding the trial, John C. Montgomery and A. D. Bond each set off for Hillsboro on the same mission—to secure a place for their loved ones to stay for the duration of the trial. Although it was the county seat, Hillsboro was not the largest town in Montgomery County. Its population in 1880 was about eighteen hundred, somewhat lower than nearby Litchfield's. But the good people of Hillsboro were ready to tackle the challenges the trial would present, the biggest of which was to provide lodging for the onslaught of visitors who were about to descend on their town. Many of the residents viewed the trial as an unexpected windfall; with hotels and boarding houses booked to capacity, out-of-towners were scooping up the rooms being offered by private citizens. Those who failed to plan ahead would be forced to board in outlying villages. A few optimistic witnesses hoped to make the trip, testify, and then return home in the same day, which might be possible, depending on the weather and how long they were on the stand.

With so many visitors planning to stay in Hillsboro, it was a miracle that Emma's father found suitable accommodations so quickly, but a kind resident opened his home to the entire Bond family. The place would suit Emma well, allowing her some minimal degree of privacy. Knowing that the curious would be everywhere, hoping to catch a glimpse of his daughter, Bond was satisfied with these arrangements. Nothing further was noted in the press regarding Montgomery's search for rooms. His wife, Mattie, would be attending, even though that would mean bringing their son Harold, not yet two months old. Luckily, other relatives would be on hand to help her out with the baby.

Unlike prosecutor Drennan, who had addressed the press in November, the defense was slow to put its own spin on the upcoming case. On the day the trial was set to commence, the following appeared in the *Tribune:*

> Enough has leaked out to show that [the defense] will attempt not only to prove an alibi, but to so conduct their side of the case as to create a suspicion, at least, that Miss Bond is the victim of her own indiscretion. Rumor has it that if in her testimony she identifies them, they will attempt to weaken her evidence by proving that her father has frequently said that she could not recognize them; also that they intend to show that it was impossible for her to have been taken up into the attic and placed where she says without breaking the plastering. After this attempt to break her testimony they will, it is said, endeavor to show that it was a case of abortion or a miscarriage and that the cry of rape was raised to shield her.[16]

While the American justice system aspires to a clean legal fight, the ugly truth is that sometimes things can get dirty. If that's what this case demanded, then apparently the defense was prepared. It supposedly had witnesses who had heard Mr. Bond say that Emma "did not believe that Montgomery, Pettus, and Clementi were the parties who outraged her."[17]

Before either side could step into the ring, however, a large segment of Christian County's population would have to transport itself to Hillsboro. The first day of the trial—Monday, December 10—was to be devoted to jury selection. Almost everyone—victim, defendants, lawyers, and witnesses—planned to travel by train to Hillsboro that morning. Thus it was inevitable that some of them would end up on the same train.

The travelers had two options. The Baltimore & Ohio train from Springfield ran through Edinburg (just west of the Grove), Taylorville, and then on to Pana, where a train change would take riders west to Hillsboro. The total distance by rail was more than fifty miles, though Hillsboro sat less than forty miles away. For those living in the Grove proper, that was by far the best option, as long as they could get to Edinburg by 7:20 A.M. That would land them in Hillsboro by midday. For those living east of the Grove, the obvious choice was to catch the Wabash in Blue Mound. But the train from Decatur was equally slow as it made its way southwest through Christian County and on to Montgomery County. That option required switching to an eastbound train in Litchfield for the final ten miles of the journey, another very indirect and inconvenient route.

Had it been summer, many would have probably gone by wagon or horse-back. But anyone with a lick of sense knew that venturing too far afield on country roads in cold, unpredictable December could spell disaster. Bad weather could suddenly blow in out of nowhere. Horses and humans caught in an unexpected blizzard could lose their way or get stuck in a waist-high snowdrift—only to be found days later, frozen dead in their tracks. But even if one was daring enough to take the risk, it was a thirty-five-mile journey, which could take the better part of a day. So, all things considered, the trains made the most sense for the hundreds of witnesses and determined trial-goers who would soon be heading to Hillsboro.

4

THE TRIAL

December 10, 1883–January 2, 1884

17

Miss Bond, her mother, sister, and father arrived this morning from Tay-lorville. . . . Miss Bond was closely veiled and leaned on the arm of her father.
—Chicago Tribune, *December 11, 1883*

Monday, December 10, 1883. It was a mild winter day by all standards as the victim and her family moved swiftly and discreetly through the throngs of train passengers in Hillsboro. They headed straight for their private lodging, where Emma was tucked safely away. Her father then reappeared and was immediately overtaken by reporters. At first, he was reticent to answer their barrage of questions, but to placate the journalists, he acknowledged that his daughter was doing well and was ready to testify. Then he spoke of a recent, troubling occurrence at his home: "It appears that last Saturday night about ten o'clock, Miss Bond was awakened by a noise at her window. She screamed to her father, who was sleeping in an adjoining room and he came at once and found her in a great state of excitement and fear. An examination of the window showed that someone had been trying to get into her room. The slats in the blinds had been cut and tracks were seen on the ground outside."[1] With the mild December temperatures, Emma's window might have been left ajar; but cutting the blinds seemed strange. Assuming this was another attempt to silence the victim, whoever had sought to accomplish it had failed miserably.

Those lucky enough to squeeze into the Hillsboro courtroom that Monday were met with disappointment. Some of the key players were absent, forcing Judge Phillips to declare a one-day postponement. Whatever their reasons, weather was not one of them, as the lightest of winds and clearest of skies graced the day. The *Tribune* blamed the delay on "the non-arrival" of the two most experienced attorneys involved—Judge Vandeveer of the prosecution and Judge Thornton of the defense. Former governor of Illinois John M. Palmer—a late addition to the prosecution team—was also a no-show, although he was now expected to withdraw from the case.

There had been some other changes to the State's team since the hearing. Montgomery County's state's attorney, Amos Miller, would join Drennan, Vandeveer, and Taylor while esteemed former judge Ben Edwards would be taking Governor Palmer's place. And for good measure, another private attorney from Hillsboro, G. W. Paisley, would assist them. The defense team had also been expanded. Thornton, McCaskill, and McBride, who had worked so well together at the hearing, would share their table with two more private attorneys—a Mr. Truitt and a Mr. Steven.

The nation's editors were sorely disappointed as well—expecting, as they were, some sensational news to splash across their front pages on Tuesday. Their readers yearned for particulars—anything that would make up for the recent drought in the Bond saga. But because of Monday's unexpected hiatus, journalists were forced to tap into their more creative sides. Accordingly, they poked around Hillsboro, seeking comments from any of the main participants. Not surprisingly, the families involved were not cooperative. One correspondent tried to downplay the touchy situation: "The Montgomery brothers had a thing or two to say to the journalists. John C. Montgomery was accompanied by his wife and child. Pettus's mother came with him. They say they will be acquitted and that there is nothing to the case. John C. Montgomery's brother expressed a general contempt for newspapers and reporters."[2]

The pursued were plainly fed up with their pursuers. In the absence of anything better, the press offered suppositions: "It is thought that the defense will not be satisfied with proving an alibi, but will attempt to smirch the young lady's character. . . . Just what effect this line of defense will have is not known, but some think it very indiscreet on the part of the accused."[3]

In a society that still relied on the printed word to spark its imperfect imagination, good descriptions were paramount. Early on, John C. Montgomery had been portrayed in the simplest of terms as "a man of medium height, probably weighs 160, wears chin whiskers, and has the general appearance of a farmer."[4] Now, with the trial underway, one writer offered his readers a more satisfying depiction: "There is nothing very striking in the appearance of John Montgomery. . . . A detective would hardly take him to be a criminal. His features are Irish in the outline and their Hibernian aspect [is] intensified by the presence of a thick brown and stubby beard on a heavy chin."[5] Another report noted that he bore "a rather hang dog expression and seldom looks one straight in the face."[6]

An 1882 description of Lee Pettus said only that "he has quite a youthful appearance . . . and looks like the average farmer boy of the west."[7] Now the details were getting a bit more explicit: "Lee Pettus looks to be about twenty-four years old and is by no means prepossessing in appearance. He is a perfect picture of a healthy, ignorant, and insolent country boy."[8] The press had also managed to dig up something new on him and couldn't wait to share it. This was first given cursory mention in the *Tribune* on December 8. Two weeks later, its follow-up article, "A Man Who Didn't Like Pettus," revealed that a civil charge against Lee had once been initiated by John Hill—the man who had killed himself over his daughter's plans to marry the defendant. This second article explained: "It is said that Pettus once figured in a seduction case and that judgment for $2,000 was obtained against him. John Hill, a very respectable farmer of Christian County, committed suicide not long ago because his daughter kept company with Lee Pettus and said she was going to marry him. The marriage has not taken place yet; but the girl's father killed himself on account of his daughter's strange action."[9]

This suggested a deep rift in the Hill family; apparently, the discord between the young couple and her father had started long before Lee's arrest. Seduction cases—also known as "breach of promise" cases—weren't unusual in the nineteenth century. They generally played out like this: a young man, eager to consummate a physical relationship, would entice a young woman into a premature and passionate encounter by vowing to marry her afterward (the promise). Of course, once he got what he was after, all bets—and promises—were off (the breach).

Such trickery was deplorable (from a father's point of view), immoral (from a religious point of view), and illegal (from a civil point of view). So, although such liaisons were often consensual and far more common than anyone cared to admit, premarital sex was nevertheless verboten. Hill had tried to make Lee Pettus pay for debauching his daughter, and apparently things had gotten even uglier when daughter Allie had declared her intent to marry her lover anyway. Hill's suicide, of course, was blamed on Allie's defiance. After that tragedy, tensions between the headstrong girl and her stepmother apparently escalated until the former, whether by choice or by edict, left her family home and moved into the Pettus house.[10] John C. Montgomery had testified in the seduction case on behalf of his brother-in-law, but his contribution had failed to offset the evidence against Lee, and in the end, the court had awarded Mr. Hill the settlement.

Of the three main defendants, least was known of the peripatetic Spaniard. One journalist composed this illuminating sketch on the outsider: "Emanuel Clementi was born in New York City and picked up part of his education in the Military Academy at Yonkers. While impressing the looker-on as foolish or half-witted, he is really shrewd and intelligent, and a man of fair education. About five years ago he opened a barbershop at Mt. Auburn. He left for a short time, but finally turned up at Mrs. Pettus's."[11] It wasn't clear where Clementi had spent the preceding four or five years; however, the June 1880 census indicated that he had worked for James Armstrong that summer.[12] James was the brother of Bill Armstrong, and Bill was married to Emma's aunt Becky (Housley). As for the "Military Academy," Clementi may have volunteered that part of his background with an eye to misleading the reporter. The actual name of the school was the Yonkers Military Institute, and it sat across the river, just a few miles from its more prestigious counterpart, West Point. However, its reputation was nothing like its neighbor's. A small boarding school for boys, it produced only a handful of notable teachers and graduates throughout its many years of existence. An 1874 appraisal of the Yonkers Military Institute in the *National Quarterly Review* implied that it was the kind of place that catered to the wayward: "Its students, military and non-military, form a total of nearly a whole score, whom some are unmannerly enough to call 'urchins.'"[13] Classified ads that ran frequently in the *New York Times* throughout the 1860s and 1870s all confirmed that the school was geared toward straightening out the ornery and the disobedient.

The boarding school would have been the perfect antidote for a young troublemaker from the big city. As a student there, Clementi would have been subjected to the discipline of a strict headmaster and to the rigorous demands of the school's drill sergeant. But given his poor reputation in 1882, perhaps he lied about being enrolled there, or he hadn't stayed long enough to reap the expected benefits. As to his physical characteristics, the *Tribune* now described him as "about twenty-eight years old, of slight build, medium height, and pale features, and a thin blonde mustache ornaments his upper lip."[14] He was almost never seen without his favorite "broad-brimmed, slouch hat" atop his head.[15]

Tuesday, December 11, 1883. That morning, all of the attorneys were present, seated at their respective tables. As "hear ye, hear ye" was proclaimed, Judge Jesse J. Phillips entered and seated himself at the bench. An 1880 publication described him as "yet a comparatively young man, with little experience upon the bench." Although he was forty-six at the time, because of his brief tenure on the bench, the author withheld the typical accolades reserved for longer-sitting judges. Instead, he paid Phillips a modest compliment: "[He] has given evidence of being eminently qualified for the position."[16] By 1882, the praise was more generous, with the judge described as having "a well-stored and finely balanced mind, with intellectual and oratorical attainments of a high order."[17]

While it remained to be seen what kind of legacy Phillips would leave as a judge, there was absolutely no doubt about the reputation he'd brought to the court; this, he had earned during the Great War while fighting with the 9th Illinois Infantry. As a soldier, he'd risen quickly through the ranks to lieutenant colonel. So outstanding was his performance as an officer that after his return to Illinois he'd been awarded the commission of brigadier general for "gallant and meritorious service."[18] His courage, commitment, and leadership on the battlefield were laurels he could rest on forever. But the Bond case would test his skills in an altogether different way.

Tuesday's session was supposed to begin at nine o'clock, but nobody—Phillips included—had foreseen another delay. One of the trains from the west, said to be carrying numerous witnesses, was running late. With his hands thus tied, the judge decided to begin by hearing motions, which included the legal posturing for which epic trials are so well known. Defense attorney Thornton started by asking that Pettus and Clementi be granted a separate trial. His strategy revolved around the witness Mattie Montgomery. She would not be allowed to take the stand for her husband. Pettus and Clementi, however, needed her to testify to their whereabouts on June 29. Phillips ruled quickly, quashing the defense's request.

When the late witnesses finally arrived around noon, the voir dire process finally got underway. In November, Phillips had issued "a *venire* for 150 jurors."[19] At the time, that number had seemed excessive; but in retrospect, it seems the judge may have been too conservative: just four hours into the process, the initial pool of forty men had already been depleted, with only three surviving the scrutiny of both sides. At this point, the court called in its second batch of potential jurors. Three more hours dragged by. The winter sun set, and courtroom lamps were lit, their flickering light playing across the weary faces of the remaining men in the jury pool. If each potential juror possessed even half a mind, he had to be praying he would not be among the chosen and that come the end of the day he would be sent home. It was common knowledge that Judge Phillips was not averse to letting his court run well into the evening; thus, the lawyers dug in their heels and the interviews continued.

When Phillips finally brought down his gavel later that evening, only eight men had been inducted into the brotherhood of Bond jurors. This meant that the full panel of twelve would not be seated until Wednesday—if then. The day was summed up: "The examination of the jurors was spirited but deliberate. Counsel on both sides held frequent consultations in regard to the competency of jurors. No juror who said he would not convict on circumstantial evidence was accepted by the prosecution."[20]

Wednesday morning, December 12, 1883. Judge Phillips had every intention of keeping the case on track, so voir dire resumed promptly at nine o'clock. The victim was expected to make her first public appearance that day, and attendees were excited over the prospect. Emma, who "was neatly and tastily dressed and wore no veil," showed up early in the company of one of her married sisters and her stepmother, Delia.[21] She looked serene as she passed through the crowds of onlookers gathered outside the courthouse. But the crowds, so eager to get a close look at her, got more than they expected when Emma entered the courtroom. Montgomery was hidden from Miss Bond's view until one of the attorneys leaned left, exposing him to Emma's gaze. He lowered his eyes and, trembling, he attempted to hide his face with his hat. But he was too slow. "The sight of the face of the man who she believes to have done her so terrible a wrong utterly prostrated her, and she fainted and, amid murmurs of sympathy, was carried from the courtroom."[22]

The reporter who dispatched the story seemed under the impression that this was Emma's first encounter with Montgomery since the crime. But it was not. There'd been a commotion on the train ride to Hillsboro on Monday morning. The trip turned out to be anything but pleasant for the Bonds—especially Emma. They—like the Montgomerys—chose to travel via the Wabash. And when Emma and family boarded the train in Taylorville, things fell apart in short order: "The car they entered was pretty well filled by the Montgomery crowd, who had gotten on at Blue Mound and Stonington. Miss Bond was shown to a seat and John C. Montgomery placed himself just opposite, sitting on the arm of the seat. He was within five feet of her."[23]

Naturally, this upset the girl's father beyond all reason, and yet John made no attempt to remove himself. Mr. Bond finally asked some of the lawyers in the car to intercede. A couple who witnessed the entire incident claimed that Emma's father "threatened to shoot."[24] For someone who'd shown such steadfast restraint, that seemed out of character; however, every man has his breaking point. Under pressure from the attorneys, Montgomery finally agreed to remove himself to another car. But it was impossible for all his relatives to do the same; there were just too many of them. When the conductor stepped in and found a new seat for Emma at the far end of the car, Mr. Bond calmed down and the trip progressed without further incident.

Upon seeing Emma's reaction to John Montgomery, Judge Phillips had her taken into his chambers so that she could have some privacy and time to recover. Order was quickly restored, and voir dire continued. It was slow going, however, as the two teams wrangled over who would fill the remaining vacancies.[25] By the time the panel of twelve was finally assembled, it was nearly three o'clock.

Very little was written of the chosen men—as a group or individually. But the 1880 federal census provided a fascinating overview of the jury.[26] For purposes of simplicity, one must discount those named Henry Hill and William Blackwood (since two men with each of those names lived in the county and it is unclear which ones were chosen). The most common thread among the remaining jurors was that they were all married, except for Levi "Daniel Boone" Isaacs, twice widowed and the father of eight. Obviously, Boone needed a new, and preferably younger, wife to help care for his brood, which was probably why the nearly fifty-year-old man had recently become engaged to a much younger woman.

Geographically, the men represented a good cross-section of Montgomery County. There were jurors from the larger towns of Litchfield, Hillsboro, and Nokomis and from the tiny hamlets of Fillmore, Grisham, Butler Grove, Witt, and East Fork. Other than Thomas Card (a Hillsboro mail carrier) and Edward Barringer (a music dealer from Litchfield), all were farmers. Since farms still dominated the American landscape, this balance was to be expected.

Beyond that, the men were all fathers as well. Juror Elza "Elzie" Cannady and his wife, Mary, had been childless for many years but had finally become parents shortly before the trial. Larger families were the norm, especially among farmers, and most of the other jurors bore this out. Several had produced six or more children, and some of the younger jurors already had four or five. Even Frank Huddleston—who at thirty-two may have been the youngest member of the jury—had one child at home.

The elder of the panel was Pete Davenport, who had sixty-two years and a lot of living under his belt. But like so many other farmers who had reached their seventh decade, things had yet to get any easier for him. His wife, Frances, was fourteen years his junior, so there was a good chance she was at least wife number two (if not three or four). Some of his children were already grown and gone, a couple were nearing that point but still living at home and doing their share, and some were definitely young enough to need their father for a good while longer. His youngest—a girl—was only eight years old. The sum of Pete's life experiences was bound to come in handy when the jury got around to deliberating.

Of the remaining jurors, Robert Travis, George Beck, Robert Moore, and Thomas Card were all in their mid-forties, and Ed Barringer, Elzie Cannady, and James Short were in their mid-thirties. (As to the uncertain jurors, the older Henry Hill was about fifty-three and the younger one thirty-three. The two William Blackwoods in the county were father and son, ages fifty-five and twenty-five.) But what was most noteworthy, considering the nature of the case, was just how many females could be counted among the jurors' offspring. From school-age girls to blossoming young teens to fully grown women, there was no scarcity of daughters. Four of Beck's five children were girls, ranging in age from eighteen down to nine. Moore, father of six, had four daughters—aged sixteen, fourteen, eleven and five. Old Pete still had two girls at home—a teenager and the eight-year-old. Short had only two children, but both were girls: Cora was a teenager, and Ida trailed close behind. (Of the undetermined jurors, both of the Henry Hills had daughters, and the older Mr. Blackwood had one in her twenties and another nearing twenty. The younger Blackwood was a newlywed.)

The collective number of daughters produced by this jury seemed to bode well for the prosecution. And of course, every man on the jury had once been nurtured by a mother. The love of all these significant girls and women would surely come to bear on their thinking. No female in the world deserved what Emma had gone through, and there was a strong chance that this particular group of men would have no trouble imagining one of their own girls in Emma's shoes.

Wednesday afternoon, December 13, 1883. By the time the official swearing-in of the jurors was completed, it was almost three thirty. To the judge, that meant several more useable hours, definitely enough time for opening statements. Drennan, the young state's attorney from Christian County, took the floor first. He began with Emma's unexpected arrival at the Pettus home early on June 30. He then went over the suspicious things the two younger defendants had said and done in the aftermath, pointing out their apparent indifference to Heinlein's suggestion that they alert the neighbors. He further charged that Clementi was trying to sneak off to St. Louis when arrested. He touched on Montgomery's concern over whether Clementi had ratted on him, pledging to revisit that and the defendants' strange remarks the day after the crime. Also, promised Drennan, the State would build a case on more than just circumstantial evidence. The victim would positively identify one of the defendants as her assailant and "assert her belief" that the other two took part.[27] With that, he sat down.

John C. McBride stepped onto the stage for the defense. Looking the jurors squarely in the eyes, he declared that the defense would show that all the defendants—Montgomery included—had solid alibis. Without explicitly saying so, he also tried to put to rest the rumor that the defense intended to vilify the victim. Emma may have missed that part; she and her family entered the courtroom during the prosecutor's opening remarks, but she appeared wan and anxious. Consequently, the Bonds stayed only a few short minutes and then departed.

Other than Emma's courtroom appearance, the only major drama of the day turned out to be jury selection. The *Atchison Globe* called the group "one of the best and most intelligent ever impaneled in Christian County."[28] It was irrelevant that the *Globe* had the jurors' county of origin wrong; the more important message was that this was an honorable group of men—a collection of souls worthy of the burden that now rested on their shoulders. There was one other matter concerning the jury that the papers failed to note but which was confirmed in the court record: "They retire in charge of a sworn officer and court adjourns until tomorrow morning, nine o'clock."[29] In other words, the jury was to be sequestered for the duration of the trial.

With so many witnesses standing by, Thursday promised to be a productive day. It had been eighteen long months since the unthinkable had happened, and Emma was scheduled to testify first for the prosecution. The stage was now set for a classic showdown between some of the state's best legal minds, but since this was a rape case, it would undoubtedly come down to the word of the victim against the word of the defendants.

18

It is now reported that he has worked up a chain of evidence too strong and too well knit together to admit of a doubt as to the guilt of the parties under indictment.

—Chicago Tribune, *December 10, 1883*

Thursday, December 13, 1883. It was the day Emma's family had long been dreading—she would have to tell her side of the story. Her stepmother, Delia, and at least one of her sisters planned to be with her constantly. But having to watch helplessly from the pews while his daughter relived her nightmare would verge on the excruciating for her greatest protector, her father. That was probably why he did not accompany Emma to court that particular morning. Certainly, A. D. Bond understood that her appearance was necessary. Since rapes don't usually have witnesses other than the victims and the perpetrators, there was no way around Emma's testifying. Nobody in the world could shoulder that burden for her if there was to be any chance of a conviction. Hence, Thursday promised to be a harrowing day not only for Emma but for those closest to her.

At exactly nine o'clock, Emma and her family arrived to find scores of people pushing their way into the courthouse. Incredibly, the session started on time. As the first order of business, all of the witnesses were ushered in from the hallway and sworn in en masse. The task was accomplished in short order, and then the group's members were escorted back out to the hallway to await their turns—out of earshot of the proceedings.

The State called its first witness. Emma entered and moved slowly up the center aisle on her stepmother's arm. A large rocking chair awaited her at the stand. If her testimony took hours, her back pain might become unbearable, so someone had placed pillows on the rocker for her added comfort. Judge Ben Edwards, a former circuit court judge from Springfield, was to question her. At age sixty-five, he brought decades of legal experience to the case. Moreover, he had earned his law degree at Yale, a more prestigious school than those most of his colleagues had attended. And, like some of his older peers here, he had once counted Abraham Lincoln and Stephen A. Douglas among his friends.

Edwards stood and approached the witness, asking her to take her time and speak distinctly so the jury could hear all of her words. After asking her name and place of residence, Edwards led his witness through the events of June 29, 1882.[1] She began by saying that she'd taught at the Montgomery School for just three months. On the last day of school, she had just one pupil, Charlie Masters. At ten thirty, she had sent him out for recess so she could go across the road to practice some songs with Minnie and Ona Pettus. When Emma got there, they told her they were busy and asked her to come back in the afternoon. When asked, she said she saw no one else at the house but heard some men talking in the kitchen.

Edwards directed his witness to the afternoon hours. She said she helped Charlie with his lessons from one o'clock until two thirty and then went back to the Pettus house. She and the girls practiced for half an hour. She heard no men in the kitchen that time. Then, she returned to the school about three o'clock. Charlie was waiting on the fence, and the two went back inside to finish his lessons. Shortly before four, she sent him on his way. Then she swept the floor, shut the windows, and prepared to leave. She put her shawl over her left arm and picked up her handbag. As she reached for the doorknob, she heard a noise behind her, like someone dropping down from above. Before she could turn, a man grabbed her by the throat "with a heavy clutch."[2] His grip was so tight that she began to feel faint. He slammed her face, hard, into the door and then threw something over her head. He tied her shawl around her waist, knotting it tightly on her right side, and used a chair to boost her up toward the scuttle hole. There were two men waiting in the loft above. They pulled on her while the first man pushed from below.

As Emma told of being dragged through the scuttle hole into the attic, tears welled up in her eyes. What happened next caught everyone—including the suspects—by complete surprise. She turned toward the defendants and, in a voice rife with emotion, she described pulling the cover off her eyes and getting a look at one of the men. Here, she paused, raised her arm, and pointed directly at Montgomery, saying: "And there sits the very man. I will swear that is the face I saw."[3]

She made the charge with such conviction that an audible gasp rippled through the gallery. Judge Phillips called for order in the court. Emma drew in a breath and continued: "He wore low shoes, red stockings and had chin whiskers about three inches long."[4] He asked the man below to hand up her purse and hat, so that nobody would know she was still there. As she came to the next part, the look on Emma's face revealed how difficult the memories were, but she pushed on. They carried her to a platform toward the rear of the loft. When she realized what was to come, she begged them to kill her instead. Here, Emma paused. Edwards gave her a moment to compose herself, and then she continued: "One of the men swore and said that was easy enough to do."[5] He took out a knife and put it to her throat and cut her nine times, on her neck and throat. Then, she thought, she fainted.

When she awoke, she knew she had been outraged. Whenever she would start to come around and try to talk, they would give her more chloroform and "repeat the treatment." If she begged for mercy, they told her to shut up, and if she didn't, they swore they would kill her. She knew they would do it; they'd already cut her neck and wrists. Here, Emma was asked to slip off her gloves and hold up her wrists so that all could see her scars. As she pulled her gloves back on, he asked about her other injuries, to which she replied that "her back was very much bruised and her knees and arms and shoulders bore marks where her assailants grasped her."[6] At this point, the unavoidable subject was broached. The *Tribune* handled it as delicately as possible, noting only that the fiends had "subjected her to nameless indignities."[7] Shielding the girl from further embarrassment seemed the unwritten editorial rule of the day: not a single newspaper carried anything more specific on the matter. So perhaps Emma was spared the embarrassment of having to describe those "indignities" in front of the packed courtroom.

The lawyer sought to clarify a few points with his witness. He asked whether she knew how long the men stayed in the loft. She replied that it seemed like two or three hours and recalled that "one of the men said they would have to leave at sundown," so they "cut a hole in the rear end of the loft so that they could see when it was sundown." They applied the chloroform at least twice by dousing her handkerchief and holding it over her face. When he asked if she knew how many times she was outraged, she only knew that it had been multiple times. Edwards then led her through the events of later that night; this was how the *Tribune* reported it: "About one o'clock in the morning she became conscious again and found herself on the schoolhouse floor under the scuttle hole. She was covered with blood and was very weak. She attempted to get up, but fell, injuring her face and nose. She finally made out to get to the house of Mrs. Pettus; aroused her and fainted away. Was carried into the house and there told Mrs. Pettus what had happened."[8]

Edwards addressed an important point. Had she asked to go home? She replied that she begged to be taken home at once, but she wasn't, because Mrs. Pettus told her the boys were worried her father might suspect them. After covering the delays—first at the Pettus house and then the detour to the Montgomery house—Emma repeated the description of her assailants that she had given to her father upon her arrival at home. When queried about the items stolen from her at the schoolhouse, she mentioned her pocketbook and her engagement ring. Suddenly, her face changed and she dissolved into trembling and tears, prompting the judge to call for the midday recess. It had been an exhausting morning for the young woman, with several intermissions taken so that she could rest or because she broke down in tears. Evidently, she was not alone in the latter, as one journalist remarked that there was not a dry eye among the many women in attendance that morning.

After the break, Miss Bond returned to the stand, looking somewhat refreshed. Now it was Thornton's turn to interrogate the witness and probe for any weaknesses in her version of events. And what a fine line he was obliged to walk—trying to make points for his clients while not appearing to lay into the victim too harshly. The *Tribune* presented a summary of the cross-examination:

> She said she usually closed school about four o'clock but the day the outrage occurred she closed a little earlier. She said the little boy had told her that afternoon when she was over at the Pettuses' he heard a noise in the loft, but she did not think anything about it much; told the boy she guessed it was rats; said the man who lifted her into the loft had on low shoes, red stockings, and wore thin chin-whiskers. Heard a buggy going by while they were dragging her up in the loft, and heard a buggy while she was in the loft. The latter she recognized by its rattle to be William Montgomery's vehicle.[9]

If Emma was correct about the second wagon, the time was around six in the evening or shortly thereafter, based on the hearing testimonies. According to William's servant girl, he'd gone to pick up his family at three o'clock, making his first pass of the schoolhouse before the time Emma was in danger. Still, there'd been a few inconsistencies regarding his whereabouts on that Thursday afternoon—specifically between three and six o'clock. Of course, since William had already faced his final judgment, the State had no intention of trying him in absentia. Thornton turned his focus to some as yet unaddressed points.[10]

He prodded. Wasn't it true that shortly after the outrage, she told Mr. Drennan and his wife that she was not sure that the defendants were the guilty parties? Emma didn't recall. He asked if she remembered telling Mr. Sharpe that she was "not certain they were the men?"[11] She didn't. Thornton turned up the heat a few more degrees, asking if her father had ever instructed her to accuse Montgomery. Emma gave no sign that she was taken aback by the question, answering that "her father had never told her that she must swear that John C. Montgomery was the man, but had told her if she could identify him, she must do so. No one told her to point him out. When she saw Montgomery, she knew she knew him."[12]

Thornton changed course. Did she know any of the defendants before the attack? She replied that she didn't. John Montgomery might have nodded to her once, but she didn't really know him then, or when he pulled her into the loft. When she saw him in the courtroom the day before, she recognized his face as belonging to the man in the schoolhouse. Thornton then raised an odd question. Hadn't she spoken with John Montgomery back in April? No, said Emma. It wasn't exactly clear where Thornton was headed with that line of questioning, but if there was any significance, the press did not reveal it. With that, Emma was allowed to step down. As she departed, she appeared "perfectly calm." Her family and friends later expressed relief that she had "passed through the ordeal so safely."[13]

According to the press, there were two key moments in Emma's testimony. The first was her admission that "although it was true she had told Mrs. Pettus and her father that only two had outraged her, she [was] now satisfied there were three." The second was "her identification of John Montgomery," which the *Colorado Springs Gazette* labeled "full and complete." In total, the paper deemed her testimony on Montgomery to be "straightforward" and "unshaken." Still, there did seem to be some confusion over her remarks about Pettus and Clementi. As the *Gazette* put it, "The other two defendants she could not swear to."[14]

Emma's cross-examination lasted two hours. During that time, the audience hung on every word that fell from her lips, shared every twinge of pain that flashed across her face. The *Tribune* gave all the details: "The witness herself was often overcome and went into paroxysms of grief. . . . It was one of the most piteous and dramatic scenes ever witnessed here. Strong men could hardly keep the tears back. Her conduct on the witness stand was that of a brave but broken-hearted young girl, yet she showed herself to be a woman in every sense of the word."[15]

With the day winding down, Judge Phillips decided to allow just one more witness. Martin V. Swick—one of the first three men to arrive at the crime scene—was called in from the corridor. Yes, he knew all of the defendants. He was first asked how close each lived to the schoolhouse. Then he gave the distances from the schoolhouse to the train depots in Blue Mound, Stonington, and Edinburg. Since he had lived in the area for more than twenty years, his answers were accepted as accurate. The next part of his interrogation was more pointed. Had he spoken to Pettus on the day after the outrage? Yes, he talked with him in the Grove the following afternoon. While Lee was describing the appearance and condition of Miss Bond's clothing and underclothing to him, John walked up and joined the conversation and Lee suddenly stopped talking.

Asked about his conversation with John on June 30, Swick told of the defendant's eagerness to know whether Clementi had talked about the writing on the blackboard and who had done it. When Swick replied that he didn't know, John asked him "to find out what, if any, statement Clementi had made, and whether he was implicated in it."[16] At some point, the defense sought to exclude part of Swick's testimony. Exactly which part they objected to was not noted, but it's a fair guess that it had to do with John's expressed concerns over Clementi's blabbering. The objection turned into a drawn-out discussion, with both sides arguing heatedly. Judge Phillips ultimately ruled against the defense, declaring that all of Swick's testimony could stand.

The audience's spontaneous response caused another delay in the proceedings, as spectators cheered and clapped in loud approval. This behavior did not sit well with Judge Phillips. Determined to keep order in his courtroom, he called a half dozen or so of the noisiest offenders up to the bench, including some "old, gray-headed men."[17] If they caused any further disruptions, warned Phillips, he'd have them all escorted out of the courtroom, slap them with a big fine, and lock them up for a week—minimum. Swick's testimony finally resumed, taking up the rest of the day. When court adjourned early that evening, the crowds dispersed in haste. Temperatures had been dropping steadily all day, in advance of a cold front sweeping in from the northwest; thus, nobody was inclined to stand around and hash over the day's events, much less stir up trouble.

Friday, December 14, 1883. Before the trial ever got off the ground, rumors floated that the State's key witness, Laurence Heinlein, had taken off for parts unknown. If it had been true, few would have blamed him. Heinlein—who had been so uncooperative at the hearing that he'd come close to being labeled a hostile witness by the State—had finally admitted, under oath, to being threatened by John Montgomery. He had also confessed he was afraid Montgomery would make good on his threats.

The rumors of Heinlein's flight were put to rest when he showed up in the Hillsboro courtroom on Wednesday. Sitting there listening to the prosecutor make his opening statement was the easy part for the reluctant witness. Facing him was going to be the hard part. A *Tribune* headline entitled "Belief That Heinlein Is Afraid to Tell All He Knows" revealed just how conflicted the man felt about testifying—*for* the State and *against* his relatives.[18] That he was an uncle to Lee and to John's wife, Mattie, and was willing to go against the family did raise some rightful concerns about his safety. But if the State could get Heinlein to open up, what he had to say would indeed be compelling.

Laurence Heinlein, a longtime area resident, worked a tenant farm southeast of the Grove. His son, thirty-year-old Sammy, was a druggist in the village as well as its postmaster—the same man who'd first alerted the Decatur papers about the outrage on Friday, June 30. Now his father approached the stand with obvious trepidation, fully cognizant that whatever he said might unleash a furor between him and his in-laws. The prosecutor established the basics: that the witness lived a mile and a half from the school and that he had known the defendants, Pettus and Montgomery, all their lives. The lawyer then turned to the predawn hours of June 30. He had to constantly nudge his witness along, but, slowly, surely, Heinlein gave up the answers. He had first heard about the outrage just before daylight, when Margret, Lee, and Clementi stopped by his place on their way home from the Bond farm. When Heinlein tried to find out more about the affair from his nephew Lee, he didn't want to talk. So the witness suggested that the two boys go out and alert the neighborhood; however, they didn't want to.

After they left he got dressed at once and headed to the schoolhouse, stopping to pick up Mr. Swick. The school looked deserted at first, but then they noticed a man standing out in front. It was just before dawn. As they got closer, they recognized him as William Montgomery. The three went inside the school together. Though there was enough light to see around the classroom, they had to send William for a lantern so they could see in the loft. When he returned, Swick and Heinlein went up to look around. The first thing they saw was the victim's hat and parasol near the opening. Swick and Heinlein handed them down to William and then continued their search. They found a section of a Chicago newspaper and, further back, on the platform, a scarf-pin. The platform, said Swick, was "made out of five pieces of weatherboarding laid alongside of the stay plank, which ran east and west across the schoolhouse." It was "about six feet long and three or four feet wide."[19]

During the preliminary hearing, a lock of hair had been mentioned—but just one. The papers had called it red hair—presumably yanked by the victim from the head of one of her rapists. Now Heinlein told of finding two clumps: "a lock of hair near the hole" and "several bunches of hair on the north side of the platform on which Miss Bond had been laid by the assailants."[20] The latter was stuck under the edge of the platform, explained Heinlein. It sounded as if, at this point in the interrogation, Heinlein himself produced the hair sample but "was not then permitted to exhibit it in court."[21] If this was true, it was a sorry commentary on the quality of the investigation. That a critical piece of evidence may have wound up in the hands of a layperson would have obviously precluded its admission as evidence. None of the news articles had much to say about the locks of hair—suggesting that the subject was glossed over, just as it had been during the hearing.

Heinlein continued, telling how he and Mr. Swick then noticed the small rectangular opening in the attic's west-facing wall. He described it as nine

Emma Bond. (Courtesy of
Muriel Bywater)

Emma's father, Abner Dobbins
Bond II. (Author's collection)

Emma's stepmother,
Delia Delile Sabine
Bond. (Author's collec-
tion)

Justice James B. Ricks,
who presided at the
hearing. (Courtesy of
the Abraham Lincoln
Presidential Library and
Museum)

Judge Jesse J. Phillips, who presided at the trial. (Courtesy of the Abraham Lincoln Presidential Library and Museum)

Christian County Courthouse (1856–1901), Taylorville, Illinois. (Courtesy of the Abraham Lincoln Presidential Library and Museum)

Montgomery County Courthouse, Hillsboro, Illinois. (Courtesy of the Lake County Discovery Museum/Curt Teich Postcard Archives)

John G. Drennan, State's attorney, Christian County. (Courtesy of Catherine Drennan)

Judge Amos Miller, State's attorney, Montgomery County.
(Courtesy of the Abraham Lincoln Presidential Library and
Museum)

Judge Horatio
M. Vandeveer,
senior member
of the pros-
ecution team.
(Courtesy of the
Abraham Lin-
coln Presidential
Library and Mu-
seum)

Judge Anthony J. Thornton, lead defense attorney. (Courtesy of the Abraham Lincoln Presidential Library and Museum)

J. C. McBride, defense attorney. (From J. C. McBride, *Past and Present of Christian County, Illinois.* Chicago: S. J. Clarke, 1904.)

Shelby M. Cullom, Governor of Illinois, 1877–1883. (Courtesy of the Abraham Lincoln Presidential Library and Museum)

Palmyra Sanitarium in Palmyra, Wisconsin. (Courtesy of the Palmyra Historical Society)

John C. Montgomery and family, 1911. (Copyright www.historicmapworks.com)

Delia Sabine Greene (1889–1984), Emma's niece and A. D. Bond's granddaughter. (Author's collection)

or ten inches wide and a couple of inches high, certainly large enough for a man's hand to fit through. The witness believed it was "freshly cut and by a dull knife."[22] A long, narrow chunk of wood was then produced and entered into evidence. Heinlein identified it as the cut-out piece, discovered near the rear of the loft. Next, he was asked about the blood in the downstairs classroom. The bloodstain he saw was directly under the scuttle hole and was roughly three inches by two inches. Heinlein noticed no blood in the loft but pointed out that the light there was very poor.

Next came the tough part—dealing with what John C. Montgomery had said and done on Friday, June 30. This was where Heinlein had been reticent during the hearing, for fear of what Montgomery might do to him in retaliation. The witness told of seeing Montgomery late in the afternoon in the Grove and how the defendant wanted to know if Clementi had implicated him. When Heinlein replied that he had, Montgomery said that "he didn't see how that could be."[23]

He and Swick also ran into Montgomery later that day, in the evening, on the road just outside of the Grove. John was with Pettus's brother George, and again, he asked what Clementi had said about him. Then somebody mentioned the cuts on Miss Bond's neck and said something about Clementi's finger being bitten, and Montgomery exclaimed, "My God, what shall we do?" By this time a crowd had gathered, and the group stood around and talked with Montgomery for some time, with everyone urging him to come clean. It was suggested that maybe he and Pettus should "put it on Clementi."[24] Montgomery said he needed to make sure Pettus didn't "give anything away."[25] He wanted someone to talk to him.

The state's attorney pushed Heinlein through question after question. Montgomery feared a mob, said the witness, so he told him that "the people didn't think he was in the thing, but that he caught the other boys, Lee Pettus and Emanuel Clementi, in the schoolhouse."[26] Montgomery wanted reassurances and asked if he "would be protected if he would give it away."[27] Here, the witness paused. The prosecutor urged him on. He responded that somebody promised Montgomery he'd be escorted safely into Taylorville if he would tell what he knew. When prodded further, Heinlein hesitated again, before saying that he wasn't exactly sure who promised. Nor was he sure what the defendant replied.

Here, the defense raised a vigorous objection, asking the judge to strike all of Heinlein's testimony on the roadside meeting, since he seemed unsure about so much of it. The jury was escorted out, and considerable time was lost in argument. The State maintained that Heinlein should be allowed to "give the substance of the talk."[28] Finally, the jury was ushered back in, and Phillips made the call: Heinlein's recollections of the conversation "might go in for what they were worth."[29]

The prosecutor tried one more time. Had Heinlein discussed anything else with Montgomery? No, not really, because the constable showed up and arrested him about that time. The witness was then asked if he'd talked with Mr. Montgomery after his arrest, and he said he had, at the jailhouse on Sunday. When Edwards asked what the two had discussed, Heinlein said that Montgomery indicated that Clementi was good, that he "hadn't given anything away."[30] They had also discussed the handwriting on the blackboard, with Heinlein urging Montgomery to share whatever he knew of it.

Judge Thornton handled the cross-examination, intending to clarify some vital points. The question of William and the pocketbook incident was addressed. Heinlein confirmed that he and Swick had "made no special search in the schoolhouse" as they waited for William to return with the lantern. But then confusion prevailed. William had either found the pocketbook on the floor or on a desk near the scuttle hole; Heinlein wasn't sure. But William did say that he had opened it, "examining as to its contents" before he handed it over to the older men.[31] Heinlein affirmed that he had first seen William Montgomery out in the road, directly in front of the schoolhouse.

The lawyer wanted Heinlein to be more precise about the time of his Friday night roadside encounter with John. Witness stated it was just after dark, between eight and nine o'clock. Also present, at first, were Martin Swick and George Pettus. But as the group talked, quite a few others happened by and stopped. The witness was vague when asked if Montgomery had admitted any guilt. Thornton pressed further: Didn't Montgomery state that "he had no hand in the outrage?" Heinlein agreed that the defendant may have said something to that effect. Next, the attorney asked whose idea it was for John and Lee to "make a confession and throw the crime upon Clementi." The witness confessed that it might have been Martin Swick's idea. Suddenly, Heinlein's memory started to improve. He decided that it *was* Swick who told Montgomery about Clementi's remarks—and Swick who told him that Clementi had "scratches on his face, a finger bitten, and blood on his shirt" when arrested.[32] Before the witness was excused from the stand, Thornton managed to make the point that maybe Montgomery was so afraid for his life that the promise of protection led him to say things that weren't really true.

Heinlein was done. His testimony had taken the entire day. In defense of the exhausted witness, the *Review* stated, "Heinlein has been quite sick lately and his mind was not clear. Thornton succeeded in befuddling the witness even more and [Heinlein] was compelled to leave the courtroom to gain a breath of fresh air."[33] Obviously, the long wait for the trial had been difficult for a man who knew that sooner or later he'd have to stand up and sing counterpoint to the entire chorus of his in-laws.

Even though the week was coming to an end, the journalists had work to do. The race was on to finish up their bylines, get to the telegraph office, and fire off updates to their hometown papers. A *Tribune* correspondent sent in this assessment of Heinlein's performance:

> His testimony was given in rather a broken, hesitating way. He seemed to have a defective memory, and he frequently had to wait some time before he could go on. . . . He seemed to be holding something back all the time. He gave some very strong circumstantial evidence, but left the impression that he knew a great deal more than he cared to tell. It is generally thought . . . that Heinlein's testimony alone would convict the defendants if he would only tell all that he knows. There ought to be some way of pumping Heinlein dry.[34]

The witness had come across every bit as guarded as he had at the hearing, and his reluctance to open up would, no doubt, work in the defendants' favor. So, too, would the fact that Alonzo Huggins, "a very material witness" for the State, had recently died. Although Huggins had not testified at the hearing, he had been pegged "to swear that he was in a store the day before the outrage and saw Dr. Vermillion go behind the counter and get some chloroform at a time when Emanuel Clementi was in the place."[35] Then, two weeks before the trial, the twenty-three-year-old had succumbed to tuberculosis. The timing of his death was most unfortunate, considering what he might have done for the case against Clementi.

Saturday and Sunday, December 15 and 16, 1883. With court recessed until Monday, many of the witnesses departed for their homes on Friday evening. The strain of travel didn't appeal much to the Bonds, so they settled in for the weekend. Although Emma did not attend Friday's court session, she had survived her time on the stand no worse for wear. Certainly, her positive identification of John C. Montgomery had left her friends, family, and supporters feeling confident. Several of her friends stayed in Hillsboro that weekend, also, to keep her company.

Of the three defendants, only Montgomery left town that first weekend, supposedly to attend to some business connected to his case. Pettus and Clementi stayed behind in Hillsboro, perhaps with an eye to doing a little carousing. Clementi had friends living in the nearby village of Irving, just outside of Hillsboro.

The head of that family, Bartholo Leon, was a local merchant and fellow Spaniard. Bartholo and his much younger wife, Theresa, had several children. The oldest, Bartholo Jr., was about the same age as Lee and Clementi, so it may have been his company the two boys planned to seek over the weekend.

Late on Friday, the mercury began to drop dramatically. It showed no signs of rebounding even with the coming of daylight. The cold was so extreme, in fact, that almost no one ventured outside all of Saturday. That evening, however, one hardy journalist was roaming the deserted streets when he spotted A. D. Bond. He stopped to ask how Emma was doing. Bond replied cordially, "Her health is good and she is very calm and cheerful."[36] That was precisely what the world wanted to hear.

As compensation for being sequestered, the jurymen were treated to haircuts on Saturday. Judge Phillips had issued them some very specific orders for the weekend. Naturally, he forbade them to discuss the case. As an added measure, he ordered them not to attend Sunday church services; there was always a chance that the preachers, from their pulpits, might call for the defendants' eternal damnation. And that was not the kind of thing Phillips wanted his jurors to hear. As it happened, had the twelve been allowed to go home that weekend, the snowstorm that was about to descend on central Illinois would surely have prevented their timely return. For on Sunday, Hillsboro awoke to find itself buried beneath a six-inch blanket of pure white—the first heavy snowfall of the season. Everyone gladly embraced the distraction. Men hurried to transform their wagons into sleighs by replacing the wheels with smooth metal runners; instead of the usual clip-clopping of hooves on hardened mud, the jingle-jangle of sleigh bells filled the streets. Right after church, youngsters were bundled up and sent outside to enjoy their favorite winter pastimes. Of course, all of this only served as a reminder that Christmas was just a week away.

In Hillsboro, unlike Taylorville and most other county seats, the business district did not surround the courthouse square. Instead, it was strung out along Main Street, which ran perpendicular to the front entrance of the courthouse. As was customary, all stores and services were closed on the Sabbath. But in the coming week, merchants were anticipating a surge of holiday shoppers. Shelves had been well stocked with candies and nuts and oranges and apples, woolen mittens and scarves, and simple wooden toys for the children. Velvet mufflers and delicate lace collars and cuffs would be the most sought-after items for women while, for the men, it was the ever-popular fur-lined caps, suspenders, handkerchiefs, and tobacco. The shops were more than ready for the gift-giving season; but whether those involved in the trial would be able to enjoy the season was an altogether different matter.

By now, almost no one believed the trial would conclude before Christmas. This, of course, had people wondering how Judge Phillips would handle a holiday break. But on Sunday at least, the enchantment of fresh snow brought serenity to the town that had of late been the scene of so much tension. After church, a group of local women paid Emma a visit; they wanted to welcome her personally and let her know they were praying for her recovery and for the conviction of the three defendants.

Fortunately, there was only one minor altercation over the weekend. Reporter F. M. Whitman of the St. Louis evening paper had been caught carrying concealed weapons.[37] He was fined $25, and that amount was subsequently reduced to $10, which he paid. Perhaps this reporter was the same one who'd written so fervently in defense of the suspects in August 1882 and had wrangled the interview with them right after their near-fatal lynching. That reporter, from the *St. Louis Republican,* had done little to mask his support of the accused. Beyond that one incident, however, nothing untoward marred the quiet of the weekend. There were no drunken brawls in saloons, no loud gatherings on street corners, and, most importantly, no mob activity of any kind. The citizens of Hillsboro could thank the good Lord for all of those things and, more precisely, for sending the kind of weather that fostered a spirit of peace throughout the weekend.

19

Montgomery, who had been out of town and was by some not expected to return, was promptly in his seat. He said he expected to be acquitted and there is nothing to run away from.
—Decatur Daily Republican, *December 18, 1883*

Monday, December 17, 1883. The second week of the trial was slow in getting underway. Knowing that many of the trial's participants were going home for the weekend, Judge Phillips had announced on Friday that court would not resume until eleven o'clock on Monday morning. Of course, he had no way of knowing that half a foot of snow would hit the region, that in its wake temperatures would plummet to ten below, or that because of the bad weather Monday's trains would run way behind schedule. As a result, only a few witnesses were interrogated that day, but each did add a tiny piece to the larger puzzle.

Sam Mossier was one of the men present on July 1, 1882, when the nail paring was compared to John Montgomery's big toenail. He described a ridge down the middle of the paring that, in his opinion, seemed to line up with the one on John's toenail. On cross-examination, he stated that at no point did Montgomery object to the comparison. Charles Dickerson then testified that he was the one who found the paring—about six feet from the platform. According to the witness, he picked it up, looked at it, and then handed it to William Montgomery, who gave it to Constable Eltzroth. Ed Montgomery had observed this, said Dickerson.

Next came Emma's uncle, Bill Armstrong, who told of running into William and John Montgomery and their father near the schoolhouse on the day after the crime. He said that around three in the afternoon he had stopped to talk with all of them. During that conversation, William kept insisting that he had seen his brother John and their father at the schoolhouse on Thursday, even though John Sr. and John Jr. kept denying it. Then William had said, "I'll bet $10 you were both there!"[1] John Jr. then told Armstrong that he was only there fifteen or twenty minutes.

The next witness, Charles Jacobey, contradicted John's claim. According to him, Montgomery told him he and his father stood talking for nearly an hour by the coalhouse on Thursday afternoon, within feet of where the attack was in progress. The next witness, Benjamin Burg, also ran into Montgomery the day after the outrage and said to him, "John, that's a devil of a scrape you got into last night." John's reply was, "How did you find out? Who told you?" Burg answered, "Egli told me." To Burg, John had also said, "Father and I stood between the schoolhouse and coal house and talked till six o'clock; we talked about an hour."[2]

At some point in the investigation, it was decided that the person wielding the knife during the attack was left-handed. That may have been determined by the position of the cuts on Emma's cheek and neck or from the carved opening in the loft—or both. So the State, in a logical approach, set out to show that Montgomery was a leftie. Sam Sadler—one of the five men who had helped debunk John Sr.'s hearing testimony—was the first to be questioned on the matter. He insisted that the younger Montgomery was a leftie because his "right hand was crippled," that he'd watched him whittle many times and he always used his left hand.[3]

Next came the three men who had joined Clementi early on Friday morning to help hunt down the two suspected tramps. Their stories did not vary in the least from their hearing testimonies. Pleasant Venters recalled how the farmhand laughed when speaking of the crime. Then he told of how Clementi suddenly decided to cut across the fields "to see if he could find any trace of the ravishers." When the other three agreed to rejoin him down the road, he took off alone across the Pettus pasture. When he didn't show up as promised, the men backtracked to find him and finally caught up with him "about a mile and a half south of the schoolhouse." But, noted the witness, "Clementi was gone a good while to only travel the distance he did." The other two members of the search party corroborated Venter's story:

> [Knight] and the others had followed the tracks of Clementi's horse across the field from Pettus's pasture . . . to a bridge a quarter mile from the Pettus pasture where the tracks of a mule and a second horse were found with those of the horse Clementi rode. A stand was made at the end of the bridge where the three animals remained some time, the weeds having been tramped and nibbled away. Witness knew Emanuel Clementi's horse because it belonged to Housley and had on plate shoes. Clementi had taken the short cut across the field and should have reached Armstrong's residence on Blue Mound road before [the witness] did.[4]

On cross-exam, Knight repeated the defendant's statement that he had not shaved off his whiskers the morning after the attack nor was he leaving town because he'd gotten into "a scrape with a girl."[5] The third member of the search party, James Wickens of Mt. Auburn, recalled Clementi's insistence that "two tramps" were responsible for the crime. He was also present at Clementi's arrest and heard him ask to see John Montgomery.

George Housley, Emma's uncle, confirmed that Clementi came to his door very early on the morning of the thirtieth, at about five o'clock. Clementi asked to borrow one of Housley's fast horses so that he could "go to Blue Mound to hunt some tramps who had outraged Miss Bond at the schoolhouse."[6]

So far, the State had focused on Clementi and Montgomery. Now, a number of witnesses came forward to describe what Pettus had been wearing on the day of the outrage. They all agreed: "a blue dotted shirt and low shoes and red-striped stockings."[7] The footwear closely resembled what the victim had described both early on and then at the trial. However, if Emma had ever mentioned the dotted shirt, it was not reported. The papers all covered the same testimonies from Monday's session, suggesting that those were the most significant of the day.

The rumor mill, so omnipresent right after the crime, was beginning to start up again. Since the beginning of the trial, there'd been the buzz about Heinlein running off to escape John Montgomery's ire. Then came the rumor that Montgomery had planned to skip out over the previous weekend. The stories, of course, all proved false. The Pettuses weren't being shortchanged in the gossip department either. The newest contention was that Lee's sister Cora was upset over having lost the Montgomery School teaching position to Emma. That was said to have "caused a secret feeling of bitterness in the Pettus family."[8] True to form, the papers weren't limiting their fishing expeditions to the dark waters surrounding the suspects. They had also reeled in some hearsay about the usually restrained father of the victim: It was reported that Mr. Bond "had sent a threatening letter to Judge Thornton, the defense counsel." This, however, was "emphatically" denied.[9]

Tuesday, December 18, 1883. A. D. Bond was the only member of Emma's family to attend the trial on Tuesday, which turned out to be a very busy day in Judge Phillips's courtroom. James Armstrong took the stand first and explained that he lived a short distance east of the Montgomery School. He told of seeing Clementi just after five o'clock in the morning on Friday, June 30, 1882. When he stopped to talk with him, Clementi told him that Emma Bond "had been outraged by some tramps at the schoolhouse until about one o'clock in the morning" and that she'd been robbed of "her engagement ring and $10 in money."[10] Armstrong confirmed that Clementi was on horseback but did not recognize the horse he was riding.

Ed Housley, at nineteen, was slightly younger than his cousin Emma and the defendant against whom he was about to give testimony. He stated that he'd run into Lee Pettus on the morning of June 30, at the Montgomery schoolhouse around ten in the morning. The two soon decided to go swimming, at Lee's suggestion. But when they reached the creek on the Pettus property, stated Ed, Lee, without giving a reason, "refused to go in and did not take off his clothes"[11]

What the State had in mind next was a gamble of sorts. But the worst that could come of it was that the jury would completely ignore what the next two witnesses had to say. The men seemed to be enjoying their stay in town, since their accommodations were a trifle better than their usual ones at the Southern Illinois Penitentiary in Chester. The prison warden had delivered Edwin Burritt and Charles Meyers into the capable hands of the Montgomery County sheriff—thanks to a writ of habeas corpus filed by Drennan, ordering the inmates to appear at the trial.[12] The former jail mates of Montgomery, Pettus, and Clementi appeared in handcuffs—acting smug, as if they had a prized secret to spill.

Burritt was brought in first. After stating his name and place of residence, he was asked why he was doing time at Chester. Three years for burglary and larceny, responded the witness with a smirk. Sure, he knew the three men sitting at the defense table, because they'd all been in the Taylorville jail together, summer before last. He described the cell arrangements at the jail, specifically the prisoners' proximity to one another, and how during the daytime all of the inmates were allowed to congregate outside of their cells, in the center hallway. The questioning then turned to the day the Bond defendants were booked. That day, said Burritt, he could hear the three defendants talking—about the Bond case and the piece of toenail found at the schoolhouse. He heard Clementi say "he had let a toenail grow long, and had lost it shucking corn in June." Then Montgomery said, "You couldn't lose it shucking corn in June."[13] This was an entirely new twist, since the toenail had always been considered a link to Montgomery—not Clementi. Also, Burritt claimed that Clementi had a newspaper and was reading it out loud to his friends. When he read the part about Miss Bond's underclothes being torn, Pettus called it "a damned lie" and said they were not torn. To this, Clementi replied, "Shut up, you little fool. What do you know about it?"[14]

The prosecution had anticipated trouble and, sure enough, here it came—from Thornton. Jumping to his feet, he shouted, "You may just as well rake hell for witnesses as to take them from the penitentiary. The introduction of a witness convicted of one of the highest crimes to testify against men of good standing is infamous." Burritt was "wholly incompetent," decreed Thornton, and his remarks should be struck from the record.[15] This led to ninety minutes of arguing back and forth, with Thornton objecting to the admission of any and all of Burritt's testimony and Vandeveer countering that ample precedent existed for allowing a convicted man to testify. The judge listened patiently, and in the end he ruled that Burritt's testimony was admissible. The convict was excused, and the sheriff came forward to escort him back to his temporary cell on the first floor of the courthouse.

Obviously, if Burritt's word was to be admitted, then the testimony of Charles Meyers would also be allowed. Because of his part in John McKinney's murder, Meyers was almost as notorious in central Illinois as the three men on trial. Courtrooms were familiar to him, so he looked quite at ease when he entered. After explaining the unpleasantries that had landed him in Chester for ninety-nine years, he told the court that he knew the Bond suspects from their time together in the Taylorville jail—in the summer of 1882. He had also overheard them discussing the Bond outrage right after they were put in their cells on July 1. According to the witness, John told the others to "stick together and tell the same story."[16] He did not hear Pettus and Clementi's responses, however.

When asked about the toenail discussion, Meyers told a slightly different story than Burritt. According to him, Clementi had said, "I don't know how I came to lose that toenail," and Montgomery had replied, "I suppose you lost it husking corn in June."[17] That sounded only slightly less incriminating than Burritt's version. Given both men's statements, perhaps the more relevant question was why had there been no attempt to fit the paring to Clementi—or anybody other than Montgomery? Meyers also heard the three defendants' discussion on Emma's clothing, and Clementi telling Pettus to shut up about it. Thornton minced no words in cross-examining the witness. He asked Meyers if he'd ever spoken to anyone from the prosecution team about the three men currently on trial. He admitted that, yes, he had talked with Judge Vandeveer, who'd been his own defense attorney, and the lawyer had advised him to share whatever he knew about the Bond suspects.

Thornton chipped away at the convict's story. He demanded to know whether Meyers had told two other inmates he was going to "fasten guilt on the defendants" in exchange for "mercy." The witness replied he had never said anything of the sort. Nor had he attempted to "draw" information out of Montgomery, Pettus, or Clementi. He also did not concur with Thornton's assertion that "the prosecution was pushing him hard and that he was sorry he and Burritt made up a story on the defendants."[18] As denials tumbled from the convict's mouth right and left, it became clear to all that Thornton's patience was wearing thin. And so, too, was the judge's. He called a recess.

After the break, Thornton was calmer and ready for his second go at Meyers. He began by inquiring about a man named John Dunn, who had also been locked up in the Taylorville jail in August 1882. Meyers denied ever discussing the Bond case with Dunn during their incarceration. Here, Thornton stepped closer and ratcheted up the rhetoric, asking if the witness had ever told Dunn that he was going to "put up a job on the defendants." Meyers said he had not. Nor had he ever made a similar claim to a Mr. Parks. Without warning, Thornton changed course again, asking how many times the witness had discussed the Bond case with Judge Vandeveer. It was only once, said Meyers. "Judge Vandeveer told him that if he could honorably tell what he had heard the defendants say it would be of great use to the prosecution and it won't do him no harm. It would do him good."[19]

Thornton returned to his chair, looking thoroughly disgusted. Meyers and Burritt would soon be on their way back to Chester, and it would likely be Meyers's last glimpse of the outside world—ever. The State knew that using the convicts was a risky move and that the jurors might scoff at their testimonies. But the prosecution needed to build a solid mountain of suspicion, regardless of whose help that required.

Tuesday afternoon brought forth a man with an intriguing tale of bribery. J. T. Ferguson was asked if he had ever served on a grand jury in Christian County. Yes, said the witness, he'd served on the one that had returned the indictments in the Bond case. And he had known the defendant, John Montgomery, for eight years. Evidently, Montgomery had approached Ferguson on the day the Bond indictments were handed down, saying, "You get Miss Bond's statement to the Grand Jury and give it to me in writing. Whatever you charge, the money is ready." It caught Ferguson so off guard that all he could think to say was that he'd have to "see about it."[20] This sounded like fodder for the defense, but Ferguson quickly reassured the court that he never gave Montgomery any information, nor did he take any cash from the defendant.

Thornton tried to divert attention from the damaging comments, by asking the witness if he knew whether John Montgomery was right- or left-handed. Ferguson "noticed John used his right hand since the outrage." That latter part wasn't exactly what Thornton was expecting to hear. With a little effort, he got the witness to admit that he wasn't sure "whether John used his left hand before or not."[21] Maybe, reflected the witness, he just "uses his right hand more than his left." Thornton couldn't let that one stand, either, and asked what kinds of things he had seen John do with his right hand. Ferguson thought for a moment, then answered, "He makes gestures with the right hand. Cuts tobacco with a knife in the right hand. Uses his right hand in cutting a hedge."[22] Those were pretty keen observations and seemed to even the score: one vote for left-handed and one for right-handed—or at least right-handed more recently.

Witness Oliver Harlan was asked if he was acquainted with Clementi. Harlan said he was and pointed out the suspect sitting at the defense table. His testimony centered on a remark Clementi had made to him in August 1882, at the time of the hearing. Clementi told Harlan he didn't do it but he knew who did. Harlan was followed by Isaac Ward, a man in his early forties. His twenty-six-year-old wife was the former Amanda Montgomery, another of John's many cousins. But like Laurence Heinlein, he was going against the family grain by testifying for the State. His testimony for the prosecution gave further confirmation of John's close proximity to the crime scene on June 29. According to Ward, Montgomery told him that "he and his father were standing by the coal-shed when Miss Bond was being outraged."[23]

With that, the judge called for another recess so the prosecution could consult about whether to bring its remaining witnesses to the stand. At three o'clock, everyone reentered the courtroom, expecting to hear more testimony. Instead, Vandeveer stood and announced that the prosecution was resting its case. The State was apparently confident in its four-day presentation.

At this point, the defense made a last-ditch effort—well, actually two official motions. The first was "that the evidence of the witnesses Heinlein and Swick be excluded from the jury on the grounds that their testimony was in the nature of a confession." The second asked "that the evidence against Pettus and Clementi be excluded on the grounds of insufficiency."[24] The arguments dragged on into the evening. Finally, a weary Phillips decided the court had heard enough for one day.

Wednesday, December 19, 1883. The two teams of attorneys in the Bond case were living proof that the long-windedness of lawyers should never be underestimated. Judge Phillips may have planned to make a swift decision on the defense's motions, but that turned out to be wishful thinking. The first thing on Wednesday, both sides picked up where they'd left off the night before. To the spectators, so eager to hear some tantalizing testimony, this came as a huge disappointment. Instead, they were subjected to a lot of legal gibberish—the kind that can quickly numb the brain of the average layperson. Taking pity on the bored audience, Phillips called for a recess at noon, adding that he would render his rulings when court resumed.

When the three defendants, their attorneys, and the plethora of onlookers filed back into the courtroom at two o'clock, a much calmer atmosphere prevailed. The judge addressed the first motion—the one seeking to throw out Swick's and Heinlein's testimonies. He overruled it, explaining that "it was not apparent . . . that Montgomery made the confession to Swick and Heinlein because of the threats of the mob." There simply was no mob. Not anywhere close by, at least. In the judge's opinion, any statements Montgomery made were of his own free will. Hence, Swick's and Heinlein's testimonies would stand. Phillips also ruled against the defense on the second motion—the one calling for the dismissal of charges against Pettus and Clementi. "The court can allow evidence to go to the jury and then instruct the jury how to act upon it." Furthermore, explained the judge, "If the court decides in favor of the motion, [the] defendants [can] never again be prosecuted for the crime."[25] Ultimately, it was up to the jury to determine whether the State's evidence against the two men was adequate.

20

The defence depends upon proving an alibi and expect to break down the testimony of Miss Bond; but the opinion is freely expressed that that will be a dangerous experiment and, should it fail, be fatal to their case.
—Decatur Daily Republican, *December 18, 1883*

Wednesday, December 19, 1883. If the defense was even half as efficient as the State, there was still a good chance the trial could wrap up by year's end. The State's third witness was called back as the first witness for the defense. Laurence Heinlein entered the courtroom again, looking haggard. The State had put him through the wringer the previous Friday. His inquisition at the hands of the defense was much shorter and not nearly as clear-cut. Heinlein admitted that, yes, he had "assisted in raising a subscription of $124 to help defray the expenses of the prosecution."[1] This brings up an interesting question: was making private donations to the prosecution once an accepted practice? Today, the financial burden of trying a case falls entirely to taxpayers; but perhaps in the late nineteenth century the local taxing bodies didn't have enough resources to cover the cost of a trial of such magnitude.[2]

The defense didn't seem to be suggesting anything illegal on Heinlein's part; other citizens were known to have contributed to the prosecution's cause. Rather, it sounded like the defense was inferring he might have had some sort of hidden motive for supporting the State's case. Before being excused, Heinlein turned to Judge Phillips and asked if he might "correct a statement that he made on the direct exam."[3] The defense vehemently opposed the request, and Phillips concurred. So whatever Heinlein wanted to get off his chest would forever remain a mystery.

Beyond that, the Montgomery and Pettus clans had to be upset with Heinlein for having sided with the State. Though he was portrayed as an uncooperative witness, it took considerable nerve to do what he had done. Of course, he wasn't a blood relative of the Pettuses or the Montgomerys, but his wife of three decades was Margret Pettus's sister. His aiding of the enemy almost certainly affected his marriage and his relationship with his in-laws.

A long stream of witnesses followed. Unlike Heinlein, they were clearly partial to the defense. Only a handful were unrelated to John and Lee. A number of married Montgomery and Pettus women, along with their husbands, took the stand. So, too, did several of their children. Of those witnesses with ties to both families, John's wife Mattie had to be in the least enviable position. To add to her burden, she had to bring her two-month-old infant to the trial, cradled in her arms.[4] That she would not be allowed to testify for her husband was a minor setback, however, since so many other relatives were standing by. It was going to be an extended family collaboration, and a multigenerational one, at that.

A host of family members waited in the second-floor corridor, out of earshot, of course. The prudence of this measure quickly became apparent with the next witness—Hiram Linn Montgomery, age twenty-four. Hiram was the son of John's uncle Levi and aunt Jane. Levi had been dead for years, but Jane had a whole brigade of sons to help her work the family farm, which sat just northeast of the Pettus land and the Montgomery School. Hiram's testimony was the beginning of an unending flood of contradictions. By the time all of the defense witnesses had finished, what remained was a muddied field of evidence, so deep that almost nobody could wade through it, least of all the jurors. Not that the confusion was intentional; undoubtedly, the passage of time was partially to blame. Eighteen months was a long time for the human mind to retain minutiae.

Thornton's questions centered on the day after the crime. Had he gone to the schoolhouse on Friday morning? And had he seen John there? Did John go into the loft that morning? Hiram answered all three questions in the affirmative. He and John had also gone up into the loft together, where he witnessed John cutting an opening in the wall at the west end. When asked which hand John used, Hiram said it was his left. W. C. Montgomery—another of John's cousins—followed. He, too, was asked about his visit to the schoolhouse on Friday morning. Like Hiram, he told of seeing John carve a hole at the far end of the loft, but using his right hand. Now, if anybody on the jury was keeping track, so far they had heard—from State witnesses—one vote for John being left-handed from Sadler and one vote for him being right-handed (at least since the outrage) from Ferguson. Now, for the defense, here were two of Montgomery's own cousins—one claiming he was left-handed and the other the opposite. Perhaps John C. Montgomery was ambidextrous.

The defense needed to throw in a few voices not related to the accused. George Miller of Blue Mound fit that bill, and he was up next. Of course, nobody mentioned that he was "a staunch friend of Montgomery."[5] George's wife,

Hattie, was a Heinlein, however, so maybe he was distant family.[6] His contribution to the defense was hard to categorize. Thornton interrogated him about the Friday morning discussion in Blue Mound on the two tramps. Miller was handed a small piece of paper and asked to read it aloud to the court: "Blue Mound, June 30, 1882.—A. D. Bond, care of City Marshal, Taylorville, IL: Parties answering description were seen here at 10:15 last night. Think went west on freight at 1:20 this A.M. E. P. Clementi." The witness confirmed this was the message he saw Clementi send to Bond that Friday morning at "9:20 A.M."[7] When asked whose idea it was to send the telegram to Mr. Bond, he said it was Clementi's. Thornton thanked the witness and sat down.

State's Attorney Amos Miller—no relation to the witness—took over for the prosecution. He asked the witness if he had ever heard Montgomery say that "if they had not been in such a hurry in arresting him, he might have told them something." The witness answered that he hadn't. He was also present when Clementi and the posse first rode into Blue Mound on the thirtieth and stated that several men, himself included, were standing around talking about the outrage. Clementi, as far as Miller could remember, said nothing about tramps.[8] Regarding the train mentioned in the telegram, George conceded that he had no idea if there was such a train that night.

Late Wednesday afternoon, a light, soft snow began to fall. From where Judge Phillips sat, looking out over the town, the fresh dusting of white was a reminder that Christmas was less than a week away. In November, he had expressed his belief that the trial would run until Christmas. Now he had to consider his options. In the worst-case scenario, if the trial dragged on at its current pace, he would be forced to call an extended break from Friday evening, December 21, until the following Wednesday, December 26. Most people were expecting precisely that. However, if he were to implement a more aggressive schedule for the remainder of the week, then it might be possible to wrap things up more quickly. It was a long shot, but worth a try, so the judge laid out a new plan, which called for shorter supper breaks followed by extended evening sessions, starting at seven o'clock. The revised schedule would begin that day, and depending on how things progressed, he might ask the jury to deliberate over the coming weekend, in hopes of getting a verdict by Sunday or Monday. Monday was Christmas Eve, so, ideally, everyone would be home in time for the holiday. Well, maybe not everyone: two or three could wind up going south—to Chester.

The trial's first nighttime session brought forth Dr. J. S. Cussins, one of the men present for the toenail comparison. He expressed the same opinion that he'd given at the hearing—that the paring did not fit John's toe. His belief was based on a slight variation in thickness, though he admitted on cross-exam that

John's toenail looked like it had been scraped down, which might explain the difference.

To discredit Burritt and Meyers, the defense called jailer George Murphy and Deputy Sheriff Hamel.[9] The two were asked about the jail's cell layout and living arrangements. According to both men, Meyers occupied a cell on the east end of the jail block. Each believed there was no way Meyers could "see the defendants who were at the west door, and slept under the west windows the night they were brought there."[10] Of course, that didn't mean Meyers didn't hear them; the cell block wasn't long—just five cells down each side of the center hallway. In cross, the State elicited that very fact from the witness—that it was possible for the Chester inmates to have overheard the Bond suspects talking to one another. Hamel also confirmed that during the daytime, prisoners were allowed to mingle in the center hallway.

The defense introduced John Dunn, who had also been in the same cell block as the Bond suspects the previous year. Now a free man, he told a different story than Burritt and Meyers. The attorneys asked him if during his incarceration he had ever talked to Meyers about the defendants in this case. Yes, he recalled Meyers saying that "some prisoners wished to put up a job on the defendants." Dunn refused to be a part of it, however. The value of Dunn's testimony was subtle—the word of one acquitted man was bound to be worth more than the word of two convicted men. On cross, the State planted its own subtleties by asking Dunn to tell the court why he was in jail during the summer of 1882. He answered that he was accused of rape. The State then asked if he sympathized with the three men on trial. He had "no fellow-feelings for the defendants," declared Dunn.[11] In the end, it was up to the jurors to decide which questionable characters were the most believable; or, of course, it could ignore every one of them.

It was nearly impossible to tarnish the credibility of the next witness. Lawyer Joseph Creighton explained he had been one of the defense attorneys for convicted murderer Charles Meyers. Creighton indicated that Meyers told him he had made up the story about the defendants because he and Burritt hoped to "secure favor with the prosecution."[12] He thought if he helped convict the suspects in this case, it might work to his advantage in his own case.

Before Wednesday night's adjournment, the trial got sidetracked by another controversy. The defense wanted to question some additional people who were on the State's list of witnesses; however, the prosecution had decided not to use these particular witnesses. The State argued fervently against allowing it, but Phillips ruled in favor of the defense.

Thursday, December 20, 1883. That morning, a slew of people were waiting to testify. The first was Sheriff Haines, who described what the suspects were wearing when they were booked. On examining their clothing at the jail, he hadn't noticed anything out of the ordinary. He described Clementi's clothing specifically: "The shirt was of red and buff striped goods. The red stripes had run somewhat," but there was no blood on it. Haines continued: "I was not satisfied so on the next day I examined them again and found no stains on the shirt or underclothing." According to the sheriff, there was nothing suspicious on Pettus's clothes, either, and none of the suspects appeared to have changed their clothes recently. All, including Montgomery's, looked as if they'd been "worn several days."[13]

When Thornton asked what time the prisoners had been booked into the jail on July 1, Haines said it was around sunrise, though they were not taken to their cells until later in the day. Pettus and Clementi were put in their cells in the early afternoon, and Montgomery went over to the square to look for bail and didn't go into his cell until later that afternoon. He confirmed they were all put in separate cells, although Haines was not there to lock them up personally. He also agreed with his deputy's statement that the suspects could not have communicated about the case nor could Meyers and Burritt have overheard them talking. In the end, each side spent an inordinate amount of time trying to prove or disprove the statements of two convicts who were of highly dubious character anyway.

Next to the stand was John Stumpf, proprietor of the hotel located near the Blue Mound depot. He remembered that two men he didn't recognize came into the hotel around ten o'clock on the night of June 29, 1882. He described them both: One was lean and tall. He wore dark clothes and sported chin whiskers. The other was shorter and had a smooth face. He was wearing dark clothes and "quarter shoes and red socks."[14] He offered these other sketchy details on their attire: "The man with whiskers wore a light colored hat and pants of a color not exactly black" and the other "a black hat and colored pants."[15] After they left the hotel, said Stumpf, they went toward the depot. And yes, he mentioned that to the group who gathered the next morning to discuss the outrage. When someone in that group mentioned Miss Bond's description of her attackers, he recalled seeing the two tramps on Thursday night, around the time the freight bound for St. Louis came through the village.

Attorney Edwards, on cross-exam, questioned the accuracy of Stumpf's memory. Apparently, the witness wasn't exactly sure how he had described the two strangers at the preliminary hearing. The lawyer, glancing down at his notes, asked if he had described them as "neatly-dressed, nice-looking men." The witness thought that sounded right. Edwards, again referring to Stumpf's earlier testimony, asked if he remembered saying that he "did not notice any-thing peculiar about them," and that "their shirts were clean and their boots were dry"?[16] He conceded to having made both statements, or at least something to that effect. Edwards's point was a sound one: Was the jury supposed to believe that the two tramps—supposedly on the run from a violent crime scene—had hiked nine miles in the dark, across muddy fields, and arrived at their destination looking "well-dressed and with dry feet?"[17] Clearly, common sense was all the jury needed to apply to that scenario.

Stumpf would have been better off if he could have excused himself at that point. But Edwards had one more question: What color facial hair did the man with the whiskers have? Stumpf looked stumped. His response must have confused even the journalists, who reported that "the man had either light, sandy or dark whiskers."[18] Evidently, the witness wasn't exactly sure what he'd seen, and his uncertainty obviously carried over to those listening in the courtroom. One reporter wrote that the witness identified the stout man as the one with chin whiskers, while another thought that Stumpf had assigned the whiskers to the taller, leaner man. Even so, the defense apparently accomplished what it set out to do in regard to the two strangers. Their similarities to the men in Emma's description—combined with their proximity to the crime scene—might be enough to plant a seed of reasonable doubt in the jurors' minds. And whether Stumpf had simply forgotten the crucial details over the course of time or had been unsure of them from the very start, he firmly established that two strangers were seen within a few miles of the crime scene on the evening in question at a most unusual hour. And those who lived in tiny villages almost never saw outsiders loitering in their communities at such a late hour.

The defense called Thomas Hart, unmarried and in his twenties. His brother Owen was married to Lee's sister Cora. He was one of the many who'd been at the Montgomery School on Friday morning, June 30. Thornton took him straight to the heart of the matter and asked him to tell the court about the experiment he, Deputy Hamel, and Charley Dickerson conducted at the schoolhouse that morning. Hart began by saying that Dickerson weighed 135 pounds—about the same as Miss Bond. So Deputy Hamel went up into the loft. Then a shawl was tied around Dickerson's waist, and Hamel and Hart tried to raise him into the loft. Hart stood below and pushed while Hamel grabbed the shawl from above and pulled. When that didn't work, he got a chair and climbed on it to try and lift him higher, though he was unsuccessful. Asked about his own size, Hart stated that he was "one-hundred and seventy-five pounds" and "six-feet two."[19] In their two attempts, the men never got Dickerson closer than two feet from the ceiling. Thornton asked "if it was difficult to lift [Dickerson] up." This brought a loud objection from the prosecutor—Judge Phillips wanted to know where this line of questioning was headed. "Here are two men," said Thornton, gesturing toward Pettus and Clementi, "neither one bigger than a woman and yet we are asked to believe that one of them thrust Emma Bond up into that scuttle hole. It seems to me there's an issue."[20] The judge sided with the State, and Thornton was forced to drop the matter. Hart was excused.

Sam Funderburk, another participant in the lifting experiment, came next. He gave his size as "five feet nine inches in height and weighing 180 pounds." He participated in another attempt to lift Mr. Dickerson into the attic. After Mr. Hart tried and failed, Funderburk offered to try. He told the court: "I could lift him as high as my head." This was not exactly what Thornton was after, so he tried again. "Did this require all your strength?" The State raised an objection, and the judge sustained it. Thornton reworded his next question carefully, to which Funderburk replied: "I used both hands in lifting him up. Don't think I could have put him up with one hand." Sam did indicate, however, that "Hamel could reach and catch hold of the shawl around [Dickerson]." Thornton persevered: "If the man had made any resistance, could you have put him up?"[21] This prompted another strong objection from the State, and again, it was sustained.

Emma testified that she thought she had fainted from the chokehold on her throat, so whether she had been in any condition to put up a struggle was a matter of conjecture. Furthermore, there was no way to honestly compare the strength of Deputy Hamel to that of the man who had done the lifting during the crime. In fact, if two criminals had pulled from above, then any comparison to Hamel's solo effort was meaningless. Finally, there was the matter of the shawl. Apparently, the State made no effort to ascertain what shawl had been used in the experiment. If the shawl that Mrs. Pettus had struggled to untie from Emma's waist had gone home with the victim, then the men could have been using a substitute shawl—and possibly a shorter one.

The day's witnesses kept coming, until finally only one remained to be questioned before the midday break. What this one had to say ranked near the top in relevance. Of course, there wasn't a soul present who didn't feel sorry for the scared youngster who approached the stand, slowly and timidly. Any child in his shoes would have done the same, but, by December of 1883, little Charlie Masters was not nearly as little or as vulnerable as he'd been the previous August. Still, the hour and a half he was about to spend in the witness chair was bound to produce some fidgeting in a boy of his age. Sitting still on a hard wooden chair for that long while fielding question after question would feel like an eternity to any child. In addition, the time elapsed since that fateful June day truly *was* an eternity for a child. Asking him to recall details from so long ago was going to be like asking him to sit still for an hour and a half.

The boy scooted his small frame to the back of the imposing chair next to the bench, his feet dangling just above the floor. Though he had grown in the intervening time, he was still dwarfed by the setting. That he looked ill at ease was an understatement. Thornton greeted him with a reassuring smile. Mustering his softest and calmest tone for the boy's benefit, the lawyer asked him for the basics. The boy responded that he was Charlie Masters, he was nine years old, and he went to the Montgomery School. Thornton's questioning turned to the day of the crime, with Charlie confirming that he remembered his last day of school the June before last. His teacher that year was Miss Bond. He wasn't positive she was already at school when he arrived, but he thought so. He remembered that he had been using the second reader that semester. Thornton nodded his approval. In answer to Thornton's next questions, Charlie explained he was the only pupil that day, because he needed to complete some reading and spelling lessons with Miss Bond. Then at recess time, she sent him outside while she went over to the Pettus house. It didn't seem like she was gone very long.

When asked about his midday break, the witness said he took his lunch pail into the schoolyard to eat. Based on newspaper accounts, however, Charlie had some trouble recalling other details about the noon hour. At one point, he said Miss Bond also ate her dinner at school. But then he also stated that she went over to Ed Montgomery's for her meal. Either the boy was confused, or his delivery of the details confused the reporters. When asked what he did after eating, the boy said that he just laid around on top of the coalhouse, waiting for Miss Bond to come back. That response seemed to imply that Emma had indeed left the school during the noon hour. Charlie also stated he did not go inside the schoolhouse at any time during his noon break.

Thornton gently led the youngster, step by tiny step, through that distant day, guiding him closer to the critical afternoon hours. He asked if Charlie remembered what happened that afternoon. According to the boy, after reciting a few lessons, Miss Bond gave him another recess while she went back to the Pettus house to practice with the girls. When asked how long his teacher was away this time, Charlie wasn't sure. But while she was gone, he "staid around the coal-house and did not go far away from there." He saw no one else during that recess except "Old John and young John." And yes, he had talked to them: "Young John asked me why I wasn't playing with the school children." The boy told him that "there wasn't any." Then young John said to him, "Well, wait and I'll come back and wrestle with you."[22] The witness also recalled that the younger man was on foot, and the older one was riding.

When Miss Bond came back from her break, the youngster told her he heard noises in the loft and maybe there were some tramps up there. She assured him it was just rats. Charlie also testified that the scuttle hole was "open all day" and that there was mud on the wall beneath it when he arrived that morning. This he pointed out to Miss Bond, saying, "Look at that." She didn't say much in response, according to the witness. Thornton addressed one last detail: he wanted to know if there were any trees in the schoolyard, and the lad responded that there weren't.

Charlie had done okay, considering. But his testimony was not without its share of problems, and the prosecution seized on his inconsistencies during its cross-exam. The prosecutor asked him where exactly he was sitting while Miss Bond was at music practice, and he replied that he was "on the end of the top of the coalhouse that fronted toward Mrs. Pettus's."[23] Doing what? "Kicking up his heels."[24] And evidently, trees or no trees, the school's front entrance was not visible from the boy's vantage point. When asked if he stayed on top of the coalhouse for the whole afternoon recess, Charlie hesitated, seeming unsure. The prosecutor urged him to think very hard about whether he had done anything else. He answered that he did go to the Pettus well to get a drink but wasn't gone for very long. He then returned to the coalhouse roof and laid there listening to the music coming from across the way.

The State had pressed the boy hard about the day's timeline. With three separate recesses that day, Charlie seemed fuzzy, at best, about the timing of some of the relevant events. At one point, he claimed that he went to the Pettus well while Emma was inside the schoolhouse and that he "did not hear any singing or playing while he was at Mrs. Pettus's getting a drink."[25] And yet, according to his own testimony he'd gone to the well at a time Emma was known to be practicing songs with Minnie and Ona. This probably had the jury puzzling over how much stock to put in the boy's statements. There was simply no getting around fact that he'd been only eight years old on the day in question.

At noon, Judge Phillips announced a recess. Spectators filed out of the room, donning their winter coats. Overnight, the region had been hit by more snow, which a brisk north wind and plunging temperatures had chased off. Despite the biting cold, Hillsboro was a hotbed of activity. Out-of-town visitors mingled with local shoppers as they went in search of hot meals to satiate their winter-driven appetites. Trial-goers knew that speed was of the essence if they wanted to get a seat in the afternoon session; with the defendants due up next, space would be at a premium.

When the courtroom doors reopened, the gallery quickly filled to capacity and then some. Clementi's name was announced. The defendant stood, loped around the defense table and up to the witness stand. He'd already placed his hand on the Bible and sworn to God to tell the truth. Given his legendary shortcomings in matters of honesty, the chances of his keeping that oath seemed slim. He settled into the witness chair with an air of nonchalance.

He gave his name as Emanuel Clementi and said he had lived in Christian County since 1879. He stated that in June 1882 he was working for Mrs. Pettus.

On the twenty-ninth, there had been a wheat harvest going on, but because of the big rain the night before, there wasn't much to do. After eating his dinner at the Pettus house at noon, he'd spent the rest of the afternoon with Lee. When the two went to the barn to feed the horses, they noticed some "cattle swimming across the branch, sixty or seventy rods southeast of the house," so Lee fetched a horse and crossed the creek to bring them back while Clementi watched from the fence.[26] After he was done, he turned his horse loose and the two sat down and talked for a bit. After that, they climbed into the wagon where, according to Clementi, he fell asleep right away and didn't wake up until suppertime, around seven.

The witness seemed to have near-perfect recall. But in an apparent blunder, he mentioned that "John C. Montgomery and wife took dinner at Mrs. Pettus's about five o'clock that evening." Just how he would have known that bit of information was a mystery, given his claim of having been asleep in the wagon from mid-afternoon until seven. And both remarks conflicted with his original 1882 statement, in which he'd told Officer Crowe that he'd eaten supper at six o'clock that day. The witness was led through the events of later that same evening. The *Republican* gave this interpretation of Clementi's testimony:

> He did not go to bed as early as usual. Pettus called him during the night. When he got downstairs he saw Miss Emma Bond, Mrs. Pettus, Lee and Minnie Pettus. He went up to Miss Bond and looked at the cuts on her wrists and face. Mrs. Pettus said Miss Emma wanted to be taken home, and he told her that she was not in a condition to be taken home. He then went to the kitchen to put on his boots, and Mrs. Pettus said she must be taken home, to which he replied that he was afraid Mr. Bond would blame them.

So, as instructed, he and Lee rounded up the horses and prepared the spring wagon. When Emma was loaded into the back, with Mrs. Pettus seated next to her, the group departed. They made a slight detour to old man Montgomery's so they could send Charlie to keep an eye on Lee's sisters, and then they headed for the Bond farm. After Emma's father carried her inside, he returned to give them his daughter's description of her assailants: "two large men dressed in dark clothes; wore white shirts; one had whiskers."[27]

Clementi's lawyer walked him through his activities of the following morning, including his hunt for the two tramps. The defendant was also quizzed about his arrest in Blue Mound and his first day in jail. His answers sounded as cut and dried as a bale of hay. As the *Tribune* put it: "The witness told a very nice story, but it is the general opinion that he made it too nice."[28] His answers on cross-exam raised more than a few eyebrows: "In some material points, [he] contradicted the

testimony of the jail officials, who were placed on the stand to contradict the statements of the convicts brought here by the state."[29] The defense had spent considerable time trying to dismantle Burritt's and Meyers's remarks, only to have their
own client come along and carelessly shoot off his mouth to the contrary.

Friday, December 21, 1883. It was the last day of the work week, the tenth day
of the trial, and just four days before Christmas. Lee Pettus was to testify, followed by several members of his family. Behind them waited the third and final
defendant—the one bearing the brunt of the suspicion. But the Bond trial was
now so far behind schedule that it was obvious it would run past Christmas—
quite possibly, into the New Year.

On Friday morning, Pettus was guided through a cogent thread of his whereabouts on the day of the crime. Asked when he'd first learned of the outrage, he
said it had been late on Thursday night. Thornton directed him back to the beginning of the day, with the defendant explaining that he had spent all of that Thursday at home. He didn't do much in the morning because of Wednesday night's
hard rain. First, he milked the cows, and then he noticed some of the mules and
horses had jumped the fence in the pasture and broken it, so he went out and
nailed it up. He took his dinner at the house, between twelve and one o'clock.
John and his sister Mattie were there, as were Cora and her husband, Owen. Also
present at dinner were Minnie and Ona, Clementi, and Pettus's uncle Rob.

After eating, he fed the horses. Then he noticed some of the cattle had gotten across the branch so he got a horse, swam it across, rounded up the cattle,
and brought them back. Yes, his clothes had gotten wet, but he didn't change
them. He confirmed that these were the same clothes he was wearing when he
was booked into jail on Saturday, July 1, and that he had not changed them on
Friday. According to Pettus, Deputy Hamel examined them at the jail. Since
Lee had admitted to getting his clothing wet while crossing the creek, it seemed
peculiar that the deputy had not noticed any telltale water marks on his pants,
since Wednesday night's heavy rain would have made the stream muddier than
usual. Pettus said that next, he sat down with Clementi on the fence and talked.

After that he "went back to the house, got a paper, and went and sat on the
wagon in the seat." When asked whether he had fallen asleep in the wagon, he
replied, "Don't remember whether I went to sleep or not. I was there half an
hour. Then I left the wagon and went back to the house." There, he sat around
waiting for supper. He did no more work that day "until late in the evening,"
when he cut some weeds around the fence corners. Both Montgomery and Clementi saw him doing this. The lawyer then asked whether he'd cut any weeds
near the schoolhouse, and Pettus replied that he had not. He reiterated that he'd
been on his farm the entire day. Apparently, by "late in the evening," he meant

five or six o'clock, because he proceeded to explain that he ate his supper *after* chopping weeds. Here again, the prosecution may have missed a chance to trip up the defense. For if supper was at seven, as most of the witnesses had stated, then there was no way Clementi could have seen him cutting weeds, since Clementi had claimed to be asleep, right up until supper was served at seven.

Present at the evening meal, according to Pettus, were mostly the same people who were there at dinner. He also stated that Mattie and John left right after the evening meal. Here, the prosecution cut to the chase.

> Thornton: Did you go to that schoolhouse that Thursday and ravish Emma
>   Bond?
> Pettus: No sir.
> Thornton: Did you conspire with others to ravish or outrage Emma Bond?
> Pettus: No sir.

Thornton turned to Emma's late-night arrival at the Pettus house. It was in the middle of the night, said the defendant, when his mother called him to the parlor. When he entered and saw Miss Bond lying on the sofa, she had a shawl around her waist, and his mother was trying to untie it. He noticed Miss Bond's light dress had some blood on it, and that she was holding a bloody handkerchief. Pettus saw cuts on her wrist and the left side of her face. She had little to say, other than "two tramps in dark clothes and white shirts had cut her in the schoolhouse. She said she wanted to go home."[30] Pettus assured her he'd take her in a little while.

The witness proceeded to give basically the same details as Clementi had given about the late-night trip to the Bond farm. When they arrived there, said Pettus, Clementi hollered out for Mr. Bond. He must have been sound asleep because Miss Bond finally had to call for him. Her father then came out and carried her in. When asked about the assailants' description that Mr. Bond had given them before their departure, Pettus recalled slightly different details: "One she said was a large man with black chin whiskers. The other was a smaller man, dressed the same way."[31] She said both were wearing white shirts and dark pants. Mr. Bond wrote out that description and handed it to Pettus, who then went out and woke up Laurence Heinlein, Jacob Yockey, Jones, and Samuel Heinlein. Clementi went along, but he got out after a half mile or so, leaving mother and son in the wagon. When Pettus got home, he and Charley Montgomery went up to Ed Montgomery's to tell him what had happened. Then they went to the schoolhouse, where there was already a crowd.

Thornton guided the defendant through a brief account of what he had seen and done at the school on Friday morning, conveniently skipping the part about his trip to the creek for a swim. He asked Pettus what kind of shoes he was wearing on the afternoon of June 29, and Pettus replied he wasn't wearing any; he was barefoot. Finally, he said he had gone to bed about nine thirty. Thornton needed nothing further from his client and turned the floor over to the prosecution.

On cross, Pettus was asked if he recalled telling Swick about the "pattern of Miss Bond's underclothing." He denied it. The prosecution then wanted to know if he and his codefendants discussed Miss Bond's underclothing at the jailhouse. He denied that, too. The prosecutor next turned to the morning after the crime, when the witness had refused to go swimming at the creek with Ed Housley. Asked why he had initiated the swimming idea and then refused to go into the water, the defendant replied: "The reason I did not go in swimming with the boys was that the water was too deep. I could not swim." Pettus was then quizzed "as to distances, and put on record as to the sex of the stock, their number, shape and style of wagon . . . with the purpose of making him contradict what Clementi had said."[32]

Pettus was excused, and his sister Mattie Montgomery was called in from the outer hallway. She, as the judge reminded the court, could only testify on behalf of her brother and Clementi. Anything connected to her husband was off limits. After ascertaining that she was at her mother's home on June 29, from eleven in the morning until "about sundown," Thornton asked if she had seen her brother Lee and Clementi that day. Yes, they were "in and around the house all the afternoon." Had she also seen Miss Bond that day? Yes, she came to practice with the witness's sisters around three in the afternoon. Where were Lee and Clementi at that time? "Clementi was then in the wagon and Lee around the house," she replied. About sundown, in and around the house, all the afternoon. Mattie's answers were less than compelling. Had she eaten supper at her mother's home that evening? Yes, and Lee and Clementi were present. The time, said Mattie, was seven o'clock.[33] Having been excluded from the courtroom along with all the other witnesses, Mattie had no way of knowing that Clementi had given five o'clock as the hour she and John had eaten. She spent ninety minutes in front of the jury, during which time, according to the *Tribune*, "it was impossible to tell whether the prosecution made any points off of her as her testimony was so closely identified with that of the defendants."[34]

Lee and Mattie weren't the only Pettuses who'd kept a close eye on the time on June 29. Their sisters Minnie and Ona were in general agreement on most points. Everyone—including the defendants—had eaten dinner together at the noon hour. Emma came to practice at either two thirty or three o'clock. She stayed thirty minutes. Supper was at seven. John and Mattie left for home at sundown. And yes, both girls recalled seeing their brother Lee and Clementi that particular day. Not surprisingly, their individual statements to the court had an all-too-familiar ring. Each attested to having seen the boys "in and around the house during the afternoon."[35] On the one hand, it's quite possible that the phrase "in and around the house" was a popular one at the time; if so, there may have been no significance to its repetition. On the other hand, maybe it was just another way of saying "the boys were here and there, part of the time, but we didn't have our eyes on them all of the time"? And perhaps the similarities of their answers also indicated some coaching.

Only Ona, the youngest, vacillated on one major point. Asked if she had seen the defendants *later* that same day, she stated that she saw all three there through the evening, up to nine or ten o'clock.[36] This represented another contradiction, given that John and Mattie supposedly ate at seven (or five, according to Clementi) and then left for home at sundown, which on June 29 was around seven thirty. But nine or ten o'clock? Even on one of the longest days of the year, the time Ona was proposing would have been well past dark, when John was supposedly home in his bed, sound asleep for the night.

Friday's session was drawing to a close, and many defense witnesses—including John Montgomery—had yet to speak. So there was simply no way around it: there would have to be a hiatus for the Christmas holiday. Phillips announced that court would reconvene the day after Christmas, at eleven o'clock. The four-day interruption was bound to have an impact on the momentum of the defense, only halfway through its case.

21

Miss Emma Bond will be married after the conclusion of the trial now in progress at Hillsboro.
    —Decatur Daily Republican, *December 23, 1883*

Friday night, December 21, 1883. Court let out a little early, and a mass exodus began. Everyone—attorneys, witnesses, and spectators alike—couldn't wait to get home. The holiday season would be a welcome, tranquil interlude. Unfortunately, the departing throngs were met with great frustration, due to the sheer numbers trying to get out of Hillsboro. As a result, many were forced to delay their escapes until Saturday. Unbeknownst to them, however, another fierce snowstorm was preparing to sneak in overnight and dump several more inches of fresh powder atop the old and crusty snowbanks.

The jurors, to their mutual chagrin, were not going anywhere. Phillips had little choice in the matter. And one of the twelve—Frank Huddleston—was feeling under the weather, so the mandatory confinement might speed his recovery. The news that he would have to remain in Hillsboro was difficult for juror Cannady to take; his bad luck had begun when his only child had fallen ill in early December. According to the *Daily Republican*, "When he was drawn, he had come to town for medicine [for his child] and asked to be excused from jury duty, but as he said that the child was not dangerously ill, he was permitted to take his chance with being selected along with the rest of the panel. Since that time his child has grown worse and this fact, together with [the] peculiarly irksome character of his services on the jury, makes his position anything but enviable."[1] To say that he was "permitted to take his chance" sounded like a poor choice of words. Maybe the paper should have said he was "required to take his chance." Of course, he might have altered his statement that his child was "not dangerously ill" if he could have seen the future.

No one, of course, could have anticipated the gifts Mother Nature had in store for Illinois over the extended weekend. One of her very best efforts loomed just to the west, waiting to slam headlong into the travelers so anxious to get home to their warm hearths. In fact, she was about to unleash her vengeance not only on Illinois but on the entire Midwest and eastward through the Ohio Valley.

Saturday and Sunday, December 22 and 23, 1883. The snow that fell overnight on Friday left Hillsboro cloaked in a glorious mantle of glistening white, but it was only a whisper of things to come. Still, it was enough to convince the Bonds to cancel their plans to go home, even if that meant the family would be apart on Christmas Day. Saturday's report on Emma had her doing well and playing the piano. And there was more good news; an article that had appeared a week earlier in the *Tribune* signaled a potential end to Emma's long uphill battle. Until then, there'd been a conspicuous void regarding her fiancé Adams, but now there were some new details:

> Before the terrible experience in the schoolhouse Miss Bond was the betrothed of a young man named Adams, who belongs to one of the best families in Christian County. He is a stock-raiser in the West and was absent at the time of the occurrence in the summer of 1882. Afterwards he returned and proved his fidelity by offering to marry Miss Bond then. By the advice of friends, the marriage was postponed until after the trial and the restoration of the lady's health. She is so much better now that the lovers have begun to talk about a date. Miss Bond's intended is not here, but is on his ranch. It was thought prudent that he should not be present during the trial, as friends feared he might not be restrained as well as Mr. Bond has been. The marriage will probably take place after the holidays.[2]

Whether the advice had come from his friends or hers, it had its obvious wisdom. But certainly, Emma was way overdue for a little happiness. On December 22, a second article confirmed what the *Tribune* had reported: "The Macon *Independent* is authority for the statement that Miss Emma Bond will be married after the conclusion of the trial now in progress at Hillsboro. Her husband will be Mr. Hitch, a young cattle drover of the West, who is said to be a wealthy and most worthy young man. How soon after the conclusion of the trial the event will occur the *Independent* does not state."[3] The only hitch, of course, was that the fiancé's name was now being given as "Hitch." Perhaps the reporter had been told the young man's name was Hitch and then mistakenly assumed that to be his surname. In fact, it sounded more like a nickname. In any case, Adams seemed to be Emma's ticket to a happier tomorrow. And it now looked as if that tomorrow would soon come.

Like the Bonds, the two youngest defendants also decided to stay in Hillsboro for the holidays. Clementi, it was reported, was staying because his new fiancée, Miss Ona Pettus, was staying. And Lee Pettus was staying simply because his buddy Clementi was. John, however, had his family to think about—especially since there was a strong chance he might not be home for many Christmases to come. Initial reports had him departing Hillsboro early on Saturday. But he and everyone else who trudged to the depot that morning were met with the news that all train travel had ground to a halt, because of the big snowstorm.

Though a twelve-inch accumulation was not unusual for the region, the whipping winds that came with it had free rein on the flat Illinois prairies. They piled the snow into deep and impassable drifts, clogging thoroughfares and trapping man and beast alike. The storm raged across the entire state all of Saturday and into Sunday. Then came the very thing midwesterners dreaded the most: the temperature rose and hovered near freezing. City and country dwellers alike shook their fists at the heavens—and with good reason. The *Tribune* gave a tongue-in-cheek account of Chicago's messy predicament: "The [snowstorm] was followed by a sleet storm and then the sun came out briefly and melted the snow banks turning everything into damnable masses of slush. Then came rain and when temperatures fell at night, everything refroze creating a 'skating rink.' . . . Hundreds of folks measured their lengths on the sidewalks and said all manner of unpleasant things. Folks stayed home from churches, leaving the pews empty. The theatres did not suffer to any extent and the saloons did a thriving business."[4]

Like a runaway train, the blizzard churned eastward, picking up steam as it passed through Indiana and Kentucky, before plowing full-force into Ohio. In Cincinnati, the whiteout began on Saturday, burying the city under two feet of snow before it was done. Then, as temperatures rose on Sunday, a thick and merciless fog rolled over the river town—along with five inches of rain. Communications in the city went down, and by Sunday evening, the accrued weight of the precipitation caused many rooftops to give way, sending torrents of water pouring into the buildings' interiors. It was a depressing preamble to what should have been a joyful holiday weekend. Back in Hillsboro, the storm finally began to let up on Sunday—prompting Emma and her parents to reconsider their holiday plans. Hearing that the trains would start running again on Monday morning, they decided to go home after all.

Monday and Tuesday, December 24 and 25, 1883. Bright and early on Christmas Eve, the Bonds—along with John Montgomery and the many others who had found themselves stranded in Hillsboro—caught the train to Litchfield. There, the Bonds transferred to the Wabash and continued on to Taylorville. However, in an apparent revision of his own plans, Montgomery disembarked in Litchfield to wait for a northbound train to Springfield. The purpose of his detour drew plenty of speculation. Some attributed his decision to prudence, saying "he was afraid to pass through Taylorville."[5] In truth, that was a very real possibility. But others believed there was a different explanation—one that carried dark repercussions for Emma.

The members of the jury, not by choice, spent a quiet Christmas Eve with only each other as company. Though it gave them little solace, they were treated to a sumptuous Christmas feast of "turkey, oysters, and all the delicacies of the season."[6] At the Bond farm, the entire family came together over a splendid turkey dinner—the main course harvested from the family's large flock. Their tradition called for the meal to be followed by a spirited celebration of music, replete with singing, piano playing, and, of course, a lively dose of Pa Bond's fiddling. But try as they might, they could not marshal their usual holiday exuberance.

They weren't the only ones for whom the holiday proved less than joyful. John Montgomery, who had detoured to Springfield, never made it home, leaving Mattie and their children to spend Christmas without him. A wire from downstate to Chicago on Christmas Eve indicated that when Montgomery left Springfield, he returned directly to Hillsboro, where he passed the holiday with his fellow defendants. Recent talk had emerged that the defense was concerned about its case and thus was contemplating a new plan of attack. On Christmas Eve, the *Tribune* leaked the rest of the story—that "as a last resort," the defense was going to introduce the "abortion theory."[7] Montgomery's side trip was for the alleged purpose of talking to Emma's Springfield doctor, in hopes of garnering proof that she had undergone an abortion. It was an obvious act of desperation—on Montgomery's part, if not the defense's. Here it was, the most blessed season of the year, and the rumors were growing ever more sinister. Previously, the nastiest ones had targeted the defendants—their behavior, their alibis, their character. Only on rare occasions had the Bond family found itself in a similar corner.

While the suggestion of an abortion was ugly enough, unbeknownst to the Bonds, more nefarious rumors were about to surface, and the press had no qualms about peddling the worst of them: "EMMA BOND. Belief That Her Mental Condition Will Be Questioned by the Defense. Statements Derogatory to Miss Bond's Character Attributed to the State's Attorney. The Defense Said to Have Some Startling Developments in Reserve—an Attorney's Letters." It looked like readers were going to be treated to every detail of the scheme to discredit the victim:

A paper published in Springfield contained an article which purports to have come from a couple of Taylorville gentlemen, and contains some statements which, it is said, came from the lips of State's Attorney Drennan. The article in question says that shortly after the outrage, Mr. Drennan and his wife went out to see Miss Bond and that while there, Mrs. Drennan had a private talk with the unfortunate Miss Bond, in which the latter asked Mrs. Drennan's advice, saying: "I have gotten myself into a terrible fix and don't know what to do. I don't like to make up a story, but will have to or they will find it all out, and in that case I would be ruined." The article says that Mrs. Drennan told her husband and he told others, so it leaked out.[8]

Drennan issued a prompt and potent denial, stating that the story was pure bunk and that he "had never said anything that could by hook or crook be so construed." What's more, he was willing to sign "an affidavit that his wife had never told anyone else anything of the kind." Maggie Drennan issued a disclaimer of her own, also volunteering to give an affidavit swearing that she "never spoke to Miss Bond about her trouble." Obviously, the press knew how to boost its readership—put out any salacious story that was making the rounds, then dispute its validity. The *Tribune*'s rebuttal came in the next paragraph: "The paper that published and the parties from whom the story emanated are being thoroughly denounced today, everyone saying that never before was such a lot of lies published."[9] Decatur's *Republican* backpedaled, too, noting that the Drennans were "very indignant over the report alluded to." Where it had originated, they had no idea, but they believed it was most likely the work of "someone who desired to acquire a little newspaper notoriety."[10]

It also sounded as if the defense might go so far as to question Emma's mental stability. Of course, the shadowy specter of hysteria had already been raised in the same breath as Emma's name. Only this time, she would be lucky to escape intact, if the latest report was true: "The physicians have all been notified to appear at court again this week to give expert testimony as to Miss Bond's mental condition. It is understood that McFarland of Jacksonville has been consulted and will probably go to Hillsboro to tell what he knows."[11] Although this said that McFarland was "consulted," more than likely it was he who approached the defense and offered to share his expertise at the trial. Certainly, his fame had diminished after he was snubbed as a witness at the Guiteau trial. But the Bond case had the power to propel him back into the headlines, both near and far, and he knew it.

So much hearsay: Emma had had an abortion, John Montgomery was after the proof, and Drennan and his wife were keeping secrets; Emma was mentally unstable, and Dr. McFarland was ready to say so. If that wasn't enough, an older attorney, B. F. Burnett of Taylorville, was promoting a theory that there had been no rape at all—just a lot of lies from the victim. Burnett, who had ties to Springfield, was being convincingly linked to a handbill recently distributed in the capital city: "Burnett has a letter-head, on the back of which is printed a circular claiming the innocence of the defendants, one paragraph of which is printed in black type, and says that no outrage was ever committed on Miss Bond. In sections where this is not known, his letters poison the minds of the people and they have looked upon Miss Bond's story with considerable distrust."[12]

Burnett had been following the case from the very beginning. He had attended the entire hearing in Taylorville, and not a day went by that he wasn't sitting in the pews of the Hillsboro courtroom, taking notes. The man seemed to have an obsessive fascination with the case; he had followed its every nuance and turn, had considered every legality and all of the pursuant ramifications. Though a lawyer, his interest far exceeded that of his peers.

In addition to Burnett's theory that no rape had occurred, another was being advanced by a young lawyer who claimed to have inside knowledge of the defense's plans. While this person wasn't naming any names, he was predicting some new surprises in the case:

"Why," said he, "before Saturday night the Judge, jury, and attorneys will be perfectly willing to let at least two of the present defendants loose."

"Do you think someone else had a hand in the ravishment of Miss Bond?"

"Well, yes; I think two of the men on trial are innocent and will go free, and when they do, then look out, for it will not be long until a witness who has been on the stand is brought back and made to answer for this crime. There is another man up in that neighborhood that is none too good to take a hand in just such a crime, but his name I will not give out just at present. You can depend on the new development."[13]

The informant was tight-lipped about his source. But the *Tribune* had some thoughts on the identity of the man called "none too good." It reported: "Mr. Drennan declared that the story that Sammy Heinlein was concerned in the outrage of Miss Bond and that his father, Laurence Heinlein, was cognizant of the fact is equally as absurd . . . if required to do so, he will bring forward a dozen witnesses who will swear that Sammy Heinlein was in Grove City the entire day and night of the 29th of June, 1882. There have been half a dozen other reports concerning the case in circulation, which it has been ascertained have no foundation whatsoever in fact."[14]

Unfortunately, not even the solemnity of the season was enough to silence the claptrap surrounding the trial. Drennan undoubtedly found no time to share visions of sugarplums with his children that Christmas, since he had his hands full trying to keep ahead of all the rumors.

22

The defendants do not intend to rely wholly on an alibi, but will endeavor to show that Miss Bond is HYSTERICAL and therefore of unsound mind and not to be relied upon.
    —Chicago Tribune, *December 26, 1883*

Wednesday, December 26, 1883. The holiday break over, Christmas was quickly downgraded to a warm memory. Evidently, the widely read *Tribune* had jumped the gun with its McFarland prediction. The *Republican* set the record straight: "Dr. McFarland will be remembered as the Illinois physician who offered to testify at the Guiteau trial at Washington. It is said that he has a theory that the greater portion of mankind is insane to some degree, and it was feared by the friends of the prosecution that if he was called, he would declare Miss Bond a lunatic. He will not be called and this fear, therefore, is unnecessary."[1]

Obviously, McFarland's outspokenness could still generate controversy. But, given his tainted reputation, not using him in the trial had to be one of the defense's better decisions, although he was probably bristling over the exclusion. For defense attorney McCaskill, the first order of business on Wednesday was to gather the press members and assure them that his team had no intention of calling or recalling any medical experts, including Emma's personal physicians. Such an approach "was not warranted by anything he or his associates knew."[2] It sounded as if Montgomery had decided to poke around Springfield without the sanction of his attorneys.

At eleven o'clock that day, everyone was back in place and eager to get on with it, especially with the New Year looming. The only people missing were the Bonds; Emma and her family did not return to Hillsboro until that evening. However, there was no shortage of Montgomery and Pettus kin waiting in the wings. Minnie Pettus was recalled to answer a few more questions about her brother. She established that he was wearing dark pants on June 29, as was Clementi. Both wore the same clothes all day. Minnie also confirmed that her brother had not changed his clothes, even after swimming the cattle across the branch.

Owen Hart, Lee Pettus's brother-in-law, followed. He testified that on June 29 he had returned to the Pettus house to pick up his wife, Cora, at approximately five o'clock. At that time, he had noticed both Pettus and Clementi in the wagon. When asked whether he'd seen Montgomery there too, he admitted that he had not lain eyes on him the entire day. Again, something seemed amiss, since several had testified that Cora and Owen were both present at the noontime meal, along with John and Mattie. When the defense inquired as to how long he had stayed that evening, he responded that he had been there just long enough to get Cora.

Like Pettus, Montgomery had a brother-in-law ready to vouch for his whereabouts on the day of the crime. James Allen, who lived at John Sr.'s house with his wife, Amanda (John's sister), told of seeing John Jr. there around one o'clock, when the defendant stopped by to help hive the bees. Later, Allen saw Montgomery talking to two men near the Pettus house, between six and seven. The witness's next remark, however, must have caused a stir in the courtroom—unless the *Tribune* misprinted it: "On cross-exam, the witness said he saw Miss Bond at old man Montgomery's that afternoon about three o'clock. Montgomery went away but witness did not know whether he left before Miss Bond did or not."[3] With each passing day, the number of contradictory statements grew more and more mind-boggling. What was to blame for all of the inconsistencies? Was it the scarcity of clocks, the frailties of human memory, or the duplicity of the witnesses?

Three of Lee's sisters—Mattie, Ona, and Minnie—had already testified. Now it was Cora's turn. Yes, she'd spent that Thursday at her mother's home. And yes, she had seen her brother-in-law John there. In the morning. She stated that Clementi had spent part of the day in the wagon and "part of the time lying on the kitchen steps." But unlike her younger sisters Minnie and Ona, who insisted that Emma came to practice between three o'clock and three thirty, Cora thought the teacher had come by somewhat earlier—"between two and three o'clock." She did agree with her sisters on one thing: Emma had stayed only thirty minutes. And she had seen her brother and Mr. Clementi *after* Miss Bond left: "Lee was sitting on the kitchen steps and Clementi was in the wagon."[4]

Wednesday's session had kicked off late—just before noon. Nevertheless, Phillips wanted to keep the day short, perhaps because the participants—the lawyers in particular—needed to ease themselves back into the mindset that a serious trial required. Thursday's pace would be much more demanding. The Bonds would be in attendance again, and, like everyone else, they could not wait to hear what the last defendant would have to say.

Thursday, December 27, 1883. At last, it was John C. Montgomery's turn. He gave his age as thirty-three and acknowledged that he was married and the father of three.[5] He stated that he had lived in the same area nearly all of his life and that his current home sat a couple miles east of the Montgomery schoolhouse. Thornton proceeded to throw one question after another at the defendant. All required only short answers—a good way to avoid opening the door for the prosecution. What time had he taken his family to the Pettus home on June 29? Between ten and eleven in the morning. He ate dinner there at noon and visited for awhile before leaving for his father's house, up the road three or four hundred yards. Had he seen anyone there? Yes, Sherman Yockey. The defendant and his father left there together, about three o'clock, headed down the road to Joe Younker's. Did they see anyone else? Yes, little Charlie Masters was sitting on the coalhouse at the school. The two men didn't stop to talk, but the defendant called out to the boy. When asked about the location of Joe Younker's place, Montgomery said it was about a quarter-mile south of the schoolhouse.

According to the witness, when he got to Younker's, a number of people were already gathered there. Besides Joe and his wife, Mattie, there was Joe's brother George. It was unlikely that Thornton asked Montgomery about his relationship to the Younkers, but, in fact, they weren't just neighbors. They were also relatives—Joe and George Younker were first cousins of the elder John Montgomery. And the relationship was even more complicated: Joe's wife, Mattie, was John Jr.'s sister. The defendant gave a longer answer than usual as he described his visit at Joe's. Shortly after arriving, he went into the field to check the corn with Joe and George. About that time, John Morgret happened by. All of them "went to the wheat field and looked at a cradle and tried to work it but could not." So they sat on the fence in the field and talked for awhile. When asked what the group had talked about, the defendant replied, "About Guiteau, who had been hanged the day before."[6] If this really was Montgomery's remark, apparently no one—not even the prosecutor—caught the error. For on Thursday, June 29, 1882, the convicted assassin Guiteau was still a full day away from his appointment with the gallows.

Thornton continued to bombard his client with questions. How long did everyone remain together? About ninety minutes. Then what did they do? Montgomery replied: "We all went to Morgret's house. George Younker and his wife then left for home and I started for Mrs. Pettus' house." What time was that? "The sun was then about an hour from setting."[7] On a day the sun set at about seven thirty, John's own estimate placed his departure for the Pettus home around six thirty.[8] The defense lawyer continued to lead John through a timeline of what he'd done after parting company with the other farmers. John remembered it this way: "I met Sherman Yockey and my father in the road. On arriving at Mrs. Pettus's, I heard her say that Lee was mowing. Emanuel Clementi was there. I got out my team, took supper, and left with my wife and

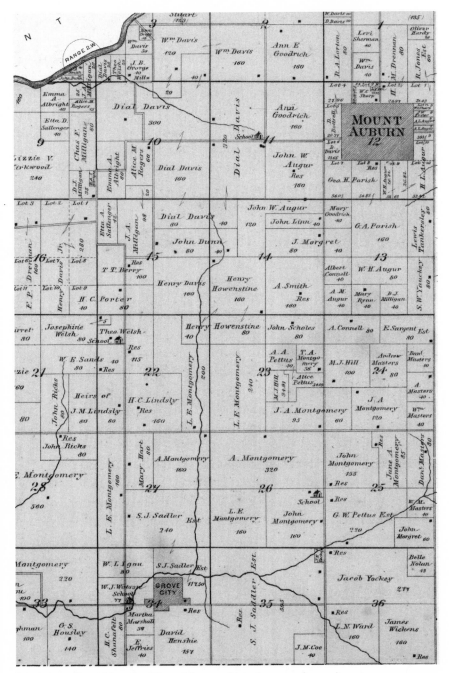

Mt. Auburn Township, 1891. (Copyright www.historicmapworks.com)

children for home. The sun was then down. I saw John Campbell as I was driving home, also John Morgret on horseback. I got home at dusk and shortly after went to bed. I was never in the schoolhouse loft until the next morning and never pared a toenail there."[9] Part of this statement contradicted what he'd told several others—that is, that he was talking with his father right by the schoolhouse between five and six o'clock and from there walked over to the Pettus house. That part, he completely omitted. Furthermore, if John had seen Lee mowing weeds, as others claimed, why hadn't he said that specifically? Instead, he stated that he heard Mrs. Pettus say it. Clearly, certain details didn't add up. But Montgomery had served up plenty of names of people he had encountered, people who could presumably back up his story.

Thornton jumped to Friday, quizzing the defendant about his visit to the crime scene. How long had he stayed at the schoolhouse that morning? "Three-quarters of an hour." He continued, "I was in the loft with others when someone asked me to cut a piece of wood from the inside boarding; [I] cut out the piece of board; [it] had nothing to do with the Emma Bond outrage." Montgomery testified that he'd used his right, adding that he "could use a knife easily with his right hand." Later, he explained, "I left [the school] with my cousin and went south to Grove City where there was also excitement about the rape.... I stayed at Grove City until four o'clock in the afternoon and then went home."[10]

Here, Thornton asked his client to describe the clothes he was wearing on June 29. He described overalls and a colored shirt, mostly brown with small white stripes. He'd worn the same thing all week, said Montgomery. On his feet he wore boots; he didn't wear shoes in the summer. He remembered that neither Clementi nor Pettus was wearing a coat. Both had on dark shirts. If by "dark," John meant red and buff striped for Clementi and blue and white dotted for Pettus, then his testimony aligned with what others had already stated. Thornton quizzed Montgomery about the comments he had allegedly made right before his arrest. These questions, according to the press, were aimed at "getting denials and explanations for a swarm of little circumstances upon which the prosecution seem[ed] to rely for his conviction."[11] In answering, the defendant refuted every charge—across the board—that had thus far been leveled by the State's witnesses: "Montgomery denied he ever told Heinlein or Swick to tell Lee Pettus to stand firm. Or that he said, when told Pettus and Clementi had been arrested and the former made a written confession implicating him, 'My God, what shall I do?' He did not remember saying any such thing. He never told the crowd that people were in two [sic] great a hurry to arrest him and if they had waited a while, they would have got something out of him, but now they would not get a thing."[12]

Nor did his repudiations end there. He also never "told Charles Jacobey and William Armstrong that he and his father were standing by the schoolhouse while the outrage was going on."[13] As for the jailhouse conversations reported by Burritt and Meyers, those never happened either. In answer to a final question, John emphatically denied being at the schoolhouse and having any hand in the outrage. His interrogation took an hour and a half. But if he was telling the truth, several prosecution witnesses were at risk of being charged with perjury—foremost, Swick and Heinlein. Nothing was said in the papers about the State's cross-exam of the lead suspect. Either Montgomery had done enough damage to his own case without the State's help, or the cross-exam had been so ineffective that there was nothing worth reporting.

The Younker brothers followed Montgomery to the stand. Joe swore he was with the defendant continuously between three thirty and six thirty Thursday afternoon. According to the *New York Times*, "He was cross-examined very closely and has proved to be the best witness the defense has yet had." George Younker's statements further corroborated Montgomery's alibi. George "was minutely cross-examined but his evidence was unshaken."[14]

The case appeared to be coming together for the man at greatest risk. But all of that was about to be undone by the next witness. The bailiff walked to the back of the room, opened the imposing door, and called out for Mrs. Sarah Younker. This was George's wife. What she was about to say as a defense witness was sure to cause a rumble. Sarah, it seems, had gone with her husband to Joe's on the day "the events and circumstances as given by the Younker brothers and John C. Montgomery" had taken place. But she didn't remember that day as Thursday, June 29—the day of the outrage—as the others had declared; rather, insisted Sarah, her visit to Joe's actually took place on Friday, the day after the outrage. She cited certain memories that seemed to add weight to her belief—namely, it was the same day she learned of the outrage. And she'd first heard that news from Joe's wife, Mattie. Further, Sarah was adamant that "she had not been [there] nor seen Mrs. Joe Younker for some days before and did not see her for three weeks afterwards."[15] Of that, she was positive. Although the defense did its best to break Sarah, she was resolute.

Then again, if what Sarah believed was true—that all the neighbors had assembled at the Younker farm on Friday—it was harder to explain Montgomery's presence in Grove City the day after the crime. Several prosecution witnesses had already testified to seeing and speaking with him in the Grove that afternoon. True, other than Montgomery—who said that he'd gone there midday, directly from the schoolhouse, and stayed until around four—none had given specific times. Was Sarah just forgetful? Or confused? Or was she a lone voice in a dense forest of orchestrated lies? She was, in fact, the only person out of the two Younker couples who was not a blood relative of John Montgomery. Also, there was Montgomery's inadvertent reference to the discussion of Guiteau's hanging on Thursday, which was an impossibility, since Guiteau had not been hanged until high noon on Friday, June 30.

Joe's wife, Mattie—John Montgomery's oldest sister—testified next on her brother's behalf. She did not agree with Sarah, insisting that Thursday was the day her brother had come by. Compounding the confusion, however, Mattie also stated that Thursday was when she told Sarah about the outrage. And that, of course, was another impossibility. The longer Mattie was on the stand, the deeper the quagmire became. By the time she was finally excused, she had also claimed that "Mrs. George [Sarah Younker] was at her house Friday and brought her children to go to a picnic."[16] Clearly, one of the Younker women was suffering from a profound memory lapse. Lara Younker, Joe and Mattie's sixteen-year-old daughter, took the stand and sided with her parents and Montgomery. But when the prosecutor delved further, comparing her trial statements with the ones she'd made at the hearing, the girl's recall seemed deficient.

The defense managed to reclaim some lost ground with its next witness, John Morgret. As positive as Sarah Younker was that the gathering at Joe's took place on Friday, Morgret was equally convinced that it was Thursday. The men—Montgomery included—lingered in Younker's wheat field that day, said Morgret. And not once did he "lose sight of Montgomery during the time he was supposed to have been in the loft with the unfortunate school mistress."[17] While Morgret was the father of one of Miss Bond's pupils, he was also one more in the long list of defense witnesses who had familial ties to the Montgomerys. His sister Harriett had been the wife of John's uncle Ira, though the couple had long since passed away.

Several others came forth to back up John's alibi. Granted, some of their statements covered only small segments of John's day. But taken as a whole, the testaments to his whereabouts on the day of the crime seemed to bode well for John. The defense felt it had proven "a very strong alibi, chiefly through the statements of John Morgret." State's Attorney Drennan didn't see it quite that way, though, vowing to the press that he could "completely impeach Morgret's testimony."[18]

With Thursday winding down, Thornton announced that he wanted to bring back a handful of people, after which the defense would be done. The State, in turn, told the judge that it had only a few witnesses to call in rebuttal. Here, Phillips reminded everyone that court would be held on Saturday. The judge had made every effort to keep the trial moving, but there was simply no way to predict how long the closing arguments would last, especially since several of the talented lawyers who sat before him were known to have penchants for making long speeches. Sunday, of course, was the Lord's Day—a day of rest. And then it would be Monday, the last day of the calendar year.

But the end was definitely near, and with it came a resurgence of talk about what the jury might do. Days earlier, the *Tribune* had opined that the outcome still seemed a fair certainty: "The best lawyers here do not see how the defense can hope to save him [Montgomery] after Miss Bond's positive identification of him as one of the men who assaulted her and that if he is guilty, there seems little doubt of the guilt of Pettus and Clementi as the three were almost constantly together."[19] But then the defense had gone on to do an adequate, if not remarkable, job of shoring up John's story. As a result, the public's confidence in a guilty verdict was starting to slip: "Thursday's evidence makes the action of the jury less a matter of course than has hitherto been acknowledged. No one looks for an acquittal, but unless the state can break [John's] testimony, it will be no surprise if the jury disagree."[20]

For the defendants, a hung jury would be a far cry from total exoneration; however, it would be preferable to a conviction. Considering the public's long-standing rancor over the case, a hung jury might be the suspects' last, best hope. But even that could end in disaster; a great many still hankered for their own brand of justice, should the jury fail to deliver. Anyone who doubted that need only look at the glut of mail Mr. Bond had been receiving. Throughout December, letters had poured in from all over the country with offers to provide assistance to carry out what the August 1882 mob had failed to do. The latest had come from Galveston, Texas; its author described himself as the "chief of an organization for the punishment of crime," and he promised "to furnish forty men on short notice to hang the three defendants if Bond desired." Of course, Emma's father wasn't about to accept that kind of help. As a Montana paper pointed out: "Bond gives no countenance whatever to such communications."[21] Still, if the jurors did not see eye to eye, there was the risk of another uprising.

Friday morning, December 28, 1883. When court opened on Friday, the prosecution told Judge Phillips it would call nine to fifteen people in rebuttal. Based on both sides' revised estimates, it looked as if the actual testimony would conclude on Saturday. The defense finished with Lee's brother, George, the only Pettus not at his mother's home on June 29.[22] George testified that he had seen Montgomery on Friday, the thirtieth, first at the schoolhouse and then in the Grove later that afternoon, when he was talking to Swick and Heinlein. When asked about the latter, the witness remembered something slightly less incriminating than what the prosecution had represented. According to George, Montgomery asked him to tell Lee "that a warrant was out for his arrest and that he had better come to Grove City." And yes, his uncle Laurence did ask him "to tell

Lee that if he knew anything about the others, he had better give them away."
George testified that Lee's response was that "he didn't know anything."[23] By
mid-morning, Thornton had run out of witnesses, although he kept glancing at
his pocket watch every so often, as if waiting for someone else to appear. When
no one did, the defense rested its case. The time was ten thirty in the morning.

23

If they could impeach Miss Bond's testimony no jury could convict the defendants. They failed at this, and now are fighting at every vulnerable point of the evidence submitted in rebuttal.
—Decatur Review, *December 30, 1883*

Friday afternoon, December 28, 1883. When Emma was called as the first rebuttal witness, she was nowhere in sight. Her father stood, saying he would have to get his daughter, who was resting nearby. As if on cue, spectators began pouring into the courtroom, taking up every last inch in the gallery. As the room buzzed in anticipation, the room's rear door opened. All heads turned—expecting to see the victim. Instead, in came John Montgomery's wife, Mattie. It was a timely appearance, to be sure. She was the perfect maternal portrait. Even the staunchest Bond supporter could not help but feel empathy for the young mother as she walked slowly up the center aisle, cradling her two-month-old son. A space was cleared for her directly behind her husband. Moments later, the door creaked open again. This time, the paternal-looking Mr. Bond entered with Emma on his arm. She wore a light cloak and a dark red hat, her bangs peeking out from under its brim. He guided her gently up the same aisle, past the same sympathetic gazes from the same curious onlookers. Past Mattie, past Montgomery, past Pettus, past Clementi. Drennan waited patiently while Emma settled herself into the witness chair.

The prosecutor directed her to the afternoon of Thursday, June 29, asking if she had noticed the wagon in the Pettus yard that afternoon. She had seen it on her way to the Pettus house and again when she left. How close did she come to "the wagon in which Clementi and Pettus claim to have been during the afternoon"? Thornton bellowed an objection. As the two sides went back and forth at length, Emma began to feel faint. The judge excused her, and she was taken into his chambers. When she reappeared, Phillips overruled the objection. The prosecutor repeated his question, and she responded that she had come "within a few yards" of the wagon.[1] And she hadn't seen Mr. Pettus or Mr. Clementi in the wagon, either time; she hadn't seen anyone there at all.

Drennan turned to a critical part of young Charlie's testimony. Under direct examination, the lad had first stated "that he did not leave the schoolhouse during that afternoon recess." But under cross, he had vacillated—admitting to a short absence. Drennan wanted to ascertain what, if anything, Emma knew about that. She responded that Charlie had told her that he went to get a drink from the Pettus well while she was rehearsing. It didn't take much to figure out the logic behind that line of questioning, but the *Tribune* spelled it out: "This point is quite important as it is the theory of the prosecution that Miss Bond's assailants affected an entrance into the loft during the afternoon recess. If Charlie Masters went to Pettus's at the afternoon recess, this would leave the road [open] for the men to get into the loft and not be seen."[2]

At this point, Thornton "submitted an affidavit saying he gave notice, before the evidence was taken, that he would introduce one particular witness." Apparently that witness, who was to have testified on Friday morning, had suddenly taken ill. After forty-five minutes of haggling and getting nowhere, he motioned for a continuance until the next term of the court. The missing witness, Mrs. Nellie Woodruff, had some very relevant information "affecting Miss Bond's identification of John Montgomery," argued Thornton.

The State countered that Nellie's testimony had "no bearing upon the question of identification . . . that it was solely for the purpose of impeachment and that a continuance could not be granted for such purpose." The judge concurred with the State and denied the motion. However, Phillips did allow a written statement from Nellie to be entered into the record. And what was Nellie supposed to tell the jury, had she made it to Hillsboro? Well, if the *Review* was correct, it had to do with something Emma had supposedly said to her—to the effect that "she did not see her assailants because she was drawn into the loft so quickly and that she only knew who they were by supposition."[3]

Who was Nellie Woodruff? The *New York Times* referred to her as Mrs. Woodruff. The 1880 census revealed that, in all likelihood, she was the widow Ellen Woodruff—a milliner from Taylorville who was a dozen years older than Emma.[4] Based on the age difference, she was probably not a close confidante of the victim but more likely someone who'd sold hats to the Bond sisters. When Nellie's written statement was read back to Emma for comment, she flatly denied having made any such remark. She was excused.

Martin Swick was then recalled. He confirmed that he had passed the schoolhouse on the afternoon of the twenty-ninth, around three thirty. He had seen a wagon in front of the Pettus house when he went by, and "looked in the wagon but saw neither Clementi nor Pettus."[5] He saw nobody in the yard. But he did remember seeing Miss Bond and little Charlie at the school door.

Drennan also brought back mail carrier McNeil, who explained that he followed a regular route, passing the same places at approximately the same time every day. And he always passed the Montgomery School at about three o'clock. On June 29, he looked in the direction of the Pettus yard but didn't see anyone there; however, he "met old man Montgomery forty or fifty yards from the schoolhouse." He stated that the man was alone. Next, James Armstrong and Rufus Housley were recalled, and each affirmed that there was a four- to five-foot hedge on the east side of the school, near the road.

Friday's final witness provided one of the more detrimental testimonies against John C. Montgomery. Dr. J. G. Harvey of Grove City was asked about a comment the defendant had made to him in August 1882, regarding the day of the outrage. The doctor remembered the conversation vividly, saying that he asked Montgomery if "he could account for his whereabouts on the afternoon of June 29." The suspect "said he could, all but about an hour and a half, and that was what hurt."[6] Montgomery seemed his own worst enemy, considering that a large part of the case against him stemmed from his own offhanded remarks. Of course, there was also the other thing—Emma's dramatic and compelling identification of him during the first week of the trial. The *Review* weighed in on his chances: "The defense has proven a strong alibi for Montgomery but whether that alibi can overcome the strength of Miss Bond's identification of Montgomery is a question which worries the defense. If they could impeach Miss Bond's testimony, no jury could convict the defendants. They failed at this and now are fighting at every vulnerable part of the evidence submitted in rebuttal."[7]

Friday's session pushed on into the evening hours, but progress slowed as motion after motion was raised, each demanding its own germane argument. As the minutes ticked away, it was obvious that the lateness of the hour was affecting everyone's clarity of thought. Phillips saw no alternative but to adjourn for the night with a handful of rebuttal witnesses still sitting in the outer hallway.

Saturday, December 1883. The main disagreement Friday night and Saturday morning centered on the State's effort to put stenographer John T. Montgomery on the stand as a rebuttal witness. The prosecutor saw the transcript of evidence as an extremely valuable tool, and he wanted the court reporter "to read two or three questions, and answers as given by Mattie Montgomery at the earlier hearing." The defense jumped all over that move, and a lengthy battle erupted over "the reliability of the stenographer's notes."[8] That seemed strange coming from the defense, considering that just two days earlier Thornton had asked John T.

to read back parts of Swick's and Heinlein's hearing testimony. However, the State was now asking that the court reporter be sworn in as an actual witness, something the defense called "an unheard of proceeding."[9]

To impeach Mattie Montgomery, said Drennan, the jury needed to hear all of her previous testimony. After a lengthy discussion on Saturday morning, Phillips ruled that "the notes could be used by the prosecution, but all of the testimony and not just the part given by Mrs. Montgomery must be considered for the purpose of impeaching the testimony of Mrs. Montgomery."[10] So John T., with bulky transcript in hand, seated himself on the stand and read back witnesses' testimony from the hearing. The result: "Nearly the entire morning was taken up reading the notes of the former [hearing] where the testimony conflicted with that given here, the counsel for defense making objection after objection on account of alleged irrelevancy."[11] The *Tribune* praised the State's move, saying it provided a substantial boost to its case.

The prosecution needed to address one last matter: Clementi's honesty, which nearly everyone who knew him agreed he was sorely lacking. The State called several men from the Grove City area, and each affirmed that the suspect had a distinct knack for distorting the truth. Sam Sadler—one of the most respected men in the neighborhood—said that when it came to telling the truth, Clementi's history was very poor. James Wickens, James Armstrong, Rufus Housley, and Jacob Yockey expressed even stronger opinions. Wickens told the court that "of all the people he knew, he would be slower to believe Clementi than anyone else, unless it was corroborated by substantial people."[12] Armstrong's words also carried significant weight, since he had once been Clementi's employer. But when the State tried to call a sixth character witness, the judge sided with the defense—five was enough. So, with the afternoon mellowing into evening, the State announced it was done. Immeasurable looks of relief spread across the faces of the jurymen, only to evaporate when the judge announced that summations would begin immediately after the supper break.

But first, the two factions and the judge had to hash out a lineup for the closing arguments. In a show of compromise, the two teams agreed to alternate turns. Amos Miller, Montgomery County's prosecutor, would take the floor first. He would be followed by John McBride for the defense, and then back and forth it would go. Evidently, there was a lot of bickering over who would get to speak and when. After all, this was an opportunity for each lawyer to showcase his own talents, and at least one had his eye on a political future. By the time the speaking order was finalized, the reporters—who had taken notes feverishly during the discussion—were completely lost. As a result, at least four different versions of the agreed-upon agenda appeared in newspapers around the state. One reporter from the *Republican* was apparently so confused that his paper's

Monday edition carried two different schedules—neither of which matched those in the *Decatur Review* or the *Chicago Tribune*. No matter the order, one thing was certain—several attorneys from both sides would be addressing the jury in closing. Knowing lawyers, and Phillips did know most of this group personally, it was obvious that the end was still several days away; there were just too many stage-hungry orators vying for a piece of the third and final act.

Certainly, another extended break for the New Year would only prolong the agony of all concerned. So Phillips polled his jurors about a second holiday interruption. In a show of unanimity, they agreed to forge ahead with no further breaks. They seemed to know that nothing short of a miracle would get them home before the New Year, anyway. So it was set. Right after the supper recess, closing arguments would commence. Then, come Monday morning, the speeches would resume and continue throughout New Year's Eve and New Year's Day, or however long it might take. But, other than for the Sabbath, there would be no more delays.

Had the jurors known the estimates the papers were already preparing—of how long each lawyer might speak—they would have been totally demoralized, assuming they weren't already. McBride, it was predicted, would consume at least four hours. And then there was this formidable forecast: "It is estimated that Judge Vandeveer will speak for at least six hours, and those who know him best predict that he will require twelve hours in which to make his argument."[13] It was hard to imagine what all of the other capable attorneys had in them. As it turned out, the press estimates weren't too far off target.

24

Now that all the evidence has been heard, the popular question is, what will the jury do? No one . . . can be heard to say they believe the jury will acquit.
—Decatur Daily Republican, *December 31, 1883*

Saturday night, December 29, 1883. The State had used four days to present its case, the defense six. Opening arguments and rebuttals had consumed one day each. And though much of the witness testimony had been riveting, the summations were expected to be the climax of the entire show. With those set to begin right after the evening break, the courtroom emptied out quickly, and when it reopened an hour later, the same large crowd filed back in for the evening encore.

Outside, temperatures hovered near zero while inside, State's Attorney Amos Miller delivered a heated plea for conviction. The audience sat in rapt silence for four long hours as he paced back and forth in front of the jury box. By the time McBride finally took the floor for the defense, it was getting very late, and yet not a single spectator rose to leave. The lead-off man for the defense could have gone on for an additional four hours; but Phillips decided to call it a night, just two and a half hours into McBride's speech. He would have to finish his argument on Monday.

Sunday, December 30, 1883. The Sabbath—a day for prayer, rest, and loved ones. But for the legal giants involved in the Bond case, Sunday was the day of final preparation—a chance to collect their thoughts and fashion their winning arguments. One day seemed hardly enough; yet had they been given thrice the time to prepare, it would not have been sufficient.

Neither side lacked in motivation. One side understood that the freedom of three men hinged on its skills. The other's goal was nothing less than obtaining retribution for a young woman's suffering. So the lawyers all stayed in Hillsboro that Sunday. Although lengthy speeches from both McBride and

Vandeveer were predicted, neither of these men would carry the larger burden for his respective team. For the defense, that task would be handled by Judge Anthony Thornton, considered the "heavyweight" of the defense team. For the State, the responsibility would fall to Judge Ben Edwards. And if, by some fluke, any of their team failed to address a pertinent detail or overlooked some critical argument, Edwards and Thornton would step in at the last minute to sway the jurors with their eloquent rhetoric.

For the jurors, Sunday was given over to quiet contemplation. Still banned from attending worship services, they had ample time to consider the finer points of the case and reflect on who was lying and who wasn't, whose memory was reliable and whose wasn't. As for the accused, only the good Lord knew what they were thinking about on that Sunday. If they were still hoping for salvation, perhaps there was a glimmer of hope in this assessment of the select few who controlled their fate: "The twelve jurors . . . are men of apparent inflexibility of character. There is not a vacillating outline in the makeup of any of them. Those who know these twelve . . . say they are men of strong personal convictions. It is generally thought they have already made up their minds. . . . It is believed that should the jury fail to agree at the outset, there will be no possibility of their ever arriving at a conclusion. Their unyielding dispositions will grow firmer with opposition, resulting in an agreement to disagree."[1]

The rest of the country probably spent Sunday second-guessing how the jury would vote. For a large percentage of the public, belief in the defendants' guilt had not faltered; if anything, it had grown stronger throughout the course of the trial. Nevertheless, in a few minds, subtle doubts did exist. The *Republican* dared to give voice to them: "The defense [claims], and not without some show of reason, that Miss Bond may be mistaken, that her extremely disturbed nervous condition made her liable to err when she attempted to pick out from among a hundred faces that of one of the men engaged in an assault upon her. If it can be impressed upon the minds of the jury that there was a probable mistake in the identification, the strongest point against a verdict of not guilty will have been overthrown."[2]

Part of the premise Mr. McBride had introduced in his Saturday night monologue, though he offered no proof, was that "possibly the wrong men [were] accused, and that others were concerned in the affair that [had] been to some extent under suspicion since the trial opened." It was always an effective way to interject doubt—by casting aspersions on the opposition's leading witnesses:

> Mr. McBride commented pointedly upon the testimony of Martin V. Swick . . . and called attention to his movements about the time of the outrage, characterizing them as at least very strange. It was shown that on the night

of the outrage, Mr. Swick went to a Justice of the Peace at Mt. Auburn and offered to pay a fine of $5, saying that he had been engaged in a fight near the Montgomery school house and had whipped a man. It is reported that there was blood upon his shirt at the time . . . while on the witness stand here [he] admitted that he had offered to pay a fine, but said that he had had no fight. This matter has never been explained fully and is looked upon as having some bearing, however remote, upon the Bond case. Mr. McBride claims that Swick and Laurence Heinlein have taken a very active part in the prosecution of Montgomery, Pettus and Clementi and that they constituted themselves detectives to ferret out the perpetrators of the crime immediately after its occurrence. Hints have been dropped that an investigation is now in progress which promises startling developments.[3]

Of course, this plan B strategy is as old as the legal profession. Any experienced and shrewd lawyer knows how to use it for utmost effect. And McBride was decidedly both. If he could plant a tiny seed of doubt, it might take root and grow, especially if the jury became hopelessly mired in the muck of deliberation.

For a handful of witnesses, a dark cloud hung heavily over the Sabbath. For, depending on the jury's decision, it was quite possible that their lives would be forever changed: "Several of the witnesses . . . have declared their intention of leaving the county in case [Montgomery, Pettus, and Clementi] are not convicted. Among these witnesses is Laurence Heinlein, an uncle of John C. Montgomery, and whose testimony was so damaging to Montgomery. He has his things all ready to ship to Missouri. Several witnesses against the accused have been threatened."[4] It sounded as if Heinlein was not alone in his plan to hightail it out of the area if the defendants walked free.

For the victim and her family, at least, Sunday fulfilled its promise as a day of rest and prayer. In fact, prayer was just about the only thing left in their arsenal. Emma and her parents did attend church that Sunday. Mr. Bond's most exalted prayer that day was almost certainly offered on behalf of his daughter—that she would soon be able to put the past behind her and move on with her life. His next plea may have echoed that which he had openly called for in the immediate aftermath of the crime: that the justice system would do its job and return a guilty verdict. Only then could he and Delia and his other girls let go of their angst for Emma. Last, he may have asked blessings for his cousin Sonny, truly the brother he'd never had, the man who had given so unselfishly of himself throughout the family's eighteen-month struggle.

Monday, December 31, 1883. Predictably, a great horde descended on the Hillsboro courthouse on the last day of the year. A good portion of those who came were from north of Taylorville. But a new faction was represented as well: many interested attorneys were in attendance, having come from near and far to observe, firsthand, one of the premier legal dramas of their day. It was the perfect opportunity to witness several of Illinois's finest in action.

Although Hillsboro was packed at an early hour, visitors continued to stream into the town throughout the day. Passengers deposited at the local depot scurried off to the courthouse—keen to escape the biting cold and even more so to catch the performances taking place inside. Waiting for Judge Phillips to enter, the defendants and their legal advisors whispered back and forth while the prosecution huddled in its own last-minute consultations. Extra deputies were strategically stationed around the edge of the room and at the doors—ready to thwart any potential outbursts, verbal or physical. Emma arrived in the company of her stepmother, Delia, and her father. When the doors were slammed shut at nine o'clock, an expectant hush settled over the gallery. Judge Phillips entered, took his place at the bench, and instructed McBride to resume his closing argument. The day's speeches unfolded as anticipated: "J. C. McBride finished . . . this morning and was followed by J. M. Taylor of Taylorville on behalf of the prosecution . . . these two gentlemen occupied about nine hours altogether. Mr. Taylor was followed by Judge McCaskill for the defense who spoke nearly five hours tonight and tomorrow morning Judge H. M. Vandeveer of Taylorville will reply to Judge McCaskill's speech."[5]

If McBride and Taylor used nine hours and there were the usual midday and suppertime breaks, then by the time McCaskill took the floor, it had to be eight o'clock, if not later. That meant Monday's session did not conclude until well past midnight, which suggests little heed was paid to the passing of the old year and the arrival of the new. No newspapers remarked on whether Monday's speakers were able to hold the jury's undivided attention for those fourteen hours. In all likelihood, they were not; even the most engaging of orators would be hard-pressed to do so.

Tuesday, January 1, 1884. It was reported that on New Year's morning juror Barringer was not feeling well. Perhaps Monday's extended session had been too much for him. Or maybe he had found his second wind after Monday's late session and decided to celebrate the New Year after all. Regardless of the root of his discomfort, he and his fellow jurors were all present on Tuesday morning. And at least the other eleven were eager to finish their civic duties, ready to return home and enjoy a belated Christmas with family. Other than the jurors and the accused, the only people more anxious for the trial's end had to be the Bonds, who let it be known that they would be staying in Hillsboro until a verdict was reached, no matter how long that might take.

Mr. Vandeveer spoke first on New Year's Day. Regrettably for the jurors, he possessed more stamina than most men half his age. For nearly five long hours, he paced back and forth in front of the jury box, hammering home point after logical point in favor of conviction. His appeal resonated throughout the halls of justice and commanded the full attention of all present, all except for Clementi, who sat reading a newspaper and feigning total indifference. Finally, his insolence became too much for Vandeveer. Turning toward the defense table, the lawyer reminded his audience of Clementi's remark that "he did not know who his bondsmen were." The defendant "dropped the [paper] and glared ferociously at his accuser." Having gotten the reaction he wanted, Vandeveer couldn't resist rattling off some of the man's other brash comments. Each sounded like an "expression of guilt."[6] When the lawyer got to the one in which Clementi ordered Pettus, "Shut up you little fool, what do you know about it?" the gallery erupted into thunderous applause. Each subsequent chide from Vandeveer set off a louder outburst than the one before. When the situation started to get out of hand, deputies were called upon to restore order. When the veteran attorney finally finished his speech, the court took a dinner break.

With appetites satiated and legs stretched, minds were once again able to focus. Thornton was to address the jury next, followed by Edwards. Fort Wayne's *Gazette* touched on the high points of Thornton's summation:

> He said that according to Miss Bond's story, a man dropped down from the loft and choked her, had to go to the other side of the school room for a chair, that while he was gone and when he first grabbed hold of her, Miss Bond made no outcry, though the thing was done in broad daylight and Mrs. Pettus's house was only 200 yards distant; that no outcry was made while this villain tied the shawl around her and handed her up to the man above. Then he said it had never been proved beyond Miss Bond's statement that an outrage had been actually committed. He said that the law made it very essential that the prosecuting witness should always be corroborated.[7]

Naturally, rapes seldom have witnesses—other than the victims and the assailants. Yet, as Thornton so astutely pointed out, "the two witnesses who could testify to [Emma's] condition when she got home that night, Mrs. Bond and Dr. Cornell, had never been presented by the prosecution." He then posed the very valid question: "Why not?"[8] It merited the jury's consideration. Why had the prosecution failed to put either one on the stand? Those were decisions seemingly devoid of rationale—particularly the failure to call the doctor. Today, a gynecological examination is usually done when a rape is alleged, but perhaps that wasn't standard practice in Emma's day. But at the least, the doctor or Mrs.

Bond, if not both, could have confirmed Emma's other injuries and her state of mind. Since the State had called Dr. Cornell at the preliminary hearing, his absence at the trial seemed all the more perplexing.

After five hours of commanding the stage, Thornton exited with a flourish, leaving the jurors with the compelling thought that maybe there had been no rape. A brief recess was taken, and then at precisely seven o'clock, Judge Ben Edwards stepped forth to deliver his final argument. This was the State's last chance to undo any damage left in Thornton's wake. Not one to be outdone by his peers, Edwards turned in what would later be called the trial's "most eloquent and forceful speech."[9] By the time he finished, the clock showed ten. There was nothing left to be said—by either camp. All the allegations had been leveled. All the unprovens had been addressed. For those who had watched, there was a sense of having witnessed a well-choreographed masterpiece. But it was the twelve reluctant souls of the jury who would now have to decide which troupe had turned in the best—and the most believable—performance.

The jurors would get their instructions first thing Wednesday morning, said Judge Phillips. And with a tap of the gavel, the day was over. Not everyone had stayed until the end; those who did filed quietly out into the night, only to be hit by a blast of air so cold that it hurt to inhale. Snow had come down heavily throughout most of the morning and afternoon, veiling the landscape in a fresh, ethereal white, but there was no moonlight to reflect off of its pristine surface. Not a soul cared to linger, and within a few minutes Hillsboro's Main Street stood desolate and dark.

The half-foot of snow that had fallen on the first weekend of the trial had been greeted as a welcome change from the barren gray of early winter. A lesser snowfall had followed that midweek. Then, during the Christmas recess, the messy blizzard had come through, and, all too quickly, the merry music of sleigh bells and the soft shushing of blades on powder had lost all their magic. Now, bitter January had already delivered its first hard punch, piling several more inches of aggravation atop the old. Although the New Year's storm made a rapid retreat on Tuesday night, by Wednesday morning, thermometers would plunge to twelve below. Fortunately, with the verdict imminent, the Bonds were exactly where they needed to be. Unfortunately, life—like the weather—can be unpredictable. And when it is, circumstances beyond anyone's control can intercede and change everything.

Along with Emma and her family, most of those with an interest in the case had braved winter's hardships to be present for the verdict. One exception was cousin Sonny. On New Year's Day, he bundled himself up in his warm woolen overcoat and spent the afternoon hoofing around the Taylorville square, settling his business matters from the previous year. It was a practical way to begin any new year. About two o'clock, he stopped at Milligan's Store to buy some cotton rope for his farm. After chatting briefly with the owner, he headed for his home on the northeast edge of town. He arrived to find the new snow piled up on his front porch, so, despite the falling temperatures, he traipsed out to the barn to fetch his shovel. Like his older cousin, Sonny was a large man, and yet it took him only a few minutes to clear his front steps and porch. Then, in the dwindling afternoon light, he trudged back to the barn to return his shovel to its hook.

By five o'clock, the darkness was all encompassing but the snow was showing signs of tapering off. With supper on the table, Lizzie grew impatient and sent the hired man out to the barn with a lantern to see what was taking Sonny so long. When he entered, he glanced around but saw no one. Then, as he turned to leave, something caught his eye. He raised his gaze, and there, dangling life-less from the rafters, hung Lizzie's husband.

Wednesday, January 2, 1884. The arrival of a new year brought a renewed optimism to most people's lives. But that was not the case for A. D. Bond and family. Bond awoke early on Wednesday and went directly to his daughter's side. On this day—one that had been so long in coming and one that should have brought relief to the girl and her family—he had the unenviable task of telling Emma about Sonny's death. The family members, reeling with grief, packed their belongings and left at once for the depot.

Bond had learned of his cousin's tragic death late on Tuesday night—from the state's attorney. Drennan had received the unexpected telegram from Taylorville at eight o'clock but was forced to withhold its gut-wrenching news until Judge Edwards had finished speaking. "The announcement" wrote the *Herald*, "shook Abner Bond beyond the power of words to tell." The same article expounded on Sonny's life and his generous contributions to the Bond case:

> He was foremost among those who assumed the work of hunting down the ravishers of Miss Bond, and spent money lavishly for that purpose. It was at his house that Miss Emma Bond stayed all last winter after her examination by the Grand Jury . . . , and it was there that the alleged attempted abductions were made. "Sonny" Bond was fifty years of age, a wealthy man of family with five amiable, lovely children. He lived in Christian County for thirty years. It is reported that at one time he offered $10,000 for a clew leading to the arrest of the real ravishers.[10]

Neither the holiday nor the weather had the power to delay a coroner's inquest. Coroner Blount and his jury of six men gathered in Sonny's barn that frigid Tuesday evening to determine cause of death. Their report was conclusive:

"We the undersigned jurors . . . do find that he came to his death by suicide by hanging in his barn . . . cause of said suicide is unknown to the jury."[11] It described the victim as male; six feet tall; with light complexion, hazel eyes, and light hair. After Sonny's hefty frame was lowered to the barn floor, the following personal effects were removed from his pockets: $50.00 in currency, $5.05 in coins, a pocket knife, and a wad of small papers, including one showing a $300 deposit to A. G. Barnes's bank, four notes made out to Bond, totaling $361.80, and a receipt showing his recent tax payment of $18.14. These things were usually given to the spouse, but the coroner added this note in his book: "Deposited or turned over to Wm. Dalby by me this 1st day of January." As the husband of Lizzie's sister, Mary, Dalby was family.

Those present that evening maintained the utmost discretion, leaving the desperate news corps wanting for answers. As the *Republican* reported: "The matter is kept very secret here, and none of the circumstances beyond the fact of his suicide can be learned." In lieu of confirmation, the paper surmised that the trial had "preyed upon his mind so much that he killed himself."[12] Other publications postulated along the same lines, using phrases like "his anxiety and worry over [the trial], it is thought, was the cause of the suicide," or "it is supposed his mind was unbalanced by his cousin's troubles."[13] One reporter secured information that "the deceased [had] acted strangely of late."[14] If family members and close friends knew the reason behind Sonny's fatal decision, they weren't talking.

As untimely as the death was, Judge Phillips would not—nor could he— postpone the trial for the Bonds' benefit. It had to go forward without them. And with the end so near, everyone was issuing predictions. Even State's Attorney Drennan got in on the act, declaring, "If the jury does not return by five o'clock this evening, there will be no verdict." In the town that had hosted the trial, citizens were even less optimistic, opining that the twelve men would reach a stalemate within three hours. For those with a bent toward gambling, perhaps the best tip to be had called it "2 to 1 all around that it will be a hung jury."[15]

A half-hour after court convened at ten o'clock on Wednesday, the jurors were ushered in. As Phillips read them their guidelines, they and the audience listened closely. At ten forty-five, the twelve were handed a copy of the indictment and led off to the jury room by Deputies Burns and Miller. Around noon, Burns was dispatched to check on their progress. He found them in agreement on just one thing: they were all hungry and wanted to break for a meal. Phillips brought them back into the courtroom to give them the necessary admonition to discuss nothing about the case while they ate. They devoured their food and returned quickly to the jury room. At three o'clock, word came that no decision was forthcoming.

Of course, it was far too early to give up hope on this particular panel, as only a few hours had elapsed. A full day or two or three might be required. A hung jury would be a truly disappointing finale for a trial that had lasted twenty-three days and cost the county $10,000. Judge Phillips set six o'clock as the next mark for a jury update. Five o'clock came and went, leaving observers to wonder whether Drennan's prediction had been right. At the scheduled six o'clock update, there was still no verdict. Before long, the judge would have to start thinking about calling it a night. He knew how mentally exhausting the discussions could be for those locked behind jury doors, and it was imperative that the twelve have clear frames of mind during their deliberations. With their entire futures at stake, the accused deserved nothing less. And then, at approximately seven thirty, came the news that the whole nation had been awaiting. The jury had reached a verdict—less than ten hours after being handed the case.

Nobody had ventured too far, just in case. So when word spread that the jury was ready, the courtroom filled as if by some preordained wave of a wand. Judge Phillips appeared shortly before eight o'clock to address the restless audience, warning that "no sign of approbation or dissent would be tolerated from the audience."[16] He then ordered that the jurors be brought in. Everyone in the room scoured the twelve somber faces as they entered, single file, but their faces bore no visible clues. When the jury was seated, the foreman handed a small slip of paper to the bailiff, who then handed it to the judge.

Phillips scanned it quickly before asking the three defendants to stand. He then read the inscription on the paper: "We the jury, find the defendants not guilty as herein charged." A heavy silence permeated the courtroom. Not a cry, not a murmur, not a whisper, nor a single objection arose from the stunned observers. They sat immobilized, transfixed, trying to absorb the unthinkable. "Gentlemen, is this your verdict?" asked the judge.[17] Even though all answered in the affirmative, the clerk was instructed to poll the jurors individually. One by one, the twelve names were called, with each man responding, "Not guilty, your Honor." The judge nodded and thanked the men for their service.

He turned back to the defendants, telling them they were free to go. In a rush, their friends and relatives surged forward to congratulate them. The majority of those present, however, could do nothing but stare in disbelief as the celebration unfolded around the defense table. The jurors tried for a hasty departure but were instantly besieged by a throng of journalists, seeking details on the deliberation process. And they got what they were after. The jury's first vote had been seven to five, in favor of acquittal. By six o'clock or so, it had risen to ten for acquittal. Ultimately, explained one juror, it was the alibi testimony that saved the defendants. And, as reported in the *Decatur Daily Republican*: "They also considered it impossible for Miss Bond to have recognized John Montgomery as she said she did under the circumstances."[18]

One renegade reporter sought the judge's opinion, writing that Phillips "heartily approves the verdict and adds that time will prove that justice has been done."[19] Asked by the press about their immediate plans, the ex-defendants indicated they would spend the night in Hillsboro and leave Thursday morning, taking care to add that they weren't the least bit worried about a lynch party. Their departing remarks, however, hinted that they had some scores to settle when they got home—that they would "make it hot for some of the witnesses who testified against them."[20]

Before the courtroom completely emptied, telegraph lines snapped to life, carrying the shocking news to nearby towns and points beyond. Word soon spread that a lynch mob was already on its way from nearby Litchfield. The local sheriff had anticipated that possibility, so he and his deputies herded the main targets—Montgomery, Pettus, and Clementi—along with their twelve liberators, off to the second floor of the courthouse. There, sequestered in a strong room, the unlikely group passed the long night together under the protection of several heavily armed deputies. The overnight conversation in that room must have made for some fascinating eavesdropping, although the guards would later refuse to share a single word of it.

At least one thing worked in the sheriff's favor that evening: the sub-zero weather. The bone-chilling cold sparred with the many idlers who milled about on Hillsboro's Main Street. It first nipped at exposed skin, then gnawed at extremities until, finally, it chased away any and all thoughts involving rope. By midnight, the potential mob had dissipated in search of warmth. Only a few hangers-on lingered into the deepest hours, fortifying themselves heavily with alcohol. But by four o'clock the next morning, even those hardy souls had surrendered to the harshness of the night.

The unforeseen verdict prompted a rash of editorials not only in Illinois but across the nation. The *Republican's* contribution was a fair representation of what newspapers everywhere were saying:

There has never been a more melancholy case in the history of crime in Illinois than that which has just ended at Hillsboro. . . . There the efforts of the law must cease . . . unless new developments tending to fasten the guilt upon someone else come to light, it is likely that the case will speedily fade from the public mind, and the perpetrators of one of the vilest outrages ever committed will go unwhipt of justice. . . . [W]e can have no other method of determining the guilt of accused parties except by the judgment of a jury that has heard the evidence. The jury may err but when it has once acquitted, there is no tribunal that has the power to review the case, except the mythical and often mistaken one called public opinion. There is no safety in any well regulated community except in a peaceable acquiescence in the decisions of courts and juries, even though there may sometimes be doubt of their justice. . . .[M]any. . . will still believe that the three men just acquitted are really guilty, but the twelve "good men and true" who listened to all the evidence were not willing to say so, and from that verdict there is no appeal. All talk of visiting public wrath upon the acquitted defendants ought to be silenced at once.[21]

The case had been allowed to play out in the judicial system in the proper manner and the end result, be it right or wrong, demanded unequivocal acceptance.

5

RUMORS, RAMIFICATIONS, AND NEW REVELATIONS

After 1883

25

The funeral of Abner Bond took place this afternoon from the Christian Church. Notwithstanding the intense cold, an immense crowd was present.
—Fort Wayne Daily Gazette, *January 4, 1884*

The citizens of the county, the state, and the entire nation expected the trial to clear up at least some of the puzzling aspects of the Bond case. They were sorely disappointed when it didn't. Sonny's death, of course, only added to the intrigue. So closely intertwined were the two stories that the *Herald* called his death "the most sensational feature of the whole case" and one that "adds wonderfully to the interest in the trial." To soften that harsh reality, the paper had the decency to add: "The attorneys here [say] it goes to make the whole tragedy deeper and more sorrowful."[1] Everyone agreed that Christian County had lost one of its finest public servants, and accolades flowed from all quarters. Sonny's close friend Jesse W. Hannon—who'd led the grand jury in the Bond indictments—shared his thoughts: "He was one of the best men I ever knew . . . one of the best citizens of the county. I haven't been so shocked for years and years. He was a man of good property, worth over $100,000. Emma Bond was at his house all last winter. It will nearly kill the poor girl. Mr. Bond was a supervisor on the County Board for years. I understand he offered $10,000 for the conviction of these men."[2]

Sonny's generosity was attributed to his firm belief that the right men were on trial. As to what drove him over the brink, that was blamed on "the intense mental strain consequent upon this trial . . . he probably concluded that the jury would acquit the defendants." At least that was Drennan's opinion. Naturally, nobody took the news of Sonny's death any harder than A. D. Bond. His reaction upon learning the news spoke volumes: he "sank down in his chair utterly broken in spirit, saying, 'I've lost my best friend.'" Though the case had occupied the news for over a year and a half, there was still some confusion over how the two Abners were related, with the *Herald* stating that "nearly all the money for the prosecution of this case had been furnished by the deceased brother."[3]

As the people of Christian County struggled to make sense of Sonny's suicide, what the papers were writing only served to compound the mystery:

The Abner Bond Suicide.

The Taylorville *Republican* thus speaks of Bond, who was an uncle of Emma Bond. "Mr. Bond was a man of strong and vigorous mind . . . he had not a personal enemy on earth. He was known as the most popular man in Taylorville. So far as is known, there was no cause for the suicide. His domestic relations were pleasant. He was in independent circumstances financially, owning over a thousand acres of the best land in the county and valuable city property. He was . . . of robust and vigorous health. His family reports that in the last few days, he was worried a great deal in regard to the Bond outrage trial at Hillsboro. It will be remembered that [Emma Bond] was at his home at the time of the alleged abduction . . . whatever may have been the cause of the suicide, one of the best and noblest men of this section of Illinois has passed away. Mr. Bond was about 50 years of age. His estate is supposed to be worth $50,000 to 100,000.[4]

The coroner's inquest report did hint at another possible explanation for Sonny's death. Remarks on the inquest report read: "Leaves family of wife and five children in good circumstances. Mr. Bond was a man of high standing in the community, respected by all, and I am of the opinion that Temporary Insanity of Imagined Financial Embarrassment induced him to commit suicide. D. C. Blount, Coroner."[5] Financial ruin—imagined or not—was probably the most common cause of suicide in nineteenth-century America. And yet nobody, other than perhaps Sonny himself, believed he was in desperate straits. In any case, his death had left Lizzie a widow with five young children to care for; her eldest was just twelve and her baby, Abner Faye Jr., barely two. Fortunately, she had the love and support of her own relatives, most of whom lived nearby.

Despite the unrelenting cold snap, Sonny's funeral was well attended. Abner and Delia and their six girls were among those present to honor the man who had tried so valiantly to secure justice on Emma's behalf. For her family, that day could not have been worse. They had learned of the acquittal just hours before the funeral. But as death has a way of doing, it allowed them to put things in perspective. As one paper noted: "Their grief over this loss deadened them to the verdict."[6] One plucky journalist approached A. D. Bond the morning of the funeral, asking for his thoughts on the verdict. Bond gave his honest appraisal, saying he believed the alibi testimonies had swayed the jury.

The journalists were still hanging around Hillsboro that Thursday morning, waiting to pounce on the jurors. When the twelve finally emerged from the safe room, the impatient press corps immediately swarmed them, eager to learn more about the deliberations. At first, the jurors grappled with how to respond. But slowly, they opened up. Their first revelation was that they believed the defendants were probably guilty but that the State had failed to prove it. Then, one brave member stepped forward to say that Emma's testimony "was practically thrown out by the jury." When pressed further, another explained, "Miss Bond's evidence was simply weighed against that of the sisters of Lee Pettus and the verdict determined by the preponderance of evidence."[7] Nobody could deny that this was precisely what the law demanded, and the jury had followed that directive exactly. In their collective mind, the preponderance of evidence had boiled down to numbers: the word of one against the word of many. Of course, that neglected the cruel reality that a rape victim is usually the only person other than the aggressor with any firsthand knowledge of the crime.

Judge Phillips, after having slept on it, clarified his opinion on the trial's outcome, stating that "from the evidence, he thought the jury could not well have done otherwise." The newsmen, as usual, wouldn't let it go and pushed him for his personal view of the verdict. He carefully sidestepped the matter by saying "he was not prepared to state whether he thought the men were guilty or not."[8] Naturally, judges are expected to wear a robe of one color, and Judge Phillips was wearing his well.

In Hillsboro, the frustration was tangible, and that had law officers on edge. The town's residents weren't about to tolerate the presence of the ex-defendants any longer than necessary. So, under the leadership of a prominent citizen named Mr. Glenn, a resolution was quickly drawn up, demanding that the three men be gone no later than Friday morning. Evidently, Glenn didn't know that one of them had already left town. Pettus had caught a train headed for "the west" at seven o'clock that morning. This turned out to be nothing more remote than the rail crossroads in Litchfield, where he transferred to a northbound train and passed safely through Taylorville before disembarking at Blue Mound. Once back in his own neighborhood, he and his mother took shelter—not at the family home but at George and Effie's place.

Wisely, the other two ex-defendants were keeping a low profile in Hillsboro. Besides trying to avoid reporters, they had no desire to be at the receiving end of another public eruption. Their getaway plans called for sneaking out of town at different times and in different directions. At eleven o'clock Thursday morning, Clementi went to the depot to buy a ticket to Irving, the tiny village six miles northeast; he planned to take shelter at the Leons' home. As he waited in the depot full of glaring antagonists, however, he began to sense that he was at risk. So he shoved his ticket into his pocket and slipped out of town on foot, hiking all the way to Irving. He reached the village in a couple of hours and quickly made his way to Bartholo Leon's house, relieved that his journey had been without incident. But that relief was short-lived, as this telegram makes clear:

Irving, IL, Jan. 3—To J. R. Chattacomb, Hillsboro, Ill.: Clementi . . . reached here a little after two o'clock and put up at B. Leon's. On his arrival becoming known, a crowd quickly gathered, and he was given five minutes in which to get out of the town. He left at once, going toward your place. Give this to all citizens.[9]

News that the outcast was now on his way back to Hillsboro caused a commotion. The townspeople had seen all they cared to of Clementi, and they were not going to take his return lightly. Between three and four o'clock that afternoon, a reporter spotted the lone man approaching the outskirts of town, walking along the railroad tracks. He intercepted him and asked about his banishment from Irving. Clementi, always happy to talk about himself, told of being chased out of the village by a hostile group. The reporter asked, "Did the crowd have the appearance of a mob?" Clementi responded, "Yes, it did; there were 75 or 100 persons in the crowd. Several of them cursed me and I saw a revolver in the hands of one man. One of the leaders said that the walking was too d——d good for me."[10]

Clementi snuck back into the secure room at the courthouse sometime after dark. There, he and Montgomery hatched a new plan. This one involved stealing out in the dead of night and catching an eastbound train to Pana. They slipped away safely Thursday night, with nobody aware of their departure. The *Republican* reported that the two split up in Pana, with Clementi heading to Chicago and then possibly on to Milwaukee, where his mother lived.[11] Either big city was a good place to disappear. Montgomery rode to Decatur on a route that passed well to the east of Taylorville, thus circumventing a possible confrontation; there was no point in tempting fate a second time. In Decatur, he curled up in the station overnight to await the early morning train to Blue Mound.

All was still when he disembarked in the deserted village just before dawn. Hunching down into his coat collar, he hurried out of town, walking at a brisk pace. But with the cold wind assaulting every inch of his exposed skin, he turned instead toward the home of George Miller, his close friend and unflinching supporter. Miller and his wife, Hattie, lived in Pleasant View, just outside of Blue Mound. Their home offered a warm stopover and, more importantly, a place to pick up a weapon. If vigilantes were on the prowl, if an ambush was in the works, it would surely take place on the road to the Grove. Luckily for John, he made it home later that day without so much as an encounter.

It was good that he and Clementi had launched their getaway when they did, or there'd have been no trains to take them anywhere. Proof of that appeared in Saturday's headlines from Decatur where on Friday night the thermometers had fallen to a dangerous thirty-two degrees below zero: "It must have been thirty-five below on the prairies . . . the horses were covered with a white coat of frost and there was frost on their eye-winkers and hanging from their nostrils. . . . Potatoes, apples, water and milk froze in dwellings . . . all the store windows are coated with thick coats of frost and the merchants have had to scratch off the white coating to see out. . . . The South train on the Central Road, due here last evening, was fifteen hours late."[12]

Once again, as painful as it was, the weather had provided a blessing in disguise: no man in his right mind would saddle his horse and ride out to join—much less organize—a lynch party in such extreme conditions, no matter how he felt about the verdict. To Montgomery's and Pettus's relief, by the time the mercury crept back up to a more tolerable level, the urgency for retribution had subsided. Thus it was that the two settled in for the winter, guardedly resuming their former lives. But tucked away in the backs of their minds was that subtle admonition issued by the *Republican,* which wrote, they "will hardly sell out and run away from the neighborhood where they have lived for so many years. Their flight would be taken by some as a confession of their guilt."[13]

The disappointed public had plenty to say in the immediate aftermath of the trial. In Taylorville, the general feeling was that "justice can no longer be obtained from the courts."[14] One week later, the community most deeply affected by the trial, Grove City, held "an indignation meeting." There, at the schoolhouse, the scene of the crime, fifty residents came together to pass a resolution denouncing the acquittal as "an outrage on the people and justice." On behalf of the victim, the attendees "resolved that the character of Miss Bond was above reproach." Before concluding, they organized a group of male volunteers "for the protection of females."[15] In Assumption, the tiny town where the irate band of farmers had organized to march into Taylorville in August 1882, the verdict was "unqualifiedly condemned."[16] One angry resident, calling for retaliation, was said to be busy gathering weapons.

Of all the towns in the region, Montgomery and Pettus were probably safest in Blue Mound, where they were said to have a "large circle of friends." But some of its residents declared that that large circle constituted only a small portion of the town's population. The Decatur press was more restrained, concluding that the jury had no choice but to acquit, "and that settles the case as far as the law is concerned."[17]

Two hundred miles north, in the teeming metropolis of Chicago, talk of the big trial predominated. There, the Moral Education Association of Chicago met at the Grand Pacific Hotel within days of the verdict, for the sole purpose of discussing the outcome. It was a vocal assembly, marked by livid speeches and damning resolutions. Members decried the increase in violence against women and children, calling the verdict a "blot upon the impartiality of the common law."[18]

Without a doubt, the most regrettable behavior was that directed at the jurors. Each had performed his duty as prescribed by law, but the law also allowed for the freedom of speech. And when the public spoke, "the execrations cast upon the heads of the jurors were loud and deep."[19] Unfortunately, harsh words weren't all the twelve men had to endure. They'd no sooner left the courthouse, thinking the worst was behind them, than they were given a taste of reality. The public's displaced bitterness made them instant outcasts, shunned by even their closest friends. On Friday, January 4, a raucous Hillsboro crowd tried to hang them in effigy at the courthouse. The local sheriff halted the attempt, but three weeks later, their situation had not improved much, according to a story entitled "Much Afflicted Men," which appeared in the *New York Times*: "The jurors in the late Emma Bond case are suffering under peculiar afflictions, having been almost completely ostracized by the indignant people. One of the twelve is subject to peculiar crying spells, while another has become so frightened that he runs away whenever any one approaches him. Mr. Boone Isaacs is in the worst predicament of all. He was engaged to be married to a beautiful young lady, but she refused to speak to him after the verdict of acquittal and has broken off the engagement, which has caused Boone to be almost overcome with grief."[20]

Dr. McFarland, dubbed the "insanity crank of Jacksonville," also had to have a say, even though nobody was inclined to listen. In a letter to the *Review*, the self-proclaimed authority on mental health declared that "the whole affair was only imaginary and that Miss Bond [was] evidently insane." But the *Review* wasn't buying that assessment, countering that "Dr. McFarland got cranky when he was bounced as Superintendent of the State Hospital for the Insane in Jacksonville and he has been at oats with humanity ever since. His mania runs in his thinking that everybody is crazy except himself, when it is the very opposite."[21] Like McFarland, not everyone sympathized with Emma and her family. Friends of the ex-defendants were finally speaking out more freely than they had in a long time, expressing their wholehearted support for the jury's courageous decision.

26

All who desire to add their mite to the Emma Bond fund can do so by leaving their dollar with Dr. J. W. Davis at the Sanitarium. He who adds to that fund for the benefit of that unfortunate woman will have done a good act.
—Palmyra Enterprise, *January 16, 1884*

After Sonny's funeral, Emma and family went into seclusion on their farm to grieve the death of their relative and the disappointing verdict. To the public's credit, its displeasure with the verdict quickly mellowed into something more constructive. Even before the acquittal, there'd been talk of assisting the Bonds in whatever way possible. Now, an altruistic plan was taking shape in Wisconsin: "A movement has been started here to create a fund for the benefit of Miss Emma Bond. . . . It was decided to solicit subscriptions of one dollar each from all parties in the county, the fund to be placed in the custody of John W. Davis and John H. Davidson of the Palmyra Springs Sanitarium in this city."[1]

The initiative quickly gained a foothold and spread, with towns across the Midwest and beyond jumping on the bandwagon. In Illinois, Bloomington was the first to take up the cause, with Decatur's *Review* chiding its citizens for not doing the same. Leading Bloomington's effort was a professor named Sue M. D. Fry.[2] On January 7, she issued an appeal to the educators in her town in hopes that their generosity would encourage teachers everywhere to join the crusade. In Iowa, the *Davenport Gazette* issued this petition: "Miss Bond . . . has lost the little all she before possessed, besides suffering the greater despoilment of that which was more dear to her than all else except life, while her father has impoverished himself in mortgaging the inevitable expenses attendant upon the effort to discover and bring to punishment the criminals who ruined his daughter. . . . In every city in the land an 'Emma Bond Subscription Fund' should be opened."[3] Professor Fry aimed her appeal at the rural segment of the population, where country schoolteachers formed the backbone of education. She wisely pointed out the inherent risks women like Emma faced:

They labor in schoolhouses, on country roads remote from town or village. Almost invariably, these schoolhouses are located on section corners at long distances from any habitation . . . school duties impel the faithful teacher to presence in the lonely schoolhouse both long before any of her pupils reach the premises and long after they retire. . . . How many of these noblest of all laborers for the public good are anywhere sure of immunity from the grossest of possible wrongs? . . . Therefore, let the teacher in the country schoolhouses be much more thoughtfully regarded henceforth than she has been heretofore.[4]

If that loquacious plea didn't produce results from an array of educators, nothing would. On January 14, Hillsboro announced its own charitable fund, bragging that it had already collected $400. The town's stated goal was to pay off the mortgage on Bond's farm, so he would not lose it. Closer to home, several benefits were organized, with donors being entertained in return for their contributions. In Taylorville, the nearly complete Vandeveer Opera House was the site of a lavish benefit on January 17, where a record-setting crowd dug deep into its pockets, netting another $400 for the victim's family.

The competition escalated as cities vied for the title of "most generous." Each time a new place announced its fund-raiser, a neighboring town would be inspired to do its part. When Decatur still had nothing in the works by January 22, the *Review* urged its citizens to action by invoking guilt: "An Emma Bond fund is being raised in Springfield. Why can't Decatur do something for the deserving young lady?"[5] The good people of Decatur were dragging their benevolent feet; perhaps an earlier remark made by the *Republican* had something to do with this. For although the Bonds were running out of money, the paper had stated that the victim's father had "emphatically" turned down other large donations. That message probably had Decatur's citizens wondering if their donations would even be accepted.

Two days after the *Review* had chastised its readers, the *Republican* issued its own challenge: "Decatur ought to give and give liberally. . . . Who will be the first to give?"[6] The paper implored residents to drop off their contributions at its office. And in case anyone still harbored doubts about Mr. Bond's finances, the paper sought to set the record straight, by including another fervent appeal from Professor Fry:

Letters from responsible people in Taylorville say that all assertions representing Mr. Bond as well off are untrue. . . . Let there be mass meetings, personal solicitations, voluntary contributions, benefit entertainments—whatever will suit your place and people the best, but let every place and everybody do something. Do not forget to report the amounts to Dr. John

W. Davis of Palmyra, Wis. who has generously offered everything at his sanitarium free of charge, as long as she wishes. . . . [Amounts] should be reported to the Palmyra headquarters of the fund so that a complete record can be kept. Let the friends of the afflicted and of truth and justice send on their contributions.[7]

Fry did not name the "responsible people" vouching for Bond's ailing finances. And the directive to report the collected monies to Davis in Wisconsin seemed odd. Did he need the extra funds to cover the free care he had offered Emma, or was he hoping to drum up some free publicity for his sanitarium by linking its name to the Bond fund?

By February, the contributions began to slow. One of the last benefits to be held took place in Pana on February 3, where the home talent put on a stellar benefit at Hayward's Opera House and collected $200. An entire trainload of Taylorville residents traveled to show their support—or maybe they had gotten wind of the plan to hang Judge Phillips in effigy that evening, in downtown Pana. The visitors' return trip was interrupted when it was discovered that someone had placed railroad ties across the tracks in an attempt to derail the train carrying the attendees back home. Luckily, the deed was uncovered in the nick of time, narrowly averting another tragedy. Late in February, a final donation trickled in from faraway Atlanta, with Southerners giving a generous $350.

The Bonds weren't the only ones facing a shortage of cash. That the Pettus family had mortgaged the family farm to cover Lee's defense was common knowledge in and around the Grove. The Montgomery and the Pettus families had each dropped a bundle on their gaggle of top lawyers. But with their men now free, not a one among them dared complain that the money hadn't been well spent. A. D. Bond wasn't the only man with a cooperative and generous relative. It seems John C. Montgomery had his own version of a Sonny Bond, and, coincidentally, *his* savior was also *his* first cousin.

Lewis Montgomery, son of John Sr.'s brother Asa, was a year and a half older than his cousin John. Like A. D. Bond's benefactor, he was an entrepreneurial spirit who speculated in land. And, thanks to some lucrative transactions out west, he had done quite well for himself. Thus, he kicked in a generous $5,000 in support of his cousin's defense. Nevertheless, it amounted to only half of what it cost to get John off the hook. The defendant and his father covered the balance. As it turned out, $10,000 was also what it had cost the State to prosecute the case.

Other people's money, or lack of it, always made for interesting gossip. But something even more interesting had recently surfaced. When the *Republican* first broke the story on January 7, it came as quite a shock—even to those who knew the families best:

It is not generally known that the Bonds are related by marriage to the Montgomerys, as everybody in this section of the state appears to be, and the fact has never been made public. One reason given for the manner in which mysterious features were developed in this case was the fact that nearly all the interested parties were related in some way to the Montgomerys. The Bonds were supposed to be the only ones not connected with them even in the remotest degree. It now appears that "Sonny" Bond, who committed suicide at Taylorville on Tuesday and is a cousin of Emma Bond's father, was a brother-in-law of Lewis Montgomery. It is said that the ties of relationship have prevented the unearthing of a large number of facts which would shed a glaring light upon this still most mysterious case.[8]

If this detail had been purposely suppressed, it was now out in the open. It was also undeniably true. Lewis Montgomery's wife was the former Emma Hall, and Sonny's wife was her sister, the former Lizzie Hall. The possibilities triggered by this disclosure set off a whole new round of speculation. Had Sonny and Lizzie somehow compromised Emma's safety, knowingly or unknowingly, on the night of the failed abduction at their home? What allegiances did the two sisters feel to their respective in-laws? And were their loyalties such that either of them or their husbands might have interfered with the investigation or, worse yet, attempted to influence the outcome of the trial? Or was this just another in a long line of strange coincidences, seized on and blown out of proportion by the press? If answers existed to these questions, no one was talking. If something untoward had taken place between any combination of the four, to the detriment of either side, no one was talking. The paper promised more pertinent facts would soon be revealed, shedding additional light on the "mysterious features" of the case. Once again, it faltered, but at least this time it had gotten the family relationships right.

By spring, the news coming out of Christian County ground to a halt. The two local ex-defendants returned to their fields and picked up their plows, happy to put their energies into their land and even happier to put their nightmare behind them. In late March 1884, Lee Pettus finally married Allie Hill, nineteen months after her father's suicide had sidetracked their original plans. Nothing stood in their way now—no irate father, no iron jail bars, and no nagging worries over Lee's future.

At some unknown point, Emanuel Clementi had returned to Christian County. In May, a representative of the *Republican* stopped by the Grove to chat with local resident J. W. Watson, who was quoted as saying that Montgomery and Pettus were busy on their farms but that Clementi "goes about doing nothing."[9] Right away, Watson asked the paper to issue a correction. Three days later, it obliged: "What he claims he did say was that he sees Montgomery and Pettus near Grove City nearly every day, but has not seen Clementi since the Emma Bond trial but hears of him occasionally . . . and that Emanuel Clementi is also laboring in their neighborhood."[10] Watson apparently didn't want the farmhand to think he'd called him lazy. That Clementi returned to Christian County at all was somewhat astonishing. Perhaps the reason was the relationship he had developed with Ona Pettus.

By early spring, Thornton was being suggested as a candidate for the state's top office. He'd long been a dedicated public servant, having already given three years of his life to Illinois's highest bench. But it was undoubtedly his performance in Hillsboro that catapulted him back into the spotlight. By 1884, every voter in the state knew the name of Judge Anthony Thornton, lead defense counsel in the Bond case. And although he was touted as the one man who could give the Republicans a real run for their money in the upcoming governor's race, he decided to turn down his party's offer. Again, his love of private practice guided his decision.

Like Thornton, Judge Phillips was also encouraged to throw his hat into the political ring. And so he forfeited his seat on the circuit bench in hopes of winning a seat in the U.S. Congress. Much to his dismay, his support fell through, and he was forced to withdraw from that race. Ultimately, Phillips did return to the halls of justice, sitting on the Illinois Supreme Court bench from 1893 until his death in 1901, serving proudly as its chief justice for most of that time. On June 29, 1887, exactly five years to the day after the crime, the *Atchison Daily Globe* bragged that the venerable Mr. Amos Miller of the Bond prosecution team was an honored guest in its city. So while the famous trial had depleted any number of bank accounts, it had also inflated the careers of every lawyer who had been a part of it. Their names would not soon be forgotten.

27

*The unwanted penetration of one's body is an invasion of the mind and of the
heart and of the soul. And the scars of this crime endure if it is left untreated.*
—Raymond B. Flannery, Post-Traumatic Stress Disorder:
The Victim's Guide to Healing and Recovery

Life went on, leaving the victim and her family to fend for themselves in the
aftermath. While the word "victim" is usually reserved for the person against
whom a criminal act is committed, in a very real way, the victim's closest family
members are victims as well. The Bonds were no exception, and, not surprisingly, A. D. Bond took one of the hardest hits. For eighteen months, he'd put up
his best front, not just for Emma's sake but for that of his entire family. With the
disappointing verdict, his deepening money deficit, and the tragic loss of his
dear cousin, he sank into a deep depression, taking to his bed for days on end.

For the victim, life continued to look bleak. The much-talked-about wedding never materialized. And although her outward appearance had improved
dramatically, Emma's back pain was an ever-present torment. Worse yet, her
emotional progress was slow and excruciating, marked by the proverbial two
steps forward and one step back. It soon became obvious that Emma needed
more help than her local doctors could give her. So in February 1884, A. D.
Bond decided to place her under the care of Dr. Davis, who had initiated the
Emma Bond Fund at the Palmyra Sanitarium and had generously offered her
his services and free care at the facility.

The small town of Palmyra lies in southeastern Wisconsin, twenty-five miles
north of the Illinois state line. There, in 1871, a fellow named Bidwell had picked
up a piece of land just east of town, specifically because of its mineral hot
springs. Knowing of their therapeutic value, he took on a partner, Dr. G. C.
Wood of Michigan—a longtime proponent of the hydropathic approach to
treating illness. The two men erected a building near the hot springs, and thus
began the enterprise known as the Bidwell House. Though the place sat well
off the beaten path, by 1873 it was attracting many locals in search of cures for

whatever ailed them. Of Bidwell's six springs, two produced superior drinking water—healthy, pure, and crystal clear. They each contained a different mix of minerals and varied slightly in temperature. The list of chronic illnesses thought to respond to their curative powers included everything from epilepsy to diabetes to arthritis.

In the late 1870s, Dr. John W. Davis of Lansing, Michigan, took over as manager of the retreat, renaming it the Palmyra Springs Sanitarium. Davis had a reputation as a freethinker—someone who had "a natural bent for independent investigation" and who "fearlessly ignored precedent" in his approach to disease.[1] The sanitarium was the perfect vehicle for such a man, and, under his guidance, it flourished. In 1884, he was joined by a Colonel Davidson, whose talents leaned more toward the business end of things. The two complemented each other, and together, they added a large new wing to the sanitarium. This housed not only a lecture room but a large dance hall, which did double duty as a roller-skating pavilion. These inviting new features were luring a growing number of visitors from further away—all seeking modern cures for their ills.

The place soon became so popular that "ten trains ran east and west bringing guests to the Sanitarium, some from as far away as New Orleans, New York, and San Francisco." When Emma arrived at the sanitarium on Friday, February 15, 1884, the place was being promoted as a destination for "summer visitors, pleasure seekers, and invalids" alike.[2] Emma clearly belonged to that last category; her father escorted her there by train and placed her in the capable hands of the "sympathetic and charitable" Dr. Davis.[3] It is uncertain whether the doctor's goal was to ease Emma's habitual back pain or to ease her off of the restoratives so freely prescribed by her hometown doctors.

The term "restoratives" was definitely a misnomer; they had done absolutely nothing to restore Emma—quite the opposite, really, for the drug that her doctors had so casually administered to her for now going on two years was the opiate morphine. By the time she was deposited at the Palmyra Sanitarium, she'd been a slave to its numbing effects for way too long. Now the thought of doing without it was beyond unbearable.

The method for extracting the drug from opium had evolved decades earlier, and it had quickly earned a place in the satchels of many caring doctors. Its popularity was spurred on by the 1853 invention of the hypodermic syringe by Scottish physician Alexander Wood, who believed that "taking opiates through the mouth, and the act of swallowing, created an appetite, like other forms of food or drink," whereas "if the drug was injected rather than swallowed, patients would not hunger for it."[4] As the world has since learned, Wood was dreadfully mistaken.

Even more disastrous than Wood's misguided theory was its timing, for the Civil War gave doctors plenty of good reasons to administer morphine; it was the panacea for the pain of lost limbs and gaping body wounds, as well as chronic diarrhea. Unfortunately, what had been a godsend in the arenas of hell turned into a curse in the hamlets of home.

In the postwar era, opiate abuse soared. Many war survivors and Victorian physicians smoked their way into stupors using opium pipes, while others recklessly doctored themselves with laudanum. Morphine itself could be had as an elixir for drinking, as a powder for licking, and—for a privileged few—as an injection for instant gratification. Doctors freely gave it to their female patients for menstrual pain, morning sickness, postpartum depression, and hysteria. Within a decade of the war's end, in fact, the majority of morphine abusers were female. There is no way to know how the drug was administered to Emma; however, it's almost certain that her small-town doctors did not fully understand its dangers.

Even as late as the 1880s, "narcomania" was still a little-recognized problem. In fact, it took another thirty-plus years for the word "addiction" to push its way into the common vernacular. But with the amount of morphine Emma was fed in the summer of 1882, it was inevitable that narcomania would grab her. Her doctors used it to ease her physical pain, having no idea, however, that it was also dulling her psychological pain.

In the early days of her addiction, Emma would have experienced a pronounced feeling of peace and euphoria and possibly some nausea. As her dependency increased, she would have taken on a gaunt appearance and lost interest in all normal physical and mental activities. Martin Booth—in *Opium: A History*—describes the deterioration that comes with long-term opiate abuse:

> The first symptoms of physical decline are inflammation of the mouth and throat, gastric illnesses and circulatory disorders which can weaken limbs so far as to paralyse them . . . appetite for food is lost: the voice grows hoarse, constipation develops with amenorrhoea and sterility in women. . . . Medical complications include hepatitis and liver damage, blood poisoning . . . respiratory diseases, tuberculosis, psychosomatic disorders, advanced tooth decay and nervous tremors. The memory is impaired . . . hearing and sight, however, become acute: tiny noises are amplified and bright lights are painful. Waking hours may be filled with hallucinations with sleep bedeviled by nightmares.[5]

Some of Emma's symptoms surely came from her physical injuries, while others were undoubtedly the result of her psychological trauma; yet there is no denying that more than a few were probably drug-induced. And with all the restoratives she had been given while on the witness stand, there was a very real chance that her testimony had been unwittingly compromised.

The focus of Emma's treatment plan in Palmyra could have been her back injury or her drug dependency—or both. One 1884 advertisement that ran repeatedly in a Wisconsin newspaper suggested that the sanitarium geared its treatments to the standard physical ailments: "A Wonderful Cure—A lady having a cough for twenty-five years and bedridden for eighteen years, from spinal and other complaints, has been cured at the Palmyra Springs Sanitarium in Palmyra, Wisc."[6] However, some sanitariums did cater to addicts. Whatever the nature of her treatment, Emma's progress there was erratic at best. Just a few weeks into her stay, she experienced "a serious relapse when it was thought she would die, but she rallied and at last accounts she had grown stronger."[7] Two months later, on the ninth of July, Palmyra's local paper announced that the famous Emma Bond—after spending nearly five months at the sanitarium—was on her way home. With luck, she would return to Illinois with a renewed outlook on life and the demons of her past forever banished.

There was another who wished to be rid of the demons from his past. For two years, John Montgomery had carried around a seething resentment over his brush with death. In early August 1884, he decided to do something about it. He wanted somebody—actually several somebodies—to pay for what they'd done to him. And so he approached his attorney, Judge Thornton, about the possibility of suing the "parties who took [him] and his companions from jail and strung them up to a tree."[8] The press did not reveal the names of those rope-toting individuals; but apparently, Thornton convinced him to let it go. And with the fading of his plan for revenge, interest in the Bond case dried up. One brief reference to Emma appeared in a Decatur paper in October. It said that the famous victim was visiting a friend, Mrs. Henry Kreider, in Blue Mound. If nothing else, this was a good indication she had finally gotten her life in order.

Fall bowed to winter, and three more months passed uneventfully. And then there it was again, something about Emma. In mid-January 1885, she took a bad fall at her home. A Bismarck, North Dakota, newspaper dispensed the details, stating that she was "now in a dying condition from the effects of a fall a few days ago while ministering to her sick father. Miss Bond swooned on striking her head upon the floor, producing a concussion of the brain."[9] That she had fallen while not doing much of anything wasn't proof-positive that her body was once again in the clutches of morphine; and yet, it might explain why a woman of her age was so unsteady on her feet. In any case, the fall sent her into another downward spiral.

The trusted Dr. Cornell was again called to attend to her. A week later, he announced, "She is still unconscious most of the time and has almost entirely, at least for the time being, lost her sense of hearing and smelling." Nevertheless, he was hopeful that he could "bring her through her present spell."[10] Shortly after that, Mr. Bond spoke to the Taylorville press, saying that his daughter's condition had, indeed, gone from bad to worse. Though she had regained consciousness, she now suffered from complete paralysis on her right side. And not only were her hearing and sense of taste and smell gone, but she couldn't speak either. In late February, the *Washington Post* mentioned another disturbing symptom. It seems her "jaws [were] locked, with the mouth partly open."[11]

While these seemed like most unusual side effects for a fall, even a hard one, they were fairly commonplace in those stricken by hysteria; she had experienced similar symptoms in the fall of 1882. Then came the news that she had suffered a stroke. On a positive note, her hearing and other senses were slowly returning and her locked jaws were improving; at least she could eat solid food. But neither of the offered explanations—the head injury from the fall or the possible stroke—accounted for her newest symptom, described thus: "Between ten o'clock a.m. and 1 p.m. and from two to four in the afternoon, [Emma] lies in a stupor from which not even an electric battery can awaken her."[12] The stroke, surmised her doctor, was caused by a blood clot at the base of her brain. There was talk of summoning a well-known St. Louis physician to attempt cranial surgery to relieve the pressure in her head. But that plan was soon dropped. In the meantime, she was having trouble sleeping, every tiny noise of the night intruding upon her sacred rest. If anything smacked of renewed morphine abuse, it was this.

February and March came and went with little change. Then in April, after three long months confined to her bed, Emma took a marked turn for the better. Her hearing was back to normal, and that allowed her carry on conversations. She was even sitting up in bed. May brought both good and not-so-good news. The good was that she was up and about, moving around the house. The not-so-good was that she was now suffering from amnesia. A clergyman named Hoy, who visited with the patient, described her latest affliction: "The poor girl has no recollection whatever of events happening or acquaintances made previous to the injury and has even forgotten her knowledge of music. She remembers nothing of the outrage of 1882 and her family hopes she may never recall the affair. She still uses crutches and the necessity of doing so she attributes to the fact that she is getting fleshy."[13]

With so many factors at play in Emma's body and mind, there is no way to know which symptoms resulted from what—the accidental fall, the stroke, the ravages of morphine, the original back injury, the implacable hysteria, or the trauma of the rape. Several of her responses fit within the parameters of today's post-traumatic stress disorder diagnosis; modern scholars have long puzzled over the similarities between nineteenth-century hysteria and twentieth-century PTSD. Volumes have been written about the complexities of both, with experts noting a degree of overlap between their causes and effects. Suffice it to say that

Emma bore some very deep and serious wounds that might never heal. Add to that the perpetual clamor for details on her personal life, and it is easy to understand why her life remained so out of control. One insightful editorial made perfect sense: "The poor girl's worst affliction is those newspapers who continually parade the unfortunate girl before the public. For two years she has been the subject of their talk. Since her misfortune, she has never been able to visit a city or town without all the papers chronicling the fact, and not content with this, reproduce the facts of the horrible outrage, until it is no wonder that the poor girl is constantly reminded of her fearful experience and kept in a state of nervousness and ill health."[14]

In time, the predictions that she might not recover from the fall and the resulting head injury proved false—just like the grim predictions of 1882. Nevertheless, as the summer wore on, the amnesia persisted. Although she recognized family and old friends, she could remember nothing else of the previous three years. All memories of the rape had been mercifully obliterated. Walking was still difficult, but with the support of a cane, she was making every effort to carry on. Yet, if asked why she needed it, she'd usually say that she didn't know.

Then one afternoon in September 1885, all of the sickening scenes that she had so carefully locked away in the deepest recesses of her mind suddenly exploded back into her consciousness. Emma described her transformation in a letter to a close friend:

My memory has at last returned to me. I have been sleeping an unnatural sleep many afternoons during this summer until Saturday last (August 29). Then I went to sleep as usual but just before it, my nose bled and I had a dreadful headache. When I awoke, everything seemed so strange to me. I remembered something dreadful had happened to me while at the school house. The recollection came back to me as if it had been yesterday. It was an awful shock. I could think of nothing else and it was not long before I was unconscious again.

My people all hoped I would never remember again. They never told me of how it happened I was so lame, and Father was in constant fear that someone would tell me. God knows what is best for me and has given me my mind again. I try now to be more patient than ever, for I believe I am destined to be a cripple all my life. Oh, how I hope and pray that I may someday walk for I did not know how to appreciate walking before.

My sisters were all here yesterday except Etta, and they rejoiced that I could remember again, for they said there were so many funny things that happened up at the old home, and they did not want me to forget them. Sometimes I can't control my thoughts and have to look with sorrow on what has happened but I try to be cheerful. You must excuse this letter for I can't write with a pen and ink.

This is the first I have written since last fall and it was so difficult for me to write that I never tried. Besides, everyone seemed a stranger, and I could not tell what to write about. All I did this summer was to grow, practice on the piano, and hunt crickets for my pet turkey. I would hobble around on my crutches and sometimes go over to sister Maggie's alone. I never thought of being afraid, I was so happy.

My head is all right now—I mean my brains—for I have headaches all the time.[15]

The letter indicated that the family had relocated to a different house on their property. This other home, considerably smaller, sat on a distant corner of the farm, a couple miles southeast of the family's original home; living there put more distance between them and the Grove. Whether Bond was downsizing and selling off land because he needed the cash, or whether it was the logical move of an aging farmer with a dwindling brood is unclear. His property, both the house and acreage, was valuable, and its sale would have gone a long way toward wiping out his debt. And with the three oldest girls out of the fold, the smaller house actually suited the Bonds. By 1885, A. D. and Delia had six grandchildren. Belle and Hank had three girls; Maggie and Lester, two; and Etta and Charles had a son, with another baby on the way. The last two Bond girls had blossomed into fine, young women. Josie, the youngest, was now eighteen.

Though it would have been easy to do so, none of the other families involved fled the county either, in spite of the ever-present risk of running into their adversaries. Like the Bonds, the Montgomerys and Pettuses had called Christian County home for so long that none could fathom leaving. They had invested too much time and energy in their respective properties to walk away. John C. and Mattie Montgomery appeared to have weathered the storm without any lasting impact on their marriage. Thanks to John's father and his cousin Lewis, no long-term financial obligations hung over their heads. Only one dark cloud had come along to dampen their spirits.

In November 1885, a John Montgomery was indicted on charges of perjury. Apparently, the matter created a good deal of confusion because of the name listed on the indictment. Decatur's *Republican* automatically assumed that it was the ex-defendant, but the *Pana Gazette* had it right. The person charged was the father of the former suspect. According to five reliable witnesses, the elder John Montgomery had lied on the witness stand during the 1882 hearing. In December 1885, the *Gazette* reported that the perjury case would be continued until the next session of the circuit court. However, there were no records to show that the case ever went to trial, suggesting that the charge may have been dropped.

As for the Pettus brothers, try as they might, they just couldn't seem to get their feet back on solid ground. The family had borrowed heavily against its farm to pay for Lee's defense, and in September 1886, it appeared as if time were running out: "All the heirs to the Pettus estate signed a mortgage to the farm and now the mortgage comes due and remains unpaid."[16] The farm was advertised for sale. However, an 1891 plat map of the township showed that the land still belonged to the Pettus estate, which indicates that the family members had somehow scraped together enough money to save their farm and their futures.

28

*He is now preparing an extended address on the case, which will soon be
published. Mr. Burnett says the address will shock the world.*
  —Decatur Daily Republican, *May 15, 1886*

By the mid-1880s, change was in the air. Although rural dwellers still arose before dawn and still retired at sunset, the industrial revolution was in full swing,
and with it came some remarkable new inventions. The big change for Decatur arrived on February 20, 1886. As one of the major cities in central Illinois,
it had prepared itself for the coming of the newest convenience. Towers had
been raised and wires had been strung, and then, in a flash, it happened. On a
Saturday night, with one flip of a switch the town suddenly basked in the tran-
scendent glow of electric light.

The downtown streets were the first beneficiaries, but it wasn't long before
stores, public buildings, and private residences were also enjoying the benefits
of nightly illumination. On that dark February evening when power surged
through Decatur for the first time, one man—the city's lamplighter—became
an instant relic. Early that Saturday morning, he had trudged from post to post,
mindlessly snuffing out the flickering gas lamps, just as he'd done for years.
Then, in a single day, it was over. If only the lingering sparks of interest in the
Bond case could have been extinguished that easily—and permanently. But no,
this was a story that had to rekindle itself every so often.

In spite of the legal finality of the jury's decision, the real verdict was still out.
The unanswered questions continued to hold everyone's imagination. In May
1886, Benjamin F. Burnett, the elderly Taylorville lawyer, reawakened interest
in the case; it seemed his obsession with the mystery had never subsided. He
had attended every day of the hearing and trial as an observer and had taken
copious notes throughout. Now, he was ready to give a public presentation of his
theory on what had really happened. The *Republican* called him "a clear-headed
old man who has been a lawyer for more than fifty years." Clear-headed, maybe.

Old, definitely. Burnett was born in 1807, which meant that he'd been around longer than both Vandeveer and Thornton. In an interview with the *Republican,* he called the Bond case "nothing more nor less than a damnable deception."[1]

His theory sounded every bit as wicked as the accepted version of events. He claimed there had been no rape. Rather, "Miss Bond was betrayed and an abortion was produced to shield her betrayer, who has since left Grove City and cannot be located." That betrayer had belonged to "a well-known secret order" whose members had conspired to protect him. Their influence had been "at work" throughout the trial. In addition, claimed Burnett, "there were men in the [lynch mob] crying 'hang them, hang them!' even though they knew the accused were as 'innocent as unborn babes.'"[2] Burnett's theories didn't stop there. He further asserted that Emma's wounds were done with "surgical instruments" and that she wasn't seen by a doctor until forty-six hours after she returned home. Burnett insisted that the cold facts would support his theory, and he encouraged the skeptics to conduct their own investigations.

While it may have been coincidence, the old lawyer did live next door to Emma's doctor, D. K. Cornell.[3] Presumably, the physician would not have shared any private details regarding his patient. However, he might have let something slip, inadvertently. But since there is no evidence Burnett ever made his public presentation, his argument remains a premise without substance. To his credit, he did call his opinion a "theory"; nevertheless, his use of certain terms—like "damnable deception," "alleged outrage," "abortion," and "her betrayer"—could never be taken back.

Despite the mystery's revival, it was obviously time for the infamous Bond case to take its place on the back shelves of history. In October 1886, the *Atlanta Journal* noted that Miss Bond had made a full recovery, adding, "She is still a beautiful girl and is the belle of the neighborhood."[4] In Decatur, the *Review* proclaimed the story to be "a thing of the past." But it couldn't usher out the era without making one last mention of the victim: "Miss Emma Bond has recovered her former strength and activity . . . [and] was in attendance at a camp meeting in this city last week." Nor was Emma's father exempt from mention. He was said to be "living happily on his farm" and working hard at making a financial recovery.[5]

In May 1887, with Emma's name finally fading from the news, Mr. Bond decided she should visit her uncle and aunt, Levi and Jane Housley, in Kansas. The Housleys owned a farm near tiny Hepler, in the southeastern corner of the state. Levi and his brother Dan, who had recently given up his stake in Grove City's dry goods store, had taken up Kansas land under the 1862 Homestead Act. Kansas—most of it anyway—was no longer the wild place it had been in the 1860s, when it had been the site of some bloody skirmishes between northern and southern sympathizers. But, by the late 1880s, it was drawing a new breed of single young men, who flocked there in droves, lured by the promise of a fresh start on virgin land.

Bond no doubt had reasons for sending his girl off to Kansas. For one, it would do her good to get away from her past. For another, maybe there was an honest, hard-working young man there who would be thrilled to have Emma as his wife. Even if her visit turned out to be nothing more than a restful sojourn, sending her to Kansas would be money well spent. Just how long she stayed is unknown; but she was back in Illinois by early 1888. As far as her family knew, the trip had produced neither beau nor even the slightest possibility of a future union. That did not stop the guessing games, however. Her holiday provided plenty of fodder, with paper after paper asking: Was Miss Emma Bond now engaged? And if so, to whom?

In January 1888, the *Springfield Monitor* announced that she was engaged to a California millionaire. The *Republican* quoted the *Monitor* but speculated: "Is this another sensational yarn?"[6] Four months later, the *Republican* declared that Miss Bond was "soon to wed a wealthy cattle dealer in Texas."[7] Again, no proof was offered. Two months later, the paper mentioned the rumor that Emma "had left Taylorville last year and had gone to California or Nebraska to become the wife of a young ranchman." That sounded like a throwback to her first fiancé, Mr. Adams, who had been a "stock-raiser" out west. Then, in its first honest assessment of the matter, the *Republican* called the rumor "a canard . . . probably the outcome of the imagination of some romantic writer."[8]

The summer following her Kansas trip did prove an enjoyable one for Emma. Having been cooped up for so long, she was starved for a little taste of what life used to be. So when her old friend Eva Stare invited her to spend a few days in Decatur, Emma jumped at the chance. On a balmy July evening, the girls took in a band concert at a local park and were later seen strolling up and down city streets, visibly enjoying themselves. Someone recognized her and relayed the sighting to the press, describing Miss Eva's visitor as "a healthy, rosy-cheeked young woman . . . in good spirits."[9] Her frame had filled out from its alarming low of 75 pounds to a much more Rubenesque and wholesome 165 pounds. Wholesome in more ways than one, perhaps: that she was now thirty-five pounds above her original weight suggested that she had finally kicked her morphine habit.

With the passage of time, the famous victim apparently believed it was safe to wander freely about the city. So when Eva suggested she have her picture taken at a photographer's studio, Emma liked the idea. As the proprietor was writing up the bill, he asked for her name. When she answered that it was Emma Bond, he nonchalantly asked where she was from. "Though of a retiring disposition and naturally anxious to obscure her identity and keep her name and history out of the newspapers," she politely informed him that she was from Taylorville.[10] That was all he needed to hear. The *Republican* told the rest of the story: "The photographer said that he had been anxious for some years to procure a negative of the young lady, and that he would give her a reduction on the price of the order she might make. This angered Miss Bond at once, and she proceeded to deliver a lecture to the amazed photographer, whose place she left without sitting for the picture, going to another gallery where the artist was less curious and inquisitive."[11] The gallery owner, though not named as the paper's informant, seemed the most likely candidate. If the story was true, he probably wanted to kick himself for misjudging his customer. Emma, however, had displayed a feistiness many thought would never be seen again from the once-broken girl. She was showing she was willing to stand up for herself, in no uncertain terms. Nobody, especially a man, would ever take advantage of her again.

This was not the end of the dispute. The following day, the newspaper printed a retraction: "Miss Emma Bond, who is still in Decatur, denies that she has had any racket with any Decatur photographer. She ordered some pictures and got them at the only gallery she visited. The party who told the story was wrongly informed."[12] If that was true, somebody had fabricated the events, perhaps with an eye to grabbing a few minutes of glory by riding on her skirt tails. If it was not true, and Emma really had stormed out of the gallery, who could blame her for denying the whole incident? She probably wanted nothing more than to slip away, unnoticed.

Later in the summer an unexpected letter—postmarked Hepler, Kansas—showed up at the Bond farm; however, it was not for Emma, who had spent much of the previous year under the watchful eyes of her uncle and aunt. Instead, it was addressed to Mr. and Mrs. Lester Sabine, Emma's sister and her husband, from Uncle Levi. Uncle Dan, Levi's brother and partner, had a wife and children who had stayed behind in Illinois, but Levi and Jane were childless. And neither man was getting any younger; Dan was fifty-eight, and Levi was right behind him. So the rigorous demands of running a farm were beginning to wear them down. Their solution: invite their niece's ambitious young husband to join them.

The Housley brothers knew all they needed to about Les. He was a hard worker; Mr. Bond thought the world of him; he was in his prime at thirty-three; and, moreover, his family was young enough to withstand the journey to Kansas. Above all, they knew how much Les longed for a farm of his own—a long shot in Illinois, since his father had given up farming in favor of carpentry and cabinet-making. Since he would inherit no land, Lester could work his fingers to the bone, teaching full time and tending a leased farm on the side, but he was going to need a miracle to save enough to purchase his own farm. Of course, he was the kind of person who would die trying. And that was exactly the kind of man Dan and Levi wanted at their sides.

They made Maggie and Les a generous offer: if the couple would bring their family to Kansas, the Housleys promised them "a chance to farm on their shares." To sweeten the deal, "[Lester] would not have to furnish all the seed or equipment as he did in Illinois. Uncle Levi would furnish half, and would leave the land to them when he and Aunt Jane died."[13] The young couple could hardly say no. Though Les had just received his first teacher's raise in seven years (from $50 to $60 per month), he liked the Kansas idea. So he resigned from the Stonington School, just two months into the fall term.

Once the harvest was in, Sabine sold his crops and the bulk of his stock, paid off his local debts, then hopped a train for Hepler—riding in a boxcar surrounded by all of the family's household belongings; his beloved dog, Shep; and what was left of his herd. Maggie and their two young girls stayed behind, to spend Thanksgiving and Christmas with her family; they planned to follow him right after the New Year. Shortly before Lester's departure, Emma set off on a trip of her own. The now twenty-seven-year-old apparently had a clandestine meeting with somebody in St. Louis. A week after her departure, she was back in Christian County. It is hard to imagine how she managed to conceal her destination and purpose from loved ones, but she did just that.

In January 1889, Maggie and her two little girls said their goodbyes and climbed aboard a passenger train bound for Kansas. Several months went by, and Emma's grand deception continued. And then in late spring, the *Los Angeles Times* dropped a sensational scoop:

> In 1887, Miss Bond visited friends in Hepler, Kansas and while there met a Mr. Justus. The meeting culminated in something stronger than friendship and last October they met by agreement in St. Louis and were married. For reasons best known to themselves, they decided to keep the marriage secret and succeeded in doing so until a few days since, when a misplaced letter conveyed to the wife's relations the first information which they obtained of the situation. Mr. Justus was then conducting the business of a wool merchant at Hepler, and his wife was at her home in Illinois. The discovery of the letter was followed by an avowal of the truth and arrangements to live together.

It was certainly an unorthodox way to begin a marriage. Perhaps Emma harbored a fear that her father might disapprove of her marriage to Clarence Justus, a man he did not know. Not even her two uncles in Hepler, who surely knew the groom, were aware of it. The *Times* explained that the couple had since reunited:

"On Sunday Justus reached Nevada and waited here until his wife arrived today [June 12.] They will visit friends of the husband for a few days, and then go to Hepler to live. Mrs. Justus has apparently recovered from the effects of the brutal treatment which she suffered."[14] Nevada was a small town in far western Missouri, near the Kansas state line and just thirty-five miles from Hepler.

If A. D. Bond had any misgivings about his daughter's secret marriage, he kept them to himself. If nothing else, he had to be relieved that she was going to be living in Hepler, so close to Maggie and Les, her two doting uncles, and the kindly Aunt Jane. Outwardly, the new Mrs. Justus looked every bit the part of the perfect Victorian bride—serene face, statuesque body, translucent skin, refined in both demeanor and dress. Many a young man would have been proud to call her his wife. But inwardly, a storm raged; this was still a very troubled woman whose invisible scars were more raw than anyone imagined.

Emma discovered all too soon the challenges of being a proper wife. Caring for a spouse and a prairie home required strength and stamina. Though she'd come through a long and arduous recuperation, she still suffered from severe back pain and still required the use of a cane. This undoubtedly hampered her in her daily household duties. Plus, there were the other, unspoken duties a bride was expected to provide for her husband. Any young woman about to climb into bed with a new husband experiences some degree of apprehension. And victims of sexual assault almost always bring more complex issues to their marital beds: feelings of fear, anger, shame, and guilt—things buried deep within the mind as a means of self-preservation. So, for someone like Emma, the physical side of marriage was bound to hit a snag or two.

Even for today's victims—who have the benefit of counselors, support groups, and a wealth of information on the subject—it is not easy to overcome the trauma of rape. In Emma's and Clarence's day, however, the problem was theirs alone. Obviously, her husband's sensitivity—or lack of it—would have been a critical factor for someone as fragile as Emma. There is no way to know what kind of approach Clarence took with his new bride; yet, suspiciously, the marriage began to unravel almost at once.

Hepler, Kansas—with its two churches, one general store, small weekly paper and a population of just two hundred—sat isolated on the "undulating prairie." Other than the Missouri Pacific Railroad line, which passed through the town, the place had little going for it. In his 1883 compilation on Kansas, William Cutler wrote that Hepler "makes up in solidity of growth what it lacks in speed of development."[15] The out-of-the-way village was Emma's new home, and having her sister Maggie close by should have been a godsend. However, Maggie had recently given birth to her third daughter, Delia, and the demands of caring for a

228 · NAMELESS INDIGNITIES

newborn left little time for her sister. As a consequence, the new Mrs. Justus—a young woman who thrived on music, books, and the camaraderie of friends and family—struggled to adjust. Clarence may have been a kind enough husband, but that didn't lessen his workload as a busy wool merchant. Motherhood might have provided the perfect antidote to Emma's isolation; indeed, it would have kept her busy for many years. But months went by, and no pregnancy came to pass, raising the question: Did they, in fact, consummate their marriage? And if so, why was there no conception? Then, to make matters worse, Maggie was growing homesick. Her daughter Delia Sabine Greene later revealed:

> Mamma did not like it there. The wind blew too hard and constantly. There was always the fear of cyclones and she missed her family. When a storm was brewing, Mamma said Uncle Dan would take "the baby" [me] and go to the cyclone cave to wait the storm out in safety. Sometimes, the rest of the family would join us, Mamma carrying her silverware tied in a white flour sack for safekeeping. People had respect for those Kansas cyclones. Aunt Jane [Uncle Levi's wife] was sweet and motherly, but the two of them shared the house and the household duties, not always an easy thing for two women.[16]

Because of this, just as soon as the growing season came to an end, the Sabines returned to Illinois. With the departure of her beloved sister, loneliness and boredom took over Emma's days. In early November, the couple's first wedding anniversary came and went. Winter winds whipped across the desolate prairies, sharpening her melancholy and haunting her days and nights. Cut off from all of her interests, Emma grew more deeply depressed as the holidays approached. She fought to get through them, keeping up appearances as best she could. But in the end, it became too much to bear. She packed a small bag, and, without so much as a goodbye to her husband, she walked away from her life in Hepler, just two days after Christmas and barely six months after she'd joined him in Kansas. He would never again lay eyes on her.

Thirty miles northeast of Hepler as the crow flies, the bustling community of Fort Scott, Kansas, beckoned to the runaway bride. Known as the "Metropolis of Southeastern Kansas," the town had a lot to offer—certainly more than Hepler. As its name implies, it began as a military outpost, in 1842. Thirteen years later, the government disposed of the original buildings in a public auction, and a new community sprang up where the army post had stood. The town sprouted factories and stores, hotels and newspapers, civic organizations, good schools, even a college. And people came. Lots of them—of varied religions and races and backgrounds.[17] For someone setting out on her own, without a penny to her name, Fort Scott was an attractive destination. It was the kind of place where one could find steady work and cheap living quarters. And it was the kind of place that could provide other things—like anonymity, for instance. It was also the kind of place where one could forget whatever one needed to forget.

29

The Emma Bond sensation has been recalled in a very unexpected manner at Joplin, Mo.
   —Decatur Herald-Despatch, *January 30, 1892*

Maggie Sabine was relieved to be back in Illinois, where her two youngest sisters had reached marrying age in her absence. In 1891, Josie wed a local boy named Obadiah Baughman. Two years later, Francie married Joe Henson—a popular Taylorville man. By February 1893, A. D. Bond's grandchildren numbered fourteen. The family missed Emma terribly; her sudden departure from Hepler in late 1889 had left them bewildered. Then, right before Christmas 1895, an unexpected package arrived at the Bond farm. It contained modest gifts from Emma for each of her fourteen nieces and nephews—many of whom she'd never met.

Apparently the family had no clue where Emma had gone or what she'd been up to until the gifts arrived. But had any of them picked up the Decatur paper on January 22, 1892, they would have learned far more than they cared to know about her new life. The story, entitled "Gone to the Bad," was as alarming as any connected to the crime and trial: "The discovery of the body of an infant in an alley at the rear of a house of ill repute at Joplin, Missouri brought to light the astonishing fact that Emma Bond, under the name of Linn Leon, was an inmate of the place and had been since she parted from her Kansas husband. Emma was the mother of the child. It died and was given to a party in the house to bury. Instead he threw it in the alley."[1] Until this tragic story broke, all previous rumors and theories—even those that had surfaced after the trial—had made only a minimal impact on what people were willing to believe about the famous victim. This latest account, however, dealt a crushing blow to Emma Bond and her once pristine reputation, and it would be used against her, harshly and retroactively. Henceforth, any concessions previously granted her would be called into question.

What doubtless stuck in the minds of readers was that the former school-teacher had turned to prostitution and was using an alias. In an almost unbeliev-able twist, she had chosen the surname "Leon"—the same name as Clementi's Spanish friends in Irving. How he had come to know the Leons was never told, and there was certainly no indication that Emma had ever known them. So just why she happened to pull that name out of the air was also a mystery.

Heaping disgrace upon disgrace, Emma had given birth to a child out of wed-lock, conceived in prostitution. Worst of all, the baby had died. The article didn't need to spell everything out. The public knew how to read between the lines, and the message was clear: Emma must have done something to cause her child's death; at the very least, she must have allowed the infant to die through neglect. It didn't help that she and her abandoned husband, Clarence, had produced no offspring, either, which suggested she had never acquiesced to his needs and desires. And yet she had turned around and sold her body to other men.

The story was laden with unspoken condemnation. If she had shunned the sexual aspects of her marriage—as many rape survivors do—something more powerful must have driven her to prostitution. Virtually every detail in the article pointed to one thing: Emma had never shaken her craving for morphine. Few people other than family members knew of her ongoing battle with the drug—let alone its side effects. That was the only detail missing from the Joplin article, and its omission made it that much easier to blame the former schoolteacher for her skid into the dark side of life.

Given her history, it's a safe bet that Emma's need for morphine was what lured her to Fort Scott. In tiny, remote Hepler, opiates would have been hard, if not impossible, to come by. But in larger communities, like Fort Scott and Joplin, she would have had no trouble getting her hands on such drugs. Like-wise, there would have been no trouble finding work in that age-old profession. It appeared Emma had become hopelessly tangled in a web of cause and ef-fect: violent rape; external injuries; internal anguish; constant pain; unresolved fear; drug dependency; a failed marriage; reckless prostitution; abject poverty; an illegitimate birth; and—most tragically—the innocent, dead baby. Sadly for Emma, the world had yet to conceive of such ramifications in a rape victim.

Her new life also gave her another excuse for using morphine: in the world of prostitution, opiates were thought to provide protection against pregnancy. Long-term morphine use is known to interfere with ovulation, but this was a far-from-reliable birth control method. So for Emma, like for most prostitutes of her day, it was only a matter of time until the inevitable came to pass. When she figured out that she was with child, she would have had no idea her baby was doomed because of the opiate, as virtually nothing was then known of the effects of hard drugs on a fetus. Such knowledge, however, would probably not have stopped her from the destructive course she was on. She was a wretched addict, and very few have ever been able to put their children's health above their own cravings.

Chances are, the child was stillborn or born so prematurely that it had no chance of surviving. If it was born at full term, the birth would have sent the infant into life-threatening withdrawal. Although it would be easy to blame the baby's death on his mother and her addiction, it should be remembered that during this time women were often given morphine during both pregnancy and delivery. Mothers in even the best homes doped their colicky babies with opiates—with no notion of how much was too much. Such practices surely led to infant distress and, in some cases, death.

Saddest of all was what occurred after the baby died. With her mind most likely clouded by morphine, Linn Leon made the mistake of giving the baby to "a party in the house to bury." That person was probably a departing client and, clearly, not someone any rational person would have entrusted with such a serious task. But Emma was no longer rational, no longer in control of her own body and mind. The entire story was unimaginably grievous—from start to finish.

The 1892 exposé gave a lengthy summation of the Bond case, followed by this astounding declaration: "The general opinion now is that the men were innocent of the crime, and some of the best physicians advance the belief that she was a victim of the worst form of hysteria. After being the inmate of several questionable houses in Joplin, she left for Pittsburgh, Pa."[2] The dramatic shift in public opinion between 1882 and 1892 probably had nothing to do with the ex-defendants and virtually everything to do with Emma herself. Although she had once enjoyed the unwavering support of almost everyone, now even her staunchest allies would be hard-pressed to defend her. Many had to be wondering if this ordinary country girl had pulled off a great sham. Sadly, she'd fallen into drug dependency not by choice but because of her doctors' efforts to ease her pain. But for those unfamiliar with the pitfalls of morphine addiction, this latest installment in the Bond saga was beyond comprehension.

As for the defendants, in 1882 there'd been only a handful of people who had believed in their innocence. Now, a decade later, it sounded as if only a handful believed in their guilt. In all fairness to the accused, ten years was a long time to wait for their due presumption of innocence. In the U.S. justice system, that should have been theirs from the very start and until proven otherwise. But even when the jury had declared them innocent, few had accepted it.

The article's statement about Pittsburgh was almost certainly an error. Emma knew nobody in that city and did not have the financial means to get there. In fact, there is no evidence that Emma Bond (or Linn Leon) ever spent one day in Pennsylvania. Rather, the likely explanation is that on hearing the mention of

Pittsburgh, an overzealous reporter wrongly assumed it was the large and more familiar East Coast city. Her destination, however, was undoubtedly Pittsburg, Kansas—just across the state line from Joplin. That much smaller Pittsburg (with no "h") sat midway between Joplin and Fort Scott, not far from Hepler. That entire area was one with which Emma was quite familiar. Plus, there is existing evidence that she lived in various parts of eastern Kansas in the coming years. But thanks to one reporter's eagerness to inflate the scandal, the obvious was overlooked.

As to the vague comment on medical opinion, one thing was undeniable. The phrase "worst form of hysteria" carried a more damaging connotation than did simple hysteria. There was a large faction of the medical community that still believed hysteria in its worst form could cause a woman to engage in a wicked game of deception, which included the feigning of symptoms. So who, exactly, were these so-called best physicians who had branded Emma? With news of the case reaching far and wide, doctors everywhere probably discussed the mental and physical afflictions of Miss Emma Bond of Taylorville, Illinois. Yet it seems highly improbable that any of them, including the very best ones, ever saw or spoke with her. The names of her physicians are known, and they all—with the exception of Dr. Davis in Palmyra, Wisconsin—had ordinary practices in the Taylorville-Springfield area. In all likelihood, these "best physicians"—whoever they were—reached their conclusions in absentia. In any case, their opinions had to be conceived at a great disadvantage. To make a serious analysis of someone's state of mind without examining her was, at the very least, unprofessional. At the very most, it was unscientific.

Dr. McFarland's name immediately comes to mind as among those unnamed physicians. His post-trial letter, in which he declared that Miss Bond was "evidently insane," was probably the first medical opinion to appear in print—so perhaps this started the ball rolling. But by the time the "worst form of hysteria" remark appeared in 1892, McFarland was dead—having hung himself the previous year at his private hospital in Jacksonville. However, there was another Emma critic within the medical community.

In 1885, Dr. James G. Kiernan of Chicago wrote a damning evaluation of Miss Bond for the prestigious *Journal of Nervous and Mental Disease*. Although Kiernan never used the exact words "the worst form of hysteria," he did pay tribute to the famous victim upfront by calling his article "Hysterical Accusations: An Analysis of the Emma Bond Case." Despite the title, he was addressing the broader subject of hysterical women who falsely accused men. Moreover, based on the bitter tone of his first paragraph, it sounded as if he had a personal ax to grind: "HYSTERICAL accusations against physicians are so far from being infrequent, that a recent little poem in *Punch* speaks of living hysterical scandals 'down' in a way which denotes that such scandals are a necessary concomitant of a medical man's life. That laymen should also suffer from such scandals is to be expected, although from the circumstances of the case they do not suffer as frequently as physicians. The recently decided well-known case of Emma Bond seemed to me one of this character."[3]

That rant off his chest, Kiernan launched into specific cases of other hysterical women. Finally, on the fourth page of his five-page diatribe, he got around to his thin analysis of Emma Bond. It was blunt and disparaging, with the cornerstone of his premise being that her accusations were the "product of a diseased brain." He further asserted that women such as she were "capable of deceiving a whole community." As proof that Emma belonged to that particular class of charlatans, he harkened back to the photograph fiasco, which in his opinion, exemplified "her craving for public notice." He labeled her paroxysms as "convenient" because they always occurred "whenever public interest in the case began to abate." Then he alluded to the "insane and eccentric members of the Bond family"—an unmistakable reference to Sonny.[4]

Kiernan evidently believed he had enough information—on both Emma and the case—to draw his conclusions. By the time he was done spelling everything out, he had maligned not only Emma and her family but her attending physicians for playing along and the "scandal-loving" people of her community for buying into her charade. He concluded: "It is to be regretted that Miss Bond did not fall into the hands of a similar sensible physician soon after the alleged outrage. In that case, this poor girl's affliction would not have been made the property of the public."[5] By "affliction," Kiernan obviously meant "the worst form of hysteria."

In stark contrast to Kiernan's 1885 submission, there was another reference to Emma's case in contemporary medical literature. It came from Dr. John H. Kellogg, a member of the well-known Battle Creek family. His popular book, *Plain Facts for Old and Young: Embracing the Natural History and Hygiene of Organic Life,* was one of the earliest forays into sex education. It debuted in 1879, and by the time his reworked sixth edition came out in 1891, it had sold well over a hundred thousand copies. While many of Kellogg's expressed views were typical of the nineteenth century, a few were ahead of their time. He espoused equality for the sexes and encouraged openness in discussing matters of the human body with children. In his chapter entitled "Social Evils," he quoted from an 1885 speech given by Frances E. Willard, president of the National Women's Christian Temperance Union. It was a chastisement of society's tendency to look the other way: "When we remember the unavenged murder of Jennie Cramer, of New Haven, and the acquittal of the ravishers of Emma Bond, a cultivated school-teacher of Illinois; when we reflect that the *Pall Mall Gazette* declares 'the

law is framed to enable dissolute men to outrage girls of thirteen with impunity'
. . . it is a marvel not to be explained, that we go on the even tenor of our way,
too delicate, too refined, too prudish to make any allusion to these awful facts,
much less to take up arms against these awful crimes."[6] Kellogg's inclusion of
Willard's words left no doubt about which side he was on. Unfortunately, his
support came too late for Emma; her life was in free fall by then.

The diagnosis of hysteria, of course, was commonplace in the Victorian era,
so it was not surprising that Emma succumbed to that particular affliction. It
was what her world expected, what it acknowledged, what it knew. In the twentieth century, however, hysteria quickly faded as the ailment du jour. The numbers dropped so dramatically that by the 1930s, cases were almost nonexistent.
Eventually, the *Diagnostic and Statistical Manual of Mental Diseases* dropped
the diagnosis altogether; it has since been replaced with more delineated alternatives, including post-traumatic stress disorder and rape-victim syndrome.

In any case, it is now recognized that rape survivors can suffer from emotional
aftereffects for decades. In all probability, Emma was never encouraged to discuss
her fears and feelings about the attack with anyone—not even her sisters. If that
was true, she never stood a chance of overcoming the crime's residual damage.

Assuming that the Bonds were unaware of the Joplin scandal, it's hard to imagine nobody mentioned it to them; perhaps compassionate friends and family
wanted to shield them from the devastating news. If, however, Emma's immediate family did know of this most pitiful chapter in her life, they never spoke of
it openly. Perhaps they were too heartbroken or humiliated. Or maybe she had
pushed them beyond their limits with her deplorable choices, and, thus, they
could say nothing in her defense.

In any case, at least one of Emma's uncles in Kansas knew what his niece had
been up to since leaving Hepler. So, too, did her husband. In April 1894—more
than four years after Emma had taken off—Clarence Justus gave up on his wife
and filed for divorce. If she wasn't coming back, the only sensible thing to do
was to end the hapless union and get on with his life. In his divorce petition—
filed in Crawford County, Kansas—Justus listed three dates on which he could
pinpoint Emma's whereabouts; but by the time of the filing, he'd lost track of
her. The information he'd obtained for those three dates, however, was so specific that he must have either hired someone to find her or had a well-meaning
acquaintance who had enlightened him. The divorce papers listed five charges.
If just one were true, he had sufficient grounds for a divorce:

1. That on the 5th day of November A.D. 1888, he was married to the
   defendant Emma Justus and has ever since then conducted himself

toward defendant as a good and faithful husband, but that the said defendant wholly disregarding her marital duties toward this plaintiff did on the 27th day of December 1889 willfully abandon this plaintiff and has ever since abandoned and remained absent from plaintiff.

2. And the plaintiff for and as a further and second cause and ground for divorce alleges that said defendant did on the [illegible] day of October 1890 at a house whose owner is unknown to plaintiff, in the City of Fort Scott, State of Kansas, commit adultery with one A. B. Lycan.

3. And the plaintiff for a further and third cause and ground for divorce alleges: That said defendant did on or about the [illegible] day of March 1891 at a house unknown to plaintiff in the City Of Joplin, Missouri commit adultery with a man whose name is to plaintiff unknown.

4. The plaintiff for a fourth cause of action alleges that said defendant did, on the 5th day of September 1892 at the house of one Jordan whose given name is to plaintiff unknown, in the City of Kansas City, Missouri, commit adultery with the said Jordan and she has at divers and sundry times committed adultery with said Jordan at said place, since the date above mentioned.

5. The plaintiff further alleges that said defendant is an habitual user of opium or other opiates or intoxicants and she is habitually under the influence of such drugs or liquors and has been such habitual user of said intoxicants for years past.[7]

The only problem for Justus and his attorney, L. F. Rager, was that the divorce papers could not be served on the "defendant" because nobody knew where to find her. An affidavit filed in May read: "That service of the notice to take depositions cannot be had upon the defendant Emma Justus in the State of Kansas: that said defendant is a nonresident of the State of Kansas and the residence of said defendant is unknown to affiant and cannot be ascertained by any means under his control: that said defendant has no agent or attorney of record in the State of Kansas."[8] It's doubtful that Emma would have hurried back to Walnut, the county seat, for the divorce proceedings anyway. Still, somebody had to cover the court costs, which normally would have fallen to the defendant. So Clarence agreed to do so; if that's what it would take to gain his freedom and be rid of his errant wife and the embarrassment she had caused him, he was more than ready to pay.

It was probably just as well that Emma knew nothing of the depositions, since her uncle Dan was about to say things under oath that would be injurious to her character. While Dan Housley would have preferred not to take sides against his own kin, he recognized that Clarence Justus deserved a little help.

Thus, on June 6, 1894, Daniel W. Housley appeared before a notary in Walnut, Kansas, and gave the following sworn statement:

> My name is D. W. Housley, my residence in Bourbon County, Kansas. I am acquainted with the plaintiff and defendant about twenty five or thirty years. She left Kansas some time in A.D. 1889. She has not returned since to live with her husband. They were living near Hepler, Kansas up to the time when she left and the plaintiff has been living there ever since. I saw the defendant in Kansas City, Mo. I think it was in September 1892. I called on her. She was there living with a man named John Jorden to whom she introduced me as her husband. They were keeping house together as man and wife there in Kansas City, Mo. I cannot give the street and number. It was about three blocks from the Metropolitan Hotel on Fifth Street from what I can learn. She is still living with the man Jorden as his wife. I know that from the year 1882 the defendant has been an habitual user of morphine, opium and other intoxicants to excess nearly always under the influence of drugs during the time that the plaintiff and defendant were living together as husband and wife. Apparently, the plaintiff provided well for his wife and treated her well. I lived about two miles from them.[9]

One month later, Clarence Justus was granted release from a marriage that had been doomed from the beginning.

Unresolved questions surrounding the Bond case persisted. Without fail, whenever somebody connected to the case was present, sooner or later the subject would come up. That apparently happened a few months after the Linn Leon story broke, when the elder John Montgomery was visiting friends in Decatur. Obviously aware of the Joplin debacle, the old man thoughtfully applied his own rationale, which he shared with his Decatur hosts as well as a reporter from the *Daily Republican*: "Mr. Montgomery maintains that all the circumstances at the time and since, fully established the fact that it was simply 'a freak of fraud' on the part of that young lady. Her friends were misled into a belief that she was a victim of outrages most foul. It was a put up job to hide the shame of her own crime."[10]

Throughout the Bond saga, personal opinion was treated as fact. In this instance, the writer was serving up a hefty plate of vilification without so much as a morsel of proof. He then tossed in a comment that seemed to side with Mr. Montgomery: "While this might be true, it was not so believed at the time by the public. Her career since has been one of the doubtful character. She now lives in Pittsburgh, Penn. Five thousand dollars did not pay Mr. Montgomery's defense expenses, to say nothing of the mob violence suffered by himself and family. In any event, it proved to be a most sorrowful episode to all concerned, and the public as well. Emma Bond never was in the school house as claimed."[11]

Without a doubt, Emma's new lifestyle was feeding the backlash. Nevertheless, several earlier influences had also worked against her. Burnett's theory—that there'd been no rape, only an abortion—had sparked doubts in 1886. Chances are, the general public never saw Kiernan's 1885 professional article. Nevertheless, the "worst form of hysteria" remark did appear in a popular newspaper and was attributed to "some of the best physicians." Emma's transgressions in Missouri were, in essence, the icing on the cake.

The end result was that John Sr. now possessed a full storehouse of ammunition, some of it courtesy of Linn Leon. And there was simply no way that she, or anybody else, could deflect the assault. In fact, John Sr. could now take slow and deliberate aim at the victim—with no fear of repercussions. If he was compelled to do so, it was probably because he—like any other father—felt the need to right the wrong done to his own kin. He was really no different than A. D. Bond, who had sought retribution for the crime against his daughter, the now-disgraced accuser.

On closer look, however, some telling clues can be drawn from the wording in this 1892 article. First was the phrase "all of the circumstances at the time and since." If those last two words didn't directly refer to Emma's Joplin indiscretions, nothing did. And what about "freak of fraud"? That seems clear, especially when taken with "her friends were misled" and "it was a put up job." All smacked of redundancy, and when taken as a whole, these phrases needed no further explanation. They were simply a way of saying that Emma had engaged in pretense and lies.

Yet, an astute observer would have noticed that none of these expressions were enclosed in quotation marks, suggesting that they weren't the exact words of John Sr. but rather the reporter's interpretation of them. That reporter then hedged by saying "while this might be true." The half-hearted concession seemed to imply that the accusations were unsubstantiated; this was lost in the very next sentence, however, when he wrote of Emma's "doubtful character"—another obvious reference to her life as Linn Leon. Perhaps precise terms—like "prostitute" and "bastard child" and "whorehouse"—were too shocking for readers. But the writer's choice of words left little doubt about what he meant.

His last assertion—that "Emma Bond was never in the schoolhouse as claimed"—had to be the most confusing and disturbing of all. It was confusing because it sounded like the writer was echoing Mr. Montgomery's sentiments, yet the remark just dangled there at the end of the article, attributable to no one in particular. And it was disturbing because not a smidgeon of proof was offered to back it up. In all, this 1892 article sounded like it had come from Mr.

Burnett's earlier postulations. And if repeated often enough, any theory can take on a life of its own.

However, this particular reporter did hit the bull's-eye with one pointed observation, and nobody could argue otherwise. The crime, the attempted lynching, the trial, the aftermath—together, these things represented the "most sorrowful episode to all concerned, and the public as well."[12] No one—not even the victim—could claim exclusive rights to the anguish that had resulted from this crime. Many had endured physical pain and emotional suffering. There had been more than enough anger and animosity to go around on all fronts—the public's included. And that said nothing of the peripheral damage: the jurors shunned, the suicides committed, the families ripped apart, the ruinous expenses incurred, and all the precious time lost with loved ones. Children and wives, mothers and fathers, sisters and brothers, cousins, close friends—almost nobody had escaped in one piece. And that, quite frankly, was what made the Bond case the most sorrowful episode in Christian County's history.

30

The Emma Bond outrage, though it happened thirty years ago, is still fresh in the minds of the people who lived here then, and at the time was a feature story in every newspaper in the U.S.
—Taylorville Daily Breeze, *December 24, 1910*

As the 1800s drew to a close, the Emma Bond case and its central figure drifted into relative obscurity. In time, she did marry her lover, Johnny Jorden, but there was no record of the couple's whereabouts between 1892 and 1900. They appeared in the 1900 U.S. census in Kansas, listed as Emma and John H. Jordan.[1] Under the column "Number of years married," the census taker entered a "6," an indication that the marriage had taken place in the same year as Emma's divorce from Justus. Her appearance in that 1900 federal census for Butler County, Kansas, represents the last verifiable proof of Emma's whereabouts until her death.

That same census also revealed that her relationship with her family, while it may have been badly damaged, was mended for a time. Living practically next door to the Jordens in 1900 were Josie and Obie Baughman and their two children. A few miles away were Belle and Hank Goodrich and their four children. In a separate abode from the Goodriches but on the same property lived Delia and A. D. Bond.[2] That meant that most of the family now lived in the region just east of Wichita. But there was a glaring lack of evidence as to Emma's whereabouts after 1900. The 1910 census showed that she and her husband no longer lived in Butler County, but an extensive search failed to turn up any clues as to where they had gone. Though it was not a common occurrence, people were sometimes missed in the door-to-door census canvassing. In all probability, they were still in Kansas, but where exactly?

An earlier census listing for Emma's husband, Johnny Jorden, revealed that his middle initial was "H." The 1902 Wichita city directory listed a "John H. Jordan," a contractor who lived on Dodge Street.[3] The same man also appeared in the city's 1904–1905 directory at a different address.[4] Both listings for this John

H. Jordan put him on the edge of what was then Wichita's booming business district. Still, it wasn't conclusive proof of the couple's whereabouts, especially since his was not an unusual name. Nor did the couple show up in the 1910 census for Wichita.

So why focus on Wichita at all? Because there was irrefutable proof that this was the last place Emma lived. It was also the place where the demons of her troubled past finally caught up with her. There, in the predawn hours of a bleak winter morning, Emma was admitted to Wichita Hospital.[5] And here at eight o'clock on the morning of December 18, 1910, morphine laid claim to Emma Bond Justus Jorden for the very last time. With only her husband and her sister Josie at her side, the long-suffering woman was finally granted absolution from almost thirty years of self-persecution. Though the attending doctor listed her official cause of death as "morphine poisoning," his handwritten note in the margin of her death certificate spoke volumes. It said: "morphine fiend."[6] To be sure, hers was no careless overdose administered by an inept doctor. No, this woman had died at her own hand, though probably by accident. It was the culmination of an unbearable tragedy, born of an unthinkable crime.

The next day—a Sunday—Emma was quietly laid to rest in Wichita's Highland Cemetery. The burial was a simple one; the only people present were the same two who had been at her side when she took her last breath—her second husband and her youngest sister. The cemetery is a lovely one, but for Emma it represents a forlorn ending. Her final resting place lies amid the graves of strangers, rather than those of her loved ones. Not even the one constant in her life—Johnny Jorden—lies anywhere within the bucolic sanctuary. Emma rests alone, in an unmarked grave. And while her death should have been the final chapter in this endless and baffling mystery, amazingly, it was not.

There was yet one more shocking revelation in the case—a piece of the puzzle brought to light more than 125 years after the crime, its details previously unknown. Surprisingly, the source of this unexpected disclosure was a descendant from the family of one of the suspects. What he had to share was an unbelievable tale that went something like this: With her physically weakened body giving up its earthly fight, Emma's spiritually burdened soul was moved to give up a long-held secret. Emma, it seems, made a deathbed confession, in which she revealed the identity of her rapist.

Unfortunately, it proved virtually impossible to verify these facts. Nonetheless, the details bear repeating. First among them, Emma named a boyfriend as the perpetrator of the attack. Second, sadistic wounds were inflicted upon her during the commission of the crime. Specifically—brutal mutilation, and possibly amputation, of her breasts. This stunning disclosure rings of golden truth, for it coincides perfectly with the "nameless indignities" the newspapers had so carefully danced around throughout the case. Regrettably, the informant could not remember if the boyfriend was identified by name; however, he did recall being told by his mother that the culprit was someone Emma's parents had disliked and distrusted immensely—someone they had urged their daughter to avoid. While it is hard to understand why Emma kept her secret for so long, fear of retaliation was undoubtedly the main contributing factor. Her attacker was obviously a sadistic man. And, to a lesser degree, her naïveté and humiliation probably reinforced her silence: what nearly grown child ever wants to admit that her parents were right? Yet, had she heeded her parents' warnings, her life of heartache might have been avoided.

The manner in which these newest revelations came to light was so incredible that it can only be attributed to that elusive thing called Fate. But if these new assertions are to be believed, their unwitting discovery demands at least a cursory explanation. First, the source of the information was an octogenarian (a fact that will no doubt call his accuracy into question, even though the elderly are known to have an uncanny knack for dredging up the smallest of details from the distant past). According to this person, in the late 1930s his mother produced a newspaper clipping, on the outside chance that the prickly subject of the Emma Bond rape might someday resurface. After reading the article in which the crucial information was given, this person—a teenager at the time—simply forgot about the matter and went on with his life, as teenagers will do. As to the date of the article or the newspaper from which it was taken, the informant had no recollection. With seventy-plus years having come and gone, even the sharpest of minds would have difficulty recalling such specifics. Not surprisingly, as a relative of one of the suspects, this person also felt that the accused had been rightfully vindicated by said article, given that the victim had redirected her accusations at a boyfriend. Finally, the information from this informant was not solicited but was offered of his own accord. Understandably, he also asked to remain anonymous.[7]

This newest information added an entirely new twist to the story. Still, it wasn't the full story. There were a few more surprises waiting to be uncovered, and they were not the cryptic words of a dying woman, but rather tangible and significant clues, stowed away in the great vault of recorded history.

31

Who committed the outrage on Emma Bond?
—Decatur Daily Republican, *January 3, 1884*

Despite Emma's obscure deathbed recantation, her world was left to ponder what really happened on June 29, 1882—the day her life came crashing down. Today, the Bond case still raises the same questions that captivated the nation more than 125 years ago. Who did it? And why? Or was there some truth, perchance, to the vague but persistent charge leveled against the victim in the aftermath of the crime—namely, that absolutely nothing happened to her in the schoolhouse and that she fabricated the whole story as a cover-up for whatever circumstances she was facing?

It is essential to put this last idea to rest. First, to embrace that notion one must ignore an abundance of clues to the contrary. Young Charlie heard noises in the loft and saw muddy footprints on the classroom wall, and there was no reason for him to invent any of it. Beyond that, many clues were found in the loft itself: the carved opening, the newspaper page, the piece of envelope, the tufts of hair, and the nail paring. Emma's belongings were found not only in the classroom but in the hard-to-reach attic. Exactly how, without a ladder and a knife, would she have ascended into the loft to plant the physical evidence and carve the hole? There was also the perplexing note scrawled across the chalkboard, written in what looked nothing like her handwriting. Blood was noted in several places besides the attic platform: on the classroom floor, on the victim, and on her clothing. One might argue that a young woman desperate to save her reputation could have easily inflicted superficial knife wounds on her own neck and wrists. But that did not explain the extensive bruising on her knees, wrists, arms, shoulders, thighs, and back—all confirmed by Dr. Cornell under oath. It's even harder to imagine how the victim could have given herself the kind of neck injuries that her doctor described in this way: "The neck was considerably swollen from the pressure, and the skin showed signs of the marks of the villains' hands. The windpipe had been nearly crushed."[1] And just what manner of agonizing contortions would the victim have had to put herself through to cause that severe spinal injury? Or the fractured rib? Or the internal injuries to her abdominal area? Cornell attested to all these things at the August hearing, and he later confirmed that her spleen was enlarged as a result of her injuries.

If that wasn't proof enough that a crime had been committed against Emma, then there were the newspapers' repeated veiled references to those "nameless indignities"—wounds so repugnant in nature that the Victorian press couldn't bring itself to share the specifics. Without a doubt, breast mutilation or amputation would have fallen into that category. In the end, the omission of the goriest details mattered very little, for, when taken as a whole, Cornell's testimony left no doubt about Emma's overall condition. Her body was badly abused, and she was subjected to unspeakable atrocities. Those are the fundamental facts, and there are simply too many of them to be explained away. Likewise, it would be preposterous to ignore them just to legitimize one of the alleged alternatives.

So presuming that a crime was, indeed, committed and that the recent disclosures from the anonymous informant were true, then the more precise question ought to be: Who was this so-called boyfriend who stole not only Emma's innocence but her entire future? These newest revelations demand a closer examination of the obvious suspects: The Montgomery brothers, Pettus, Clementi, Vermillion, and the soldier Elliott Hobbs. And it would be remiss to ignore Sonny Bond, given his oddly timed suicide. Finally, there was Adams, the missing fiancé. Who among these men had motive, and who did not? And where and how did they conduct the rest of their lives? Fortunately, almost every American who has lived in this country since the mid-1800s has left a paper trail. Government records and other historical documents are bursting with clues about the past. So it wasn't surprising that these sources contained some startling and pertinent details about certain men suspected in this case.

The last two men on the list of possible suspects were, of course, never charged with anything. It seems Sonny only fell under suspicion as time went by. And if, at the time, the locals had held any thoughts on his involvement, they managed to suppress them until John C. Montgomery's death in 1918. The *Tribune*, which had covered the Bond case extensively, could not let the death slip by without note. Its comments on John were redeeming, but what it had to say about Sonny was appalling.

The paper prefaced its charge by stating that it did not want to upset the parties concerned. If by that, the publishing stalwart meant the friends and family of the deceased, then it had succeeded. If, however, it was referring to the Bonds, then its accusation would fall pitiably short of that goal. For John's obituary contained something heretofore unseen in print, something sure to offend Emma's family. It's hard to believe that by 1918, the *Tribune* didn't have an entirely new staff in its employ. Yet, someone at the paper had enough knowledge to add a new twist to the unsolved Bond case. For there, tacked onto the end of John's death notice, was a none-too-subtle reference to Sonny Bond, which read: "She [Emma] made the charge to conceal the illicit love of her uncle, who killed himself afterward."[2]

Perhaps the belated accusation did make some sense, considering when Sonny chose to end his life. What didn't make sense was why the prestigious upstate journal was just now accusing someone who'd been dead for thirty-four years. What didn't make sense was the paper's obscure wording, leaving readers to wonder if Sonny's interest had been one-sided or reciprocal. What didn't make sense was how the paper could submit such a serious allegation without offering one speck of proof. If it had that proof, why not come clean with it, instead of dishing out more hearsay without calling it by its rightful name? Numerous allegations were unleashed in the decade after the trial, though none were ever substantiated. All appeared to be personal opinions that gained wider acceptance through repetition. But not a single one ever involved Sonny Bond.

So if not guilt over the inexcusable behavior suggested in John's 1918 obituary, what could have driven Sonny to take his own life? There was one other compelling explanation—the one first revealed in the coroner's inquest report and attributing his suicide to "Imagined Financial Embarrassment."[3] Sonny's estate papers did contain certain information apparently unknown to the wider community, which suggested that such a motive was not imagined on Sonny's part. It seems the man came nowhere close to being as wealthy as everyone liked to believe. Estimates placed his net worth as high as $100,000—an amount equivalent to more than $2.3 million in today's world. But at the time of his death, Abner Faye Bond was facing genuine hardship.

The detailed accounting contained in his estate file confirmed that the keen business man had dug himself into a deep pecuniary hole.[4] Sonny was virtually broke when he departed from this earth, and his shame over that would have been enough to push such a self-made man over the edge. Unfortunately, Sonny—always so thorough in his county's business affairs—had overlooked one small but important detail in his own personal affairs. He had failed to execute a will, a grave oversight for any father of underage children. So, at the county courthouse on the Monday after his death (January 7, 1884), Richard M. Powel was appointed administrator of Sonny's estate, with the capable J. M. Taylor assigned to look after the legal interests of Sonny's children.

Lizzie surely assumed her husband's sizeable estate would provide adequately for her and her children. Thus, to suddenly learn that her protector had left her almost nothing must have been devastating. When Powel assembled all the financial records of his longtime friend, they showed that Sonny's debts far exceeded his assets. The total claims against his estate totaled $13,433.61. Powel set to work disposing of Sonny's personal property—everything "not set apart to his widow, said Elizabeth E. Bond," which consisted of the family home and its furnishings. A few people still owed money to the deceased, and Powel was able to collect on some of those outstanding debts. But, in the end, the estate was left with a shortfall of $7,412.80. Luckily, one asset—a piece of undivided farmland in Section 33 of Buckhart Township—was not included in the final accounting.

But this was where things got sticky, because Lizzie's name was not on the deed for that land. For a wife to be thus omitted was typical in the nineteenth century, but in this instance, it was going to impede the settlement of the estate. Plus, there was another complication. Bond only owned half of that property; he and local entrepreneur Albert G. Barnes had purchased it together in April 1881 with each man assuming half of the mortgage. That debt was coming due in full—along with 8 percent interest—in March 1885. Powel needed to sell Sonny's half of the land to reduce the estate's obligations, but that money was not going to be easy to come by.

Barnes, aware of the legal implications brought on by his friend's sudden death, filed a petition for partition, asking the court to divide the land equally and fairly, in both quantity and quality. That way, he could keep his share of the land and the estate could sell its share. The obligation for the unpaid mortgage of $6,000, plus interest, would be split accordingly—between Barnes and Sonny's heirs. It promised to be a legal mess, but one with no alternative. Lizzie, with dower rights, had a lawyer to represent her interests, and her five children had attorney Taylor looking after theirs. The mortgage holder—Henry Davis—was also named in the petition, so yet another lawyer was involved.

In November 1884, the court appointed a three-man commission to assess the land's value and determine the most equitable way to divide it. First, they were to set off half of the property for Barnes. Next, Lizzie would get her share of the remaining half. What was left would be divided into five equal parcels for the Bond children. Not surprisingly, the mandate to assure a balance of quality among that many disparate segments proved impossible. The commission's report stated, "Each piece and parcel thereof is not susceptible of division without manifest prejudice to the parties."

There was some good news, however. The commission appraised the property at $12,400. But the land would have to be sold as a whole, with the proceeds and debt divided accordingly. On February 14, 1885—two weeks before the mortgage was due—the property went on the auction block. It fetched an even $10,000, yet when the mortgage was paid and the lawyers and court employees were given their due, Mr. Barnes walked away with barely $1,400 (given in three $469 payments over the course of eighteen months). The total allotment for Lizzie and her children was exactly the same, but their share had to be diverted to Sonny's estate to reduce the claims against it.

Fortunately, the court granted Lizzie a token "widow's award [of] $727.27," to cover her immediate living expenses. But the man rumored to have been worth as much as a hundred grand had left virtually nothing for his family. Lizzie and children had only their house and the land on which it stood. When Lizzie passed away in 1898, her five children inherited the aging house, plus forty acres and $129 apiece—a mere pittance to show for a family once believed to be among the wealthiest in the county.[5]

Just how much the munificent Sonny dished out during the course of the Bond case remains a guess. The press indicated that he was the main donor to the State's effort. One article placed his contributions at $10,000. In total, he may have dropped a good deal more than that: the reward fund rose to $31,000, with Sonny supposedly a liberal contributor to that as well. Another unknown is just how much cash he gave to his cousin. Although A. D. Bond had prospered during the 1870s, he'd hit a streak of bad luck shortly before the outrage occurred. According to the *Daily Republican*: "There are four [sic] girls in the family, and to lift the debt and assist their father, these brave young women, Emma among the number, went to work and did all the work on the farm themselves, putting in the grain and harvesting the crop last season. They saved the old home place, and last fall Miss Bond, who was studious in her habits, went to Taylorville and passed a successful exam by which she obtained a certificate to teach at the Montgomery School, at $40 a month for a period of five months."[6]

The crime, of course, ended Emma's contributions. Maggie's teacher's income was also lost that same year when she decided to marry. Bond was so overwhelmed in the aftermath of the crime that he neglected his farm, and Sonny probably depleted his own resources by trying to help his cousin out. In any case, what the citizenry of Christian County had long held to be undisputed truth turned out to be grossly inaccurate. Sonny Bond was not sitting atop a stack of greenbacks when he died, nor had he been for quite some time.

In Sonny's favor, a broader search of historical newspapers failed to turn up any other smears on his good name. And since the boyfriend was someone whom Emma's parents distrusted, that would seem to eliminate Sonny. Still, if there was even an ounce of truth in that 1918 accusation, then yes, Sonny would have had motive—but to do what, exactly? Jealousy over losing Emma to Mr. Adams certainly would have been one, but for a much younger, jilted lover—

not for an established family man with an outstanding reputation to protect. He could have simply let the girl go and moved on with his life—leaving the world, his wife, and his favorite cousin none the wiser.

Naturally, the possibilities for his ruination were numerous if he *had* been involved with Emma, regardless of her willingness. When considered with their thirty-year age difference, the blood relationship, and a possible pregnancy, it's a sure bet that a scandal of mammoth proportions would have rocked the county. Of course, if his motive were to silence the alleged object of his affections to avoid disgrace, he could have hired a younger man (or men) to carry out the wicked act. But the logic behind that move is also difficult to rationalize, because the more people who are in on a secret, the more likely it is to get out. And that kind of risk was too great for a man like Sonny.

In the end, the most plausible explanation for the sinister charge is that it was a misguided theory, spun off of his unexpected suicide and perpetrated by gossip and speculation over the years. Nonetheless, it surfaced after Emma's 1910 demise, which could indicate that it arose from her deathbed confession. That alone makes it hard to absolve Sonny completely, despite the alternate and valid financial explanation for his suicide.

While the term "boyfriend" was the one used by the recent informant, it was not necessarily the same word Emma used as she lay dying in 1910. Nevertheless, a "fiancé" might be loosely construed to be a "boyfriend." For that reason alone, Mr. Adams requires a second look. The press provided a couple of clues on where to look for the elusive fiancé: "It was reported and generally believed that Miss Bond . . . had gone to California or Nebraska to become the wife of a young ranchman."[7] Fifteen young bachelors named Adams (those born between 1853 and 1863) resided in Christian County in 1880. Those from Prairieton Township were the closest geographically, but none lived in the immediate vicinity of the Bond farm or the Montgomery School. Alternately, it was possible that Adams had gone west well before his engagement. Many a young man of that period sought to establish a stake on the plains as a precursor to taking a wife; then he would return home to claim his girl and cart her back to his established homestead. But only a handful of men named Adams turned up in the sparsely populated states of Nebraska and California in 1880.

Of those, only one came close to being a match. That fellow—a Jesper Adams, born in Illinois in 1861—didn't own his own land or ranch but worked as a "herder" in Fairmont, in Fillmore County, Nebraska.[8] Fairmont sits in southeastern Nebraska, about a hundred miles southwest of Omaha. Assuming that this was Emma's missing fiancé, it is ludicrous and illogical to think that the man would have left his labors on the remote plains and traveled all the way back to Illinois—by wagon, horseback, or rail—just to surprise his fiancée with a sexual assault. If he had experienced a change of heart and wanted out of his commitment, he could have simply stayed out west, buffered by the hundreds of miles of open country, and broken the news to her in a letter. Nobody would have undertaken that long journey for such a purpose. In the end, however, there was just too little information on the man to prove or disprove his exact identity, much less his possible involvement in the crime.

In the decades following the trial, while Emma's life was crumbling, the main defendants in the case went on with their lives. For John Montgomery and Lee Pettus, staying put in Christian County was a gutsy decision, to be sure. Many men in their shoes might have fled to new lives in new places, but they chose to live out their days where they were both born and raised and where their family roots ran deep. Lee and Allie eventually moved to nearby Mosquito Township and produced four children. John and Mattie and their three sons stayed put in Mt. Auburn Township, just outside of the Grove. John eventually purchased the 320 acres of land he had been leasing. Subsequent censuses showed his family living in virtually the same spot, surrounded by the same people they'd known all their lives: George and Effie Pettus, the Younkers, the Morgrets, the Masters, the Yockeys, and numerous Montgomery relatives—family and friends who had come to John's defense during his trial.

Other than the earlier breach of promise charge filed against Lee, neither man had any prior troubles nor subsequent run-ins with the law. If they had any motive for the crime at all, it was thin at best. The only one given much credence was that Emma may have acted snobbish in their presence. In addition, John was married with children and Lee had a soon-to-be wife in Allie. In the aftermath, both went on to raise decent families. Both worked hard to eke out respectable livings. Both went to their graves honored by friends and loved by family. So, too, did John's brother William. Of course, tuberculosis slammed the door shut on the question of his possible involvement. But in his favor, the State had no evidence of consequence against him. In truth, his alibi appeared the most airtight of all, as Emma herself said she heard his wagon pass by as she was being assaulted in the loft. Ultimately, however, there is no way to rule out the possibility that one or more of these men may have had prior knowledge of the crime or perhaps even acted as lookouts or accomplices.

Of the original suspects, Dr. Vermillion was one of three—along with Emanuel Clementi and Elliott Hobbs—who seemed to vanish into thin air after the fact. This brings to mind Mr. Burnett's 1886 assertion that the guilty party had left the county post-trial and could not be located. Burnett also surmised that Emma's wounds had been inflicted with surgical instruments, which might raise additional questions about the doctor.

William H. Vermillion, the oldest of the accused, spent more time behind bars than all the other suspects combined—even though he was charged only with complicity.[9] But because he was a physician, it wasn't difficult to fill in the gaps in his pre- and post-trial life. After graduating from the Eclectic Medical Institute of Cincinnati in 1877, Vermillion apparently set out for tiny Fourche, Arkansas. Within months, however, he turned up in central Illinois, where he took out a medical license and hung out his first shingle in the Grove. He wed Kate Hart in 1879, and although she died in 1880, the couple was recorded in that census. It shows that her ten-year-old sister Ella and his thirty-year-old spinster sister Mary were both living under his roof that year—something that might speak well of his character.

The doctor left Christian County for good some time after the trial and before 1886, when he applied for a medical license in North Dakota. But by 1900, he was back in Arkansas, where he lived by himself in a place called Roland, northwest of Little Rock. He applied for his state medical license in 1903 and was one of four physicians who had a practice in that tiny town of eight hundred souls—nearly all of them poor, black tenant farmers. Four seemed like an overabundance of doctors for a town that size; clearly, it was not the ideal place to build a lucrative medical practice. However, it was the perfect place to escape one's past and avoid the public eye. Oddly, he did not appear in the 1910 Arkansas census. In any case, he was back in Arkansas by 1914—single, retired, and living in a Little Rock boardinghouse, his last known residence. Beyond that, there was nothing to suggest that he was anything other than a practicing, though perhaps lonely, physician throughout the remainder of his life.

On reputation alone, Clementi's name should probably be moved to the top of the list—as a potential accomplice at the very least or as the unnamed "boyfriend" at the utmost. Many of his actions were never explained to satisfaction. Among them were his reluctance to drive Emma home, his early-morning quest for a fast horse, his callous demeanor in discussing the crime, and his protracted detour across the Pettus pasture in pursuit of the culprits. That last one begs the question: how did Clementi know in which direction to ride in this noble pursuit?

News reports raised even more questions. One mentioned blood spots on his shirt, a bitten finger, and cuts on his hand at the time of his arrest. If true, these things should have set off the alarms. Another claimed he sported chin whiskers on the twenty-ninth but was clean-shaven on the thirtieth. Several pieces of evidence were left at the schoolhouse, and one was specifically linked to Clementi: that part of the *Chicago Times* found at the crime scene was said to have fit neatly into a portion of the same paper that turned up in his bedroom. And, according to the testimony of a dozen witnesses, he was seen reading that same paper on the afternoon of June 29. Another potential link was the piece of envelope found in the loft, "the counterpart of which was found on the person of one of the prisoners."[10] The press never stated which prisoner that was, but any man who had spent most of his adult life wandering from place to place was more likely to have an out-of-town letter on his person than one who'd spent his entire life in one place. He was also suspected of securing the chloroform used on Emma, but the witness who could have verified that had died of tuberculosis right before the trial.

Justice Ricks seemed to think that anybody with a ready alibi—like Clementi—was probably innocent; however, many experts might disagree. The innocent do not prepare alibis in advance, mainly because they don't anticipate the need for one. Clementi mentioned his alibi at the very moment of his arrest, suggesting he had thought about it in advance. Certainly, anyone who has had previous run-ins with the law knows the value of a strong alibi. While all of this sounds incriminating, it does not prove motive. But for some rapists, motive is nothing other than being able to overpower a helpless victim for their own sexual gratification. For Clementi—a man of highly dubious character to begin with—that may have been motive enough. However, his presence at the noontime meal at the Pettus house would seem to exclude him as the ringleader and, thus, as the boyfriend. Based on little Charlie's testimony, *that* man was probably hiding in the school loft all day, though Clementi could well have been an accomplice, if not a participant in the rape itself.

Clementi's past was fairly well covered during the trial, but he left minimal evidence of his post-trial existence. While he did return briefly to Christian County in 1884, it wasn't long before he took off again—permanently. Thankfully, Ona Pettus became wise to his ways before it was too late, or else he slithered out of Christian County without so much as a goodbye to his young fiancée. Given her age and his reputation, Ona's family must have been very relieved to see him go. He apparently spent some or all of his next four years working as a machinist in Milwaukee, where his mother, Maria, lived. And, in fact, that was where he died in 1888, just four years after his acquittal.

Elliott Hobbs, like the drifter Clementi, had no permanent attachments to Christian County. But unlike him, the army enlistee did leave an extensive and intriguing trail of documentation on his life—including censuses, military and pension files, and marriage and divorce records. Taken as a whole, they weave a tale of a man whose life was anything but admirable.

32

Hobbs . . . stated that he went from St. Louis to Mitchell, Illinois, reaching the latter place on the morning of June 28th, when he went to work for a man named Ellsworth, remained with him until he was discharged on the morning of 30th of June for oversleeping himself.
—Decatur Daily Republican, *August 24, 1882*

Private Hobbs was the last to be arrested and the first to be cleared. During the 1882 investigation, very little was written of the laborer turned soldier. His name didn't even surface until August 1, a full month after the outrage. In fact, he was mentioned in fewer than ten news articles before he was released from the Taylorville jail in September, when he was sent back to his army post, never to be seen in the Christian County area again.

Like Clementi, Hobbs was a young, single man in search of farm work, wherever he could find it. Like Pettus, his age was close to Emma's, making him someone who might have taken a fancy to the attractive young schoolteacher. He was said to have lived and worked in Christian County shortly before the crime occurred, although the exact date of his departure was never given. Not long after the outrage, he turned up in Springfield—thirty miles from Taylorville. On August 1, the *Tribune* reported that Hobbs had joined the Army there on July 21 because, by his own admission, he had just been fired from his Mitchell, Illinois, job for oversleeping. Like the timing of Sonny's suicide, the timing of Elliott's enlistment should have raised a flapping red flag.

What else can be deduced from the known facts that might point to Hobbs as Emma's mystery boyfriend? From day one, Mr. Bond seemed hell-bent on getting to the bottom of things and wasted no time in hiring Mr. Page to help. What was most remarkable about their detective work, however, was just how quickly they zeroed in on Hobbs's enlistment, and, in particular, where it had taken place. The probability that they made that Springfield connection on their own seemed remote—like the proverbial "needle in a haystack." Either their discovery was an enormous stroke of luck, or someone in the know tipped them off. The following statement revealed a lot: "Mr. Bond stated to the Sergeant that they had pretty conclusive evidence that Hobbs, who was a resident of Christian County at the time the outrage was committed, is one of the guilty parties."[1] This also raises the thought that Emma's father had not needed a crime solver so much as a suspect tracker. Perhaps Hobbs was the same man that he and Delia had disliked so intensely—the one they had urged Emma to avoid. If so, Bond's determined pursuit of Elliott Rainey Hobbs makes a lot of sense.

Assuming Hobbs was the boyfriend, what transpired in Emma's bedroom after his arrest might have been more than met the eye. One can only imagine the victim's terror to suddenly find her attacker standing at the foot of her bed. Would she have dared react to his presence, given the viciousness of the act and the verbal threats uttered during its commission? Fear of retaliation would have been more than enough to scare her into utter silence. Or, maybe she was not yet capable of rational thinking, especially if morphine was clouding her mind. And who's to say that Hobbs wasn't holding his own breath, in hopes that Emma would keep her mouth shut. That "no word was spoken" doesn't mean unspoken messages weren't exchanged between the two.[2] Hobbs could have shot Emma an intimidating look while everybody else was focused on *her* face. Further, if he was nothing more than an innocent and casual friend, as the article implied, then surely some sort of dialogue, however minimal, would have passed between the two. Hobbs might have said something like "How are you feeling, Emma?" or "So sorry to hear about what happened to you." And she might have managed a simple "Hello, Elliott" or "What are you doing here?" Yet, not a single word broke the stilted silence as Hobbs stood there, within an arm's length of poor Emma in—of all places—her bedroom, until that moment, the only remaining safe haven in her world.

Another illuminating sequence of events apparently escaped all notice in August 1882. It was reported on the eighth of the month that Sergeant Ricketts "returned a day or two ago" from Columbus.[3] Allowing for travel, he would have been in Columbus, quizzing Hobbs on August 4 or 5. These dates become more significant when considered in conjunction with the mysterious Chicago letter sent to Mr. Bond, dated Saturday, August 12—just one week after Ricketts tipped off Hobbs that he might be a suspect in the outrage. Postmarked in Chicago on Monday, August 14, the letter reached Mr. Bond on Wednesday, August 16. That same day, Page showed up in Ohio to arrest Hobbs. While the letter's timing could have been a mere coincidence, it could also have been a carefully executed ploy, meant to divert suspicions from the real culprit and seal the fate of those already in jail. The eight days between August 4 and 12 were ample time to compose a letter in Ohio and send it to somebody in Chicago, with instructions to forward it to Taylorville.

Hobbs was certainly smart enough to know from the sergeant's visit that his days of freedom were probably numbered. Yet, something about that letter seemed off at the time and still does. Whoever wrote it knew far more about the crime than he should have. First, he attempted to clear Dr. Vermillion; yet, as a mere passerby, how could he say with certainty what the doctor did or didn't *know,* much less what the doctor did or didn't *do?* It was an outrageous claim. And the author's mention of a wife sounded like a feeble attempt to cover his true identity. Furthermore, someone on the road would not have been privy to the kinds of details contained in that letter. How, for instance, could he have known that Pettus was "concealed" in the attic if he only saw Montgomery and Clementi exiting the school? Even more problematic—how could he have known the order in which the suspects took their turns at Emma? This begs the question: just how close to the schoolhouse did this tramp happen to pass? Right through the attic itself, perchance? As for calling himself "the tramp that they mentioned," what better way to discourage any further searches for the two tramps seen in Blue Mound? If ever a letter read like a hoax, it was this one.

The troubling August timeline continued after Hobbs's arrest. He was officially booked on Friday, August 18, charged with "rape of the person of Emma Bond," not complicity, as the press reported at the time.[4] That same day, he was taken out to the Bond farm, where he coughed up an alibi. On Monday, August 21, Mr. Bond suddenly backed off, saying he now had doubts about the soldier's involvement. It was also reported that Bond planned to check out the Mitchell alibi. Then, on Wednesday, August 23, Detective Page suddenly took off for Decatur, looking for an "unknown party . . . implicated in the terrible affair."[5] His destination was the Forepaugh circus, where he hung around the gate, searching the faces for someone in particular. Based on the timing of this excursion, it may have had something to do with the information Hobbs had provided.

Four days later, the *Review* decreed, "The people *are satisfied* that Hobbs is innocent of any part in the crime and the authorities would gladly be rid of him."[6] Two days after that, the *Republican* wrote: "Mr. Bond broke the spirit of the mob when he cut the rope from John Montgomery's neck. He says now he would have kept his knife in his pocket . . . had he been as sure then as he is at present of Elliott Hobbs' whereabouts the afternoon of June 29."[7] Apparently, Bond's detective was also swayed by whatever Hobbs had to say. In an interview on the last day of August, Page ranted about all of the other suspects: "I know things that the public do not know and I tell you when Miss Bond gets able to testify, if she ever does, these men and others will be convicted."[8] He then ticked off the suspects' names, omitting only that of Elliott Hobbs.

While all of this made it sound as if somebody did, indeed, follow up on Hobbs's alibi, that remains an assumption. First, the press wrote nothing more about it, other than noting that everyone had done an about-face on Hobbs.

Furthermore, if the people were so thoroughly convinced of his innocence by the end of August, as the papers implied, why was he held until September 19? Was it because investigators were having trouble tracking down his employer, Mr. Ellsworth? And if his alibi was never confirmed, the decision to release Hobbs was based solely on his own statement—that he was in Mitchell, working for somebody named Ellsworth, on the days in question.

It would also be a grave error to ignore the influence of that mysterious Chicago letter on Mr. Bond, Detective Page, and the local authorities. So eager were they to believe the right men were in custody that they did not seem to notice the letter had "fraud" written all over it. Most suspicious of all was its absolutely perfect timing: mailed from Chicago one week after Ricketts's trip to Ohio, and received by Bond just two days before Hobbs was returned to Taylorville.

When all was said and done, what seemed most frustrating was how very little was known about Mr. Ellsworth. An alibi witness is always highly relevant, and yet almost nothing was written of him. Since this was the soldier's only defense, it demanded a more thorough investigation, even though confirming it or refuting it today—more than 125 years after the fact—seemed like a long shot.

The little town of Mitchell sits on the western edge of Illinois in Madison County, five miles east of where the Mississippi begins to shoulder its way past St. Louis. But there never was—nor is there now—anything to entice a body to seek out the place, let alone to linger there. So it is hard to say just how and why Elliott R. Hobbs wound up in Mitchell, Illinois, in late June 1882. If he truly was there, as he claimed, the next logical question might be: Who was this man named Ellsworth, and was he recorded in the 1880 Madison County census?

In fact, five men with the last name Ellsworth lived in Madison County in 1880, but none in Mitchell proper.[9] And not a single one of them sounded like a potential employer for Hobbs, because of either age or financial situation. Two were young white men who worked as farm laborers themselves. The other three were mulattoes—two in Edwardsville and one in Alton. All five were leading hard lives. And this was Madison County in southern Illinois—"southern" being the operative word. It was a section of the state that had harbored many a Confederate sympathizer during the Civil War. Hence, it would have been highly unusual for a young white man to seek employment from a man of color in that region, just fifteen years postwar.

Alternatively, the alibi witness might not have been a "Mr. Ellsworth" at all; there were two males in the county whose parents had saddled them with the first name "Ellsworth."[10] But again, they were easily discounted, since one was a thirteen-year-old mulatto, and the other, at sixteen, was a coal miner. So, if this Ellsworth fellow lived in Mitchell in the summer of 1882, it sure didn't look like he'd been there during the federal enumeration two years earlier. It seemed the man named as Elliott's rock-solid alibi had slipped, undetected, through history's fingers.

Other aspects of Hobbs's alibi were equally vexing. He claimed, ever so conveniently, to have been in Mitchell the day before, the day of, and the day after the crime. Hired on Wednesday, the twenty-eighth. Fired on Friday, the thirtieth. Furthermore, it seemed remarkable that a supposedly innocent man would have such perfect recall when almost nobody can remember precisely what he was doing eight weeks prior. One other point might also be relevant. The Wabash trains bound for St. Louis—those that came from Decatur to Blue Mound, Taylorville, and Litchfield—passed right through the sleepy little town of Mitchell before crossing the rail bridge into St. Louis. One of those could have deposited Hobbs back in Mitchell in the early morning hours of Friday, June 30. Witness Stumpf even mentioned seeing the strangers right before the "freight bound for St. Louis" came through Blue Mound. Plus, there were two early-morning passenger trains that also passed through the village. The first—which arrived in Blue Mound at 4:15 A.M.—would have pulled into Mitchell at exactly 7:23 A.M.[11] A passenger on that train could have disembarked, rushed off to his bed, and pulled the blankets up over his head in plenty of time to make it look as if he'd overslept for work.

Of course, the train to Mitchell wasn't the only escape route available to the Bond rapist. There were others, including the one mentioned in connection with the bottle of chloroform found in Litchfield: "Yesterday, Mr. Freshwater of Blue Mound, who saw the fellows in that village, went to Litchfield, and securing that bottle and a further description of the men, went to Waverly in pursuit."[12] This statement, while fascinating, drew little attention in 1882. The Litchfield-Waverly clue apparently fell by the wayside, just like the actual bottle of chloroform. In fact, all trains en route from Decatur to St. Louis stopped in Litchfield. And with rail lines crisscrossing all over central Illinois, a passenger could easily go from Christian County to Litchfield and from there catch a northbound train to Waverly. From Waverly, it was a short ride into Springfield. And a passenger taking that route would have entered the capital city from the west rather than the east, which may have been a good diversionary tactic.

In fact, Waverly was so close to the capital city—barely twenty miles away—that any able-bodied man could have covered the distance on foot in less than two days without looking any worse for the wear. And then, with a flourish of ink on army paper, he could have literally disappeared—whisked away by his superiors to some far-off garrison. That would have been the expectation, anyway. But it seems Hobbs was forced to hang around Springfield for almost two weeks before being transported to his Ohio barracks. If he was in a big rush to get out of central Illinois in July 1882, that delay must have felt like an eternity.

Thus, given the suspicious timing of the Chicago letter, its even stranger content, the rail lines linking Christian County to Mitchell and Springfield, plus the possibly unproven alibi, granting Private Hobbs his freedom may have been a gross error in judgment. Of course, with all of the other missteps made during this case, such a prospect wasn't entirely out of the question.

33

I, Elliott R. Hobbs, desiring to enlist in the Army of the United States for the term of five years, do declare that I have neither wife nor child; that I am of the legal age to enlist, and believe myself to be physically qualified to perform the duties of an able-bodied soldier.
   —Declaration of Recruit signed by Elliott R. Hobbs, dated July 3, 1882

Hobbs, an Indiana native born in 1861, appeared in the 1880 census in Omaha, where he was working as a teamster and living in a large boardinghouse with dozens of other young men who did similar work.[1] Strangely, the census trail for Hobbs went cold after that year. His name did not appear in any subsequent federal censuses through 1930 (the most recent one released to the public). However, veterans' records can be a virtual gold mine of information, and Hobbs's file was.[2] Though it contained only five pages, those held many valuable and startling clues about the former Bond suspect.

When he signed on with the army in Springfield, Hobbs was noted to have brown eyes, light hair, a ruddy complexion, and a height of six feet, one-half inch. His papers also revealed that his middle initial was "R," and that he was born on November 7, 1860, in Delaware Station, Ripley County, Indiana. The file gave his exact date of enlistment, which was *not* July 21 as originally reported by the *Tribune,* but Monday, July 3, 1882—just four days after the schoolhouse attack.[3]

Hobbs was assigned to Company G of the 14th U.S. Infantry and was first stationed at the army's Cantonment Uncompahgre in Colorado. His next assignment took him way out west, to Washington Territory, where he spent time at both the Vancouver and Seattle Barracks. His file also indicated that he enlisted for a second tour of duty in the mid-1890s. But the most helpful clue of all was the one found on his "Statement of Service Reference Slip." Written just above his name was an astounding note that explained why Elliott Hobbs had been impossible to find in every post-1880 census. When he reenlisted, he did so using an alias—his new name: Elliott R. Harding. This clue was the key to unlocking the rest of the man's life. Knowing his alias, his exact name and age, and other details allowed access to his complete pension file.[4] The information contained therein made it possible to trace Elliott Rainey Hobbs/Harding for an additional forty-nine years.

The rest of Hobbs's story began with his discharge from the army in Washington Territory on July 3, 1887, five years to the day after his enlistment. He left the military as Elliott Hobbs and wasted no time changing his name. Nine months later—on April 7, 1888—Elliott Harding took a bride. Young Lena Taylor was just sixteen when she married the twenty-seven-year-old. The groom signed their marriage certificate as Harding, so there's a strong chance that Lena never knew her husband's real surname.[5]

Territorial censuses showed that when Hobbs was released from the army, Lena still lived at home with her parents, J. V. and S. Taylor, and her younger brother, Kester.[6] In the next territorial count in 1889, she was recorded as Mrs. Lina Harding.[7] The head of her household was listed only as a "Harding" (a "laborer" with no first name given). The couple lived in Seattle's Ward Two with their five-month-old infant son. Lena was counted twice that year, which wasn't unusual; what *was* unusual was the nature of that second entry.[8] It showed her living in her parents' home where someone—possibly Lena herself—gave her name to the canvasser as "Lena Taylor." Her baby was likewise recorded as a Taylor, with no first name given. (The baby's name was James Merlin and he had arrived in January 1889.[9]) Since she had married Harding just a few months earlier, this seemed most irregular.

Both census entries for Lena and her child were recorded on the same July day, and both houses were located in Seattle's Ward Two, but they were sixty-four pages apart in the census book. While there's no way to determine the proximity of the two homes, they were probably close enough for Lena to scurry back and forth between them. That didn't explain, however, why mother and child were recorded as Taylors at one house and as Hardings at the other. Was it possible young Lena had already left or was in the process of leaving her new husband?

The 1889 census highlighted another discrepancy. It gave Harding's occupation as "laborer." However, three consecutive Seattle directories—starting in 1888—hinted at a deceptive streak in the man. All three gave his occupation as a "police officer" or "policeman."[10] Other than these instances, he was never listed as anything other than a laborer or carpenter. The explanation may be tied to the E. R. Harding found in Washington's "National Guard Enlistment Register."[11] The information on that man perfectly matched Elliott Harding: aged twenty-eight at enlistment, a height of six feet and one-half inch, a carpenter, born in Indiana. If this was the same man—and it surely was—he had joined the guard in the same month that he married Lena. At the time, National Guard units operated strictly as volunteer militias, charged with controlling the occasional outbreak of civil unrest, so to equate sporadic guard duty with full-time police work clearly embellished the facts.

In 1892, Elliott turned up in the same Seattle ward where he and Lena and their baby had first appeared together in 1889.[12] It would have been nice to discover, at least for Lena's sake, that the two were making a go of their life together. But instead, there was only more proof that something was terribly wrong in the marriage. For Elliott now lived in the home of a younger brother—who was also using the last name Harding.

E. H. Harding, age twenty-nine, was listed as the head of their household. He had a young wife, Idella, age twenty-one, and a baby girl, still unnamed at two months. In addition to Idella, a second young woman lived in the expanded Harding household. She was recorded only by the initial "B.," but the ditto marks next to her name (underneath E. H. Harding's) implied that she was also a Harding. This was definitely not Lena, though. First of all she was twenty-five, and Lena was only twenty-two that year. And "B." was born in Wales—a long way from Lena's birthplace of Colorado. Further, there was no child named James (or Merlin) in the home. And by this time Elliott Harding had fathered another child with Lena. Little Nola Fern Harding had entered the world on December 3, 1890; but there was no Nola in the Harding household, either.

It's hard to say who "B."—occupation "housekeeper"—was. If her last name truly was Harding, perhaps she was Elliott's second (and unlawful) wife. That she was born in Wales strongly suggested that she was not a blood relative.[13] But if she was even a distant one, why weren't Lena and her two small children with Elliott? And, furthermore, why was the younger brother now using the same last name as Elliott? The older man had changed his immediately after his 1888 discharge. Maybe he would have done it sooner, but the army wouldn't let somebody change his identity midstream. While it wasn't hard to come up with a theory on Elliott's alias, his brother's name change was more difficult to explain.

In December 1894, Elliott reenlisted in the army, as Elliott Harding. He spent the next three years at the Port Townsend and Vancouver Barracks, his duties coming to an end on December 19, 1897. However, civilian life was not to his liking for long; barely a month later, he turned up in San Diego, where he signed on with the navy. It's hard to come up with a good reason for his being thirteen hundred miles away from Lena and his two children. On January 31, 1898, he reported to work as a ship's carpenter on the steamship USS *Albatross*—moored in San Diego Harbor. Three months later, he was discharged. His navy papers included another physical description: brown hair, hazel eyes, and dark complexion. Also, scars were noted: "on the left arm, the right thigh, the right leg, the left leg, and small scars on both hands."[14] Even for a carpenter, that seemed like a lot.

Until this point, the only indication that Harding ever intended to fulfill his fatherly and husbandly obligations was that 1889 census, when James Merlin was a newborn and Lena was undecided about her last name and where she lived. It looked like their marriage was—and always had been—a pretense. Still, the June 1900 census suggested there'd been a reconciliation: Lena told the census taker who came through her Ballard City neighborhood that her husband, Elliott, was living in her household.[15] He was actually nowhere close that summer; instead, he was up in Port Valdez, Alaska, from April until September.

That village port sprang up initially as the starting point of an alternate route into the Yukon during the 1898-99 gold rush. But the place was soon overrun with starving and destitute miners, ravaged by the extreme weather conditions. When army units arrived to cut in military roads, lay telegraph and telephone lines, and build Fort Liscum, the government hired many of the waylaid miners. So there's a good chance Elliott went to Alaska initially as a prospector, before signing on as a carpenter in Port Valdez. He was counted twice in the 1900 census—in Ballard City, Washington, and in Port Valdez, Alaska.[16] In the latter, the census listed him as one of the many construction workers living at the government's work camp. Oddly, Elliott's brother E. H. was nowhere to be found at the turn of the century, nor were his wife Idella and their little girl. One thing was certainly becoming clear—the Harding brothers didn't like any dust to collect under their feet.

The Harding brothers definitely warranted some further investigation, especially since both had changed their last names. The obvious step was to backtrack to their childhoods in Indiana, in hopes of determining how they'd come up with the new last name. It could have been their mother's maiden name or some other familial name. Although nothing was found to prove that, there were some new revelations buried in the 1870 and 1880 censuses that indicated that the two had come from a very difficult family background. In 1870, both were school-aged boys, and their middle-aged father worked as a farm laborer.[17] This was unusual, since farm laborers were almost always young, unmarried men—not family men with wives and children to support. Further, John Hobbs owned no real estate and his personal assets amounted to only $100. The Hobbs family was dirt poor.

Another telling clue turned up in the 1880 census. That year, the family—or at least the parents and the two youngest of their five children—should have still been living together on their Indiana farm. But they were not. Instead, the father, John, had taken up residence with his own mother in neighboring Ripley County, Indiana, where he was recorded as a married man.[18] Mother Susan was now working as a live-in servant for a wealthy family near Cincinnati, and her marital status was given as "widowed/divorced."[19] She obviously held a much different view of her state of matrimony than did John. And why were their two youngest children—both girls, by then fifteen and thirteen—nowhere to be found that year? Although the first three siblings—all boys—were all old enough to have been on their own, something was definitely amiss. It seemed that the Hobbs family had been ripped apart at the seams sometime between 1870 and 1880, and the reason was a mystery. A rampaging illness having claimed the two young girls wasn't the happiest of explanations, but it was far better than the other, more disturbing possibilities—those having to do with the father's temperament and behavior.

Without a doubt, the most shocking discovery turned up in the 1870 census. That listing for the Hobbs family began with the head of the household: John, farm laborer, age forty, born in Maryland. Susan was next: age thirty-three, born in Kentucky. Toward the right side of the form, in line with her name, were checks under "cannot read" and "cannot write." Then came the names of the five Hobbs children. The oldest was Elias W., age eleven. He, like his father, was working as a "farm laborer." While checkmarks by the other four young-sters' names showed that they had all attended school within the year, no such marks appeared next to Elias's name. Elliott R., age nine, was next. And under him were the names of the three youngest Hobbs children: Elsworth H., Ida M., and little Emma—ages eight, five, and three.

So Elliott had a brother whose name was Ellsworth! When he named his employer Ellsworth as his alibi, he never said a word about the man being a relative, much less a brother. But here was an Ellsworth, a man to whom Elliott had blood-thick loyalty. Was this the missing piece of the puzzle? It certainly had all the earmarks of being so. Given his age, this "Elsworth H. Hobbs" was obviously the same man as the E. H. Harding with whom Elliott had lived in Seattle in 1892. What else was there to be learned of this brother? Indeed, there was a good deal more, starting in July 1883.

That month, one year after his older brother's enlistment, Ellsworth H. Hobbs walked into an Indianapolis recruiting office and also signed up for the army.[20] He was twenty-one at the time. Military records noted his physical fea-tures: brown hair, brown eyes, dark complexion, and five feet eight inches in height. Somehow, the younger brother finagled an assignment to the 14th In-fantry, Company K, stationed at the Vancouver Barracks in Washington Terri-tory. Once there, he got himself transferred to Company G—Elliott's company. And so the Hobbs brothers were reunited. The older one wound up in the Pa-cific Northwest because the army had kindly deposited him there. The younger one, with time on his hands, apparently waited to see where his older brother would land, then followed him to the remote northwest coast.

Ellsworth had also signed on for five years, so his discharge trailed Elliott's by one year. By the time the younger brother was released in July 1888, the older had already assumed the Harding name and was married, with a baby on the way. Perhaps it was then, at the his brother's urging, that E. H. took on his new identity. If the two men wanted to make themselves hard to find, this was the prudent thing to do.

34

The deed had been DELIBERATELY AND CUNNINGLY PLANNED.
—*Chicago Tribune, July 6, 1882*

In view of these surprising discoveries about the Hobbs brothers, it isn't hard to envision a scenario that may have unfolded something like this: While working as a farm laborer in Christian County, Hobbs took a fancy to the young schoolteacher named Emma Bond. He may have flattered her with attention, and she may have been smitten by his charismatic ways. However, her parents were not pleased that their daughter was attracted to a drifter. So Emma rejected him, at her parents' insistence. She broke the bad news to him in April 1882, by announcing she was going to marry Adams. Some time in the next two months, Hobbs left the county—mad as all get-out. Mr. and Mrs. Bond breathed sighs of relief, thinking the unsavory character was now out of the picture and Emma had put her life on the right course. But as the weeks went by, Hobbs's anger intensified as he brooded over the rejection. It was bad enough that another man was going to walk away with the object of his affections, but it was even more galling to think he'd been unable to control the damned girl.

Elliott soon linked up with his younger brother in or near Mitchell, Illinois. There, he concocted a plan for revenge and convinced Ellsworth to help carry it out. He sent word to his buddy Clementi, telling him of his plan to get even with the teacher who had rebuffed him. He would return by train, a day or so before Emma's school let out for the summer. In the meantime, he wanted Clementi to get some chloroform from Dr. Vermillion—he would need it to keep his victim quiet. When the set day arrived, Elliott boarded one of the three daily northbound trains on the Chicago & St. Louis line. Two stopped in Mitchell, while the third stopped at nearby Edwardsville Junction. One required a transfer and a two-hour wait in Litchfield, but any of the three would eventually get him to his destination.

Elliott probably made the trip ahead of his brother. This assumption is based on a comment in the *Republican* on July 12, 1882, which referred to the two tramps and some evidence, thought to be connected: "Two days after the outrage was committed, the station agent at Taylorville found a bag in the waiting room that contained clothing, and a newspaper on the margin of which was written words referring to the Montgomery schoolhouse and describing its location."[1] As a former county resident, Elliott would have known the exact location of Emma's school. But Ellsworth, unfamiliar with the area, would have had no idea how to get there. And so, before leaving Mitchell, Elliott grabbed the nearest piece of paper and jotted down directions for his brother. Really, what were the odds that anyone other than one of the guilty parties would have been carrying around written directions to the schoolhouse where the crime took place?

Late on Wednesday, June 28—their travels masked by the sound and fury of the night's thunderstorm—Elliott and his brother made their separate ways on foot to the Grove City neighborhood. There, they met their local accomplice at a rendezvous near the schoolhouse. That accomplice then led them to a hiding place not far away but out of view of the road—perhaps a secluded spot on the Pettus property, in a dip near the creek. Clementi had already stashed the requested supplies there, in a makeshift camp for his comrades. There was some food to tide them over, the essential bottle of chloroform, maybe a blanket or two, and, quite possibly, some dry footwear—since their shoes and socks would have been soaked from tramping through fields saturated by the evening's wild weather. They'd each brought a change of shirt and pants, which they would save for their incognito getaway, in case the victim's blood wound up in places it shouldn't. The brothers then hunkered down on the damp weeds to catch some much-needed rest before daybreak.

When the faint glow of approaching dawn began to dance across the eastern horizon, their advanceman returned and the plan for the day was finalized. There is no way to know whether Clementi brought anyone else. In any event, he was sent to scout out the schoolhouse before it got too light. When the coast was clear, the Hobbs brothers were smuggled inside. With a boost from Clementi, the two ascended into the dark realm above. But in the dim interior, none of them noticed the muddy footprints they'd left on the school's wall. Clementi then departed, and the two predators settled down for the day, listening for the arrival of their special prize. Before leaving, however, Clementi expressed a desire for a piece of the action, too—surely he deserved something for all the trouble he'd gone to! Hobbs had no argument with that, so it was agreed Clementi would rejoin the brothers during afternoon recess. He would get Minnie and Ona to postpone their practice with Emma until mid-afternoon.

Meanwhile, Clementi made sure to be seen throughout the day so that his absence in the afternoon would not be so obvious. He also told Lee Pettus and John Montgomery who was in the attic and what they were up to. Thus, he decided to enlist the help of one or more of his friends (be it Lee or John or William). Maybe he asked one of them to act as a lookout or to give him a boost into the attic—just in case the Hobbses's outstretched hands weren't enough to lift him. But, warned Clementi, the window of opportunity would be very narrow, so the task had to be accomplished quickly.

Shortly before two thirty, Clementi slithered out of the wagon where he'd been resting, snuck across the road, circled behind the coalhouse, and hid at the rear of the schoolhouse until the coast was clear. When he heard teacher and pupil exit at two thirty, he hurried around to the front of the building—edging along on the side opposite the coalhouse. It's possible that the plan also called for Montgomery to act as a decoy, to distract Charlie so that Clementi could slip inside, unseen. But the lad was lounging on his back on top of the coalhouse, already distracted by the lilting music coming from across the road. When Montgomery came strolling by, calling out to little Charlie, he saw that the boy was preoccupied and had no direct view of the school door anyway. So he sauntered on down the road, checking back over his shoulder to keep an eye on the boy. Then, he saw Charlie hop down and take off for the Pettus farm. This may not have been unexpected, for at least one paper reported that as John went by he asked Charlie to fetch a bucket of water from the Pettus well.[2] And then he'd be right back to wrestle with him.

Montgomery, of course, was nowhere to be found when Charlie returned. So, decoy or no decoy, Clementi had no trouble getting inside. At some point that day, Clementi asked to borrow Montgomery's knife, and he willingly lent it. Of course, that knife was among the most powerful evidence against Montgomery, for he admitted owning a dull knife with a telltale nick in it, like the kind supposedly used to carve the opening in the rear of the loft. It was also said that one of the culprits was a left-handed man. This was evidently based on the carved opening and on the locations of the cuts on Emma's body. Yet in spite of the State's protracted efforts at trial, the question as to whether Montgomery used his right or left hand went unresolved. The explanation may have been quite simple: maybe a left-handed Clementi borrowed said knife from the right-handed Montgomery.

When Clementi joined the Hobbs brothers in mid-afternoon, he carried with him the nicked knife and the Chicago paper he'd been reading in the wagon earlier. The latecomer's arrival produced a bit of noise as the three men shuffled around in the attic, trying to settle themselves before Emma's return. Charlie heard that commotion and tried to tell his teacher about it when she returned. But, of course, she could not conceive of anything other than rats being in the attic. So at three o'clock, the final minutes of the vigil began. Slowly, the clock ticked down to the end of the school day, the end of the school year, and the end of life as Emma knew it.

The deed was accomplished quickly, thanks to the chloroform. Clementi took his turn with the unconscious schoolteacher, then said goodbye to his friends, dropped down to the main floor, and slipped out the door or a window. He retraced his steps, behind the schoolhouse and coalhouse and back to the Pettus home, being sure to go by way of the wagon where he had supposedly snoozed away the afternoon and early evening. He arrived back at the house just in time for supper at seven o'clock. As it was, the house sat so close to the school that the hired hand could have remained in the loft until just a few minutes before seven and still made it to the Pettus house in time for supper without showing any signs of having rushed. John and Lee also ate supper there, probably at seven, according to most of the witnesses.

While supper was being served, Elliott and Ellsworth Hobbs were undoubtedly still busy in the loft with Emma. When they were done raping and threatening and torturing the schoolteacher, they applied another dose of chloroform, snatched her watch and her engagement ring, and left her lying unconscious. After dropping down to the classroom, they rummaged through her purse and helped themselves to its cash before tossing it aside. In a moment of bravado, they decided to taunt the law by scrawling a vague and threatening message across the chalkboard.

They had no problems leaving the schoolhouse. With local farmers all at home having supper and dusk settling in, they escaped the crime scene as easily as they had entered it. Dashing from the school door, they squatted behind the hedgerow out front to listen for approaching wagons. Hearing none, they scurried across the road and headed out to their crude campsite on the back acreage of the Pettus farm. By the time John Montgomery and his family left the Pettus house, the two brothers were safely out of sight.

There was never any argument about what time Montgomery took his family home. That was—by all accounts—right at sundown, at 7:29 P.M., Lee Pettus chopped weeds "late in the evening," although his interpretation of that phrase later turned out to mean "before dinner." Clementi, in his own words, went to bed *about* nine thirty that night. Pettus said that he retired around the same time. Montgomery went straight home to bed and did not return to the Pettus farm at all that evening—unless Ona Pettus was right: she claimed to have seen the three friends together around nine or ten o'clock that night. Since this was in contradiction to everyone else's testimony, Ona may have been the only one who was confused *or* the only one who was being completely honest. Actually, there were so many discrepancies regarding the comings and goings at the Pettus house on

June 29 that it was virtually impossible to make heads or tails out of what really took place there and at what hour.

When Emma finally came around, her attackers were long gone. Realizing that she had to get herself down from the attic, the injured and still-groggy victim ended up crashing to the wooden floor below, where she again lost consciousness. More time passed before she became fully aware. Only one question remains at this juncture: When the brothers left their victim, was her breathing so shallow that they assumed she was already dead?

While waiting for Clementi at their hidden campsite, the Hobbs brothers changed into clean clothes—dark pants, white shirts, and coats. They actually looked quite respectable. Back in the Pettus kitchen, their accomplice wolfed down his evening meal; then, while everyone else was telling Montgomery and family goodbye, he slipped off to the creek-side encampment. With the gathering dusk blanketing the prairie, the Hobbses heard him approach before they saw him. He brought some hoofed transportation and extra food, snatched off the kitchen table. The three then took off toward Blue Mound, riding quickly and staying off the main road so as not to be seen.

The moon lit their way. The trip was not quite seven miles, a distance easily covered by a trotting horse in an hour. They didn't ride all the way into the village though; that would have attracted too much attention. Instead, after five or six miles, the brothers dismounted to proceed the rest of the way on foot. Clementi bid his friends farewell and turned back toward the Pettus place, borrowed mount (or mounts) in tow. It was now approaching nine o'clock. With the two brothers safely on their way, Clementi began to feel weary as he rode home in the dark. After the long day, he was more than ready for a good night's sleep, so he decided the abandoned campsite could wait until morning. Later that night, or very early on Friday, the "two tramps" hopped a train in Blue Mound. In all likelihood, this was the freight train bound for St. Louis: the sooner they could distance themselves from the crime scene, the better. In Litchfield, they hopped off the freight to await the early morning passenger train to Mitchell—the one that had left Blue Mound at 4:15 A.M.

A widespread search was organized early Friday morning, in hopes of intercepting the guilty parties. At depots in and beyond Christian County, trains were held up while local deputies boarded them and walked the aisles. They scoured the passengers' faces, perused their clothing, noted their demeanor. That extensive manhunt probably produced the brothers' only close call. While waiting at the Litchfield depot for the passenger train, they overheard talk that lawmen were looking for two suspects. So they initiated an immediate change of plans—splitting up and ditching the incriminating half-empty bottle of chloroform near the depot.

It is hard to say what happened next. Either Elliott hung around Litchfield, waiting for the next train to Waverly or Springfield or he continued on to Mitchell, gathered up his belongings, then backtracked to Springfield. Ellsworth almost certainly went straight back to Mitchell. The first passenger train of the day—coming from Litchfield—would have arrived in Mitchell at 7:23 A.M., which would have allowed Elliott enough time to hop into bed and claim he'd overslept for his morning job. But that point is probably irrelevant, since the story was undoubtedly a fabrication that Ellsworth was prepared to endorse.

Elliott's well-thought-out escape plan to enlist in the army right away was a good one. It would get him as far away as possible, as quickly as possible. Ellsworth's subsequent actions are less certain. It's possible he was still in the tiny village when Page and Bond came looking for a "Mr. Ellsworth" two months later. However, he might have already taken off for parts unknown; maybe he had gone north to Chicago or joined the circus as a roustabout.

Back at the Pettus house, Clementi soon learned the victim was still alive. Unable to weasel his way out of taking her home, he had no choice but to go along on the ride. Then, on the way back to the Pettus house, panic set in. He decided he needed a very fast horse to make an escape. Luckily for him, he was able to borrow one. Chances are, he never intended to return George Housley's steed but, rather, planned to ride it as fast and as far as he could, without ever looking back. First, he needed to take care of the hidden encampment by the creek; he had to make sure that the Hobbs boys hadn't been careless and left behind any clues that might incriminate them—or him.

Of course, he never expected to run into that band of concerned farmers, riding along on horseback so early Friday morning. Realizing he had to lose them so he could tend to the campsite, he announced that he was on his way to Blue Mound in pursuit of two tramps. But that scheme backfired when the men offered to join him. Thinking fast, he concocted an excuse for taking a detour across the fields. After cleaning up the abandoned campsite, he had to rejoin the others and ride with them into Blue Mound—if he disappeared at this point, the entire county would be on his tail.

When Clementi and the posse arrived in Blue Mound at nine o'clock, he was surprised to hear—though he didn't show it—that his two cohorts had been spotted near the depot the previous night. When someone suggested he wire Mr. Bond about the two tramps, Clementi gladly played along. This was no time to be tipping his hand, and a helpful telegram would put him in better stead with the upset father. He could make his getaway later, when things cooled down.

Clementi was evidently the originator of the story that the two tramps were bound for Blue Mound, and that from there, they went west. Did he offer up "west" as a diversionary tactic, knowing his friends were actually headed southwest to Mitchell? Or did he say "west" to sacrifice them and buy himself more time, knowing Elliott was headed to Springfield? Ultimately, saving his own neck was much more important than protecting the identities and destination of his coconspirators.

In spite of Clementi's loose tongue, the two tramps did manage to escape. By the time Elliott got to Springfield, he was breathing a lot more easily. In the coming weeks, he even convinced himself that he and his brother had pulled it off— that is, until his enlisting officer showed up at his barracks, pumping him about what he knew. After Ricketts's departure, Hobbs decided to initiate a preemptive strike. So he sent word to his brother Ellsworth to get to Chicago (if he wasn't already there) and mail (or forward) that anonymous letter to Mr. Bond. Which of the two brothers composed it, however, would be a guess. But its message was unmistakable: the men already in custody in Taylorville were absolutely the right ones. At first, it appeared this was a scheme hatched too late, because, within a few days, Detective Page came calling for Private Hobbs. Yet, to the soldier's relief, by the time he was booked into the Taylorville jail, the letter had already begun to work its spell, redirecting all suspicions back onto Montgomery, Pettus, and Clementi.

When Hobbs finally came face to face with Mr. Bond, he was ready with an alibi. Since Ellsworth's was an unfamiliar face in Christian County, Elliott offered him as that alibi. There are two possible explanations for this. Either Elliott Hobbs knew his brother had already left Mitchell and that anybody who went looking for him there would come away empty-handed, or he knew Ellsworth was still there but was prepared to cover for him with a bogus story the two had concocted earlier. Regardless, the alibi apparently worked, since Elliott was released in short order and sent back to Ohio, with everybody thoroughly convinced of his innocence.

Meanwhile, the remaining suspects held their tongues in fear of retaliation— a fear not unlike that which kept Emma's mouth sealed for decades. It is hard to explain the resolute silence maintained by both the victim and the other suspects, considering what all of them endured. However, the most logical explanation for their steadfast refusal to reveal the truth was probably something like this: Hobbs threatened to harm not only them but their loved ones if the truth ever came out. And not one of them dared take that risk, given the man's obvious sadistic nature.

Elliott's army duties soon put hundreds of miles between him and the tumult in Illinois, and any further thought of his involvement faded quickly from the public's mind. As for loyal Ellsworth, he kicked around the Midwest for another year before his path led him to Seattle as well. As soon as the army was done with them, the two brothers made the name change: if somebody did eventually spill the truth, or if somebody's father did eventually figure out that the alibi was a hoax, they would both be better off. Endless miles of rugged western terrain and their new last name would serve as formidable buffers. Gradually, the glances over their shoulders grew less and less frequent, until finally they stopped altogether. Months turned into years and years into decades, and the two men continued to go about their lives, enjoying their freedom.

35

When he found that she was engaged to Mr. Adams, he changed his tune and began writing the young woman threatening letters and asserting boldly that Miss Bond would never marry Adams.
—Decatur Daily Republican, *July 5, 1882*

It was fairly remarkable how Elliott's and Ellsworth's lives followed such parallel paths over the years.[1] As Emma faced her final wretched days, they surely knew nothing of her struggles nor cared in the least. Indeed, they seemed to care very little about the own wives and children. Although the 1900 census hinted at a future for Elliott and Lena, that was not to be. Soon after that, the couple parted company for good. The largely absentee father probably never again laid eyes on his first two children, James and Nola. Ellsworth was nowhere to be found in the 1900 census, with his young wife, Idella, and their little girl having apparently vanished as well. But both men turned up next in southern California, which suggests they had made the trip together.

Now, if ever a pair of brothers shared the same abiding proclivity for women, these two did. Apparently, neither one had any trouble wooing younger members of the fairer sex. On February 3, 1903, in the charming coastal town of Santa Barbara, Elliott remarried. At forty-two, he was old enough to be the father of his new nineteen-year-old bride, Sadie Henderson. The following January, she gave birth to a son—Earnest Rainey Harding. Two years later, baby Gladys arrived. Like his older brother, Ellsworth transitioned very quickly from his first wife to his second. In 1901, with Idella and his daughter out of the picture, he remarried. Like Elliott's Sadie, Ellsworth's new bride, Susie Cook, was many years his junior—twenty, to be exact. Over the next nine years, he and Susie produced three children. At some point during this same decade the Harding brothers finally went their separate ways. Obviously, the older one had come to trust the younger with the secrets of their past.

In 1910, the year of Emma's demise, Elliott and Sadie were ensconced in Santa Monica, where he worked as a carpenter. Ellsworth and Susie had set up housekeeping farther south, on a dusty little farm in inland San Diego County. While only one hundred miles separated the two brothers, in that time and place, they might as well have been a world apart. And yet, the striking similarities in their lives continued. The first sign that something was awry for Ellsworth came in the 1920 census, when he was counted twice. By then, he and Susie had abandoned their farm; added another child to their ranks; and moved their family into the sleepy, two-bit town of Escondido. There, Ellsworth and his eldest daughter, Ida M., found work in a cafeteria—he as a cook and she as a waitress. However, the two were also recorded in San Diego proper that year, living together in a rental abode. This entry gave his occupation as "bookkeeper in a hotel," while "May" was still waitressing. The other details in that listing left no doubt that this was Ellsworth H. Harding and his oldest girl, Ida May.

By 1930, the aging Ellsworth was back in Escondido, living with and working for a couple who owned a grocery. His wife, Susie, still lived in the same town, but at a different address, along with the couple's youngest daughter, Helen. Ellsworth's situation was reminiscent of his parents' in 1880—when his father had claimed to be "married" and his mother had considered herself "widowed/divorced." Only now, Ellsworth said he was "divorced" while a few blocks away, Susie told the census taker she was a "widow." It looked as if she wanted nothing more to do with her ex-husband, preferring instead to think of him as dead.

Elliott's pension papers revealed that he and Sadie divorced on August 18, 1923. In March 1925, less than two years later, he moved into the National Military Home for Veterans in West Los Angeles. Although he claimed he was unable to work, the military ruled that he was only 10 percent incapacitated—due to mild rheumatism. That same month, he applied for a military pension. His claim was approved in November under a 1920 act that compensated veterans of the Spanish-American War of 1898. It didn't take long, however, for the Pension Bureau to figure out that it had made a mistake; early in 1926, when Elliott applied for an increase to his pension, Uncle Sam discovered that he did not qualify as a veteran of that war, and his pension was rescinded.

From that point forward, Elliott tried repeatedly to get his pension back. But according to the 1920 act, a veteran needed ninety days of service in the Spanish-American War to earn a monthly stipend. The Pension Bureau ruled that Elliott's duties in San Diego had fallen far short: the war officially began on April 21, 1898, and Elliott's service on the USS *Albatross* in San Diego began on January 31 and ended on May 9, 1898. So he had accrued only nineteen qualifying days. The loss of benefits resulted in a stream of correspondence in the coming years. Various government forms and letters flew back and forth between Washington and Los Angeles, but the reinstatement was always denied.

The resulting paperwork showed Elliott had a clear bent for deception on his pension applications. He repeatedly glossed over the truth, gave partial or incorrect information, or completely ignored some of the questions on the forms. At times, he out and out lied. His most glaring mistakes and omissions always involved family members. Sometimes he'd name Lena as his wife, other times Sadie. And where the forms asked about divorces, he wrote nothing. Once, he defiantly supplied but a single answer on the entire form. "Are you a married man?" Answer: "No." For questions about his children, sometimes he'd list the last two (Sadie's), sometimes the first two (Lena's), and other times all four. But he never once had any of their birthdates correct. He also laid claim to James Merlin's participation in World War I but had to admit on the form that "where he served and when, unknown to me."

Elliott was nothing if not obstinate, so he applied again in 1928. That year's form asked the same questions as all the others, including: "Are you a married man? If so, state your wife's full name and her maiden name." He wrote "Yes," and then he jotted a surprising notation next to that. It said "4 times." He apparently had second thoughts and crossed that comment out. If there *had been* two other marriages, when had he squeezed them in? Before his 1888 marriage to Lena, in the short time between Lena and Sadie, or after his divorce from Sadie in 1923? Or had he been a bigamist at some point? The latter might explain the woman named "B." Harding who was living with the two brothers in Seattle in 1892—while Elliott was still married to Lena. In any case, his answers—or lack thereof—said a lot about the kind of relationships he had with his former wives *and* his four children. Furthermore, his answers were always written in his own hand, so he hadn't dictated the information to a third party who had then erred in filling in the forms.

Although the denial of benefits was explained to him time and again in correspondence, Elliott stubbornly persisted. At one point, he even fired off a terse complaint to the commissioner of the Pension Bureau, expressing his sense of entitlement: "I think you officials could find some way to take care of my case." This sounded like a man determined to get something for himself that wasn't rightfully his. Perhaps this reflected the same mind-set he had once applied to Emma Bond.

"A BLACKER DEMON than Pettus never went unhung," proclaimed the *Decatur Review*, just days after the outrage.[2] Early on, the paper had pegged Lee Pettus as the man enamored with Emma, charging that when he learned of her engagement to Adams, he began writing threatening letters to the schoolteacher, vowing that if he could not have her, then nobody could. The *Republican* also made a similar assertion: "The assault on Miss Bond was the outcome of a love affair and was done to satisfy the hellish revenge of one person who, when he found that he could not gain the affections of the young lady, planned to ruin her and blast the hopes of Mr. Adams."[3] In hindsight, it seems that the Decatur papers were on to something from the start. And while they surely had the motive right, in all likelihood it was Elliott Rainey Hobbs—not Lee Pettus—who was that "BLACKER DEMON" in Emma's life.

The last missing piece of the puzzle centers on the precise nature of Emma's and Elliott's relationship. The *Republican*'s take on the ties between the victim and her attacker contained some glaring ambiguities. On the one hand, the paper called the relationship a "love affair." On the other, it asserted that the man became upset when he "could not gain the affections" of the victim. Love affairs, of course, can be dangerously one-sided, and that seemed to be what was implied here. Hobbs may have charmed Emma with flattery and attention, and she may have encouraged him in some way—either knowingly or unknowingly. But then the more respectable Mr. Adams entered the picture, and as a solution to the problem, her parents pushed her in his direction. Unfortunately, affairs of the heart can never be fully understood by those on the outside. Whatever the truth in this matter, those who knew it took it with them to their graves.

All that can be stated with any certainty is that Emma had a colossal stroke of bad luck the day her life's path intersected with Elliott's. And she paid dearly for it, being cruelly betrayed by a man she had once trusted, if not loved. Her embarrassment at having fallen prey to the ladies' man and his charms and her subsequent fear that he might follow through on his threats probably obliterated whatever good sense she had left. So she concealed the truth not only from the world but from her father, her stepmother, her five sisters, and every other person she had ever known and loved, with the possible exception of her second husband, Johnny Jorden. It became a costly charade and one that she upheld until her final moments on earth.

EPILOGUE

Two deaths, Sonny Bond's and John Hill's, were blamed on the circumstances surrounding the case, even before the verdict was in. The premature death of stenographer John T. Montgomery in March 1887 was the third, and the first to occur post-trial. The usual particulars were noted in his obituary: age thirty-nine, married, no children, a Methodist, a Republican, a former teacher who'd taught himself the Pitman Stenographic Method. And then there was the cause of death: "Mr. Montgomery died of hemorrhage of the lungs caused by a severe cold that he caught when he was working on the Emma Bond trial in 1884 at Hillsboro."[1] True, the man had traveled back and forth between Decatur and Hillsboro during some pretty nasty weather, which might have accounted for his initial illness. But to blame a cold caught in December 1883 for a lung hemorrhage that occurred more than three years later was a medical stretch.

Although Emanuel Clementi had cheated death during the 1882 lynching attempt, he only saved himself for a slower and more miserable ending. In the late spring of 1888, he fell gravely ill from a mastoid abscess—a severe infection in the bone directly behind the ear. Today, early treatment with antibiotics has substantially reduced the mortality rate for this condition. But before antibiotics, someone suffering from mastoiditis faced almost certain doom. Scarlet fever was often the initial culprit, with the streptococcal bacteria spreading from throat to inner ear. There, the infection could simmer for days or weeks before developing into a full-blown abscess. In the worst-case scenario, the condition could progress to meningitis or even a brain abscess.

According to Clementi's death certificate—dated June 8, 1888—the "remote mastoid abscess" led to "intermediate blood poisoning."[2] In other words, his infection became so severe that it spread throughout his entire body, resulting in what had to be a most unpleasant death. Clementi probably had acute pain at the site of the original abscess. His health would have deteriorated rapidly once the infection became systemic. In 1888, there was little to be done for such a patient other than sit by and watch him go. At the time of his death, Clementi was thirty-one and single.

Dr. William H. Vermillion died of a heart attack in December 1914 at his boardinghouse residence in Little Rock. Details on his death certificate coincided with what little was known of the man: born in Fairfax County, Virginia, on June 9, 1843, a physician, and a widower.[3] The person who signed as the informant on his death certificate was probably his landlord; that person lived at the same address but was not related to the deceased and could not even provide the names of the doctor's parents. It would appear that the onetime suspect went to his grave without the comfort of a single loved one at his side.

A nagging case of pneumonia—always a hard thing to shake in the middle of an Illinois winter—dealt John C. Montgomery the final blow. His end came on January 19, 1918. His obituary in the *Taylorville Breeze* began with a long and sympathetic reminder of his connection to the famous case and concluded with: "And be it said to his everlasting credit, that throughout the remainder of his life he avoided public places and shunned the notoriety that was unjustly forced upon him by the greatest sensation in the annals of Christian County."[4] It concluded on an even higher note: "At the risk of offending friends and relatives of the parties concerned, we state that John C. Montgomery proved an absolute alibi and was vindicated by the jury as well as by all his neighbors and friends." Lee Pettus outlived John by twenty years. His wife, Allie Hill Pettus, died of a cerebral hemorrhage at the family's home on October 21, 1938. Exactly five days later, Lee followed her to the grave, struck down by the very same thing. He was seventy-eight. There was not one reference to the Bond case in his obituary.[5]

Despite all that his family had been through, A. D. Bond's troubles did not end once he reached Kansas. In the aftermath of the trial, he was forced to sell off a good portion of his Christian County land. With the new century approaching, he and Delia—along with Belle and Hank—set off for southeastern Kansas, to be near Josie's family and Emma and Johnny. (The 1900 census showed all of them living in close proximity.) Using the profit from the sale of his Illinois farm, Bond invested in a promising piece of Kansas land on the banks of Rock Creek in Butler County, which sits between Hepler and Wichita but much closer to the latter. A. D. and Delia settled in, expecting to live out the remainder of their lives on that land. Though Delia was only forty-eight, A. D. was now getting up in years, so Belle's husband, Hank Goodrich, was to carry the load of running his farm.

But something went terribly wrong during the legal process of acquiring the land. Years later, one of Josie's descendants recalled that "someone contested the land and took it and all he [Bond] had."[6] Apparently, Bond had no lawful recourse. So after pouring forty-five years of his life into farming, he was left with absolutely nothing to show for it. With his seventy-fourth birthday just over the horizon, his only option was to pack up and leave Kansas, along with Delia and Belle's family. In September 1901, the group headed back east, across Missouri, presumably bound for Illinois. But for reasons unknown, they stopped in the little town of Leonard, in northern Missouri. And there they stayed.

The journey out to Kansas and halfway back had worn the old man down. He was financially broke and spiritually broken. As a result, Leonard was his final stop on a long and futile trek. As winter settled over the Midwest, his health declined sharply; in January 1902, Abner Bond finally gave up his will to live and went in search of his eternal peace. In Taylorville, Joe Henson—widower of the former Francie Bond—received the heartbreaking news in a telegram: "Pa is dead. Will start tomorrow. Mrs. Henry Goodrich."[7]

The same descendant who recalled Bond's misfortunes in Kansas also stated that the man had taken his own life—that he had picked up a revolver and had shot himself, point blank, through the head. Whether that was true or the figment of an aging and clouded memory is hard to say, since nothing to prove that Bond's death was self-inflicted has ever been uncovered. The only hint that this descendant may have been right was her recollection that Delia and Belle had to go and identify the body. If he had died at home in bed due to failing health, there would have been no reason for family members to go anywhere to confirm his identity. A small Shelby County, Missouri, newspaper briefly mentioned his death. The notice contained no reference to a suicide and, in fact, stated that Mr. Bond had died at home. Of course, the editor might have omitted the most unpleasant details out of consideration for the grieving family. The obituary read: "A. D. Bond died at his home in this place Jan. 17. He had been in feeble health for some time. He moved to Leonard last September, having formerly lived in Kansas. He was 74 years old, was a member of the Christian Church. His remains were taken to Grove City, Ill. for burial. . . . [H]e leaves a wife and several children who have our sincere sympathy in their bereavement. 'God knoweth best.' Mrs. Bond will remain in Illinois until spring. Mr. and Mrs. Goodrich and two little boys, who accompanied the remains, returned home Thursday."[8]

Another notice of Bond's death appeared in the Springfield paper on January 21. It listed his four surviving daughters, including "Mrs. Emma Jordan of Kansas City, Mo."[9] Here, again, there was no mention of a suicide. A. D. Bond's body was laid to rest in the Grove City cemetery alongside that of his first love, Margaret Housley Bond—the mother of his six girls. Maggie and Lester were at the burial. So were Belle and Hank, along with many of Bond's friends from the old neighborhood.

Delia Bond lived for twenty-eight years after her husband's death, as a guest and welcome addition in the homes of various family members. Since she was Maggie Sabine's stepmother *and* Lester Sabine's sister, it was only natural that she spent the bulk of her time with them. She outlived five of her six stepdaughters, her death coming in 1930 in Taylorville, when she was eighty-seven. At the Grove City cemetery, her marker lies alongside the tall obelisk that adorns the graves of her husband A. D. Bond and his first wife.

As far as is known, Belle and Maggie never again saw their younger sisters Emma and Josie. (The other two Bond sisters died before the turn of the century: Etta Logan of an unknown cause in 1886, and Francie Henson of tuberculosis in 1897.) Belle and Hank eventually moved to Alabama, where Belle died in 1925. Maggie Sabine, the only Bond sister to remain in Illinois, passed away in Taylorville in 1927. She and husband Lester are also buried in the Grove City Cemetery. Josie, the youngest Bond sister, never left Butler County, Kansas. Shortly after arriving there, her husband, Obie Baughman, died, leaving her to tend to their farm and raise their two children alone. She endured the inevitable hardships of life on the prairie, never once wavering from her course over the next fifty years. She died in December 1956.[10]

The Hobbs/Harding brothers outlived Emma by decades. Elliott remained at the Sawtelle Soldiers' Home in Los Angeles until June 1931—when his life ended abruptly. While riding as a passenger in a car, he suffered a fatal heart attack. He died penniless. In a final twist, however, the Veterans' Bureau approved an allotment for his burial because he was deemed a veteran of the Spanish-American War. Ellsworth passed away twelve years later; his end came in 1943 in Orange County, midway between San Diego and Los Angeles.

Their respective death certificates revealed that the once-inseparable brothers had finally chosen divergent paths on one particular matter. It seems that daughter Gladys, the informant on Elliott's death certificate, was kept in the dark about her father's past. Where the form asked for her grandparents' names and places of birth, she wrote, "Unknown." Ellsworth, however, must have shared his forsaken family name with at least one of his children. For on his death certificate, where it asked for the name of the deceased man's father, daughter Ida May wrote the name "Hobbs." Just Hobbs—nothing more. Ellsworth, at the very least, had told her he had changed his last name. Of course, it is extremely doubtful he ever told her why he did.

Elliott Rainey Hobbs was buried in the Los Angeles National Cemetery on Sepulveda Boulevard in Los Angeles, fourteen hundred miles west of Emma Jorden's unmarked gravesite in Wichita. Back in Illinois, the once-bustling village at the heart of this story is now a faded memory. Perhaps it is a blessing that the physical entity of Grove City has all but disappeared and that the recollections of its citizens were thus scattered and lost. The encroaching fields of Illinois corn and soybeans have largely reclaimed most of the town's original buildings. Just north and east of the Grove lies the footprint of the old Montgomery Schoolhouse, which relinquished its own dark secrets to those same fields many decades ago. On the easternmost edge of the Grove sits the old Methodist cemetery. The church that founded it was leveled in 1956.

In the warmer seasons, soft breezes float across the cemetery's solemn terrain, stirring the leaves on the few trees that stand as sentinels to the dead. Walking amid the neat rows of grave markers, one can't help but notice how many of the old stones have fallen to the ground—their epitaphs lost to the ages. Of those that still stand, some tell of babies who perished in their first year, of mothers snatched prematurely from their young families, of siblings claimed by illness within days of one another. Yet none speak of that long-ago time when friends drew a line in the dirt and took up opposite sides, so consumed by animosity that they forgot the real meaning of the term "good neighbor."

Today, one can stand at the grave of Abner Dobbins Bond and shout a friendly greeting to another visitor standing at the grave of John C. Montgomery. The names on many of the old tombstones recall the very people who were once a big part of this story: Bond, Montgomery, Housley, Pettus, Younker, Sabine, Masters, Hill, Morgret—and on and on. All now rest side by side in peace, their differences buried and forgotten. If these same men and women could arise from their eternal slumbers today, they might finally agree on this one thing: what happened in their quiet, little neighborhood on that distant June day changed their lives forever, but sadly, not a one for the better.

AFTERWORD

I trust that readers will approach this story with an unbiased eye and in so doing draw their own conclusions. As to which "facts" in this case can be believed or not believed, it is hard to say—simply because too much time has elapsed, too many clues have been lost, and nobody alive today can claim any firsthand knowledge of the affair. Those who lived through it are deceased, and those who learned of it secondhand are almost certainly gone as well. That leaves those of us who inherited the knowledge at three or four removes. Unfortunately, oral history transforms itself over time. This was more than borne out by the errors contained in Delia Greene's 1977 telling of the events.

Any historical source can contain errors, but primary sources are generally considered more accurate. In this case, primary sources were scant. Luckily, there was a plethora of newspaper articles, and these became the backbone of my research. But as this story so strikingly illustrates, Victorian reporters sometimes got their facts wrong. Also, the two sources that would have shed the most light on the truth could not be located. The first, a primary source, was that twelve-hundred-page "transcript of evidence" compiled at the board of supervisors' request. The other was the newspaper article shown to my anonymous informant—the one that supposedly stated that Emma, on her deathbed, had accused a "boyfriend." Other than the court docket papers, which turned up in Montgomery County, no court records of the case could be found. Opinions were tendered—by judges, researchers, and employees of the courts—as to the possible whereabouts of that transcript. Although official case documents should have been returned to the original jurisdiction, it was never clear if the transcript fell into that category. If not, it could have gone home with one of the lawyers, the sitting judge, or even John T. Montgomery, the court stenographer (since he was apparently never compensated for it).

As for the missing article on Emma's deathbed statement, a simple clue—such as the date or the name of the newspaper—would have helped immensely. Realistically, though, it could have appeared in print any time between Emma's 1910 death and the late 1930s, when it was first shown to my informant. This almost thirty-year time span means the chances of finding it were slim indeed. Nevertheless, I scoured online historical databases for that article pertaining to Emma's death, to no avail. Emma's short obituary in the Taylorville newspaper made no mention of her deathbed confession.

I was briefly buoyed by the news that my informant had kept said article. But as so often happens, the clipping was filed in a cardboard box, which was then stashed in the attic. Decades later, when the home changed hands, everything in the attic was earmarked for the local dump. That is precisely how we lose so many valuable links to our past. Photos, letters, personal journals, news clippings, and other cherished keepsakes are carefully tucked away for future generations and then quickly forgotten. If they escape damage from water, heat, mold, mildew, insects, and time, they still face the tough scrutiny of the later generations who inherit them. Many heirs view these items as old and insignificant clutter, so out they go, along with the opportunity to truly know our ancestors.

Arguably, my theory on Elliott and Ellsworth and their role in the crime may not be the final word. Some may argue that my conclusion is based solely on circumstantial evidence, and I do not disagree. I can only hope that some determined sleuth or curious descendant will one day stumble across one or both of these two important sources that seem to have gone astray. But, until then, I am placing all my bets squarely on the Hobbs/Harding brothers.

I cannot conclude without saying a word about Fate. In my family's archives were pictures of A. D. Bond and Delia Sabine Bond—but none of Emma. In my second year of research, I did a Google search for the name "Emma Bond" on a whim—hoping to find some overlooked bit of information. Everything that came up on the first few pages of search hits pertained to a present-day woman of that name in Australia, and she appeared to be engaged in an occupation similar to Emma's in Joplin. But I continued to dig deeper into the results pages, where I eventually found a link to a popular Illinois genealogy website. I clicked on it, and there, staring back at me from my computer monitor, was the wistful face of young woman named Emma Bond, looking very Victorian. When I saw that the photographer was from Taylorville and that the words "Copyrighted by A. D. Bond—1883" were stamped across the bottom of the cabinet card, I knew I had hit pay dirt. The woman who had submitted the picture was a computer-savvy octogenarian. Unfortunately, she did not remember how the cabinet card had come into her possession. She also had no idea who Emma was; she had posted the photo in hopes of learning about her. I filled her in briefly, and she readily agreed to send me a scanned copy she had on her computer, with her blessings and a promise to send the original—if and when she could remember where she had put it. I have to believe that the other missing pieces of this puzzle await a similar discovery.

There are lessons for us all in this tragedy. The most important is that healing is never spontaneous but rather a long and trying process. Again, Fate may have had her own agenda when she placed certain Bond and Pettus family members within a stone's throw of one another. By 1910, Lee and his family were living in Mosquito Township, adjacent to the farm of Emma's aunt and uncle Bill and Becky (Housley) Armstrong. Emma's widowed stepmother, Delia Bond, was living with the Armstrongs that year. This had to be a sore situation, but at least out in the wide-open countryside, the families could go about their daily lives without so much as an encounter. Not so in the confines of a city neighborhood. In Taylorville, on pleasant tree-lined Poplar Street, other Pettus and Bond relatives found themselves in a similar predicament. In 1910, Emma's sister Maggie and her husband, Les Sabine (along with their two youngest girls, Delia and Dorothy), settled into a modest home at 1009 West Poplar. Four years later, Lee Pettus's nephew (George's son) and his new bride moved into the house next door—at 1005 West Poplar.

In 1920, the two families were still living side by side—the Sabines (now in their sixties and minus their daughters) alongside the younger Pettuses (with their firstborn child, Thelma). As awkward as this must have been, neither family opted to move elsewhere. According to my own relatives, the old animosities persisted on Poplar Street. Maggie Bond Sabine seemed unable to put the past aside, even though nearly four decades had elapsed since her sister's trouble. Then, shortly after 1920, the Sabines turned their house over to my own maternal grandparents, Clyde and Dorothy Sabine Lakin. So Dorothy, Emma's niece, now lived right next door to Shirley Ray Pettus, Lee's nephew. Dorothy and Shirley Ray were a full generation removed from the acrimony, and neither had been born until several years after the trial. The Lakins had five children—the oldest being my mother, born in 1918. The Pettuses had three—all of similar ages to the Lakin brood. Of course, these children had no knowledge of the hard feelings between their families.

This made me wonder: were these two young families able to put the past behind them and live as neighbors should? Recently, I found the answer. While repacking some old family boxes, I came across my mother's baby book. As I thumbed through its yellowing pages, my eyes fell upon an entry on the page for "Third Birthday." Listed under "Friends Present" was the name Thelma Pettus.

A little further on, under "Red Letter Days" was a notation that my mother had attended her first invitational party in the company of her little friend Thelma. My mother was just three and Thelma, five. So I had my proof. As shown by the relationship between these two innocent and unknowing little girls, the ill will between the families was finally set aside, after almost forty years and two additional generations.

ACKNOWLEDGMENTS

Were it not for the assistance of many, this book would not have been possible. Foremost among them are my two researchers, who did what I was unable to do from afar. When I first contacted Molly Kennedy, I had no idea how invaluable she would prove to be. She is a native of Taylorville who currently lives in Springfield, and as a veteran genealogy researcher, she knew firsthand whom to contact and where to find what I was after. I'm sure my endless requests grew tedious after a month or two, yet she stuck with me patiently. Her willingness to pursue my many requests went well beyond the obvious.

Joyce Wicks of Sadorus, Illinois, was my other researcher. She gave me the incentive to push forward when she visited Taylorville early on and came away with a wealth of information on specific locations, including the Montgomery School. She even sought directions to Sonny Bond's homestead site. When she set out to find the place, hoping to take pictures, the home was gone, but she photographed the location anyway. At the Christian County Historical Museum, she coerced staffers to let her rummage through boxes of old papers destined for the trash. While digging through them, she came across an old "Register of Fees Received by the Sheriff of Christian County," which included the entries from 1882 relating to the Bond case. I can't say enough about the insight and tenacity of genealogical researchers in general and of these two in particular.

Many others helped in my research. Thanks to Mary Webb, Montgomery County clerk, for tracking down the few case records stored in her county and for taking time out of her weekend to correspond with me. Finding so few documents on the case, she even sought input on their possible whereabouts from a local judge. I am equally indebted to Leon Kearns of Random Acts of Genealogical Kindness, or "RAOGK," in Shelby County, Missouri, for digging up a copy of A. D. Bond's obituary at the Shelby County Herald's office; L. J. Dean, a volunteer at the National Railway Historical Society in Philadelphia, for providing the historical train schedules and railroad maps for central Illinois; Lauretta Scheller, archivist for the Illinois Great River Conference of the United Methodist Church, for searching through baptismal records that might have confirmed Emma's birthdate; Terry and Mary Tutton of the Palmyra Historical Society for supplying pictures and a history of the Palmyra Sanitarium; Jim Angel, Illinois State climatologist with the Department of Natural Resources in Champaign, for providing weather data for specific dates in 1882 and 1883; fellow genealogist Catherine Drennan for sharing the photo of her ancestor State's Attorney John G. Drennan; and finally, Muriel Bywater, another fellow genealogist, without whom I would never have known the likeness of my great-great-aunt Emma Bond. Beyond a doubt, the most valuable material came from my anonymous informant, with whom I connected, thanks again, through my researcher Molly Kennedy.

To friends and family, special gratitude is due. Laura Aven has lent me her unwavering support, not only in this project but in all things in life. Her husband, Wes, made my old and faded family photos look new again. But it was my own family—namely, my grandfather Clyde Lakin, my great-grandfather Lester Sabine, and my great-aunt Delia Sabine Greene—who gave me the essentials for tackling this project. It seems that from them I inherited that certain genetic makeup that drives one's curiosity for all things ancestral. The memoirs and various other writings of Lester and his daughter Delia were essential in helping me construct portions of this story.

I must also thank my four grown children—Gina, Mindy, Kent, and Briana—for convincing me that this was a story worth sharing. I know there were times they thought I might never finish this book. Gina, mother of three, including twins, and Briana, mother of twins, took time out of their busy lives to read my original manuscript and offer their critiques. I am equally grateful to my better half for never once complaining about my long hours at the computer, never once grumbling about late meals, never once doubting that I would complete this book. And finally, I cannot ignore the valuable contribution of my trusty sidekick, Zoe—an old and wise black lab mix extraordinaire—whose one and only job was to remind me when it was time to take a break, go for a walk, and enjoy the little things in life (like the birds and lizards and rabbits and squirrels). She executed her tasks faithfully, day in and day out, on near-perfect schedule, thus allowing me to return to my work with renewed vigor and clear head. Sadly, Zoe crossed the bridge in March 2010, but she will remain with me in spirit, always.

PRINCIPALS IN
THE BOND CASE

Main Trial Participants and Family Members

Except for the Bond sisters, women who married before the end of 1883 are listed by their husbands' names (with maiden names in parentheses). Other than wife and children, of course, any relationships listed for the suspect John C. Montgomery would also apply to his brother, William J. Montgomery. In some cases, relationships could not be proven conclusively but are likely, based on age and census information. "ST" stands for lawyer for the State; "DF," lawyer for the defense; "SW," witness for the State; and "DW," witness for the defense.

Adams, Mr. (first name unknown; nickname possibly "Hitch")—Emma's fiancé; said to be a rancher or stockherder who was out west at the time of the crime.
Allen, Amanda (née Montgomery)—DW; wife of witness James Allen; daughter of John Montgomery Sr.; sister of suspect John Montgomery.
Allen, James—DW; husband of John Montgomery's sister Amanda; James and Amanda lived at the home of John Montgomery Sr. in 1882.
Armstrong, James—SW; brother of Bill Armstrong; former employer of suspect Emanuel Clementi.
Armstrong, William "Bill"—SW; husband of Emma's aunt Becky Housley Armstrong.
Bond, Abner Dobbins "A. D." or "Ab" (b. 1827)—Emma's father.
Bond, Abner Faye "Sonny" (b. 1832)—first cousin of A. D. Bond; member of Christian County Board of Supervisors.
Bond, Arabelle "Belle" (later Goodrich)—first child of A. D. and Maggie Bond.
Bond, Delia Delile (née Sabine)—Emma's stepmother; second wife of A. D. Bond; sister of Lester Sabine.
Bond, Elizabeth "Lizzie" (née Hall)—wife of Sonny Bond; sister-in-law of Lewis Montgomery (who helped finance suspect John Montgomery's defense).
Bond, Emma (later Justus; then Jorden)—the victim; third child of A. D. and Maggie Bond.
Bond, Frances "Francie" (later Henson)—fifth child of A. D. and Maggie Bond.
Bond, Henrietta "Etta" (later Logan)—fourth child of A. D. and Maggie Bond.
Bond, Josephine "Josie" (later Baughman)—sixth child of A. D. and Maggie Bond.

Bond, Margaret Elizabeth "Maggie" (later Sabine)—second child of A. D. and Maggie Bond; wife of Lester Sabine.

Bond, Margaret "Sis" (née Housley)—Emma's mother; first wife of A. D. Bond; died in 1868.

Burnet(t), Benjamin F.—of Taylorville; attorney who attended the hearing and trial; later promoted his own theory about the crime.

Clementi, Emanuel P.—suspect in Bond case; farmhand employed by Margret Pettus.

Cornell, Dr. Daniel K.—SW (hearing only); Emma's primary physician.

Drennan, John (G.)—ST (hearing and trial); state's attorney (Christian County); headed the prosecution at the hearing; assisted by Montgomery County state's attorney Miller at the trial.

Edwards, Judge Benjamin—ST (trial); Springfield attorney and former judge; gave the State's final closing argument at the trial.

Goodrich, Henry A. "Hank"—husband of Emma's sister Belle; son of William Augustus Goodrich.

Greene, Delia Delile (née Sabine)—daughter of Maggie and Lester Sabine; granddaughter of A. D. Bond; great-niece of Emma; teller of the Emma Bond story (as given in her 1977 interview).

Haines, William—DW; of Taylorville; sheriff of Christian County from 1880 until 1885.

Hart, Cora (née Pettus)—DW; sister of suspect Lee Pettus; wife of witness Owen Hart.

Hart, Owen—DW; husband of Cora Pettus Hart; brother of Kate Hart Vermillion (wife of suspect Vermillion).

Hart, Thomas—DW; brother of Owen Hart (married Minnie Pettus in 1893).

Heinlein, Laurence—SW/DW; key witness; husband of Elizabeth Johnson Heinlein (sister of Margret Johnson Pettus); uncle (by marriage) of suspect Lee Pettus.

Heinlein, Sammy—son of witness Laurence Heinlein; first cousin of suspect Lee Pettus; postmaster of Grove City in 1882; rumored to have been involved in the crime but never charged.

Hill, Alice "Allie" (later Pettus)—daughter of John Hill; married Lee Pettus in March 1884.

Hill, John—of Mt. Auburn Township; father of Allie and Effie Hill (both married Pettus brothers).

Housley, Daniel W.—of Grove City and later of Hepler, Kansas; uncle of Emma; brother of Maggie Housley Bond; onetime postmaster and store owner in Grove City; moved to Kansas in the late 1880s.

Housley, Edward C. "Ed"—SW; of Grove City area; first cousin of Emma; son of Rufus Housley; friend of suspect Lee Pettus.

Housley, George S. Jr.—SW; of Grove City; uncle of Emma; brother of Maggie Housley Bond; owned race horses along with his brother Hank.

Housley, Hyman "Levi"—of Hepler, Kansas; uncle of Emma; brother of Maggie Housley Bond; uncle Emma visited in Kansas in 1887.

Jorden, John "Johnny" H.—of Missouri and Kansas; Emma's second husband; the correct spelling of his surname is believed to be Jorden, although it was also spelled Jordan and Jordon.

Justus, Clarence E.—of Kansas; Emma's first husband.

Kiernan, Dr. James G.—of Chicago; asserted that Emma's accusations against the Bond suspects were false and hysterical in nature.

Masters, Charles "Charlie" (b. 1874)—SW; Emma's only student the day of the outrage; son of Andrew and Rachel Masters; nephew of William and Amy Montgomery Masters, who also had a son named Charles (b. 1879).

McBride, J. C. (John)—DF (hearing and trial); of Taylorville; private attorney.

McCaskill, Judge Alexander—DF (hearing and trial); of Taylorville; attorney; former county judge and state's attorney.

McFarland, Dr. Andrew—of Jacksonville, Illinois; former head of Jacksonville State Hospital for the Insane; later director/owner of Oaklawn Retreat, a private asylum in Jacksonville.

Miller, Amos—ST (trial); state's attorney (Montgomery County); co-lead attorney (with John Drennan) for the State at the trial.

Montgomery, Charles—DW; youngest brother of suspect John; son of John Montgomery Sr.

Montgomery, Emma (née Hall)—wife of Lewis Montgomery (first cousin of suspect John); sister-in-law of Sonny Bond.

Montgomery, John C. Jr.—suspect in the Bond case; husband of Mattie Pettus Montgomery; brother of suspect William J. Montgomery; son of John Montgomery Sr.

Montgomery, John Sr.—DW; father of defendants John C. and William J. Montgomery; first cousin of witnesses Joseph and George Younkers. The designations "Sr." and "Jr." for the elder and younger are given to avoid confusion. The men may not have used those themselves.

Montgomery, John T.—of Decatur; court stenographer in Bond case.

Montgomery, Joseph Edmon "Ed"—first cousin of suspect John; he and wife Amanda owned the home where Emma boarded while teaching.

Montgomery, Lewis—husband of Emma Hall Montgomery; brother-in-law of Sonny and Lizzie Hall Bond; son of Asa and Caroline Suddeth Montgomery; first cousin of suspect John Montgomery.

Montgomery, Martha "Mattie" (née Pettus)—DW (for Lee Pettus and Emanuel Clementi only); sister of suspect Lee Pettus; wife of suspect John Montgomery.

Montgomery, William J.—suspect in Bond case; brother of suspect John Montgomery; son of John Montgomery Sr.; died of tuberculosis in September 1883, before the trial.

Pettus, "Effie" Mae (née Hill)—wife of George T. Pettus (brother of suspect Lee Pettus), daughter of John M. Hill.

Pettus, George—DW; brother of suspect Lee Pettus; husband of Effie Hill Pettus.

Pettus, Iona "Ona"—DW; sister of suspect Lee Pettus; engaged to suspect Clementi during the December 1883 trial. Ona eventually married a Yockey.

Pettus, Lee A.—suspect in the Bond case; married Allie Hill (in March 1884).

Pettus, Margret (née Johnson)—mother of suspect Lee Pettus.

Pettus, Minnie—DW; sister of suspect Lee Pettus; later married witness Thomas Hart.

Phillips, Judge Jesse—Civil War veteran (lieutenant colonel; honorary brigadier general); circuit court judge who presided at the trial; later served as chief justice on the Illinois Supreme Court.

Ricks, James B.—justice who presided at the preliminary hearing; later served as state's attorney and as chief justice on the Illinois Supreme Court.

Sabine, Lester—husband of Emma's sister Maggie; brother of Delia Sabine Bond (Emma's stepmother).

Swick, Martin V.—SW; key witness.

Taylor, J. M.—ST (hearing and trial); of Taylorville; private attorney; also legal guardian of Sonny Bond's children (represented their legal interests in the estate settlement).

Thornton, Judge Anthony—DF (hearing and trial); of Shelbyville and later Decatur; lead defense attorney at both the hearing and the trial; a former member of the state legislature, U.S. Congress, and the Illinois Supreme Court; also a colleague of Abraham Lincoln.

Vandeveer, Judge Horatio M.—ST (hearing and trial); of Taylorville; an attorney and former judge; previously served as a circuit court judge; held numerous elected offices.

Vermillion, Dr. William H.—of Grove City; suspect in the Bond case (charged only with complicity); husband of Kate Hart Vermillion; brother-in-law of Owen and Cora Pettus Hart.

Younker, George—DW; husband of witness Sarah Atchison Younker; brother of witness Joseph Younker; first cousin of John Montgomery Sr.

Younker, Joseph B.—DW; husband of Martha "Mattie" Montgomery Younker (sister of suspect John Montgomery); brother of witness George Younker; first cousin of John Montgomery Sr. Joe's wife, Mattie, was his first cousin once removed.

Younker, Martha "Mattie" (née Montgomery)—DW; wife of witness Joseph Younker; sister of suspect John Montgomery; daughter of John Montgomery Sr.

Younker, Sarah M. (née Atchison)—DW; wife of witness George Younker.

The Jurors

The jurors' names were given in the court docket papers. The following information was compiled from the 1880 U.S. Federal Census (with 1883 ages approximated). The identities of the two jurors named William Blackwood and Henry Hill are uncertain. Two men with each of those names resided in Montgomery County in 1880. Details for all four have been included and marked with asterisks.

Barringer, Edward—age thirty-seven; of Litchfield; a music dealer; married with two sons, ages seven and five.

Beck, George W.—age forty-five; of Hillsboro Township; farmer; married with four daughters, ages eighteen, thirteen, ten, and nine, and one son, age three.

*Blackwood, William D.—age fifty-five; of Hillsboro Township; farmer; married with two daughters, ages twenty-eight and nineteen, and four sons, ages twenty-five, twenty-four, sixteen, and twelve.

*Blackwood, William F.—age twenty-five; of Hillsboro Township; farmer; married just days before the trial began (December 6, 1883); son of the older William Blackwood.

Cannaday, Elza "Elzie"—age thirty-six; of Butler Grove; farmer; married with at least one child (age and sex of child unknown).

Card, Thomas—age forty-three; of Hillsboro Township; mail carrier; married with one son, age six.

Davenport, Peter L.—age sixty-two; of Grisham; farmer; married with the following children still living at home: two daughters, ages thirteen and eight, and four sons, ages seventeen, fifteen, eleven, and ten.

*Hill, Henry—age fifty-three; of Fillmore; farmer; married with two children still living at home—a daughter, age thirteen, and a son, age sixteen.

*Hill, Henry—age thirty-three; of Fillmore; farmer; married with two daughters, ages eleven and nine; probable son of the older Henry Hill.

Huddleston, Frank—age thirty-two; of Witt; married and the father of one young son, age two.

Isaacs, Mr. Levi D. B. "Boone"—age forty-nine; of Hillsboro Township; farmer; father (by first wife) of at least two daughters and three sons (the oldest girl, circa age twenty-four); father (by second wife) of one daughter and two sons (all born in the 1870s); five children still living at home in 1880; Boone married his third wife, Maggie Brookman, in December 1885.

Moore, Robert D.—age forty-three; of Fillmore; farmer; married with four daughters, ages sixteen, fourteen, eleven, and five, and two sons, ages eighteen and four.

Short, James C.—age thirty-six; of East Fork; farmer; married with two daughters, ages thirteen and ten.

Travis, Robert—age forty-three; of Nokomis; farmer; married with two daughters, ages nine and five, and two sons, ages seven and four.

NOTES

Time played a crucial part in this case, which created some inherent problems. The hours given by witnesses were approximations, at best, since standardized time was not created until November 1883 (when the railroads synchronized their clocks from region to region to simplify scheduling).

Details on weather were derived from the Decatur papers, the *Chicago Tribune*'s statewide weather observations, or the historical records of the weather reporting station at Springfield, Illinois. Jim Angel, state climatologist for the Illinois State Water Survey of the Department of Natural Resources, Champaign, provided the Springfield reports.

Using the historical currency calculator at http://www.measuringworth.com/ppowerus/, the 1882 reward fund, which climbed to $31,000, would currently equal $704,000; the $10,000 cost of the 1883 trial would translate to $232,000 today; and the land sold in 1885 to reduce Sonny's estate debt would now be worth $241,000, while his estimated net worth of $100,000 would be valued at $2,370,000 today (all are approximations based on CPI percentage increases). The purchasing power of other dollar amounts given in the book can also be converted to today's relative values at the following rate: one 1882 dollar is now worth approximately $21.50. (All conversions are based on 2011 data.)

All the background information on the Bonds and Housleys came from the unpublished writings of the author's ancestors, unless otherwise noted. The two main sources were Lester Sabine's unpublished short autobiography, entitled "The Life of a Sucker Boy," and Delia Sabine Greene's unpublished childhood memoirs, "The Farms at Shamel Place." Delia's various other writings provided additional details on the Bond, Housley, Sabine, Goodrich, and related families. Their birth, marriage, and death dates were taken from the author's archives. (All of these are in the author's possession.)

Dates for other births, marriages, and deaths were found at the website of the Illinois Regional Archives Depository (IRAD) at http://www.cyberdriveillinois.com/departments/archives/databases.html. Family relationships were determined using IRAD records, the U.S. Census reports, and a variety of other public record databases and historical books. In some cases, exact relationships were impossible to determine; see the list of principals (page 287) for further clarification of relationships. The press frequently misspelled names of principals; the correct spelling has been substituted in all quoted material.

A majority of the historical resources used to piece this story together were accessed at the subscription website http://www.ancestry.com. Records for Washington Territory and State were found at the Washington State Digital Archives website, http://www.digitalarchives.wa.gov/RecordSeriesInfo.aspx?rsid=1.

1

1. Emma Bond's exact birth date is unknown; various sources place her birthday circa 1861–62, with the exception of the 1900 census, which lists it as July 1863. However, the most likely date is July 1861, which would mean she was just days from turning twenty-one when she was attacked.

2. *Decatur (Ill.) Daily Republican,* Dec. 22, 1883, 5.

3. *Waukesha (Wisc.) Freeman,* Dec. 20, 1883, 2.

4. *Decatur (Ill.) Review,* July 1, 1882, 1.

5. *Chicago Tribune,* July 6, 1882, 12.

6. *Decatur Daily Republican,* Dec. 22, 1883, 5; and *Stevens Point (Wisc.) Journal,* Dec. 29, 1883, 2.

7. *Decatur Daily Republican,* June 30, 1882, 3.

8. *Decatur Review,* July 1, 1882, 1.

9. Such crimes include the case of Mrs. Jane Robinson (age unknown) in Moweaqua, Illinois, as reported in the *Chicago Tribune* on March 25, 1881, 2; the Lena Zinn (age eighteen) case in Pana, as reported in the *Decatur Review* on November 20, 1882, 4; the Norma Ortman (age twelve) case in Decatur, as reported in the *Decatur (Ill.) Herald,* on November 22, 1882, 4; the Anabel Nave (age fourteen) case in Christian County, as reported in the *Herald* on November 22, 1882, 4; the Lizzie Perviance (age twenty-one) case in Attica, Indiana, as reported in the *Chicago Tribune* on November 30 1883, 6. (This last case had many striking similarities to the Emma Bond case, although there was apparently no connection. Attica, Indiana, is about 125 miles northeast of Taylorville, Illinois.)

10. *Chicago Tribune,* July 6, 1882, 12.

2

1. Sources on historic Grove City include Delores Mahan, "The Death of a Small Town: Progress, Time Take Their Toll," n.d.; Ralph Mateer, "1818–1868" (n.d.); and Cecil Showalter, "A Time of Reminiscence" (1968), all articles in a Grove City folder, Christian County Historical Museum, Taylorville, Ill. See also Christian County Historical Society, "Christian County History: Millennium Edition," pamphlet (Taylorville, Ill.: Christian County Historical Society, 1976); and Delia Sabine Greene, "The Housley Family," n.d., in the author's possession.

2. Abner D. Bond Sr. was remarried in 1859 to Rebecca Long, thirty-four years his junior. By then, his son was a husband and a father himself. Rebecca bore three children in quick succession. Abner Sr. died in December 1863 at the age of sixty-six, a few months before his last child's birth.

3. Both men had numerous land transactions recorded in the county's record books,

several within the same township. In these legal entries, Abner Dobbins Bond Jr. was listed as "A. D. Bond" and Sonny as "Abner Bond."

4. Belle was born June 27, 1857; Maggie, January 8, 1860; and Josie, August 3, 1867. Per various sources, Etta was probably born between 1862 and 1863, and Francie circa 1864 or 1865. Two other Bond children died in infancy: a son, born December 19, 1858, and a daughter, born between Francie and Josie.

5. Lester Fremont Sabine, "The Life of a Sucker Boy," 15.

6. Delia Sabine Greene, "The Farms at Shamel Place," 30.

7. Ibid.

8. Sabine, "Sucker Boy," 22.

9. Ibid., 27.

10. There was ample evidence that the Ku Klux Klan was active in central Illinois during this time and even into the twentieth century. According to the April 24, 1868, *Decatur Republican,* "We hear it whispered on the streets that an offshoot of the Ku Klux Klan is to be organized in Decatur" (3). And the August 20, 1868, issue of the same paper reported: "A democratic paper and a Ku Klux paper are printed in this city. The Ku Klux thing blathers away on Bank Ave" (1). The October 22, 1868, *Decatur Review* comments on a Saturday night when "the unearthly Ku Klux yell was unheard" (4).

11. Sabine, "Sucker Boy," 9.

12. Emma's fiancé was only mentioned by last name in three articles: *Decatur Daily Republican,* July 5, 1882, 3; *Decatur Review,* July 6, 1882, 4; and *Chicago Tribune,* Dec. 6, 1883, 12.

3

1. *Washington (D.C.) Post,* Jan. 9, 1882, 1.

2. *Washington Post,* Nov. 16, 1881, 2.

3. Ibid. The "colored" member of the jury was named Ralph Wormley. Several black men were called during voir dire. The most common reason for rejection of potential jurors was that they had already decided and/or expressed the opinion that Guiteau was guilty.

4. "C. W. Stickney," *Chicago Tribune,* Feb. 17, 1883, 7.

5. *Alton (Ill.) Weekly Telegraph,* Aug. 28, 1868, 2; *Chicago Tribune,* Dec. 20, 1867, 2.

6. Elizabeth W. Packard was incarcerated in the Jacksonville asylum from 1860 to 1863. She self-published her first book, *The Prisoners' Hidden Life; or Insane Asylums Unveiled: As Demonstrated by the Report of the Investigating Committee of the Legislature of Illinois* (Chicago: A. B. Case, printer, 1868), and followed that with *Modern Persecution, or Married Woman's Liabilities as Demonstrated by the Action of the Illinois Legislature* (Chicago: Case, Lockwood, and Brainard, printers, 1873).

7. *Chicago Tribune,* Sept. 28, 1877, 1.

8. *Atlanta Constitution,* June 1, 1877, 1.

9. *Decatur Review,* May 6, 1882, 1.

10. *Washington Post,* July 1, 1882, 4.

11. *Chicago Tribune,* Dec. 15, 1883, 12.

12. 1880 U.S. Federal Census, roll T9_181, District 76, Taylorville, Christian Co., Ill., 11 (735).

13. *Decatur Daily Republican,* July 5, 1882, 3.

14. Charles's last name was sometimes given as Dickenson or Dickinson, but "Dickerson" is believed the correct spelling.

15. *Decatur Daily Republican,* July 12, 1888, 3.

16. *Decatur Daily Republican,* June 30, 1882, 3.

4

1. *Chicago Tribune,* Dec. 18, 1883, 2.

2. *Chicago Tribune,* Aug. 10, 1882, 8.

3. *Chicago Tribune,* Dec. 21, 1883, 2.

4. Old train schedules contained travel times for each train, and there was a wide variation on any given route. Times depended on train classifications (express, mixed, mail, or accommodations.). Some made more stops and thus averaged only eight to ten miles per hour, although their actual moving speeds were probably faster. Of the six trains that ran daily the twenty-six miles between Taylorville and Springfield, the fastest made the trip in one hour and seventeen minutes, while the slowest took an unimaginable three hours and twenty minutes. To travel from Chicago to St. Louis by passenger train took about twelve hours, and freight trains operated on a much slower and unscheduled basis.

5. *Chicago Tribune,* July 6, 1882, 12.

6. *Chicago Tribune,* Dec. 18, 1883, 6.

7. *Decatur Review,* Aug. 9, 1882, 4.

8. *Chicago Tribune,* Aug. 10, 1882, 8.

9. *Colorado Springs Daily Gazette,* Dec. 15, 1883, 1.

10. *Chicago Tribune,* Dec. 15, 1883, 12.

11. *New York Times,* Dec. 28, 1883, 2.

12. *Chicago Tribune,* Aug. 9, 1882, 8.

13. *Chicago Tribune,* Dec. 15, 1883, 12.

14. *Chicago Tribune,* Dec. 17, 1883, 6.

15. The press repeatedly gave conflicting reports on the number of John's children. See chap. 20, n4 for more details.

16. Christian County (Ill.) Jail Register, volume A, 56–57, entry 122, Lee A. Pettus, committed July 1, 1882; entry 123, Emanuel Clementa [*sic*], committed July 1, 1882, entry 124, John C. Montgomery, committed July 1, 1882. The charge against all three, as entered in the register, was "Rape and Robery" [*sic*].

5

1. Calvin Goudy, *History of Christian County with Illustrations, Descriptive of Its Scenery, and Biographical Sketches of Some of Its Prominent Men and Pioneers* (Philadelphia: Brink, McDonough and Co., 1880), 57.

2. Christian County (Ill.) Jail Register, vol. A, 56, entry 118, John Dunn, committed April 28, 1882, entry 120, Edwin Burritt, committed May 9, 1882, and entry 121, Benjamin F. Scott, committed June 3, 1882.

3. 1880 U.S. Federal Census, roll T9_181, District 76, Taylorville, Christian Co., Ill., 17 (738).

4. *Washington Post,* Dec. 21, 1883, 1; and *Decatur Review,* Dec. 21, 1883, 8.

5. *Chicago Tribune,* July 6, 1882, 12.

6. (Butte, Mont.) *Daily Miner,* July 8, 1882, 1.

7. *Decatur Review,* July 10, 1882, 4.

8. *Chicago Tribune,* July 4, 1882, 3.

9. *Decatur Review,* July 15, 1882, 2.

10. *Decatur Review,* July 6, 1882, 4.

11. *Chicago Tribune,* July 6, 1882, 12.

12. *Decatur Review,* July 6, 1882, 4.

13. Ibid.

14. Ibid.

15. *Decatur Review,* July 8, 1882, 4.

16. *Decatur Review,* July 6, 1882, 4.

17. *Chicago Tribune,* July 6, 1882, 12.

18. *Decatur Review,* July 6, 1882, 4.

19. *Decatur Review,* July 22, 1882, 4.

20. *Decatur Review,* July 14, 1882, 4.

21. *Waukesha Freeman,* July 20, 1882, 2.

22. *Decatur Review,* July 8, 1882, 4.

23. *Chicago Tribune,* July 20, 1882, 3.

24. *Waukesha Freeman,* July 20, 1882, 2.

25. Christian County (Ill.) Jail Register, vol. A, 57, entry 127, William J. Montgomery, committed July 30, 1882. The charge as entered in the register was "Rape and Robery" [*sic*].

26. *Decatur Daily Republican,* July 18, 1882, 3.

27. *Chicago Tribune,* Aug. 1, 1882, 3.

28. Ibid.

29. *Chicago Tribune,* Aug. 17, 1882, 3.

6

1. Ronald D. Spears, *The Courthouses of Christian County, Illinois* (Taylorville, Ill.: William R. Kennedy, 2002), 19.

2. *Decatur Review,* Aug. 9, 1882, 4.

3. Spears, *Courthouses of Christian County,* 20.

4. *Chicago Tribune,* Aug. 8, 1882, 1.

5. *Chicago Tribune,* Aug. 9, 1882, 8.

6. Ibid.

7. Ibid.

8. Brooks and his replacement, James B. Ricks, were always referred to during the case as "justices." During the 1800s, in some states this term was used in the lowest courts to denote an official who had more limited legal powers than a judge.

9. *Decatur Review,* Aug. 9, 1882, 4.

10. Records show that John T. was born in Wheeling, West Virginia, circa 1848. John C. was born in Illinois in 1849; his family came to the state from Maryland, by way of Pennsylvania. John T.'s family lived near Elwin, Illinois, in Macon County, while John C.'s family settled first in Sangamon County and later moved to Christian County. Since

each man's father was also named John, it was unlikely that John T. and John C. were first cousins. If there *was* any familial link between the two, it was likely a distant one.

11. John G. Drennan biography, *Portrait and Biographical Record of Christian County, Illinois* (Chicago: Lake City Publishing, 1893), 315.

12. John M. Palmer, ed. *Bench and Bar of Illinois: Historical and Reminiscent,* 2 vols. (Chicago: Lewis Publishing Co., 1899), 1:579.

13. Ibid.

14. *Chicago Tribune,* Aug. 9, 1882, 8.

15. Judge Alexander McCaskill biography, *Portrait and Biographical Record,* 272.

16. John W. Smith, *History of Macon County, Illinois: From Its Organization to 1876* (Springfield: Rokker's Printing House, 1876), 139.

17. Palmer, *Bench and Bar,* 1:458.

18. *Chicago Tribune,* Aug. 9, 1882, 8; and Christian County (Ill.) Jail Register, vol. A, 57, entry 131, W. H. Vermillion, committed August 8, 1882.

19. *Decatur Review,* Aug. 9, 1882, 4.

20. *Decatur Daily Republican,* Aug. 9, 1882, 3.

21. *Chicago Tribune,* Aug. 9, 1882, 8.

22. The existence of said affidavit was mentioned in the *Chicago Tribune,* on August 8, 1882 (1) and in Delia Sabine Greene's 1977 interview, in which she stated that Emma had given an affidavit to Judge Vandeveer, detailing her assault.

23. *Decatur Daily Republican,* Aug. 9, 1882, 3.

24. *Decatur Review,* Aug. 9, 1882, 4.

25. *Chicago Tribune,* Aug. 9, 1882, 8.

26. *Decatur Daily Republican,* Aug. 9, 1882, 3.

27. *Chicago Tribune,* Aug. 9, 1882, 8.

7

1. *Decatur Daily Republican,* Aug. 9, 1882, 3.

2. *Chicago Tribune,* Aug. 9, 1882, 8.

3. *Chicago Tribune,* Aug. 10, 1882, 8.

4. Ibid.

5. Ibid.

6. Ibid.

7. Ibid.

8. Ibid.

9. Ibid.

10. William and Amy Masters (née Montgomery) also had a son named Charles Masters; however, a census comparison shows that their son, Charles H. Masters, was born in 1879, which would preclude him from being the youngster who testified. Andrew and Rachel Masters's son Charles was born in 1874, making him the age of the boy who testified.

11. *Decatur Review,* Aug. 11, 1882, 1.

12. *Chicago Tribune,* Aug. 10, 1882, 8.

13. There was some confusion about Sherman's surname. Several times, his name appeared in the press as Yo(u)nker(s). However, if the censuses are correct, his last name was

actually Yockey; thus, unlike the Younkers, he was probably not related to the Montgomery family.

14. Plat Maps of Mt. Auburn Township, Christian Co, Illinois, 1872 and 1891, indicated that the land being farmed by Joseph Younker was probably owned by his cousin, the elder John Montgomery. Leasing land to a relative was common practice in the 1800s—especially for larger landowners. For further clarification of relationships, see the list of principals (p. 287).

15. *Chicago Tribune*, Aug. 10. 1882, 8.

16. *Decatur Review*, Aug. 10, 1882, 4.

8

1. Oliver A. Harker, ed., *Annotated Statutes of the State of Illinois* (Chicago: T. H. Flood and Co., 1919), 1418–19.

2. *Chicago Tribune*, Aug. 11, 1882, 2.

3. Ibid.

4. Ibid.

5. Ibid.

6. Ibid.

7. Ibid.

8. Ibid.

9. Ibid.

10. Ibid.

11. Ibid.

12. *Decatur Review*, Aug. 11, 1882, 1.

13. *Chicago Tribune*, Aug. 11, 1882, 2.

14. Plat Maps of Taylorville and May Townships, Christian Co, Ill., 1891.

15. *Decatur Daily Republican*, Jan. 2, 1882, 2.

16. *History of Christian County*, 184.

17. Ibid., 184–85.

18. *Decatur Daily Republican*, Jan. 2, 1882, 2.

19. "Minutes of Fifth Day's Proceedings of the Board of Supervisors, July Meeting, A. D. 1882," Christian County, Ill., 305 (dated Aug. 10, 1882), Christian County Historical Museum, Taylorville, Ill.

20. *Chicago Tribune*, Aug. 11, 1882, 2.

21. Ibid.

22. *Chicago Tribune*, Aug. 12, 1882, 1.

23. *Chicago Tribune*, Aug. 12, 1882, 2.

24. *Chicago Tribune*, Aug. 12 1882, 1.

25. *Decatur Review*, Aug. 11, 1882, 1.

9

1. *Chicago Tribune*, Aug. 12, 1882, 1.

2. *Fort Wayne (Ind.) Daily Gazette*, Aug. 11, 1882, 2.

3. *Chicago Tribune*, Aug. 11, 1882, 1.

4. Ibid.

5. *Chicago Tribune,* Aug. 12, 1882, 1.

6. *Atlanta Constitution,* Aug. 13, 1882, 1.

7. *Chicago Tribune,* Aug. 12, 1882, 1.

8. Ibid.

9. *Decatur Daily Republican,* Aug. 14, 1882, 3.

10. This crime and its subsequent legal proceedings were always referred to as the Emma Bond case. This is notable, since criminal cases are usually referred to by the name or names of the accused, not the victim.

10

1. *New York Times,* Aug. 13, 1882, 1.

2. *Colorado Springs Daily Gazette,* Aug. 13, 1882, 1.

3. *Chicago Tribune,* Aug. 12, 1882, 1.

4. *Colorado Springs Daily Gazette,* Aug. 13, 1882, 1.

5. Ibid.

6. *Chicago Tribune,* Aug. 12, 1882, 1.

7. Ibid.

8. Ibid.

9. Ibid.

10. Christian County (Ill.) Jail Register, vol. A, 58, entry 132, Lee Pettus, committed August 12, 1882; entry 133, John C. Montgomery, committed August 12, 1882; entry 134, Emanuel Clementa [*sic*], committed August 12, 1882.

11. *Decatur Review,* Aug. 13, 1882, 4.

12. *Atlanta Constitution,* Aug. 13, 1882, 1.

13. *Decatur Review,* Aug. 13, 1882, 4.

14. *Decatur Review,* Aug. 15, 1882, 1.

15. *Decatur Daily Republican,* Aug. 14, 1882, 3.

16. *Decatur Daily Republican,* Aug. 15, 1882, 2.

17. *Chicago Tribune,* Aug. 15, 1882, 6.

18. Ibid.

19. *Decatur Review,* Aug. 8, 1882, 4.

20. *Chicago Tribune,* Aug. 17, 1882, 3.

21. Christian County (Ill.) Jail Register, vol. A, 58, entry 135, E. R. Hobbs, committed August 18, 1882. The charge entered in the register was "Rape of the person of Emma Bond." (For Clementi, Pettus, and the Montgomerys, the charge was "Rape and Robery" [*sic*].)

11

1. *Decatur Daily Republican,* Aug. 21, 1882, 3.

2. Ibid.

3. Ibid.

4. Christian County (Ill.) Jail Register, vol. A, 58, entry 135, E. R. Hobbs, discharged September 18, 1882 "by order of State's Atty. John G. Drennan."

5. *Chicago Tribune,* Aug. 30 1882, 1.

6. *Decatur Review*, Aug. 31, 1882, 4. By August 8, the *Chicago Tribune* was referring to Emma's doctors in the plural. On August 31, Dr. Rockwell was named along with the family's regular physician, Dr. Cornell.

7. *Chicago Tribune*, Aug. 29, 1882, 8.

8. *Chicago Tribune*, Aug. 30, 1882, 1.

9. *Chicago Tribune*, Aug. 29, 1882, 8.

10. *Atlanta Constitution*, Aug. 31, 1882, 1.

11. *Chicago Tribune*, Sept. 19, 1882, 2.

12. *Decatur Review*, Sept. 21, 1882, 4.

12

1. J. C. Paxton was married to Mary Pettus, sister of Lee, George, and Mattie.

2. *Decatur Republican*, Sept. 1, 1882, 1.

3. *Chicago Tribune*, Aug. 29, 1882, 8.

4. *Decatur Review*, Sept. 15, 1882, 4.

5. *Chicago Tribune*, Sept. 19, 1882, 2.

6. 1880 U.S. Federal Census, roll T9_180, District 67 (Grove City), Mt. Auburn Twp., Christian Co, Ill., 25–26 (598–99). This enumeration shows entry 231 as Rufus Housley, 232 as Henry Housley, 239 as O. Z. Housley, and 246 as George S. Housley. Vermillion's home was entry 237, in the middle of the Housleys'.

7. *Decatur Review*, Sept. 21, 1882, 4.

8. (Albert Lea, Minn.) *Freeborn County Standard*, Sept. 21, 1882, 2.

9. Christian County (Ill.) Coroner's Inquest Record (1882), 1:18.

10. *Freeborn County Standard*, Sept. 21, 1882, 2.

11. *Decatur Daily Republican*, Sept. 16, 1882, 3.

12. *Decatur Daily Republican*, Oct. 2, 1882, 2.

13. *Chicago Tribune*, Sept. 21, 1882, 8.

14. *Decatur Review*, Sept. 21, 1882, 4.

15. *Chicago Tribune*, Oct. 4, 1882, 3.

16. *Decatur Review*, Oct. 30, 1882, 4.

13

1. *Decatur Herald*, Nov. 22, 1882, 4.

2. *Chicago Tribune*, Nov. 18, 1882, 6.

3. *Decatur Herald*, Nov. 18, 1882, 4.

4. Ibid.

5. *Chicago Tribune*, Nov. 22, 1882, 7.

6. *Decatur Review*, Oct. 30, 1882, 4.

7. *Chicago Tribune*, Nov. 22, 1882, 7.

8. *Decatur Review*, Aug. 18, 1882, 4.

9. *Chicago Tribune*, Nov. 23, 1882, 8.

10. Ibid.

11. *Decatur Review*, Nov. 24, 1882, 4.

12. *Decatur Daily Republican*, July 29, 1882, 3.

14

1. *Chicago Tribune*, Dec. 16, 1882, 7.

2. *Reno Evening Gazette*, Dec. 16, 1882, 2.

3. *Chicago Tribune*, Dec. 5, 1882, 6.

4. Ibid.

5. *Decatur Review*, Dec. 8, 1882, 4.

6. *Decatur Herald*, Feb. 3, 1883, 2.

7. *Decatur Review*, Jan. 31, 1883, 3.

8. *Decatur Daily Republican*, Feb. 1, 1883, 3.

9. *Chicago Tribune*, Feb. 24, 1883, 11.

10. Recent medical thinking leans toward avoiding surgery for minor splenic injuries, in favor of allowing the organ to repair itself. In Emma's day, that course was followed by necessity, since splenectomies weren't done until the early 1900s.

11. *Decatur Daily Republican*, Mar. 7, 8, 1883, 2, 2.

12. *Decatur Daily Republican*, Feb. 22, 1883, 3.

13. *Chicago Tribune*, Jan. 23, 1883, 3.

14. *Decatur Daily Republican*, Feb. 1, 1883, 3.

15. *Chicago Tribune*, Feb. 24, 1883, 11.

16. *Decatur Daily Republican*, Mar. 15, 1883, 3.

17. *Chicago Tribune*, Mar. 14, 1883, 3.

18. *Decatur Review*, Jan. 5, 1883, 7.

15

1. Only three news articles mentioned Adams (see chap. 2, n12).The December 22, 1883, issue of the *Decatur Daily Republican*, made an apparent reference to the same man but called him "Mr. Hitch," which was possibly a nickname that the reporter assumed to be his last name (3). Several other articles referred to the theft of Emma's engagement ring during the crime.

2. Penelope "Nellie" Bond was then nine years old, and Mary was seven or eight.

3. *Decatur Daily Republican*, Mar. 19, 1883, 2.

4. Ibid.

5. *Chester (Penn.) Times*, Mar. 20, 1883, 1.

6. *Decatur Daily Republican*, Mar. 19, 1883, 2.

7. Ibid.

8. *Decatur Daily Republican*, Mar. 20, 1883, 2.

9. *Atlanta Constitution*, Mar. 22, 1883, 1.

10. Ibid.

11. *Decatur Daily Republican*, Mar. 20, 1883, 2.

12. It was reported in March 1883 that the case was set for the November term of the court. However, the circuit court record dated March 27, 1883, said "This cause is hereby continued until the next term of this Court." During the court's summer session, another continuance must have been granted, because it was soon announced that the trial would begin on November 30. Apparently, Vermillion was also granted another continuance.

13. *Decatur Daily Republican,* Mar. 23, 1883, 3.

14. *Decatur Daily Republican,* Mar. 19, 1883, 2.

15. *Los Angeles Times,* Apr. 10, 1883, 2.

16. Ibid.

17. The first copyright law protecting photographs, enacted on March 3, 1865, allowed photographers to transfer, in writing, their copyrights as they saw fit.

18. *Decatur Daily Republican,* June 29, 1883, 3.

19. *Decatur Daily Republican,* Aug. 30, 1883, 5.

16

1. *Los Angeles Times,* July 12, 1883, 3.

2. *Decatur Daily Republican,* July 6, 1883, 3.

3. *Decatur Daily Republican,* July 25, 1883, 3.

4. "Minutes of the Fifth Day's Proceedings of the Board of Supervisors, July Meeting, A.D. 1883," Christian County, Ill. (dated Aug. 11, 1883). Per the board's minutes, the actual amount submitted was $207.45.

5. "Minutes of the Second Day's Proceedings of the Board of Supervisors, September Meeting, A. D. 1883," Christian County, Ill. (dated Sept. 11, 1883).

6. *Decatur Daily Republican,* June 16, 1883, 3.

7. The IRAD death index gives William's date of death as September 9, 1883, while the *Decatur Republican* reported that it was Monday, September 10, 1883.

8. *Atlanta Constitution,* Nov. 22, 1883, 3.

9. Ibid.

10. Ibid.

11. *Chicago Tribune,* Nov. 23, 1883, 2.

12. *Chicago Tribune,* Dec. 8, 1883, 3.

13. *Atlanta Constitution,* Nov. 30, 1883, 4.

14. *Chicago Tribune,* Nov. 17, 1883, 13.

15. *Atlanta Constitution,* Nov. 22, 1883, 3.

16. *Chicago Tribune,* Dec. 10, 1883, 5.

17. *Chicago Tribune,* Dec. 11, 1883, 2.

17

1. *Chicago Tribune,* Dec. 11, 1883, 2.

2. Ibid.

3. *Chicago Tribune,* Dec. 10, 1883, 5.

4. *Decatur Daily Republican,* Aug. 9, 1882, 3.

5. *Chicago Tribune,* Dec. 8, 1883, 3.

6. *Chicago Tribune,* Dec. 12, 1883, 3.

7. *Decatur Daily Republican,* Aug. 9, 1883, 3.

8. *Chicago Tribune,* Dec. 8, 1883, 3. Lee's obituary stated that he was born in 1860, while the 1900 census recorded his birth as May 1862. If the former was correct, he was twenty-three during the trial. If the latter was correct, he was twenty-one.

9. *Chicago Tribune,* Dec. 22, 1883, 7.

10. Ibid. Assuming the *Tribune*'s statement was correct, Allie had been living at the Pettus home since September 1882. Mrs. Pettus moved to Decatur in the spring of 1883, leaving her farm with her two sons. A July 2, 1883, article in the *Decatur Daily Republican* noted that Lee and his "wife" were in Decatur, visiting his mother (3). But records show that Lee and Allie did not marry until after the trial, around March 26, 1884 (IRAD Statewide Marriage Index: Christian County, vol. B, 200, license 5822, listed as Lee A. Peters and Allie Hill). Although this marriage date conflicts with the 1883 *Republican* article, it appears to be correct—based on the sequential numbers and dates of the licenses, issued right before and right after their entry.

11. *Chicago Tribune,* Dec. 12, 1883, 3.

12. 1880 U.S. Federal Census, roll T9_180, District 66, Mosquito Twp., Christian Co., Ill., 28(583).

13. Edward I. Sears, ed., "Institutes, Academies and Seminaries on the Hudson," *National Quarterly Review* 28, no. 56 (Mar. 1874): 346.

14. *Chicago Tribune,* Dec. 12, 1883, 3.

15. *Decatur Daily Republican,* Aug. 9, 1882, 3.

16. *History of Christian County,* 67.

17. William Henry Perrin, ed., *History of Bond and Montgomery Counties, Illinois: Illustrated* (Chicago: O. L. Baskin and Co., 1882), pt. 2, 332.

18. Ibid.

19. *Decatur (Ill.) Saturday Herald,* Nov. 24, 1883, 1.

20. *Chicago Tribune,* Dec. 12, 1883, 3.

21. *Chicago Tribune,* Dec. 13, 1883, 3. Only Belle, Maggie, and Etta were married at the time.

22. *Atchison (Kans.) Globe,* Dec. 13, 1883, 2.

23. *Chicago Tribune,* Dec. 15, 1883, 12.

24. Ibid.

25. Circuit Court Record, Criminal, Montgomery County, Ill., November Term 1883, Dec. 11, 1883, 133. A remark in the court record for that day read: "The jury being called and *two* pannels [*sic*] selected." Apparently, a total of twenty-four men were ultimately chosen.

26. Court records gave only the jurors' names—no ages or other identifying information. All their names were found in the 1880 U.S. Federal Census for Montgomery County, the primary source for this analysis. Obviously, their circumstances could have changed between then and 1883. Wives and/or children could have died and new children could have been born, although it was unlikely their occupations had changed. Unless misreported originally, ages would be accurate to within a year. See the list of principals for more details on the jurors (287).

27. *Frederick (Md.) Daily News,* Dec. 13, 1883, 1.

28. *Atchison Globe,* Dec. 13, 1883, 2.

29. Circuit Court Record, Criminal, Montgomery County, Ill., November Term 1883, Dec. 12, 1883, 134.

18

1. Emma's testimony, as given extensively in this chapter, represents a compilation derived from various newspapers. While some of her words were directly attributed to her, others may represent the journalists' paraphrasing.

2. *Waukesha Freeman,* Dec. 20, 1883, 2.

3. *Colorado Springs Daily Gazette,* Dec. 14, 1883, 1.

4. *Waukesha Freeman,* Dec. 20, 1883, 2.

5. *Chicago Tribune,* Dec. 14, 1883, 2.

6. *Colorado Springs Daily Gazette,* Dec. 14, 1883, 1.

7. *Chicago Tribune,* Dec. 14, 1883, 2.

8. Ibid.

9. Ibid.

10. The names of all five defendants appeared on the court docket papers, even though William Montgomery was already dead and the charges against Vermillion had been recently dropped.

11. *Chicago Tribune,* Dec. 14, 1883, 2.

12. *Waukesha Freeman,* Dec. 20, 1883, 2.

13. Ibid.

14. *Colorado Springs Daily Gazette,* Dec. 14, 1883, 1.

15. *Chicago Tribune,* Dec. 14, 1883, 2.

16. Ibid.

17. Ibid.

18. *Chicago Tribune,* Dec. 15, 1883, 12.

19. Ibid.

20. Ibid.

21. *Decatur Review,* Dec. 15, 1882, 1.

22. *Chicago Tribune,* Dec. 15, 1883, 12.

23. *Colorado Springs Daily Gazette,* Dec. 15, 1883, 1.

24. Ibid.

25. *Chicago Tribune,* Dec. 15, 1883, 12.

26. Ibid.

27. *Colorado Springs Daily Gazette,* Dec. 15, 1883, 1.

28. *Decatur Review,* Dec. 15, 1882, 1.

29. *Colorado Springs Daily Gazette,* Dec. 15, 1883, 1.

30. Ibid.

31. *Chicago Tribune,* Dec. 15, 1883, 12.

32. Ibid.

33. *Decatur Review,* Dec. 15, 1882, 1.

34. *Chicago Tribune,* Dec. 15, 1883, 12.

35. Ibid.

36. *Decatur Daily Republican,* Dec. 17, 1883, 2.

37. Ibid. See chap. 8, n1 for the "Illinois Deadly Weapons" law.

19

1. (Lincoln) *Daily Nebraska State Journal,* Dec. 18, 1883, 4.

2. Ibid.

3. Ibid.

4. *Chicago Tribune,* Dec. 18, 1883, 2.

5. Ibid.

6. Ibid.

7. *Daily Nebraska State Journal,* Dec. 18, 1883, 4.

8. *Chicago Tribune,* Dec. 17, 1883, 6.

9. *Daily Nebraska State Journal,* Dec. 18, 1883, 4.

10. *Chicago Tribune,* Dec. 19, 1883, 2.

11. Ibid.

12. Circuit Court Record, Criminal, Montgomery County, Ill., November Term 1883, Dec. 10, 1883, 132–33.

13. *Washington Post,* Dec. 19, 1883, 2.

14. *Fort Wayne Daily Gazette,* Jan. 3, 1884, 3. The press disagreed over who had told Pettus to "shut up." The *Washington Post* version had Burritt blaming it on Montgomery. The *Fort Wayne Daily Gazette,* in a much more credible report, blamed it on Clementi.

15. *Oshkosh (Wisc.) Daily Northwestern,* Dec. 18, 1883, 1.

16. *New York Times,* Dec. 19, 1883, 1.

17. *Chicago Tribune,* Dec. 19, 1883, 2.

18. *Decatur (Ill.) Saturday Morning Review,* Dec. 19, 1883, 1.

19. *Chicago Tribune,* Dec. 19, 1883, 2.

20. Ibid.

21. Ibid.

22. *Saturday Morning Review,* Dec. 19, 1883, 1.

23. *Washington Post,* Dec. 19, 1883, 2.

24. *Chicago Tribune,* Dec. 20, 1883, 6.

25. *Decatur Review,* Dec. 20, 1883, 8.

20

1. *Chicago Tribune,* Dec. 20, 1883, 6.

2. The question as to which governmental body was responsible for the cost of this trial would have depended on how taxes were structured at the time. The following taxes were levied against residents of Christian County in the year 1880: state, county, town, school district, road and bridge, county railroad, town railroad, city and district road tax, per the *History of Christian County,* 59.

3. *Chicago Tribune,* Dec. 20, 1883, 6.

4. Per the 1880 census, John and Mattie Montgomery had a daughter named Birdie, born circa 1876, and an infant son named James, born circa 1879. Three more sons followed: Leonard in June 1881; Harold in October 1883 (two months before the trial); and John, born a decade after the trial. The last three sons grew to manhood, but there was conflicting information on how many children the couple had at the time of the crime and trial. In July 1882, it was reported they had one child, and yet several articles written

during the trial quoted John as saying on the stand that he was the father of three. This contradicts J. C. McBride's 1904 book, *The Past and Present of Christian County, Illustrated* (Chicago: S. J. Clarke Publishing), which states that Birdie died at the age of four and James died at fifteen months, putting their deaths ca. 1880. See *Decatur Review,* July 6, 1882, 4 ("one child"); *Decatur Daily Republican,* Aug. 9, 1882, 3 ("two children"); *Decatur Daily Republican,* Dec. 22, 1883, 5 ("took their child with them"); *Oshkosh Northwestern,* Dec 27, 1883, 1 ("three children"); *Daily Nebraska State Journal,* Dec. 28, 1883, 4 ("three children"); and *Washington Post,* Dec. 28, 1883, 1 ("three children"). See also 1880 U.S. Federal Census, roll T9_180, District 67, Grove City, Mount Auburn Twp., Christian Co., Ill., 27 (599).

5. *Decatur Daily Republican,* Jan. 4, 1884, 2.

6. That Harriet, née Heinlein, ten years younger than Laurence, lived so close makes it very probable that she and Laurence Heinlein were siblings.

7. *Chicago Tribune,* Dec. 20, 1883, 6. This article included the entire telegram.

8. Ibid.

9. Per his own signature as an enumerator in the 1880 census in Taylorville, the deputy spelled his name "Chris K. Hamel," although the press frequently misspelled it.

10. *Washington Post,* Dec. 21, 1883, 1.

11. *Chicago Tribune,* Dec. 20, 1883, 6.

12. *Washington Post,* Dec. 21, 1883, 1.

13. Ibid.

14. *Decatur Review,* Dec. 21, 1883, 8.

15. *Chicago Tribune,* Dec. 21, 1883, 2.

16. Ibid.

17. *Decatur Review,* Dec. 21, 1883, 8.

18. Ibid.

19. *Decatur Daily Republican,* Dec. 22, 1883, 5.

20. *Decatur Review,* Dec. 21, 1883, 8.

21. Ibid.

22. *Decatur Daily Republican,* Dec. 22, 1883, 5.

23. *Chicago Tribune,* Dec. 21, 1883, 2.

24. *Decatur Daily Republican,* Dec. 22, 1883, 5.

25. *Chicago Tribune,* Dec. 21, 1883, 2.

26. *Decatur Daily Republican,* Dec. 22, 1883, 5.

27. Ibid.

28. *Chicago Tribune,* Dec. 21, 1883, 2.

29. *Decatur Daily Republican,* Dec. 22, 1883, 5.

30. Ibid.

31. *Chicago Tribune,* Dec. 22, 1883, 7.

32. *Decatur Daily Republican,* Dec. 22, 1883, 5.

33. *Chicago Tribune,* Dec. 22, 1883, 7.

34. *Decatur Daily Republican,* Dec. 22, 1883, 5.

35. *Chicago Tribune,* Dec. 22, 1883, 7.

36. Ibid.

21

1. *Decatur Daily Republican*, Dec. 27, 1883, 2.
2. *Chicago Tribune*, Dec. 15, 1883, 12.
3. *Decatur Daily Republican*, Dec. 22, 1883, 5.
4. *Chicago Tribune*, Dec. 24, 1883, 1.
5. Ibid.
6. *Chicago Tribune*, Dec. 25, 1882, 2.
7. *Chicago Tribune*, Dec. 24, 1883, 1.
8. *Chicago Tribune*, Dec. 26, 1883, 2.
9. Ibid.
10. *Decatur Daily Republican*, Dec. 27, 1883, 2
11. *Chicago Tribune*, Dec. 26, 1883, 2.
12. Ibid.
13. Ibid.
14. *Decatur Daily Republican*, Dec. 27, 1883, 2.

22

1. *Decatur Review*, Dec. 27, 1883, 2.
2. *Decatur Daily Republican*, Dec. 27, 1883, 2.
3. *Chicago Tribune*, Dec. 27, 1883, 2.
4. Ibid.
5. According to his obituary, John was born in August 1849, which would have put his age at thirty-four at the time of the trial. This was one of several instances where his age was wrongly stated. See chap. 20, n4 for more information regarding John's children.
6. *Washington Post*, Dec. 28, 1883, 1.
7. Ibid.
8. Sunset in Mt. Auburn on June 29 was 7:29 P.M. CST (there was no daylight savings time yet). Civil twilight was at 8:02 P.M. and nautical twilight at 8:43 P.M. CST.
9. *Washington Post*, Dec. 28, 1883, 1.
10. Ibid.
11. *Colorado Springs Daily Gazette*, Dec. 27, 1883, 1.
12. *New York Times*, Dec. 28, 1883, 2.
13. *Chicago Tribune*, Dec. 28, 1883, 3.
14. *New York Times*, Dec. 28, 1883, 2.
15. *Colorado Springs Daily Gazette*, Dec. 27, 1883, 1.
16. Ibid.
17. *Newark (Ohio) Daily Advocate*, Dec. 28, 1883, 1.
18. Ibid.
19. *Chicago Tribune*, Dec. 17, 1883, 6.
20. *Newark Daily Advocate*, Dec. 28, 1883, 1.
21. *Daily Miner*, Dec. 29, 1883, 2.
22. 1880 U.S. Federal Census, roll T9_180, District 67, Mt. Auburn, Christian Co., Ill., 3 (587). George and his wife, Effie lived nearby on land belonging to either his mother,

Margret Pettus, or to her father, John Hill. This assumption is based on their listing in the census, just a few lines after the John M. Hill household. Theirs was followed immediately by the listings for Joseph Younker and then Margret Pettus.

23. *New York Times,* Dec. 29, 1883, 2.

23

1. *New York Times,* Dec. 29, 1883, 2.
2. *Chicago Tribune,* Dec. 29, 1883, 3.
3. *Decatur Review,* Dec. 30, 1883, 1.
4. 1880 U.S. Federal Census, roll T9_181, District 76, Taylorville, Christian Co., Ill., 21 (740). Ellen Woodruff (aged thirty-one, wife of Wm. I. Woodruff and mother of two children, aged ten and five) lived in the heart of Taylorville. Since Nellie is a common nickname for Ellen, this is most likely the "Nellie Woodruff" scheduled to appear at the trial. Her husband, William, died July 5, 1882, just six days after the crime. See IRAD Pre-1916 Death Index.
5. *Chicago Tribune,* Dec. 29, 1883, 3.
6. Ibid.
7. *Decatur Review,* Dec. 30, 1883, 1.
8. Ibid.
9. *Decatur Review,* Jan. 1, 1884, 2.
10. *Decatur Review,* Dec. 30, 1883, 1.
11. *Decatur Review,* Jan. 1, 1884, 2.
12. *Decatur Review,* Dec. 30, 1883, 1.
13. *Decatur Daily Republican,* Dec. 31, 1883, 2.

24

1. *Decatur Daily Republican,* Dec. 31, 1883, 2.
2. Ibid.
3. Ibid.
4. *Chicago Tribune,* Dec. 31, 1883, 1.
5. Ibid.
6. *Fort Wayne Daily Gazette,* Jan. 3, 1884, 3.
7. Ibid.
8. Ibid.
9. Ibid.
10. *Saturday Herald,* Jan. 5, 1884, 5.
11. Christian County (Ill.) Coroner's Inquest Record (1884), 1:2-22 (see under "Verdict of Jury").
12. *Fort Wayne Daily Gazette,* Jan. 3, 1884, 3.
13. *Bismarck (N.Dak.)Tribune,* Jan. 4, 1884, 1; *Colorado Springs Daily Gazette,* Jan. 2, 1884, 3.
14. *Saturday Herald,* Jan. 5, 1884, 5.
15. Ibid.

16. *Bismarck Tribune,* Jan. 4, 1884, 1.

17. *Chicago Tribune,* Jan. 3, 1884, 2.

18. *Decatur Daily Republican,* Jan. 3, 1884, 2.

19. *Chicago Tribune,* Jan. 3, 1884, 2.

20. *Fort Wayne Daily Gazette,* Jan. 3, 1884, 2.

21. *Decatur Daily Republican,* Jan. 3, 1884, 2.

25

1. *Saturday Herald,* Jan. 5, 1884, 5.

2. Ibid.

3. Ibid.

4. *Decatur Daily Republican,* Jan. 4, 1884, 3.

5. Christian County (Ill.) Coroner's Inquest Record (1884), 1:22.

6. *Fort Wayne Daily Gazette,* Jan. 4, 1884, 2.

7. *Chicago Tribune,* Jan. 4, 1884, 1.

8. Ibid.

9. Ibid.

10. Ibid.

11. Ibid. It's more likely that the two parted company in Decatur, as the Illinois Central ran from Pana to Decatur and then on to Chicago, where Clementi was headed.

12. *Decatur Daily Republican,* Jan. 5, 1884, 3.

13. *Decatur Daily Republican,* Jan. 3, 1884, 3.

14. *Fort Wayne Daily Gazette,* Jan 4, 1884, 2.

15. *Fort Wayne Daily Gazette,* Jan. 11, 1884, 2.

16. *Chicago Tribune,* Jan. 4, 1884, 1.

17. *Decatur Daily Republican,* Jan. 3, 1884, 3.

18. *Decatur Review,* Jan. 9, 1884, 1.

19. *Decatur Daily Republican,* Jan. 7, 1884, 2.

20. *New York Times,* Jan. 26, 1884, 1.

21. *Decatur Review,* Jan. 11, 1884, 1.

26

1. *Chicago Tribune,* Jan. 3, 1884, 2.

2. Fry was a professor at the Bloomington Normal School (the predecessor of today's Illinois State University).

3. *Davenport (Iowa) Daily Gazette,* Jan. 12, 1884, 4.

4. Ibid.

5. *Decatur Review,* Jan. 22, 1884, 4.

6. *Decatur Daily Republican,* Jan. 24, 1884, 3.

7. Ibid.

8. *Decatur Daily Republican,* Jan. 7, 1884, 2.

9. *Decatur Daily Republican,* May 3, 1884, 3.

10. *Decatur Daily Republican,* May 6, 1884, 3.

27

1. *Palmyra (Wisc.) Examiner,* Dec. 30, 1915, 9 (obituary of Dr. John W. Davis).

2. Ruth Ann Omdoll Barton, "The Sanitarium and Mineral Springs," booklet (Palmyra, Wisc.: Palmyra Historical Society, 1991), 4, 3. By the late 1880s, the sanitarium boasted a more resort-like atmosphere. Eventually, thanks to Colonel Davidson, its water was bottled and shipped out across the country. It continued to change owners and names and purposes. For a while, it was called the Spring Lake Hotel and then MacFadden Healthatorium. In the twentieth century, it served as a facility for the mentally ill, a nursing school, and finally as home to the National Druggist Association. In time, the buildings fell into disrepair and were abandoned. They were demolished in the mid-twentieth century, leaving no remnant of their contribution to Palmyra's history.

3. *Palmyra Examiner,* Dec. 30, 1915, 9.

4. Richard Davenport-Hines, *The Pursuit of Oblivion: A Global History of Narcotics* (2001; repr., New York: Norton, 2002), 100.

5. Martin Booth, *Opium: A History* (New York: St. Martin's, 1996), 88–89.

6. *Stevens Point Journal,* Nov. 22, 1884, 3.

7. *Decatur Daily Republican,* May 3, 1884, 3.

8. *Fort Wayne Daily Gazette,* Aug. 1, 1884, 10.

9. *Bismarck (N.Dak.)Weekly Tribune,* Jan. 16, 1885, 1.

10. *Decatur Review,* Jan. 23, 1885, 3.

11. *Washington Post,* Feb. 24, 1885, 1.

12. *Chicago Tribune,* Apr. 18, 1885, 10.

13. *Chicago Tribune,* May 26, 1885, 6.

14. *Decatur Review,* May 30, 1885, 3.

15. *Saturday Herald,* Sept. 15, 1885, 3. The letter quoted in the *Herald* may represent the only lengthy commentary directly attributable to Emma Bond.

16. *Decatur Daily Review,* Sept. 28, 1886, 3.

28

1. *Decatur Daily Republican,* May 15, 1886, 3.

2. Ibid.

3. 1880 U.S. Federal Census, roll T9_181, District 76, Taylorville, Christian Co., Ill., 20(739).

4. *Atlanta Journal,* Oct. 1, 1886, 1.

5. *Decatur Daily Review,* Sept. 28, 1886, 3.

6. *Decatur Daily Republican,* Jan. 14, 1888, 3.

7. *Decatur Daily Republican,* May 11, 1888, 3.

8. *Decatur Daily Republican,* July 12, 1888, 3.

9. Ibid.

10. Ibid.

11. Ibid.

12. *Decatur Daily Republican,* July 13, 1888, 3.

13. Greene, "Shamel Place," 8.

14. *Los Angeles Times,* June 12, 1889, 4. This article said the couple married in October

1888; however, the marriage actually took place on November 5, per court records of Crawford County, Kansas.

15. William G. Cutler, *History of the State of Kansas* (Chicago: A. T. Andreas, 1883).

16. Greene, "Shamel Place," 9–10.

17. Cutler, *History*. Per the U.S. census, the 1880 population of Fort Scott was about fifty-four hundred, or about twice the size of Taylorville.

29

1. *Decatur Daily Republican,* Jan. 22, 1892, 4.

2. Ibid.

3. James G. Kiernan, "Hysterical Accusations: An Analysis of the Emma Bond Case," *Journal of Nervous and Mental Disease* 10, no. 1 (April 1885):13-18. Contributors to the journal often chose topics of medical controversy. In the then-emerging field of neurology—one in which there was still widespread disagreement—this served to stir debate. However, much of the "knowledge" imparted in the pages of those early issues would not hold up under today's medical scrutiny.

4. Ibid., 17.

5. Ibid., 18.

6. James H. Kellogg, *Plain Facts for Old and Young: Embracing the Natural History and Hygiene of Organic Life,* 6th ed. (Burlington, Iowa: I. F. Segner, 1891), 210–11. Kellogg quoted the "Annual Address of Frances E. Willard, President of the National Woman's Christian Temperance Union: At Its 12th Meeting," Association Hall, Philadelphia, Oct. 30-Nov. 3, 1885.

7. State of Kansas, County of Crawford, Divorce Petition, District Court of the Sixth Judicial District: *Clarence E. Justus, Plaintiff, v. Emma Justus, defendant,* dated April 24, 1894.

8. State of Kansas, County of Crawford, Affidavit filed in Sixth District Court in conjunction with Divorce Petition: *Clarence E. Justus, Plaintiff, v. Emma Justus, defendant,* dated May 3, 1894.

9. State of Kansas, County of Crawford, Deposition of D. W. Housley before Notary Public J. M. Goff, in Walnut, Kansas, in conjunction with Divorce Petition: *Clarence E. Justus, Plaintiff, v. Emma Justus, defendant,* dated June 6, 1894.

10. *Decatur Daily Republican,* Sept. 1, 1892, 4.

11. Ibid.

12. Ibid.

30

1. 1900 U.S. Federal Census, roll T623_473, District 14, Logan Township, Butler Co., Kans. John and Emma, entry 106, 6A, 6B; Obadiah and Josie Baughman, entry 111, 6B.

2. 1900 U.S. Federal Census, roll T623_472, District 4, Rock Creek Township, Butler Co., Kans., 4A. H. A. and Belle Goodrich and family, entry 66; A. D. and Delia Bond, entry 67.

3. *1902 City Directory of Wichita and Sedgwick County, Kansas* (Wichita, Kans.: W. H. Burche, 1902).

4. *McAvoy's Wichita City Directory for 1904/05*, vol. 15 (N.p.: McAvoy Directory Company, n.d.).

5. Wichita Hospital sat within a few blocks of the John H. Jordan addresses found in the two Wichita directories.

6. Certificate of Death for Emma Jorden: State of Kansas, County of Sedgwick, City of Wichita, 834. Though her date of birth was not entered, the document gave her age as forty-nine, which would place her birth in July 1861. It also gave her Wichita address as 1120 E. Douglas.

7. Anonymous phone interview conducted and transcribed by Molly Kennedy, May 13, 2005; and anonymous taped interview conducted by Molly Kennedy, November 10, 2005.

31

1. *Chicago Tribune*, July 12, 1882, 12.

2. *Chicago Tribune*, Jan. 20, 1918, 9.

3. Christian County (Ill.) Coroner's Inquest Record (1884), 1:22.

4. Probate file for the estate of Abner Bond, Richard M. Powel, administrator (final settlement on December 6, 1888). Probate Court Journal 12:79, Christian County, Ill. The probate file is the source for this and all subsequent references to Sonny's estate.

5. Probate file for the estate of Elizabeth E. Bond, Josiah Hall, executor (filed February 1, 1899); Will Record Book 3:312, Christian County, Ill.

6. *Decatur Daily Republican*, July 5, 1882, 3.

7. *Decatur Daily Republican*, July 12, 1888, 3.

8. 1880 U.S. Federal Census, roll T9_748, District 323, Fairmont, Fillmore Co., Nebraska, 1 (450).

9. The information on Dr. William H. Vermillion was found in one or more of the following sources: Arthur Wayne Hafner, ed. *Directory of Deceased American Physicians, 1804–1929: A Genealogical Guide to Over 149,000 Medical Practitioners Providing Brief Biographical Sketches Drawn from the American Medical Association's Deceased Physician Masterfile* (Chicago: American Medical Association, 1993); 1880 U.S Federal Census, roll T9_180, Mt. Auburn Twp., Christian Co., Ill., 25 (598); 1900 U.S. Federal Census. T623_74, District 102, Roland Twp., Pulaski Co., Ark., 5A (262); Certificate of Death for W. H. Vermillion: State of Arkansas; Bureau of Vital Statistics, Volume 71, Certificate 914; IRAD: Illinois Statewide Marriage Index, 1763–1900.

10. *Decatur Review*, July 6, 1882, 4.

32

1. *Decatur Review*, Aug. 8, 1882, 4.

2. *Decatur Daily Republican*, Aug. 24, 1882, 3.

3. *Decatur Review*, Aug. 8, 1882, 4.

4. Christian County, Illinois Jail Register, vol. A, 58, entry 135, E. R. Hobbs, committed August 18, 1882.

5. *Decatur Daily Republican*, Aug. 24, 1882, 3.

6. *Decatur Review*, Aug. 27, 1882, 1 (emphasis mine).

7. *Decatur Daily Republican*, Aug. 29, 1882, 2.

8. *Decatur Review,* Aug. 31, 1882, 4.

9. 1880 U.S. Federal Census, roll T9_233, Madison Co., Ill.: C. B. Ellsworth, 379, line 9; Claude Elsworth, 8, line 19; Henry Ellsworth, 126, line 25; Hezekiah Ellsworth, 300, line 40; and Walker Ellsworth, 295, line 34.

10. Ibid. Elsworth Jones, 2C, line 21; Elsworth Mauzey, 9B, line 7.

11. "Travelers' Official Guide," 313.

12. *Decatur Review,* July 6, 1882, 4.

33

1. 1880 U.S. Federal Census, roll T9_747, District 16, Omaha, Douglas Co., Neb., 26 (168).

2. Military service record of Elliott R. Hobbs, enlisted July 3, 1882, entry 371, National Archives and Record Administration, Washington, D.C.

3. *Chicago Tribune,* Aug. 17, 1882, 3. Other articles said only that Hobbs had enlisted shortly after being fired from his Mitchell job. An actual enlistment date was never mentioned, other than the *Tribune*'s erroneous one.

4. Military pension file of Elliott R. Harding (alias Elliott R. Hobbs), File C-2 375 146, National Archives and Record Administration, Washington, D.C.

5. King County Marriage Certificates: 1855–2000, King County Archives, Seattle, #400.

6. 1887 Washington Territorial Census, roll V228_5, Ward 2, Seattle, King Co., Wash., 2, line 11 (dated July 26, 1887).

7. 1889 Washington Territorial Census, roll V228_6B, Ward 2, Seattle, King Co., Wash., 595, line 25 (dated July 11, 1889).

8. 1889 Washington Territorial Census, roll V228_6B, Ward 2, Seattle, King Co., Wash., 531, line 13 (dated July 11, 1889).

9. World War I Draft Registration Cards: 1917–18 database, located on ancestry.com.

10. *Seattle, Washington, City Directory, 1888–1889* (Seattle: Seattle Directory Co., 1889); *Seattle City Directory, 1889* (Seattle: R. L. Polk and Co., 1889); and *Seattle City Directory, 1890* (Seattle: Polk's Seattle Directory Co., 1890).

11. Washington State Military Department, National Guard Enlistment Register, 1885–1907; reference code for E. R. Harding: AR82–1–5–00192, Washington State military record series, Washington State Digital Archives.

12. 1892 Washington State Census, roll 228_7, Ward 4, Seattle, King Co., Wash., 38.

13. The brothers had only two sisters, Ida and Emma. Both were born in Indiana.

14. Military pension file of Elliott R. Harding (alias Elliott R. Hobbs), File C-2 375 146, National Archives and Record Administration, Washington, D.C.

15. 1900 U.S. Federal Census, roll T623_1743, District 58, Ballard City, King Co., Wash., 30A (78).

16. 1900 U.S. Federal Census, roll T623_1832, Port Valdez, Southern Supervisors' District, Alaska, 1B (208).

17. 1870 U.S. Federal Census, roll M593_308, Forrest Hill, Clay Township, Decatur Co., Ind., 13 (35).

18. 1880 U.S. Federal Census, roll T9_307, District 154, Delaware, Ripley Co., Ind., 30–31 (402–3).

19. 1880 U.S. Federal Census, roll T9_1022, District 95, Clifton, Hamilton Co., Ohio, 11 (306). The 1880 U.S. Census categorized civil conditions as single, married, or widowed/divorced.

20. Register of Enlistments in the U.S. Army, 1798–1914: Ellsworth H. Hobbs, 1883, 95, no. 435 (enlistment date: July 18, 1883) Records of the Adjutant General's Office, 1780s-1917, Record Group 94, National Archives, Washington, D.C.

34

1. *Decatur Daily Republican,* July 12, 1888, 3.
2. *Decatur Review*, July 6, 1882, 4.

35

1. All subsequent information on Elliott Rainey Hobbs/Harding and his family members was compiled from the sources given in chapter 33, plus the following: 1910 U.S. Federal Census, roll T624_87, District 343, Santa Monica Ward 1, Los Angeles Co., Calif., 10A; 1920 U.S. Federal Census, roll 625_116, District 598, Santa Monica Pct. 21, Los Angeles Co., Calif., 17A; 1930 U.S. Federal Census, roll 131, District 16, National Military Home, Los Angeles, Calif., 6A (228); California Birth Index: 1905–1995; California Voter Registrations: 1900–1968; Certificate of Death for Elliott R. Harding, State of California, Department of Public Health, Los Angeles County, Local Reg. No. 7092 (a copy of death certificate was included in Elliott's pension file); and U.S. Veterans' Gravesites, ca. 1775–2006.

All subsequent information on Ellsworth H. Hobbs/Harding and his family members was compiled from the sources given in chapter 33 plus the following: 1910 U.S. Federal Census, roll 624_95, District 134, Valley Center Twp., San Diego Co., Calif., 3A (270); 1920 U.S. Federal Census, roll 625_130, District 217, Escondido Pct. 2, San Diego Co., Calif., 8B; 1920 U.S. Federal Census, roll 625_131, District 313, San Diego Pct. 69, San Diego Co., Calif., 2A; 1930 U.S. Federal Census, roll 190, District 21, Escondido, San Diego Co., Calif., 10B (138); 1930 U.S. Federal Census, roll 190, District 21, Escondido, San Diego Co., Calif., 2A (96); California Birth Index: 1905–1995; California Death Index: 1940–1997; California Voter Registrations: 1900–1968; Certificate of Death (Informational) for Ellsworth H. Harding, State of California, Department of Health Services, #43036635 (3541); King County Marriage Certificates: 1855–2000, King County Archives, Seattle, Wash., #2230.

2. *Decatur Review,* July 6, 1882, 4.
3. *Decatur Daily Republican,* July 5, 1882, 3.

EPILOGUE

1. *Decatur Daily Republican,* Mar. 11, 1887, 1.
2. Uncertified Copy of Death Certificate of Emanuel Clenenti [*sic*], Milwaukee County, Wisc., 9:374, State Historical Society of Wisconsin, Madison.
3. Certificate of Death for W. H. Vermillion: State of Arkansas; Bureau of Vital Statistics, vol. 71, certificate 914.

4. *Taylorville (Ill.) Breeze,* Jan. 19, 1918, 1.

5. *Taylorville (Ill.) Breeze-Courier,* Oct. 27, 1938, 1.

6. Thelma Baughman Winzer (1916–2001), interview conducted by Joan Snyder, 1998. Thelma was the granddaughter of Josie Bond Baughman.

7. *Taylorville (Ill.) Daily Breeze,* Jan, 18, 1902, 1.

8. (Shelbina, Mo.) *Shelby County Herald,* Jan. 29, 1902, under "Leon News."

9. (Springfield) *Illinois State Register,* Jan. 21, 1902, 1.

10. Information on the deaths of Emma's other relatives is from the author's family archives.

INDEX